Mattapoisett And Old Rochester, Massachusetts

THE GRAFTON HISTORICAL SERIES
Edited by HENRY R. STILES, A.M., M.D

MAP OF
OLD ROCHESTER
TERRITORY

1 Minister's Rock
2 1st Church and Town House
3 2nd Church
4 3rd Church
5 4th Church
6 Town Mills and 1st Herring Weir
7 Old Town Road
8 Perlowtown Road
9 Old Sippican Road
10 Mattapoisett Village
11 Cannonville
12 Pine Islands
13 Hammondtown
14 Tinkhamtown and Tripp Mills
15 Neds Point Light
16 Randolltown
17 Towers Neck
18 Eel Pond
19 Cordwood Point
20 Strawberry Point
21 Indian Woods
22 Aucoot
23 Wolf Island
24 Wheel of Fortune
25 Burrbacas Ponds
26 Doggett's Brook
27 Horse Neck
28 Sippican
29 Old Landing
30 Charles Neck
31 Weweantit River
32 Sippican River
33 Happy Alley
34 Little Neck
35 Cromesett Point
36 Wareham Harbor

MATTAPOISETT
AND OLD ROCHESTER
MASSACHUSETTS

BEING A HISTORY OF THESE TOWNS AND
ALSO IN PART OF MARION AND A
PORTION OF WAREHAM

PREPARED UNDER THE DIRECTION OF A
COMMITTEE OF THE TOWN OF MATTAPOISETT

THE GRAFTON PRESS

PUBLISHERS   NEW YORK

MATTAPOISETT was set off from Rochester and incorporated as a separate town, May 20, 1857. The town voted to observe, in 1907, the fiftieth anniversary of its corporate existence, and appointed a committee of arrangements. Recognizing that the history of old Rochester-town had never been adequately presented, nor the story of "Mattapoisett Quarter" told, the first act toward this anniversary celebration was the appointment of the undersigned as a committee to gather historical data and secure its publication. An arrangement was at once made with Miss Mary Hall Leonard, of Rochester, to prepare the chapters on the early history of the old town; lists which appeared to be of genealogical or historical interest have been copied; and chapters especially relating to Mattapoisett have been added. It is hoped that the story told in this volume may give some picture of early life in one of the old towns of Plymouth Colony, and that it may set forth things, both new and old, which will be of interest to those who participate in this anniversary, and of increasing and permanent value as a contribution to local history.

CHARLES S. HAMLIN.
LEMUEL LeBARON HOLMES.
HARRIET MENDELL HAMMOND.
WILLIAM E. SPARROW, JR.
LEMUEL LeBARON DEXTER.
Committee.

MATTAPOISETT,
July 15, 1907.

"The growing good of the world is partly dependent on unhistoric facts; and that things are not so ill with you and me as they might have been is half owing to the number who have lived faithfully a hidden life, and rest in unvisited tombs."—GEORGE ELIOT.

To

LEMUEL LeBARON HOLMES

A Justice of the Superior Court in Massachusetts; a native of
Mattapoisett and a lover of her history and tradition,
who suggested the preparation of this book
and whose death, August 4, 1907,
prevented his seeing its
completion, this book
is dedicated

CONTENTS

ILLUSTRATIONS

MATTAPOISETT
AND OLD ROCHESTER

FOREWORD

A HISTORY of a locality, even if it be a brief history, is the work of many minds. The largest contributions are made by the contemporary writings of the past. The Plymouth Colony records, the Old Rochester Proprietors' book, the many town books of Old Rochester covering a period of 160 years, the ancient church and parish books of the First and Second Precincts, two or three descriptive articles published many years ago in the Massachusetts Historical Collections, the "Memoirs" of Hon. Abraham Holmes, the private writings of several early ministers of Rochester, including the diary of Dr. Thomas Robbins — these are the prime sources from which the historical material here presented has been drawn. To these may be added a number of anniversary sermons preached by later ministers in the different precincts, the historic gatherings of William Root Bliss and Rev. Noble Everett for the town of Wareham, and the addresses given at the Rochester Bicentennial celebration in 1879.

But there are many persons besides the writers of these old records who have had a part in this history, even if their contributions were not always committed to writing. Such men as John Hammond and John Bourne Sturtevant of several generations ago, have passed on to others the facts that they had learned. Aged men of to-day, like Mr. Silas B. Allen and Mr. Ichabod Blankinship, of Marion, out of the memories of a long lifetime, have furnished historic facts for these chapters. Especially valuable has been the aid given by the late Mr. John S. Ryder, for many years parish and church clerk at Rochester Center, who through his writings and in many conversations has placed at the author's service his large knowledge of Rochester history.

There are also many younger investigators and correspondents in all the four quarters of Old Rochester and in neighboring towns who can find in these pages interesting historic items which they themselves have furnished toward the preparation of this book.

Especially should recognition here be given to the direct aid given by the Mattapoisett Historical Committee, under whose commission this work has been performed, an aid without which these chapters on Old Rochester history could scarcely have been completed within the limited time that was available for this work.

The thanks of the writer are also due to Mr. A. H. Weld, town clerk of Rochester, for personal courtesies in the laborious task of collecting historic information from the old town books and papers.

That a writing of this kind is necessarily imperfect every local historian is aware, and no one knows so well as the writer the imperfections that belong to these pages. But it is hoped, nevertheless, that they may give a generally correct as well as vivid picture of the old town of the past, and form, as it were, a worthy background for the local histories of this region that will yet be written.

To the sons and daughters and grandchildren of Old Rochester, scattered far and wide through this Union of

States, belongs the task to fill out the historic picture that
has been sketched and to continue it in a panoramic
scroll through the years that follow the period that has
been in outline covered.   Since the division of Old
Rochester into three towns at the middle of the nineteenth century, each of the parts of the old town has
had fifty years of local history added to its past.

And history is still making, and the history of the new
must be recorded by those who are the actors in these
historic events as they occur.

Moreover, the history of a town in its last analysis must
exhibit a history of the families who have composed the
town, a field which it is obviously impossible to enter
upon extensively in a book of this kind.   But every family
needs its own historian, and every family has its own
historical contribution to make toward the final history
of the community in which it holds a part.

If the preparation of these chapters should lead the
descendants of Old Rochester to search their attic chests
and desks of family papers and gather and put in order
these more intimate details of local and family history,
the best result of this brief history of Old Rochester may
be said to have been accomplished.

MARY HALL LEONARD.

MATTAPOISETT AND OLD ROCHESTER

CHAPTER I

EARLIEST TIMES

ON the west shore of Buzzards Bay are many long peninsulas or "Necks," enclosing harbors having a general southeasterly trend. Near each harbor once stood an Indian village, — as Agawam, Sippican, Mattapoisett, and Acushena, — having the same name as the harbor and also of a tract of country reaching a few miles inland.

These shores were known to white men at an early date. When Bartholomew Gosnold, the English explorer, in 1602, sailed across from Cuttyhunk and entered Acushnet River, the description given by Archer shows that it was the shores to the west of Sconticut Neck that he chiefly explored. Yet the other historian of the party, Brereton, alludes to "many harbors thereabouts," and one can easily imagine that these adventurous navigators may have caught glimpses of the easterly Necks as well. But, however this may be, the descriptions given by Brereton and by Archer of the rocks and shells along the shores, the open woods (kept free from underbrush by the Indians), the plants and animals, apply to the old Rochester lands as well as to those of Dartmouth.

In 1627 an agent from Fort Amsterdam (now New York) named Isaac De Rasières, "the chief merchant and second to the governor," was sent for trading purposes to Plymouth. He sailed up through Buzzards Bay, "accompanied by a noise of trumpets," and was met by the Plymouth people at the head of the bay, then called Manomet.

He must have had glimpses of these shores and headlands, but has left no record of what he saw.

The first definite historical reference to Mattapoisett [1] occurs in 1640-1. At that time the Plymouth Colony was entering on a new stage of civic history. Governor Bradford surrendered the patent of the colony lands into the hands of the freemen. Charters were given to the towns outside of Plymouth, which now began to send delegates to the General Court, thus forming a representative government, and certain outside tracts were now set aside for the special use of the "Old Comers." [2] It was in accordance with this new policy that the General Court passed the following act:

"May 2, 1640-1. The Court hath graunted a competent porcion of vpland & hey ground to yt sufficient for a plantacion at Mattapoyst to Mr. Charles Chauncey Mr. John Atwood & Thomas Cushman & to be bounded by such as the Court shall especially assigne therevnto wch were nominated to be Mr. Thomas Prence and

[1] In the early records, however, the name Mattapoisett is often given to Gardner's Neck, Swanzey, where in 1623 Edward Winslow visited while on his second embassy to Massasoit. It was there also that the first English blood was shed in King Philip's War.

[2] The Pilgrims who came in the Mayflower, the Fortune, and the Anne were called "Old Comers" or "Forefathers."

Captaine Miles Standish, puided alwayes that such of the purchasers as shall take vp their lands there shall not have it elswhere also."

These bounds were not laid out, however, and none of the "Old Comers" took up their lands in the "plantacion of Mattapoyst." A year and a half earlier (January 22, 1638-9) the plantation of Seppekann, east of Mattapoisett, had been offered to eight men of Scituate for the benefit of Rev. John Lothrop's congregation who had fled from London to escape the persecutions of Archbishop Laud, and tarried for awhile at Scituate. This grant was not accepted, as Mr. Lothrop's congregation preferred to settle in Barnstable; but forty years later two of the sons of Parson Lothrop and other descendants of these Scituate men became original proprietors of the lands of Sippican and Mattapoisett in the town of Rochester. In 1649 a new grant of Sepecan was offered to the townsmen of Plymouth as a place for pasturage and wintering of cattle, and in 1651 the Sepecan grant was defined as "eight miles by the sea and four miles into the land." Lands thus granted to the freemen of the colony were to be purchased from their Indian owners. The land grant gave the right to make such a purchase, but was not to take effect until the Indians had been paid for their ownership rights. Liberty was now given to the town of Plymouth, " to purchase the lands of Sepecan," and the town itself took action relating to such a purchase "when its true pprietors shall be made manifest." The town also gave liberty to seven men of Plymouth "to Imploy men in hearding and wintering the cattell at Sepecan."

In 1666, King Philip gave power to Watachpoo and Sampson, two subordinate chiefs, to sell the lands of

Sepecan; and in 1688 he made a curious drawing (which
has been preserved in the Plymouth Colony Records) to
show the lands that might be sold.

In 1669, Joseph Bartlett, who had been improving the
lands of Sepecan, agreed to pay to the town of Plymouth
forty shillings for the use of these lands and to surrender
the lease of the lands that he had held. In 1670 agents
of Plymouth town agreed with the Indian Totosin (also
called Tousand) about "a psell of Land [1] desired by him
att Sepecan."

In 1670 it was voted by the General Court of Plymouth
that the profits of the upland and meadow lands at "Agawam, Sepecan, and places adjacent," together with the
rental of the Cape Cod fisheries, should be used for the
support of a school at Plymouth, and in 1672-3, agents
from Plymouth colony were appointed to purchase "whatever lands are yet unpurchased of Plymouth graunt att
Sepecan and places adjacent."

If any such purchase was made by the colony at this
date it was not recorded. In 1674, however, the town of
Plymouth voted that "Whereas the proffits of lands att
Sepecan Agawam & places adjacent were given for the
free scool att Plymouth . . . the Towne declares that
theire graunt was only of the lands there and thereabouts
which were purchased by the Towne of the Indians before
the sd May the 20th 1672."

In 1679, when the Rochester proprietors began to nego-
tiate with the General Court of Plymouth for a township
grant, the town of Plymouth still claimed a right to these
lands and appointed "Agents to treat with the purchasers
of Sepecan concerning our title to the said lands & places

[1] This land afterwards became known as Towser's Neck.

adjacent & to leave to Composition with them Respecting the Controversy betwixt the said Towne & them about it," and also "impowered agents to prosecute a suite Respecting the premises."

It appears from these records that while various attempts were made by the colony and the town of Plymouth to purchase "the lands of Sepecan and places adjacent," and while certain tracts were really purchased, no general purchase of these lands from the Indians was ever made. In 1673, when the last attempt at purchase was proposed, the Indian troubles were already gathering, and at the close of King Philip's war the remaining Indian lands passed into the hands of the English by right of conquest.

The records of "Sepecan and places adjacent" cover to some extent "the plantacion of Matapoyst," which also was never as a whole purchased from the Indians. A year or two before the war, an interesting record occurs which shows that Mattapoisett was still under Indian ownership, and also gives the bounds of the "tract called Mattapoisett." (See Plymouth Colony Records, Vol. XII, p. 225.)

"Oct. 3, 1673, Papamo, Machacam and Achawanamett being the Right owners of the land heer mensioned doe desire to have them Recorded in the Court of Plymouth Collonie that soe wee may preserue our lands for our children: the bounds of our land are as followeth, from the Easteren bounds of Dartmouth att the watersyde to a place called Wassapacoasett: and soe into the woods to the southeast end of a pond called Masquanspust [1] which

---

[1] In Winthrop's History of New England (reprint of 1826) there is a list of Indian names which gives Musquunipash as a part of Rochester.

is about six or seauen myle; and along the south syde of
the pond to a great spruce tree marked, on four sydes,
which is the head bound, on the east syde of our land, and
from thence to a swamp which lyeth south from the Marked
tree. The swamp is called quanumpacke: and from
thence to the two Rockes lying by the Pathsyde; which
goeth from Dartmouth to Sandwich; Eastern syde of
Dartmouth bounds is the Westersde of our bounds; and
Sandwich path is our head bounds, on the west syde of our
land from Dartmouth bounds, to them two Rockes before Named, our Tract of land is called by the name of
Mattapoisett.".

Soon after this (November 8, 1673), Tuspaquin, Philip's
brother-in-law, the Black Sachem of Assawampsett, sold
for ten pounds to John Tomson, John Lothrop, and Barnabas Lothrop of Barnstable a tract of land extending
from Queetiquash River, Queetiquash Pond, Sniptuit
River and a Neck of Land, to Dartmouth; and July 2,
1674, the three Indian owners of Mattapoisett again
recorded the bounds of their land with the statement that
a part of this land had been sold by Tuspaquin to these
men of Barnstable, which sale these Indian owners had
" condescended unto."

It is hard to solve the mysteries of the old Indian names,
but a study of these records makes it evident that the
tract called Mattapoisett at one time covered the whole
of the western part of Rochester, extending on the north
to the Assawampsett region of Middleboro. The tract
in North Rochester sold by Tuspaquin to John Tomson
and the Lothrops is known as " The Tomson Purchase."
A few months earlier a large tract of South Middleboro
had been bought from Tuspaquin, which is known as

"The South Purchase of Middleboro." The agents in this South Purchase were Benjamin Church and John Tomson, who were afterwards allowed to set off for their own use a certain part of the South Purchase extending to Sniptuit Pond. This became known as the Sniptuit Purchase, and a part of this was afterwards included within the bounds of Rochester.

In 1667 the Plymouth Court granted to Hugh Cole of Swanzey, "respecting his father's grant (being an ancient freeman), and his own grant, six score acres of land between the Mattapoisett river and the eastern bound of Acushena." This land Cole purchased of King Philip in 1671, and afterwards sold it to Samuel Hammond, one of the earliest settlers of Mattapoisett.

In 1676 the colony passed an act granting to the soldiers of the Narragansett expedition of King Philip's war, lands to the value of one thousand pounds in Showammett, Assonett Neck, Assawamsit, Agawam and Sepecan, but it is not certain that any of the Rochester lands came into individual ownership under this act.

In 1679 the Rochester Proprietary was formed, which (July 22, 1679) purchased from the colony at a consideration of two hundred pounds (to be applied to the debt incurred by the war) a township grant of all the lands on Buzzards Bay, between Dartmouth, Middleboro, and Plymouth Purchase or Agawam. The whole territory is often referred to as the "lands of Sippican," but it included Mattapoisett and a large territory north of Sippican known as Menchoisett. The part of Sippican which in 1739 was set off into Wareham was also called Weweantit, and the northern part of Mattapoisett was later known as Sniptuit.

Minister Le Baron in 1738 names the parts of Rochester
as "Easterly part Sepican, Southerly Mattapoysett, Westerly Snippatuit — the middle part of Town Munchoiset";
and John Hammond (b. 1756) preserved in memory a
distich learned in boyhood which names the "Quarters
of Rochester" as

"Snipatuit, Monochesset,
Sippican and Mattapesset."

These old Indian names are significant. *Mattapoisett* has
been interpreted as "a place of resting "; *Sniptuit* means
"rocky water"; *Sippican* "the long river"; *Weweantit* or
"young bucks" is supposed to have been a place of resort
for these animals; while *Menchoisett* or "much food"
suggests that its arable lands had been used by the Indians
for planting.

After the Rochester purchase was made, there were
still some Indian claims to be satisfied. In 1667 an Indian named Charles (alias Paumpmuitt) had bought of
two sachems for the sum of eight pounds the peninsula
known as Charles's Neck. This land he now sold to the
Proprietary for six pounds. November 19, 1679, Joseph
Lothrop, agent of the company, paid to Peter Suscacow
(also called "Maniment Peeter") five shillings to satisfy
his claim. But the most important claimant appeared in
the person of an Indian named William Connett, who in
1683 laid claim to all the lands between Sippican River
and Plymouth's westerly bound at Agawam. He also
committed trespass on these lands, and "did disclaime
and defie the title of every these men called the purchasers
of Sepecan." His claim was carried to the courts, but it
was not pleaded. The parties came to an agreement by

which Connett was given a proprietor's share in the lands of Rochester. Connett's name appears later as a subscriber towards the funds for the first gristmill of the town. But it soon disappears from the town history. A point of land in Mattapoisett eastward from Angelica has recently been named Connett Point in memory of this Indian who thus stoutly resisted the claims of the white invaders.

Within the Rochester territory are various traces of the old Indian life. Northwest of Mattapoisett village is a long ridge called "Indian Burying Hill," filled with bony deposits of Indian sepulture. Under the sands along the shores are buried heaps of clam and oyster shells (known to scientists as "Kitchen-middens") which mark the spots of ancient Indian feasts.

A full description of one of these feasts has come down to us in Church's "Entertaining History of King Philip's War." It was held in 1676, and commemorates an important meeting between Captain Church and Awashonks, the squaw Sachem of the Sogkonate Indians of Little Compton. An earlier meeting between Church and Awashonks had been held at Treaty Rock in Little Compton, at which Awashonks "pledged her fidelitie" to the English and offered the services of her men on the English side. But when Captain Church went on to Plymouth, offering his services and that of these Indian allies, the authorities distrusted the sincerity of Awashonks and to test it ordered her to proceed with her warriors at once to Sandwich and "to be there upon Peril in six days." She tried to get excused, but Captain Church urged her to comply and promised to meet her on his return from Plymouth.

The place of the expected meeting was in Agawam, but
on Church's arrival there the Indians were not in sight.
With some anxiety Church left two of his companions for
a reserve and continued his journey westward. After
crossing Sippican River, and another river, he came to a
shore where there was a wide view of the bay and found the
Indians running races and holding a feast on the "Sands
and Flats." [1]

At the supper, to which Captain Church was invited,
"a curious young Bass was brought in on one dish, eels
and flatfish on a second, shellfish on a third, but neither
Bread nor Salt was to be seen at table."

Supper being over, a dramatic scene ensued which is
thus described by Captain Church:

"A great pile of Pine Knots and Tops was fired and the
Indians gathered in a ring about it. Awashonks and the
oldest of her people kneeling down made the first ring,
and all the stout lusty men standing up made the next,
and all the Rabble, a Confused Crew, surrounded on the
outside. Then the Chief Captain stepped in between the
people and the fire, and with a spear in one hand and a
hatchet in the other danced round the fire and began to
fight with it, making mention of all the several nations
and companies of Indians that were enemies to the English; and at every tribe named he would draw out and
fight a new fire brand, and at finishing his fight with a
fire brand he would bow to him and thank him. When

[1] Various localities have been suggested by different historians. Dr.
Henry M. Dexter, however, in his annotated edition of Church's History
(1875) suggests that the second river crossed was Mill Creek flowing
into Aucoot Cove, and that the "wide view of the bay" makes it probable that the place of the feast was between Aucoot Cove and Angelica,
or between Angelica and Ned's Point.

NEDS POINT AT LOW TIDE

he had named them all and fought them, he struck down his spear and hatchet and came out. Then another stept in and acted the same dance with more fury if possible than the first. When about half a dozen of the chiefs had thus done, the Captain of the Guard told Mr. Church that they were making Souldiers for him, and what they had been doing was all one swearing of them, and having in that manner engaged all the stout lusty men, Awashonks and her chiefs declared that they were now all engaged to fight for the English."

At the close of the performance Awashonks presented to Captain Church "a very fine Firelock," and he in return gave to her assurances of the confidence and protection of the English.

On the following day Captain Church went back to Plymouth, offering his services and those of Awashonks' men, which were accepted, with results which had great influence in determining the final success of the English.

In the histories of King Philip's War most of the allusions to Mattapoisett refer to Gardener's Neck, Swanzey, where was an English garrison of seventy men. But one incident, which occurred July 24, 1676, is connected with the present Mattapoisett.

Church and his Indian allies had marched from Taunton to Assawampset, then to Dartmouth, going as far west as Smith's Mills, and after various encounters with hostile Indians had turned back toward Plymouth by another route. Coming to a point where the "Country Road" divided to go around the two sides of a swamp, the party separated, the English taking one path and the Indian allies the other. John Cooke's place in Fairhaven had been agreed on as a place of rendezvous.

Church's party, however, after an encounter with an
Indian force which they captured, learned that other
Indians were at Sconticut Neck, and Philip himself only
two miles away. Fearing to meet these hostile Indians
while encumbered with captives, they "made all haste
until they got over Mattapoisett River," where they halted,
sending messengers back to meet the Indian allies who
arrived the next day, and the two parties compared suc-
cesses. It was found that the English had taken sixty-
six prisoners, and the allies had taken sixty-three and
killed three. The number being equal, it was looked
upon by Church as a favor of Providence that prevented
each party from triumphing over the other. The Indians
had taken the larger number of arms, but it was held to
be unfortunate that the parties had separated, as otherwise they might have captured Philip's force.

A few weeks later another force of Indians was captured
by Church "at or near Sippican."

Of the Indians captured during the war, some were
sold to the West Indies and Bermuda as slaves, one of
these being the twelve-year-old son of King Philip. Others,
including women and children, were made slaves or in-
dentured servants within the colony. In 1676 it was
ordered that all private persons holding adult male Indian
captives should dispose of them out of the colony, on pain
of forfeiting them to the use of the colony.

It was further ordered that all Indians who had come
into Plymouth "accepting the mercy of the Colony should
take up their abode from the westermost side of Sepecan
River and sow easterwards to Dartmouth bounds, and not
to go off the aforesaid limits but by order of some magee-
strate." Three Indians, Numpus, Isaake and Ben

Sachem (alias Petenunuitt),[1] were to have the inspection and control of these Indians, and "Matters most momentous" were to be referred to Mr. Thomas Hinckley for decision.

In the southern part of Rochester, extending up from Mattapoisett and nearly surrounded by the great Haskell swamp, is the strip of upland known as Towser's Neck. The name is a corruption of Tousand, one of the names of Totosin, who has already been referred to as obtaining the use of this land from the Plymouth authorities. He was a fierce and famous fighter, a terror to the Plymouth colonists during King Philip's War, and in the intervals when he was not fighting he made this Neck his haunt and hiding-place. Many stories of his treachery and his bravery, and finally (after the death of Philip) of his capture and death, are told in the histories of the time.

From the time of the pasturage grant of 1651, there are traces of white occupation in the Old Rochester lands, but most of the early occupants were probably herders with only temporary habitations.

In the southern part of Rochester, reaching down into Marion and Mattapoisett, is an extensive woodland, now wholly uninhabited; but some ancient roads can be traced through this woodland, and one may find an occasional choked-up well or cellar, some fallen bricks or a wild apple tree, marking a spot where once stood a human habitation. But the name and the history of most of

[1] Petenunuitt was the second husband of Queen Weetamoe, who had been the wife of King Philip's brother. Numpus was afterwards the captain of the remainder of Awashonks' tribe of Indians, which for many years had a settlement, including a church and congregation, at Little Compton.

those who once lived in this forest have long been forgotten. It has been said that certain families from Dartmouth who were friendly to the Indians settled here before the coming of the Rochester proprietors. But authentic evidence as to exact facts seems lacking.

It seems probable that a few white people were living on the lands of Sippican when the Rochester purchase was made. Yet for the most part this was virgin territory when in 1679 the men of Rochester chose it for their future home.

Some Indians were left in the Rochester territory at the time of white settlement. In 1682 the colony passed a law that the Indian men left in the towns should be numbered in groups of tens, one of whom should be appointed overseer of the other nine; and that each town should have a general white overseer of the Indians. Settlement was then begun in Rochester, but the town was not incorporated, and no record occurs of any Rochester action under this law; though the provision for the three Indian overseers of 1676 was in general agreement with this policy. A regulation was afterwards passed by the town that no Indian who had not lived in town for three years should be allowed "to hunt or catch deer" within the town limits.

In 1690 King William's War was giving trouble to the colonists, and Captain Church was sent with a force of Indian men to the Coast of Maine, where some slight engagements took place. Each town of Plymouth Colony was required to furnish its quota of men (either white men or Indians), and of arms for this war. With the exception of Falmouth, incorporated the same year, Rochester was the youngest town of the colony, and its quota was

MATTAPOISETT RIVER NEAR THE SEA

"1 man and 1 arms," the required arms being "a well fixt gun, sword or hatchet, a horn car-touch-box, suitable ammunition, and a snapsack."

In 1746 the General Court of Massachusetts appointed a committee "to provide a place for the reception of the Pigwacket Indians now at Fort William" (in Boston Harbor). This committee reported that a place had been provided at Assonomock [1] Neck, in Rochester, under the care of Captain Noah Sprague and Benjamin Hammond, Jr. It was further provided that twenty-five pounds in money should be given to said Sprague and Hammond for a boat, tools, provisions, and other necessaries for the support of these Indians. The later history of the Pigwacket Indians is lost; but a tract of land in Rochester mostly unoccupied and given up to woods and huckleberry pastures — a tract lying northwest of the Witch Rock Corner, and five or six miles distant from Mattapoisett Neck — is known to some of the older citizens by the mysterious name of Pigwacket.

Several Indians were still left in the Old Rochester territory at the beginning of the nineteenth century. In the great woodland that surrounds the Towser's Neck region, an Indian called "Old Tony" lived for many years a hermit life. Also in these woods is shown the site of "Peter's House," once occupied by Indian Peter and his wife Meribah. Mention is made still later of "Black Frank," a man of Indian blood, who was the town butcher. With him lived for a time "Boston," a woman from the Indian village of "Betty's Neck" in

[1] On some old maps Mattapoisett Neck is called Attansawomuck Neck.

Middleboro.   Persons are now living who recall the two Indian women, Boston and Meribah.

It is many years since the last Indians disappeared from the soil of Old Rochester.

> "But their names are on your waters,
>   Ye cannot wash them out."

Nor would we wish to lose the memory of these aboriginal owners of the New England lands, who have passed on to "happier hunting-grounds."

CHAPTER II

THE name Rochester given to the new township was suggested, it is said, by the rich beds of shell-fish along its shores. Some of the purchasers, or their parents, had come originally from Rochester, Kent County, England, where was an oyster fishery, celebrated even in Roman times for the excellence of its shell-fish products. In Scituate, where these men had lived for a time, they had named one of the streets, Kent Street, for the county of their birth, and they now gave the name Rochester to the new town.

A description of the general features of the Rochester territory will throw some light on the pages of history that follow.

An anonymous writer of 1815 (who is quoted several times in these pages) gives a description of the Rochester of his date (the Wareham part being of course not included) from which an abridgment is here given:

"Rochester; — a maritime town in the county of Plymouth, lat. 40° 42' long. 70° 40'. It is bounded south on Buzzards Bay eight miles, west on Fairhaven and Freetown twelve miles, north on Middleboro eight miles, and east on Wareham four or five miles; distant from Plymouth twenty miles S. W.; from New Bedford twelve E; and from Boston fifty-two miles, S.S.E. It is an original corporation of the Old Colony, June 4, 1686, and contains the Scipican and Mattapoisett of the aborigines. Irregular in outline, it may be in area of near eight miles square, or in excess of it.

"Scipican or Rochester harbor, setting up from the south more than two miles in the center of its shore line, is formed by Great Neck on the east, and Charles's Neck on the west, expanding to more than a mile in width. There may be three wharves here, which afford nine feet of water in common tides, but at the extremity of the necks there is sufficient for vessels of burthen. The bay at large affords a depth of water of several fathoms. There is also, we are told, a wharf-landing at Great Neck. The situation of this harbor is the best in the place as to shelter.

"Mattapoisett harbor is a more exposed and far less capacious haven on the southwest extreme of the shore. Being further down the bay a greater depth of water is attained. It is an outlet of a small stream of the same name, which traverses the whole western line of the town, it may be nine miles, in a south direction to mingle with tide waters at this place; alewives in their season seek it for the sake of its fountain, Senepetuit Pond. There may be, perhaps, twelve or more feet of water in this harbor. The shores in this vicinity are rocky, and the tides in the bay rise about six feet.

"There are two islands large enough to have names, Bird and Ram Islands, both very small, the former alone of size sufficient to admit of cultivation. It is situated at the mouth of Scipican Harbor, and the other within it. Some small islands lie next the Mattapoisett shore and inlet.

SIPPICAN HARBOR

From the residence of the late Attorney-General Knowlton, at Marion

"Senepetuit, on the northwest corner of the town, is four miles in circumference. A brook, running from it, N.W. near a mile, connects it with the East Quittaques Pond, a very large pond, partly in this town, but chiefly in Middleborough. Iron ore, it is said, exists in this vicinity. This pond is reported to receive alewives from an inlet and outlet respectively from the Buzzards Bay side, and also from the very circuitous tributaries to the Taunton River. Let the reader trace this on the map, and be amused by the research.

"Merry's [1] Pond, so called, without any outlet, a round pond, a mile in diameter, of shallow waters, in an open space, near to the main road, has an entire margin of remarkably white sand, which contrasted with the adjacent verdure, the rural hamlets, and a smooth hill beyond it in the distance, will detain the traveler a few moments. It is, we think, one of those resting places which, though it may be often seen, pleases still, and is recollected to the journey's end with the same emotions. Snow's Pond and Little Long Pond are in the N.W. section of the town, and all contain fish.

"Scipican brook, arising from small sources, called there 'Black water' on the confines of Middleborough, is formed by two or more branches, which, running southerly, seem to unite in the eastern section of the town, when, turning easterly, it meets the tide waters in the vicinity of Great Neck, not so far from Wareham West boundary. From this little stream, a few miles in length, the plantation or proprietary, in early annals, took its name.

"Mattapoisett brook, perhaps of greater volume of

[1] A Mr. Merry, it is said, formerly lived in the vicinity of this pond.

water, meandering along low, swampy grounds, parallel to Fair Haven line, has already been noticed. There may be some other small brooks and ponds, but not of magnitude sufficient to be described.

"Great Hill, or Great Neck Hill, apparently a smooth pasture hill, is situated not far from the shore on the Great Neck. It must, we think, present an uninterrupted view of the back shore of Sandwich and Falmouth, together with the pleasant bay of Manomet five or six miles over. We have noticed this hill as a conspicuous and distinct object when at Wood's Hole. Queetiquash Hills are in the north part of the town near the pond and brook of the same name.

"Tataug, scauppaug, eels, are the most common fish near the shores, with alewives in their season. At several places of resort oysters have become less common; the quahaug and lesser clam are found in the place. Without the harbour the bay affords a greater variety; but not the codfish nearer than Gay Head.

"Birds of passage doubtless frequented these pleasant shores, in former days; and hence probably the name of the little island we have already noticed, while the deer walked unmolested in the boundless forests of pine. This animal has now become rare within the limits of this town. Wild pigeons annually seek these woods and are very common in this town in August. Partridges abide."

Another description of Rochester, written by Abraham Holmes in 1821, may also be drawn upon for a few passages (see Mass. Hist. Coll., Vol. X, 2d Series):

"Its breadth is about six miles from east to west, and its mean length about nine or ten miles, though to the extremity of some points running into the sea it is farther.

"The soil is very variant. Near the centre it is a light sandy soil tolerable for tillage, but indifferent for grazing. Some parts of the town are rocky, iron-bound, unfit for cultivation, and will probably be kept for wood; in other parts the soil is luxuriant, and produces good crops of grass. On the seashore are considerable margins of salt marsh, without which it would be difficult to keep the stock of cattle necessary for the use of its inhabitants.

"Quitticus [1] Pond is in the northwest corner of this town; a small part of the north end is in Middleboro, and a small part on the west lies in Freetown. This pond is pretty well stored with pickerel and perch. Formerly large quantities of alewives went into it through a small brook from Assawamsett Pond, but very few pass now. A part of Assawamsett Pond lies on the north side of this town, and the line of the town crosses two islands of considerable bigness in this pond. Assawamsett Pond is the largest collection of water in Massachusetts. In this pond is a vast quantity of iron ore, which increases nearly as fast as it is dug. In the southerly part of this pond are large quantities of fish, such as pickerel, white fish, perch, roaches, chubs, horn fish, and vast quantities of sea or white perch are taken in the fall of the year, when the young alewives can be had for bait, which is the only bait which can be used with success. The land on the southerly side of this pond is very uneven and hilly and

[1] That is, Little Quitticus. Mr. Holmes refers to Great Quitticus as Assawamsett. Both Pocksha and Great Quitticus lie in the same lake bed as Assawamsett. Thus Minister Le Baron (1786) says that "Assawamsit is the largest pond of Rochester."

the bottom of the pond is as uneven as the land to which
it is adjacent.   It is not uncommon for water to be from
ten to twenty-five feet deep, and within a few rods to be
not more than three or four feet deep.   This pond is the
source of Nemasket River, which is a considerable branch
of Taunton River.

"Sniptuit Pond is wholly in this town.   The seat of
this pond may be considered as the height of land.   Sniptuit Brook runs north out of this pond into Assawamsett
Pond, and may be considered as the first source of Taunton River.   Mattapoisett River runs south out of the
southerly part of this pond.

"A few rods south of this pond lies Long Pond, nearly
a mile in length, and from 5 to 20 rods in width.   Here
are large pickerel, but they are of a muddy taste.   Not
far from this, to the south end, lies Snow's Pond, which
has no visible connexion with any other water.   This
pond is deep and has some fish.   It contains perhaps 35
to 40 acres.

"On the right hand of the road from Rochester to
Plymouth lies Merry's Pond, a most beautiful sheet of
water, and is nearly as round as a circle.   In this pond
are a few fish of the minor species.   There is no natural
inlet or outlet to this pond, but a few years since the town
at the expense of $100, cut a canal from it to Sippican
River, hoping to induce the alewives into the pond.   No
success attended the attempt.   This pond is about three
quarters of a mile in diameter.

"There is no run of water in this town which geogra-
phers would call a river, but there are two which are com-
plimented by that name by the inhabitants.   The first of
these is Mattapoisett River, which issues out of Sniptuit

Pond and empties into the sea at Mattapoisett Harbor, after running about eight miles, including its windings. This stream, though small, is of some consequence, besides what results from the mills, namely, on account of the alewive fishery. The other is the Sippican River."

If the two writers who have been quoted had written eighty years later, they would doubtless have added to their list of lakes the little sheet of water called Leonard's Pond. This was the site of the ancient Sippican Mill privilege, where many important industries have been carried on. Although its interesting features have been developed to some extent by artificial means, it is now a lakelet of much beauty. Lewis Pond also, though primarily a mill pond, has landscape features of esthetic value. Snow's Pond, a little to the south of Sniptuit, is a lovely natural lakelet with steep wooded shores.

Several of the Rochester lakes contain islands. Those of Sniptuit are known as "High Bush," "Low Bush," and "Gull" islands.

The Sippican River, formed by two long branches, receives also the central tributary, which figures in old records as "Muddy Brook" and "Ventur's Brook." On the maps it is Doggett's Brook, but it is generally known as "The Trout Brook," from the large trout that are taken in its waters.

Mattapoisett River, above described, divides near the middle of its course, flowing around a tract of land, lying partly in Mattapoisett and partly in Rochester, and known as Wolf Island. Deacon John H. Clark for many years resided upon this island, which is now, however, uninhabited.

Near the "Lower Herring Weir" the river widens into a pond where mills were early established and many different industries have been carried on. A little to the east of the mouth of the river is a shallow sheet of saltish water known as Barlow's Eel Pond. It formerly had two outlets, one into the river, the other into the harbor, between which lay Goodspeed's Island. At these two channels, not only eels, but many sea bass and shad, were formerly caught. The railroad embankment has closed one of the outlets of the Eel Pond, and also lessened its fishing interests.

There are well-known old springs in Mattapoisett, one of which the Indians called "Mattapoisett Spring," and which is situated on the east bank of the river near the "Uncle David Gifford place." Another, which has been named King Philip's Crystal Spring, bubbles through a sandy tract in the woods a mile or so north of the harbor. It has been said that when the inland Indians used to come to the shore on their frequent journeys after eels and shell-fish they loved to linger beside these springs for rest and refreshment.

A short distance from the old Bates place, near Leonard's Pond, is another bubbling spring known as "The Boiling Spring, and not far away is the "Great Buttonwood," one of the largest of the trees now standing in Massachusetts. Mr. George B. Emerson, writing in 1846 of the Forest Trees of Massachusetts. says:

"The plane [or Buttonwood] tree is the largest, grandest and loftiest deciduous tree in America. . . . In Rochester one by the roadside was eleven feet in circumference at four feet from the ground."

The tree is still standing, more than sixty years after

these words were written. There are also many other
buttonwoods "by the Rochester roadsides." The Buttonwood (which is also called the American sycamore) is
conspicuous among our native trees from the fact that the
thin gray bark easily scales off, showing bright patches
which have a striking effect among the large green leaves.
In recent years the Buttonwoods have shown a less healthy
vitality than was the case a hundred years ago.

The most marked of the natural features of Old Rochester is the very extended shore line made by the harbors
and the enclosing "Necks." An ancient town record
names Cromeset Neck, Great Neck, Charles Neck, and
Mattapoisett Neck, as the four Necks of Rochester town.
Mattapoisett Neck, which gives to that harbor about two
miles of western shore line, is called on some of the old
maps Attansawomock Neck. Its two divisions are commonly referred to as the "East" and "West" Necks.
On the eastern side of Sippican Harbor is Little Neck
where the first Ministry lands of Rochester were located. Cromeset Neck, lying between the Weweantit
and Wankinco rivers, is now in the town of Wareham.
Certain tracts of upland that are nearly enclosed by
swamp lands within the town are also called "Necks."

If one follows on the map the long shore line from west
to east he finds minor irregularities that are also worthy
of notice. There is Brandt Island Cove, containing Brandt
Island, — said to have been named from the water-fowl
(brant) that used to frequent this spot, — and owned
(1907) and occupied in summer by George V. Brower
of New York. Other small islands along the Mattapoisett shore are Seal Rocks, Ram Island, and Gravel
Island.

On the eastern shore of Mattapoisett Harbor is Neds Point, named from a former owner, Edward Dexter, and now occupied by a small government reservation, containing Neds Point lighthouse; to the eastward of which is a curiously shaped peninsula with three projections, Angelica Point, Strawberry Point, and Goat Island; the last being a narrow serpentine strip of land nearly enclosing the little bay known as Pine Islands Pond.

Farther east one comes to Connett Point (formerly Cordwood Point), Pease's Point, and Hiller's Cove. Between Mattapoisett and Marion is Aucoot Cove (formerly spelled Orcoot), containing Haskell Island, and receiving the little stream on which the Sparrow mill is located. The eastern side of Sippican Harbor is broken by a double indentation known as Blankinship's Cove and Planting Island Cove, partly shut in by Little Neck and the low peninsula known as Planting Island. Meadow Island is a low, grassy tract within the harbor, and a little to the north of Ram Island is a tiny islet known as Little Island. The most interesting single feature of the harbor is Bird Island, which stands off the entrance, well out into the bay, crowned with the white lighthouse that adds picturesqueness to these quiet shores. Great Neck is partly divided by the deep indentation known as Wing's Cove, the western peninsula terminating in Ruggles's Point, formerly known as Butler's Point, from Butler Wing, a former resident of this Neck. Great Hill, which is east of the cove, attains a height of about 127 feet, and was made a station for the United States Coast Survey.

Although many places along the extended shore line are low and marshy, there are also various beautiful sandy beaches; among these being Silver-Shell Beach (formerly Nye's wharf beach), overlooking which many summer residents of Marion have built their beautiful homes.   Crescent beach, Pico beach, and other strips of shore in Mattapoisett, are of similar character   At Aucoot Cove, Angelica Point, and other places, are many rocks that show the results of strong glacial action.   Along the shores are the valuable deposits of quahaugs, scallops, and other shell-fish, which have been of large food value to the inhabitants from Indian times to the present.   The fishing rights to the shell-fish of the shores and the fish in the bay, as well as to the herring of the rivers, have been the subject of much town legislation, and in all town divisions the rights in these fisheries to all the inhabitants of Old Rochester have been carefully preserved.

With the exception of the hills near Sniptuit Pond, and Great Hill in Marion, there are no elevations of importance in the Old Rochester lands.   A few higher points like Vaughn's Hill, Braley's Hill, Cathell's Hill, may be mentioned, and reaching north from the central part of Cannonville in Mattapoisett is a somewhat elevated strip that has been named Oakland Heights.

The grassy land of the necks and the shore lands in general furnished to the colonists "hey grounds"; and here salt hay is still harvested yearly though less valued than of old.   They were also used for pasturage, and for years these Necks in general were held as a "common field" for the stock-raising inhabitants of the old town.

The Menchoisett region is largely a sandy plain, the deposit apparently of a great lake formed under glacial influences.   A large, level region a mile or so northeast of the center is known as Walnut Plain.

But there are in Old Rochester large swampy tracts
that have never been populated though they are valued
for timber. Some of these are in the northeast part of
the town, where the branches of the Sippican River take
their rise. There is also the old "Logging Swamp,"
midway between Sniptuit Pond and the western town line.
Several others, as Haskell Swamp (formerly Great Bear
Swamp), Little Bear Swamp, and Great Cedar Swamp,
lie in the extensive wooded tract that reaches from Rochester into Marion and Mattapoisett. Among the uplands
or "necks" that extend into, and are nearly surrounded
by, these swampy tracts are Horse Neck, Sniptuit Neck,
and Towser's Neck, where the old Indian Totosin dwelt
before and during King Philip's War.

But besides the sandy and swampy tracts there
are large sections where the light, sandy soil is closely
filled with huge boulders and smaller rock deposits,
showing how mighty were the glacial forces that were
once active in shaping the natural conditions of this
region.

There are many interesting single rocks. Of these the
one deserving of first mention is the great Minister's Rock
in Marion, which, like many another rock or stone in all
ages and countries, was made use of by the men of old
when they set up their altars of worship. Another rock
of great interest is the enormous granite boulder at the
rear of the summer home of the late Edward Atkinson
in Mattapoisett; a boulder forty-two feet in height and
thirty-six in width, divided by a vertical fissure through
which a footpath runs. The great Ward's Rock at the
shore, almost on the dividing line between Fairhaven
and Mattapoisett, for so long a conspicuous landmark

THE GREAT ROCK, MATTAPOISETT

from the sea, has in recent years been, much reduced in size by blasting.

Joe's Rock, in a picturesque locality of North Rochester, near the pumping station of the New Bedford water-works, contains Joe's cave, said to have been the hiding-place of a fugitive of the Revolutionary era.

In Central Rochester also there are several interesting rocks, among which may be named Witch Rock, on the corner beside the "Old Country Road." Further back in the woods is "Indian Pound Corn," a large table rock formation showing the indentation made by the Red Man's pestle. There is also a "Devil's Rock," which, like many other similar rocks of New England, shows the definite impress of the foot of the imp as he leaped from the boulder, although this particular Devil's Rock bears an added confirmation of its genuineness, in that William Harris, Sr., actually saw the fiend when he took the final leap.

In the woods about three quarters of a mile west of Rochester Center, running through the old Thompson and Sturtevant lands, is a curious ridge of gravel, half a mile long and wide enough for a wagon path, which is a very perfect specimen of the glacial formation known to geologists as an "esker."

In Mattapoisett is a ledge of "pink granite," which is still being quarried. Minister Le Baron, in 1786, refers to this as follows: "In Second Precinct there is a fine stone suitable for Building with wh Nantucket Market is principaly supplied, and of late some have been exported to the Southern States and used for Millstones in ye manu-facturing of rice."

The uplands of Old Rochester are still nearly covered

with forests of oak, pine, and cedar, interspersed with ash, maple, spruce, walnut, elm, beech, birch, holly, sassafras, and other trees. The white pine timber is especially valued, and by its rapid growth it keeps up the supply of material for the boxboard industry, at the numerous sawmills of the region. There is considerable undergrowth of vines, huckleberry bushes and other shrubby plants. In the early days the Indians kept the woods open by frequent burnings, so as to afford free passage for travel.

Along the country roads of the Old Rochester lands numerous native wild cherry trees hang out their white blossoms in spring, and in the late summer their clusters of deep-hued berrylike fruit. In the spring also the blossoms of the "shad-bush" give a feathery whiteness to the woodland edges, and the sandy fields and roadsides of the old Menchoisett region are covered with lupines, making a brave display of color with their showy blue racemes.

Beside the pathways and in the old pastures grows the sweet fern redolent of old New England associations; also the bayberry, valued of old as a source of "bayberry tallow," the fragrant green "myrtle-wax," formerly used for the manufacture of candles; and there is also a plenty of the wild indigo weed that countrymen use to stick above the horses' ears to keep off offending insects. In the swamps are delicious huckleberries to be had in plenty by those who can withstand the boggy wetness of the places where the juiciest berries prefer to grow. And there are low level stretches where the tiny-leaved cran- berry vines make a crimson carpet in September when thickly hung with the red glossy fruit. In ancient parlance this was the "craneberry," and, as an old writer informs us, "The craneberry is a plenteous production, and is sent to a wide vicinage, even to Boston."

Most of the small wild animals found in early days in the woods of Old Rochester still inhabit these regions. Wildcats, once numerous, have disappeared, but an occasional red fox may yet be seen. Even the deer, once apparently extinct in this region, has shown signs of resuscitation of late.

Throughout the summer months the ears of the villagers are greeted with the frequent call of the American cuckoo, while the whippoorwill sings his pathetic evening call from many an old fence or mossy stone. The woods abound with tree toads puffing their tiny bladders and uttering their trilling notes, and in the marshy places a million frogs make a croaking spring music which brings to the listeners' ears the pleasant assurance that the winter is over, and that all the glories of spring will soon be manifest.

But it is impossible to enumerate all the natural features of the Old Rochester lands, which are, after all, not peculiar to Old Rochester, but are similar to those of all the other parts of Southeastern New England.

Enough has been given to enable one to form a fairly correct general picture of the seventy or eighty square miles of territory that the men of Rochester bought from the old Colony Court in order to build thereon their future homes.

CHAPTER III

IN 1679, several persons having proposed to purchase lands in Sippican, the Plymouth Court decided to accommodate them if they "can procure some more substanciall men that are prudent psons and of considerable estates," who would settle with their families. The agents to make the purchase were Joseph Lothrop and Barnabas Lothrop of Barnstable, Kenelm Winslow of Marshfield, and William Clark of Plymouth, Governor Josiah Winslow acting for the colony. July 22, 1679, the purchasers met for the first time at the house of Mr. Joseph Bradford of Plymouth, and the deed was drawn.

The territory covered more than seventy square miles, which, after Wareham was set off in 1739, was reduced to about fifty-eight square miles.

The deed shows the eastern boundary of the purchase to have been the "Westerly Jumping Brook" (or Besse Brook) of Wareham and the Wankinco River. Some other land must have been added, however, for many acres east of the Wankinco were afterwards assigned to Thomas Clark and other proprietors.

The purchasers were thirty [1] in number, but two additional shares were set aside for "the Minister and the

[1] The number has sometimes been given as twenty-nine, the name of James Clark being omitted from some of the early lists.

Ministrie," and the name of the Indian Connett, added in
1683, made the whole number of proprietary shares
thirty-three, among which these extensive land holdings
were to be divided.

March 10, 1679, the proprietors "met at Joseph Burge
his house at Sandwitch," and ordered that "Mr. Thomas
Hinckley, Mr. William Paybody, Joseph Warrain, Samuel
White, and Joseph Lothrop Shall take a vew of the Lands
of Scippican and determine where the house Lots shall be
Layed out and if the Land will Beare it to Lay 40 ackers
to a house Lot and to have for their paines 2s 6d a piece
in mony." The report as to size of lots must have been
adverse, for April 15, 1679, the purchasers met again at
Joseph Burge's and made the first land division by lot,
giving to each proprietor twenty acres for a house lot and
forty acres of woodland, sixteen of these home lots being
at Mattapoisett and sixteen at Sippican. It was allowed
that those that "mislike" their home lots at Sippican
might take up home lots in any "Unlayed out lands from
Charles his meadow and the long swamp to Sippican
River." The first and second home lots on Great Neck,
and two lots of the best of the woodland, were also set
aside for the Minister and the Ministry.

Those who drew home lots at Sippican were the Minister, the Ministry, Elizabeth Ellis, James Clarke, William Clarke, Samuel Briggs, Seth Pope, William Paybody, Joseph Burge, Benjamin Foster, Benjamin Bartlett,
Kenelm Winslow, Ralph Powel, Joseph Dunham, Thomas
Clark, Aaron Barlow, — 16.

Those who drew home lots at Mattapoisett were Samuel
Hammond, Joseph Dotey, Samuel Davis, Samuel White,
Barnabas Lothrop, George Morton, Joseph Lothrop,

John Perry, John Bradford, John Cotton, William Bradford, John Burge, Moses Barlow, William Dexter, Joseph Bartlett, Mr. Thomas Hinckley, — 16.

In some of the lists of the early proprietors the title "Mr." (in those days an honorary title) was given to Thomas Clarke, John Cotton, John Bradford, and William Paybody, as well as to Thomas Hinckley. But with the exception perhaps of Thomas Clarke these honorable gentlemen do not appear to have taken up their residence on the lands of Rochester.

Joseph Lothrop was the first Proprietors' Clerk. He and his brother Barnabas did not live in Rochester, though they had very large land holdings, and were most active in the early proprietary affairs.

A few of the proprietors moved at once into Rochester; some sent their sons to occupy their lands; others soon sold their shares, which were often divided among several purchasers, so that the number of those owning proprietary rights was soon much increased. From time to time new lots were surveyed and drawn. In 1665 it had been ordered by the Plymouth Court that the proprietors of each town should procure a suitable book for the record of their land titles. These old Proprietors' Books, together with the colony patent and the Indian deeds, furnish the foundation for most of the land titles of New England. The Rochester Proprietary records are full and valuable, and were kept up for many years. The last record of land divisions was made in 1792. Two ancient copies of the Proprietors' Book are in existence. About 1875–1885, a copy, in four volumes, was begun by Mr. Joseph S. Luce of Marion, and finished by Noah Hammond, Esq., of Mattapoisett. This authorized copy is kept at the Registry of Deeds in Plymouth. Another copy was made by Mr. Hammond for the town of Mattapoisett.

Laws for the new township were at first made at the proprietors' meetings, which after 1694 began to be held in Rochester itself. June 4, 1686, the town was incorporated, under the name, "Rochester-town in New England." Soon after this, laws for the town began to be made by the freemen at town meeting, but the opinions of the proprietors continued to have much weight in town affairs.

Aaron Barlow, Samuel White, and Samuel Hammond were selectmen in 1690, the earliest whose names have been recorded. The town books now in existence begin with the records of 1697, but mention is made of records before this date. Mark Haskell was town clerk in 1697. At his death, a year or two later, Peter Blackmer was chosen, and held this office for many years. The honor of being town clerk was its chief emolument, but occasionally a small sum was paid as the "Proffits of the townes books." Thus, in 1711, Peter Blackmer was paid the sum of twenty shillings "for keeping the townes books for about 11 years past." The closely written old town books of Rochester have never been copied, but they form a most important compendium of local history.

To attract settlers the proprietors voted that "them that first settell and are livers" should be allowed to make ten barrels of tar apiece, "of the kind comonly called small barrells," upon the commons for their own benefit. But lest the purchasers who were not settlers should claim the privilege of making tar it was ordered that none of these should be "alowed to Burne or make any Tarr of the

pine knots or wood for the space of five years." Tar was
an important article of commerce until after the Revolution, and in 1704 a law was passed against unauthorized
"milking of the pine trees" on the common lands. It
was also ordered that no "tymber claboarding shingling
or coopers stuff" should be exported out of the town, and
if any were brought to the landing-place as if for export,
"it shall be forfeited one half to the informer and one half
to the town." "Twentie shilings" was the "penaltie"
for every tree or part of a tree thus exported.

The woods abounded in foxes, wildcats, and other
small animals. The early records have many entries of
bounties paid for "3 catts in season," "two foxes out of
scson," for crows, redbirds, jaybirds, squirrels, and other
animal pests. Foxes' heads brought "3 shillings for old
ones, and one shilling for young ones puppied this year."
The animals must be presented, however, "with both
thir ears on to be cut off." In 1694 forty shillings was
paid for "the killing of two grown woulves in our town."
In 1706 each householder was required to bring in his
animal quota of four crows and twelve blackbirds killed
by the bringer, or must forfeit twopence for each black-
bird and sixpence for each crow that was lacking. In
1738 each male twenty-one years old was required to
kill "6 crowhill Blackbirds or Bluebirds, or 4 squirrels or
2 crows all well grown," or on failure to do so, "to have
2 shillings added to their next town tax."

Dogs kept to protect sheep were often troublesome.
The white men had learned from the Indians to use herrings as a fertilizer for corn, one or two being planted in
each hill. But dogs uprooted the corn to dig for herrings.
So in 1703 it was ordered that "every dog, Bitch, or dog

kind" should be fettered on the 20th of April for forty days by "haveing one of their fore feet fastened up to their neck," and if any person should set his dog at large not so tied during that period, "any person may kill such dog, Bitch, or Dog kind."

One of the earliest needs of the town was a gristmill, and in 1683 twenty acres of land were laid out on the two sides of Sippican River as a mill privilege. Aaron Barlow and Joseph Burge were appointed to set up the mill, which was to be of "such Capacitie as She may grind the corne of the Inhabitants for twentie years." Aaron Barlow declined the commission, however, and the work devolved on Joseph Burge alone. Towards this first mill William Connett paid for himself and his brother "six barrells of tar," while the other proprietors were taxed ten shillings apiece.

The exact location of this first mill is not definitely stated, but a few years later the mills at "Leonard's Pond" were known as the "Sippican Mills," and here important industries were carried on in all the generations of the Old Town History. In 1694 permission was given for another gristmill to be set up in Mattapoisett. In 1704 the commission for the first mill having expired, a very important gristmill was erected at "Leonard's Pond." It had a perpendicular shaft, and was tended by Peter Blackmer, who was also the town clerk. Near Peter Blackmer's mill the town also gave a piece of land to Anthony Coomes on condition that he "do the work of a smith among us for seven years."

In 1685 the towns of Plymouth Colony were divided into three counties, Plymouth, Bristol, and Barnstable, and the judicial department of the government was transferred to the county. Rochester was at first included in Barnstable County, perhaps to preserve the balance of the counties, for of the twenty towns in the colony, Barnstable had six towns, including Rochester. In 1707 Rochester sent a petition to be transferred to Plymouth County, and in 1709 the transfer was made. About 1735 a petition for a new county was sent to Boston from Rochester and Dartmouth, but nothing finally came of it.

In 1689 the town of Rochester sent Joseph Burge as its first representative to the General Court of Plymouth. He was succeeded in 1690 and 1691 by Aaron Barlow. In 1690 also, two militia officers were appointed in Rochester, Lieut. John Hammond, and Ensign Joseph Dotey.

In 1692 Sir William Phipps arrived at Boston from England with the new Province Charter which united Plymouth with Massachusetts. In July of this year the Plymouth General Court held its final session, at which it appointed the last Wednesday in August as a day of general fasting and humiliation, and then adjourned. But at this final session the Rochester representative, Aaron Barlow, was not in his seat. It does not appear that the men of Rochester took, at first, a very active interest in the new province of which they had become a part. They were occupied in clearing lands, building houses, and piling up painfully the long stone walls which we still see in various localities. It was not until 1714 that Rochester sent a representative to the General Court at Boston, in the person of Samuel Prince, giving him four shillings a day "for his panes."

Although the men of Rochester were "substancial and prudent psons," there was little money in circulation. Plymouth Colony as a whole was poor, and at the end of the Indian war its debt was larger than its whole available wealth. Property was chiefly in lands and buildings. In 1692 the total wealth of the colony was 35,000 pounds, of which Scituate, the largest town, had 4360 pounds. The ratable estate of Rochester, at this era, was 367 pounds, the only town having less wealth being Freetown, which was rated at 349 pounds.

The first constables of Rochester were chosen in 1692. After this date the collection of taxes devolved on the constable, and the office became most unpopular. It was voted that if one were elected as constable and refused to serve he should be fined. Many a man did refuse, and paid the fine rather than take the difficult position. The attempt to keep the office of constable filled, occupied much time in early town meetings.

In every New England town religious worship at once engaged attention. One of the provisions of the Rochester grant required that worship should be established within four years. In 1683 agents were appointed to find "some meet person to preach the word of God at Scippican." The man selected was Mr. Samuel Shiverick, a Huguenot, who had fled from Catholic persecution in France. His first pulpit is said to have been Minister's Rock, at Little Neck. A meeting-house was soon provided, however, of which Hon. Abraham Holmes (b. 1754) has written: "It was small, and I think cost 20£. It was afterwards sold and made two corn-houses." Mr. Shiverick was given the use of certain ministry lands, and "a house or frame was got up for him." It was agreed that non-resident proprietors should pay him five shillings a year, and resident proprietors two shillings a year for "his paines" in preaching, and the next year it was ordered

that all landholders should be taxed ten shillings for his
support. But no permanent settlement as the town's
minister was ever given him, and after four years he
removed to Falmouth.

He was succeeded by Rev. Samuel Arnold, Jr., son of
Minister Arnold of Marshfield. In 1687, Mr Arnold
was invited to " settle," and was given a whole proprietary
share on condition that " he continue in the work of the
ministry among us until prevented by death." He began
his preaching in the little meeting-house by Minister's
Rock. But few new settlers were coming to this part of
the town. The flow of population was from this point
towards Great Neck, Wareham, Leonard's Pond, and
upper Sippican village. In 1685 lots were laid out " in
the woods " at Rochester Center, and before long settlers
began to find their way there, and into the more northern
parts of the town.

The year 1694 was an important one in the annals of
Rochester. About this time many changes were made
in the land holdings. Lots were exchanged, or were
thrown up, and new ones drawn. Minister Arnold now
came into possession of land that was later known as the
Sturtevant farm, and between this date and 1697 he had
built a house on it and moved to that locality. July 10,
1694, an important meeting of the Proprietary was held
in Sandwich, at the house of Samuel Prince, who about
this time bought out Benjamin's Foster " whole shear,"
and was also chosen clerk of the records.

About this time also a definite effort was begun by the
town to establish its permanent center. In February,
1694–5, Woodlot No. 17, belonging to Isaac Little, was
chosen as a place to " sett a meetinghouse." It is de-

MINISTER'S ROCK, LITTLE NECK, MARION

scribed as lying "on the west side of Muddy Brook below where the Rhode Island way goes over." But the town was not at that time ready to build, and three years later Woodlot No. 30 was chosen, the owners of which now threw it up, and received in return a like number of acres in the "undivided."

In 1697 the town exchanged its "Ministry lands by the Sea" for lands in the interior, and Samuel Briggs, an early settler of Little Neck, whose twelve-year-old daughter, Eliza, is said to have been the first person interred in the ancient burying-ground by Minister's Rock, was allowed to take up the lands around the little meeting-house, in consideration of his having allowed a cartway to be made through his lands to the "town's generall landing-place." On the new ministry lands thus chosen at the Center, the town now voted to lay out a burying-ground, and a training field, and "a place to sett a meetinghouse," while a part of the land was "to ly and remaine the Ministry." A woodlot to the north of Rochester Church is still known as "The Ministry." There were many other ministry lands, however, in various parts of the town, that were afterwards divided up among the parishes.

But although the general location of the central public lands of Rochester was decided upon in 1697, there were still some months of doubt and discussion as to the exact site for the important building which was to be the center for the town's civic and religious life.

February 2, 1699, it was "voted that the meetinghouse shall be sit on the westerly sid of the long Bridg."

This obscure and apparently incredible statement on the pages of the town's books has been one of several confusing factors which led to the loss, during several generations, of all real knowledge or agreement as to the actual location of the important meeting-house built by the town in 1699.

It did not seem possible that there was any "long Bridg" at Rochester Center. But further study has brought to light facts bearing on this question. If one follows the trout brook a few rods to the rear of Capt. Judah Hathaway's house he may find to-day traces of a very ancient road crossing the brook at this point. This is a part of the oldest road from Rochester Center toward Little Neck and Sippican, the road that was in use when the meeting-house was built. Between this point and the burying-ground much of the land is low, and though at present it is dry and arable, this was not always the case. Mr. Holmes writes in his memoirs: "One thing is remarkable. When I was young, old people said they could remember when people caught fish in a brook which ran across where the road turns to go to Deacon Dexter's, between Charles's and the meeting-house. There are now no signs of a brook there, but the vestiges yet may be traced from the brook westward until it comes nearly in range with Ruggles's house." In imagination one can seem to see a stretch of corduroy road made of pine logs, crossing this ancient brook and the trout brook and the wet lands near by, and known perhaps to the early settlers of Rochester as "the long Bridge."

But, whatever the structure called the "long Bridge" may have been, the location of the meeting-house is no longer in doubt. From independent and authentic sources we know to-day that the meeting-house stood a few rods westward from the low tract referred to, and within the limits of the town's burying-ground, which is indeed the only natural place to look for it.

In 1699 the Meeting-house was built, and with this event began a new era in the town history. The scattered interests of the growing villages were now in a measure united. At a town meeting held June 4, 1700, "The inhabitance had before them the accompts of some of the chang that necessarily is coming and hath been in sd town of Rochester, and being sensable of the necessity of mony to be Received for a town stock or Treasury, the inhabitance voted that a Rat of thirty shillings be raised to defray the necessary chang arising in sd town of Rochester, in the year 1700."

With this change in the town of Rochester in the year 1700, the period of beginnings may be said to be passed, and with the new century the town entered on its second stage of history, an interesting era of general town development.

CHAPTER IV

THE SETTLERS AND THE SETTLEMENTS

BEFORE the year 1700, settlement had spread thinly over the whole Rochester territory, and beginnings had been made toward several villages that grew up later within the town.

The two largest villages of Old Rochester, however, Mattapoisett Village and the Lower Village at Marion, were not among the points earliest settled.

In 1879 Mr. Wilson Barstow wrote of Mattapoisett:

"In 1750 there was no village on the harbor. Some four houses were located on what is now Main Street, the Deacon Tobey house; the Sherman house, on the site where Colson now resides; the Jas. Mendell house burnt some years ago, and Gideon Barstow Jr's. on the site of the R. L. Barstow house."

The earliest homes in Mattapoisett were near the Mattapoisett River and in Pine Island, Hammondtown being the oldest village.

The first homes in Sippican were at Little Neck, but this never grew into a settlement of much size. At various points on Great Neck, Wareham, and along the shores, the population increased and a village was soon formed at the "Upper Landing," which is now (by the building of new houses all along the shore) fast becoming indistinguishable as a separate village from the larger one that finally grew up at the "Lower Landing."

As the interests of the town quarter have always been largely agricultural, no very concentrated village has ever been formed within it, though many sites of ancient houses could be pointed out where to-day no dwelling is to be seen. Some of the earlier homes in this part of the town were near the mill site, at Leonard's Pond, something of a village being formed there at an early date. But over the general town territory, even to the northern border, population spread somewhat rapidly.

Two large sections of Old Rochester have never had many inhabitants, — the region on the northeast, known as Horse Neck, and the great wood containing the swampy tracts near the corner of the three towns of the present.

Of the sixteen proprietors who drew house-lots in Mattapoisett, three, Samuel Hammond, Moses Barlow, and William Dexter, settled on their lands at an early date. Several others or their descendants came to Rochester, but the place of their residence is less distinctly fixed.

The first settlers at Mattapoisett were probably Samuel Hammond (one of the proprietors) and John, his brother, who came from Sandwich in 1680 and settled in the southwest part of the town. Both were men of wealth and influence. Samuel Hammond was one of the founders of the First Church of Rochester. His land on West Neck was bought from Hugh Cole of Swanzey, who was the first white owner, but Samuel Hammond was probably the first English occupant.

John Hammond held many important public offices, and was the second representative from Rochester to the Province Court. In 1691 he married Mary, the eldest

daughter of Minister Arnold of Rochester. His home
was near to the herring weir, where about 1700 he built a
fine house which is still standing in good preservation, and
is the oldest house within the limits of Old Rochester
territory.

In 1684, Benjamin Hammond,[1] who was the father of
these brothers, and whose mother (widow Elizabeth Hammond) with her children had belonged to Parson Lothrop's congregation of Scituate, came to Rochester and
purchased for twenty-six pounds half of a proprietor's
share.

A younger son of Benjamin Hammond, Benjamin
Hammond, Jr., also came to Rochester, and with his
numerous descendants gave the name to the village of
Hammondtown, a mile or so from the harbor, where
Hammond Cemetery is located, and the first meeting-
house in Mattapoisett was built. Benjamin Hammond,
Jr., was a noted surveyor of the region. In 1723 he
became the special surveyor of the town of Dartmouth,
But he also made extensive surveys in his own town of
Rochester. At Plymouth Court-house may be seen a
book containing five hundred drawings, showing surveys
of Rochester lands, more than half of these drawings
having been made by Benjamin Hammond. They are
of especial technical interest in showing the methods
used, and the ways in which land areas were estimated.

Descendants of the Hammond brothers settled early
on Mattapoisett Neck and in other parts of Mattapoisett,

[1] Benjamin Hammond was the own cousin of William Penn, the
founder of Pennsylvania, his mother Elizabeth, the widow of William
Hammond of London, being the daughter of the Admiral, Sir William
Penn.

THE LIEUT. JOHN HAMMOND HOUSE, MATTAPOISETT HERRING WEIR

Built about 1700.   The oldest house now standing in the Old Rochester territory

some also going to Sippican where many Hammonds have lived. The name has been a prominent one in all eras of the town history.[1] Nathaniel Hammond, Edward Hammond, Gideon Hammond, and Enoch Hammond figured conspicuously in the Revolutionary history of Rochester town.

Israel Hammond (the great-grandfather of the Noah Hammond who copied the Proprietors' Books) was a prominent man in business, church, and society, and kept a slave, Uncle Tom, who held an honorable position as a member of the family. The story is told that once when efforts were being made at the Hammond Mill to catch a thief, Tom said he was afraid. "Afraid of what?" he was asked. "Afraid the thief is one of our good old honest neighbors," was the reply. A few slaves were then owned in New England, and the ships of Massachusetts towns brought them over rather freely for the southern market. Freedom was offered to Mr. Hammond's "Uncle Tom," but he declined to accept, and died a slave and a self-respecting and honest man.

Another proprietor who came early to Mattapoisett and settled near the river was Moses Barlow. The oldest of the Mattapoisett graveyards is to-day known as the "Old Barlow Cemetery." Wilson Barstow wrote:

"The Barlows and Hammonds were the ancient nobility of the place.

"Old Deacon Barlow, one of the first proprietors to lay out land, was famous in his day as a deacon, pillar of

---

[1] A "Hammond Genealogy" compiled and published in 1894 by Rowland Hammond, M.D., a native of Mattapoisett, gives much information of this family and of their participation in the town's history.

the church, and leader in society. It is said that when
the wife of Deacon Barlow died, he mourned for her with
due propriety for a year and a day. Then mounting his
horse, he rode to the house of a maiden lady, and having
knocked with his cane without dismounting, he greeted
her with 'Good morning, I am in pursuit of a wife; if you
will have me, I will come in, if not, I shall go farther.'
'Why, Deacon,' was the reply, 'How you astonish me!
Thank you, you had better come in.' A few days later
there was a wedding, and the Deacon took his new wife
home on a pillion behind him."

The third proprietor mentioned who came to Mattapoisett was William Dexter, whose descendants in town
have been about as numerous as those of Benjamin Hammond, and have figured conspicuously in both church and
town history. His home was at Pine Island, where he
had a farm three fourths of a mile square, with a brook
running through it. At the "Dexter Dam" on this
stream a sawmill and a gristmill were built at an early
date. Benjamin Dexter, who died in 1732, in his will
names the mill as a part of his property assets. A house
built some time before 1800 stands to-day on the site of
the original Dexter home, and is still owned in the Dexter
family.

William Dexter, the proprietor, died in 1694, but four
of his sons settled in Rochester, and his only daughter,
Mary Dexter, became the wife of Moses Barlow. Thomas
Dexter was an early representative, and the names of
Benjamin and John Dexter figure prominently in the
early town records. Benjamin married Sarah, a daughter
of Minister Arnold, and many of Mr. Arnold's extensive
land holdings passed finally into the hands of his Dexter

grandchildren. Constant Dexter, a son of Benjamin, was an early deacon of the Mattapoisett church. He died in military service at Crown Point during the French and Indian War. Another of Benjamin's sons, Seth Dexter, settled near the church at Rochester Center, on land still owned and occupied by his descendants. Rev. Henry M. Dexter, D.D., the distinguished leader and historian of the Congregational denomination, was a descendant of this Dexter line.[1]

Among the proprietors who drew house-lots in Sippican, the first mentioned is Mrs. Elizabeth Ellis, a widow, whose husband, John Ellis, of Sandwich, died in 1677. In 1687 Mrs. Ellis was living on her land in Sippican, but her descendants two or three generations later were clearing lands and breaking up the virgin soil in the Ellis neighborhood of Mattapoisett.

Samuel Briggs lived at Little Neck and came into possession of the old ministry lands there after the new ministry lands had been laid out at Rochester Center.

Aaron Barlow, who became the second representative of the town to the General Court at Plymouth, lived at Rochester at an early date, and in 1708 the town built a new pound close beside Aaron Barlow's house.

John Wing's home, the ancestral home of numerous Wing descendants, was on Great Neck, but later generations lived farther north in Marion, in the vicinity where to-day stands the Methodist Church. A large territory in this region was once occupied by Wing families. John Wing was a surveyor, and about 1700 he wrote a book on

---

[1] A "Dexter Genealogy" compiled by Robert L. Dexter of Mattapoisett, and others, has recently been published, from which knowledge of this extensive family connection may be gained.

surveying, which showed the methods then used. For many years persons by the name of Wing held the office of town clerk.

John Wing with Savory Clifton who lived in the same vicinity, and a few others, started the Quaker movement in Rochester. John Wing and very many of his descendants lie buried in the old Friends' burying-ground opposite the Methodist church.

The graves of these early settlers are mostly unmarked, but on a small tablet in the enclosure one may read:

> "Within this inclosure lie the
> Remains of 326 Friends:
> 200 x 67 Ft."

Kenelm Winslow, who was a nephew of Governor Edward Winslow of Plymouth, owned lands near Leonard's Pond, and in Mattapoisett and other places; but it does not appear that he ever lived upon these lands. The names Job, Thomas, and Edward Winslow, however, appear early in the town history.

Some of the Winslows lived several miles north of the Center. The "house of Capt. Edward Winslow in Sniptuit" is mentioned in 1726. The old "Whitridge House," built in 1695, and recently taken down, was originally a "Winslow House." It stood not far from Rounseville's Mill, which was originally the "Winslow Mill." The house of Mr. Andrew Fearing at the Center was also an old Winslow house, moved to its present position many years ago from the "Clapp neighborhood."

The location of some of the proprietors who found homes in Rochester cannot be distinctly traced; but families bearing the name of Clark were found very early in several

THE WHITRIDGE, OR WINSLOW, HOUSE

Near Rounseville's Mill, Rochester. Built in 1695; taken down in 1906

parts of the town. Some of the name of Pope lived near the Dartmouth line. There were Bensons in several localities, and Davises some time later in the northern section and elsewhere. Nicholas Davis and Timothy Davis were public speakers of note in the religious denomination of "Friends" in Rochester. Burge (afterwards Burgess) became an early name of Wareham. At a later date Burgess was a family name in the Town quarter. Tristam Burgess, born in Rochester, after graduating at Brown University, became a prominent member of Congress from Rhode Island. He was a man of impassioned oratory, with keen powers of sarcasm, and figured conspicuously in debates with southern members about the middle of the first half of the nineteenth century.

Bumpus (now Bump) was an early name in Wareham, along the Weweantit River on which Bumpus's Mill was situated. Among the members of the First Church dismissed in 1739 to form the Wareham Church there were eight persons named Bumpus. The same persons were also leaders in the movement for the incorporation of the town of Wareham.

Samuel White from Marshfield, of the old Mayflower stock, was one of the first board of selectmen in 1690. The most distinguished of the White descendants in Rochester was Lieut.-Col. Ebenezer White, the town representative of the Revolutionary era. The location of the White family is obscure, but in 1704 John White was owner of lands a mile or so east of Rochester Center, and at a later date White was a family name in North Rochester.

Dotey, also a Mayflower name, appears at an early

date in various land descriptions near the center of the town. It was also the name of early settlers in the vicinity of Look's Mills. In recent years, Mary Dotey, born in Rochester, has been known in musical circles as a concert singer in America and Europe, under the name of Madame Dotti.

In 1694 Benjamin Foster sold his entire share to Samuel Prince of Sandwich, who, before he moved his family to Rochester Center owned a house and land at Cromeset, which may have been Benjamin Foster's. Several Fosters of prominence were found later in Rochester. Lieut. Chillingsworth Foster, whose grave is in Rochester cemetery, was a military man of the eighteenth century, and early in the nineteenth century Dr. James Foster was a prominent physician near Rochester Center, but becoming depressed on account of financial troubles he finally took his own life.

Among the original proprietors it is probable that the two Lothrops, the two Bartletts, the two Bradfords, Ralph Powel, George Morton, Joseph Dunham, Thomas Hinckley, John Cotton, and William Paybody never took up their residence in Rochester.

The earliest list of freemen for Rochester, made in 1684, is given as follows:

Mr. Samuel Arnold, Peter Blackmer, John Hammond, Moses Barlow, Samuel White, Samuel Hammond, Joseph Dotey, Jacob Bumpus, Joseph Burges, John Haskell, —— Sprague, Abraham Holmes, Job Winslow. The names of John Wing and Aaron Barlow were soon afterwards added.

From this it appears that Mr. Arnold was living in the town before he became the town's minister. At his death, in 1709, he left one son, Samuel Arnold, Jr., who was a deacon in the First Church, and several daughters. Elizabeth Arnold, who married Charles Sturtevant, succeeded to the ownership of the family house on "Arnold's Plain" at the Center. At the time of the Rochester Bicentennial four generations of Minister Arnold's descendants were then living in the Sturtevant house at Rochester Center.

Peter Blackmer has already been named as living at the Sippican Mill Site, where he was miller as well as town clerk. His last descendant in Rochester bearing the name of Blackmer — Mr. Garrison Blackmer — died a few years ago at his home near the Acushnet border.

John Haskell, named as freeman in 1684, soon left Rochester and went to Middleboro. In 1692, Mark Haskell, a brother of John Haskell, came from Salem. It is said that he came in haste to avoid serving on the jury of a witchcraft trial. He lived a little to the west of the meeting-house, and took a prominent part in the town affairs for several years, but died in 1699, leaving four sons, from whom the different lines of Rochester Haskells have descended. Deacon Roger Haskell, the oldest son, succeeded his father at the home place, and his descendants are numerous to-day at Rochester Center. John Haskell, the second son, was a minor at the time of his father's death, and his mother took up land for him at Mary's Pond. He had many descendants, but most of his sons finally went to Hardwick. Mark Haskell, the third son of Mark, Sr., lived in Rochester, but the exact location is not clear. Joseph Haskell, the youngest son of Mark, Sr., became a man of considerable wealth. His last descendant in Rochester, of the name

of Haskell — Miss Eugenia Haskell, a woman of interesting and unique personality — died in 1907 at the age of
eighty-nine.

Sprague was a prominent name in Rochester town for
many years. Samuel Sprague, Noah Sprague, and
Nathaniel Sprague held important town offices at various
dates. Samuel Sprague, who was town representative
before the Revolution, lived a little north of the Center.
The Spragues intermarried with the Hammonds of Mattapoisett, and Sprague became a prominent name in that
village as well as in the more northern part of the town.

Abraham Holmes, whose name appears in this first list
of freemen, lived in the northern part of the town. A
little later we find the names of three brothers, Abraham,
Isaac, and Josiah Holmes, all living in the vicinity of
Vaughn's Hill, a little south of Snow's Pond. Abraham
Holmes (who was also the first deacon of the First Church)
and Isaac Holmes, known variously as Captain and En-
sign Isaac Holmes, were both among the signers of the
Covenant at the founding of the First Church. Ensign
Isaac Holmes was also in 1700 put in charge of the town's
herring weir at Sniptuit. Experience Holmes, the son of
Abraham Holmes, lived on old Weir Hill by Sniptuit.
Another Abraham Holmes, great-grandson of the first
Abraham, from whose Memoirs quotations are made in
this history, moved later to Rochester Center. Other
Holmeses went to Mattapoisett, and the name Holmes
has at some period figured prominently in all four of the
quarters of Old Rochester.

With the purchase of Benjamin Foster's share in 1694,
Samuel Prince became a most influential factor in town
affairs. In addition to Benjamin Foster's share, Mr.

Prince bought half of Samuel Lothrop's proprietary
rights.   He also made other very extensive land purchases
in various parts of the town, so that he was for some
years the largest landowner in Rochester.   The large
house which he built in 1710 stood near the trout brook
on the old road from the Center toward Marion that was
given up in 1785.   The house was called Whitehall, in
memory of a family estate in England.   In later years it
was known as the White House.   At a period long after
the Prince family had left Rochester, it stood for years as
a disused building, but during the Revolution its floors
were taken up " to procure materials for making saltpeter
for use of the army," and afterwards it was taken down.

Mr. Prince was twice married, his second wife, who
came with him to Rochester, being a daughter of Governor
Hinckley.   He was the father of many children, one of
them being Rev. Thomas Prince, pastor for forty years
of the Old South Church of Boston, and an important
New England historian.   Mr. Samuel Prince was himself
a man of education as well as of wealth, and during his
stay in Rochester he did much to promote the general
interests of the town, especially in school affairs.   He was
a Justice of the Peace, at that time an important office,
and he also held for years the office of representative to
the General Court.

The Prince family moved to Middleboro in 1723, where
Samuel Prince died in 1728, at the age of eighty.   After
his death some of his Rochester lands along Muddy Brook
were made a subject of legal contest among those who
had been his neighbors, and were voluntarily relinquished
by the Prince heirs.   One son, Joseph Prince, remained
for a time in Cromeset, and a granddaughter, who had

married in town, continued to live here; but for the most
part the Prince family, which for a few years had been
very influential, passed out of the Rochester history.

Another name that appeared in Rochester Center at a
very early date was that of Clapp. In the earliest town
records that are preserved, those of 1697, Increase Clap
is the first name mentioned as that of selectman in that
year. Major Earl Clapp was a brave and distinguished
officer in the Revolution. He was also the leader of the
party in the First Parish that opposed Minister Moore,
and for a time brought disruption into the church.

About 1725, Richard Church, a cousin of Benjamin
Church, came, with others, from Scituate, and acquired
a large tract of land at "Macedonia," its northern boundary being on the old "Rhode Island Path." A few years
later, he built a sawmill on the Mattapoisett River at
Wolf Island. The stones of the old cellar and chimneys
and a few wild apple trees still mark the site of the old
Church dwelling at "Macedonia."

Lemuel Church, son of Richard Church, was the first
of the Church name to be born in Rochester. In 1750
he married Bethiah Clapp, who outlived her husband by
sixty years, dying in 1832 at the age of one hundred years,
perhaps the first of the Rochester centenarians.

Lemuel Church built his home in what has since been
called the Church neighborhood, on the old Middleboro
path from Assawampsett to Mattapoisett, now known as
the "Mattapoisett Road" or the "Rochester Road." In
taking his corn for grinding to the mill some miles away,
he used to sling it on one side of the horse (as did all his
neighbors), balancing it by a stone of similar weight on
the other, the more modern method of "dividing the

grist" not being then invented. After the death of
Lemuel Church in 1772, his widow Bethiah opened her
house as an inn, furnishing rum and other "entertain-
ment" to foot travelers, — which was much appreciated
by the Indians, who still occasionally came this way, and
depended on this as a stopping-place.   It is said that on
one occasion a squaw who had brought her papoose on
her back strapped to a board, confused perhaps by what
she had been drinking, carelessly placed the board against
the side of the room head downward, and "in the morning
there was a little dead Indian."

In the vicinity of this Church neighborhood there were
various lands which were held at an early date in the
name of Cowen or Cowing. Descendants of the Cowings
still live here, though another Cowen neighborhood appeared later in the more northern part of the town.

To the south of the Church neighborhood was the land
of the Randalls, where Mr. Thomas Randall (one of the
survivors of the men of Forty-nine) still lives. There
have been many Randalls in this vicinity, though the
name Randall was carried to the central and northern
parts of the town as well. Mr. Jeremiah Randall, who
died at the Center several years ago, was the oldest resident and last person by the name of Randall in the old
Town quarter at that date.

Aunt Keziah Randall, a well-known Rochester centenarian, was born in 1789, near the site of the Marion
depot. She was a daughter of Jesse Parlow, and in her
girlhood it was said that "Kezey Parlow was the hand-
somest gal for miles around." After the death of her
husband, who was a soldier of 1812, Aunt Keziah drew
a United States pension and lived for many years alone in

a clearing in the woods to the north of the Friends' meeting-house, Aucoot, gaining health and enjoyment from the care of her vegetable garden.   On her hundredth birthday in 1889 (though she claimed to be six years older), she had many callers to whom she talked entertainingly of her reminiscences, saying that she remembered Mattapoisett village when it had only four houses and a blacksmith shop.

Another Rochester centenarian was Mrs. Jane Paine, who lived beside Mary's Pond, dying in 1891 in her one hundred and first year.   Paine has also been an old family name in the Mattapoisett quarter of Old Rochester.

In 1790 the first census of the United States was taken, in order to secure the population basis for representation in Congress, this being as early as it was found practicable to do it after the adoption of the Constitution.

A list of Rochester family names taken from this list, together with the towns from which these settlers had come, was afterwards published in the Massachusetts Historical Collections, in 1815, as follows:

Sandwich Names — Barlow, Sanders, Burges, Nye, Hammond, Swift, Willis, Blackmer, Ellis, Bessey, Wing, Black, Hamblin, Dexter, Gifford, Allen.

Marshfield Names — Arnold, Bumpus, Baker, Winslow, Snow, Hathaway, Holmes, Sherman, Sprague, White, Dotey, Russell.

Scituate Names — Church, Turner, Barstow, King, Foster, Cowin, Keen, Briggs.

Plymouth and Middleboro — Savory, Jenny, Tinkham, Clarke, Morton, Pierce, Sturtevant, Coome.

Barnstable — Davis, Lombard, Annable, Chase.

Yarmouth — Tilley, Sears, Rider, Hiller, White.

Eastham — Higgins.

Also a few Rhode Island names, with those of Pease, Luce, and Norton from the Vineyard.

Among the names in this list which have had many representatives in Rochester, the Nyes were early settlers at Charles's Neck and in the lower part of Marion. Some of the oldest graves at the ancient burying-ground of Little Neck also bear the name of Nye. At a later era the Blankinships intermarried with the Nyes and settled in the same region. Allen, Hamblin, Luce, and Savery also became well-known Sippican names, though Savery became also a name of Center Rochester. Mr. Silas B. Allen, Mr. Ichabod Blankinship, and Mr. George B. Nye are three men now living in the southern part of Marion at an advanced age, whose memories have preserved some of the facts relating to old Marion families that are mentioned in these pages.

The Hillers lived at Aucoot (formerly spelled Orcoot) and belonged to Quaker circles. They were important salt-makers. The Hathaways lived southeast of Mary's Pond, near the corner of the present towns of Wareham, Marion, and Rochester, though they were afterwards found in many other localities. Several Captain Hathaways were prominent among the shipmasters that sailed from Marion in the seafaring days.

Of other names given in this 1790 list, Barstow, Jenney, Pease, Sturtevant, and Tinkham took root in Mattapoisett, though Sturtevant was found at the Center also. Pease and Barstow became associated prominently with the later ship-building interests of Mattapoisett.

Swift became a name of Wareham. Pierce was found near the Wareham line, and Keen near the Acushnet border. King and Willis became well-known names at Rochester Center, though King was found in other localities also. Gifford, Sears, and Chase were found in several localities, though the Gifford neighborhood was in the northern part of the town. Sherman was an early name both in North Rochester and Mattapoisett, but became later a wide-spread name in all the town quarters. Rider was found at first in the northern part of the town, later at the Center and in other localities. Rider's Mill was east of Sniptuit. Snow was at first a North Rochester name, and later a name of Mattapoisett also. The Nicholas Snow house near Snow's Pond is one of the oldest of Old Rochester houses.

In 1851 David Hamblen furnished to the Historical and Genealogical Register of New England, a list of the early men of Rochester, including about seventy-five names. The list, however, has important omissions, and does more justice to some sections of the town than to others. Among the names given in this list that have not already been mentioned may be found: Andrews, Ashley, Blackwell, Bowles or Bolles, Claghorne, Danforth, Griffith, Haskins, Johnson, Leavitt, Marshall, Raymond, Robinson, Stevens, Stewart, Sommers, Thomas, and Wiatt. Some of the names given by Mr. Hamblen are no longer represented in the town, but Ashley and Bolles and a few others are still well-known names of this region.

Among Old Rochester names should be given also those of the descendants of the early ministers, Ruggles, Hovey, LeBaron, West, Moore, and Cobb. Also that of the early schoolmaster, De La Noy (Delano). Later ministers of Old Rochester, even if they left no descendants in the town, yet held important relations during the period of their pastorate. The names Chaddock, Bigelow, Harrington, Robbins, Thatcher, Briggs, Crandon, Brett, Sanger, Vose and Faunce are also names that belong to Old Rochester history.

From ancient graveyard inscriptions, lists of baptisms, marriages, military rolls, etc., a much longer list than has been given could be compiled, of names that may be considered as distinctive Rochester names of the eighteenth century. Fearing, Bassett, Mendell, Parlow, Spooner and Whitridge appear in town at an early date. Fearing was at first a Wareham name. Israel Fearing, a large landowner in the eastern edge of the town, was active in having that region incorporated with Agawam into the new town of Wareham. Bassett and Whitridge were prominent names for awhile and then passed out of town history. Parlow belonged to Parlow town, and later to other localities. Mendell has had a wide distribution in many parts of Old Rochester. Three persons of the name of Spooner were in Minister Arnold's first church list.

At the beginnings of the North Rochester parish it included (according to a statement made by Rev. J. P. Trowbridge) families bearing the names of Ashley, Bennett, Bisbee, Briggs, Clark, Crapo, Fuller, Haskell, Morton, Nye, Pope, Snow, Swift, White, Whitridge, Winslow, and Wood.

About 1800 (according to a statement made by Mrs. P. A. Wadhams) Coomb, Hooper, Hopestill, Perkins, Pierce, Reed, Bennett, Bisbee, Burges, Clark, Shaw, and Thatcher were family names of North Rochester, and, a little later still, Crandon, Omans, Sears, and Randall were also found there.

Among old Marion names not before mentioned may be given Deane, Gurney, Hadley, Handy, Hammett, Lewis, and Pitcher. Betsey Pitcher, who became Mrs. Elizabeth Taber, did much for modern Marion by her liberal bequests to the town and the church, and especially by the endowment of the academy that bears her name.

Among old Mattapoisett families not before mentioned are those bearing the names of Ames, Atsatt, Cannon, Eaton, Harlow, Howes, Mead, Macomber, Meigs, Purrington, Sisson, Southworth, and Stevens.

Near the beginning of the nineteenth century the names Sparrow and Thompson came into Rochester Center from Middleboro. Some of the Sparrows went soon to Mattapoisett, where Dr. William E. Sparrow was a prominent physician for more than half a century until his death in 1899.

Early in the nineteenth century the names Bonney and Leonard became prominent at the Center. The brothers Charles and George Bonney held many town offices, and also kept a store where considerable business was done. Mr. Charles Leonard did much to beautify his estate near the old Sippican Mill site, employing many men to build out of hewn stone long stretches of wall, that are a marked feature to-day of the Leonard (now the Rhodes) estate. Mr. Leonard (and later his wife) gave also liberal bequests to the town and the First Parish of Rochester.

A little before the middle of the century the Scotch names of Rankin and Smellie came into Rochester, where the Scotch name of Douglass had already taken root as an old town name.

But most of the family names that belong to the villages of Old Rochester refuse to be classified on either a local or a temporal basis. Some were in the town for a generation or two, and then passed out of the locality; as Peckham, Vaughn, Cathell. A much larger number were in the town from an early period, and either distributed themselves very soon in many quarters, or were found first in one section and later in quite another.

The following additional names will, however, be recognized by students of Rochester history as having at some time (and usually for a long time) held such town relations that they may be considered distinctively names of Rochester before the middle of the nineteenth century: Bates, Bartlett, Barrows, Bishop, Bourne, Bryant, Braley, Burbank, Cole, Cushman, Chubbuck, Denham, Dunham, Freeman, Gammons, Gage, Gerrish, Gibbs, Gillett, Hall, Hatch, Haskins, Howland, Howes, Jefferson, Johnson, Look, Lombard, Manter, Martin, Maxim, Mitchell, Morse, Norton, Nickerson, Rogers, Rounseville, Russell, Shaw, Shurtleff, Sisson, Smith, Snell, Southworth, Stetson, Taylor, Thatcher, Tilson, Tinkham, Tobey, Tripp, Washburn, Westgate, West.

And there are family names, not so old to the region, — some that came in about the period of the town divisions, and many that have come later still into the towns that have been formed out of this territory, — that are also assimilating themselves into the local history, and will figure prominently in the histories of the modern towns that may yet be written.

Among the names that have here been recorded there are not a few that have been carried by sons of Rochester into business and professional circles of other localities. It is a remarkable fact that of the present Massachusetts Judiciary, in 1907, three are natives of this old town: —

John Wilkes Hammond and Henry King Braley, Justices
of the Supreme Judicial Court, and Lemuel LeBaron
Holmes, Justice of the Superior Court. Theophilus
King is well known in Boston business circles. Dr. William H. Cobb is librarian at the Congregational House.
The four Johnson brothers, Arnold, Augustus, Joseph,
and Lorenzo, all attained distinction in the professions
or in business. In the world of letters is the name of
Elizabeth Barstow Stoddard, of Mattapoisett, and Richard Henry Stoddard, who, after his mother married
James Gallon, spent some of his boyhood days in that
village. Woodbridge R. Howes, who for a time conducted a private school in Mattapoisett, and who served
as a volunteer surgeon through the Civil War, had an
extensive practice as a physician in Hanover, Mass.
John L. Gifford attained the rank of Lieutenant in the
Navy and did daring work in command of scouting expeditions at the siege of Charleston. Among military men
were Major Rogers L. Barstow, and Brig.-Gen. Wilson
Barstow who was on the staff of General Dix. Solomon
E. Sparrow, whose father, Dr. William E. Sparrow, of
Mattapoisett, had served as a surgeon in the Civil War,
was a graduate of West Point and a captain in the
regular army. These and many others have been writing deeply on the social life of other communities the
family names of Old Rochester.

Among the interesting and ancient houses of Rochester
that are still standing are the Nicholas Snow house, near
Snow's Pond; the Bates house, the Sherman house, and
the Savery (or old Haskell) house. Historic houses that
have been taken down or burned within a few years, but
which had been well known as landmarks, were the old

Ruggles Tavern, the Whitridge (or Winslow) house, and the Bourne (or Major Gifford) house. The Sippican Hotel at Marion is in part an ancient structure. The oldest house within the limits of the old Rochester territory is the Lieut. John Hammond house at Mattapoisett Herring Weir, built about 1700. Other ancient dwellings of interest in Mattapoisett are the Hovey house, and the "Old Mansion" built by Minister LeBaron. In the village the Wilson Barstow house and some others along Main and Water streets, and various ones on Cannon and Pearl streets, are old houses. So also is the Benjamin Barstow (Samuel Dexter) house at Cannonville. Many of those now standing on the Necks are ancient, as also a considerable number at Hammondtown and Tinkham-town; and various ones scattered through Aucoot and Pine Islands either stand in their original form or have been enlarged and modernized. Although there are various gambrel and hip-roofed houses in Rochester, it is to be noted that there are none at Mattapoisett.

The effort that has been made in this chapter to bring together in brief enumeration the old families of the Rochester territory is necessarily very imperfect and in-complete. It must be the task of the genealogist of the future, one with a taste for antiquarian research and years of time at his command, to give an adequate account of the people who have lived and died and the families that have taken root on the soil of Old Rochester.

It has been shown that the names cannot be very defi-nitely localized, as most families spread themselves widely, through marriage and removals, into various parts of the town territory.

But while family names refuse to confine themselves in local or temporal relations, localities always have a marked tendency to assume some personal name and sometimes persist in carrying it even when the personality suggesting it has become a shadow of the past. For instance, what do we know to-day of the traditional "Mr. Merry," whose modified name has given rise to false legends relating to Mary's Pond?

As one looks over the maps of Old Rochester, and listens to the speech of the people, he comes upon geographical and institutional names, almost without number, that tell much of the history of families and of persons and of the general lines of the town settlement.

Thus in Mattapoisett one may hear of Cannonville, Hammondtown, Randalltown, Tinkhamtown; of the Ellis neighborhood, Tripps Mills, of Pease's Point, Goodspeed's Island, Barlow's Eel Pond; of the Barlow Cemetery, Hammond Cemetery, Hammond Street, Cannon Street, Barstow Street, Tobey Street, Dexter Street; of Purrington Hall and the Barstow School.

In Rochester of to-day one may hear of Snow's Pond, Leonard's Pond, Lewis Pond; of Pierceville, Parlow town, the Church neighborhood, the Morse neighborhood, the Gifford neighborhood, the Rounseville neighborhood; of Braley Hill, Vaughn's Hill, Cathell Hill, the Bisbee Corner, Cowen's Corner, the Sherman Corner, the Sherman Cemetery; of Look's Mills, and Cushman's store, as names of localities, — of Haskell Swamp, Bonney Hill, the Dexter Road, Old Parlow Road; the Waterman School, and the Stuart School.

In western Wareham are Fearing's Hill, Blackmore's Pond, and the Hathaway neighborhood. And in Marion one may hear of Wing's Cove, Blankinship's Cove, Clapp's Island, Haskell Island, Hammett's Cove, Nye's Wharf, Ruggles's Point, Mendell's Bridge, Briggs's Neck; of Allen's Corner, Hadley's Corner, Hamblen's Corner, Handy's Grove, and of Tabor Academy.

Thus do human lives write their names upon features of nature, and upon institutions, even while the personalities themselves fade away into the indistinct background of history.

CHAPTER V

THE EARLY CHURCH AND THE PRECINCTS

AS in every New England town, the first thought of the settlers of Rochester was to provide for the religious needs of the community, and as soon as possible to organize a church. The establishment of worship at Little Neck is in a true sense a part of the history of the First Church of Rochester, even though "for want of members to Imbody" no church was really organized in that locality. But the place has intrinsic and historic interest. In the words of Rev. H. L. Brickett, pastor of the Congregational Church at Marion:

"This place of worship at Little Neck is picturesque, with its massive Minister's Rock round which the Indians held their pow-wows, and close at hand the ancient burial-ground where sleep the early dead."

The religious impulses that started in the little temporary house of worship where Mr. Shiverick and Mr. Arnold preached for a few years have been transmitted to all the churches that occupy the Old Rochester territory.

But as the growing population spread rapidly over the whole town, it became evident at a very early date that this locality could not be the center of the religious and civic life of the town of Rochester.

The building of the town's meeting-house in 1699 opened the way for the church organization that had been so long delayed. As to the plans for this meeting-house (which stood within the limits of the town's burying-ground, laid out at the same time) the town records give considerable information. It was to be "24 by 26 Ft. and 10 ft. between joints, with a gable on each side." It was to have "a pulpit and flours and girts for three galerys, with three seats apew," and a rate of sixty pounds was voted to defray its cost, though it was afterwards decided to pay for it "by a free-will offering if that will amount to 50 pounds." The building committee were Samuel Prince, Peter Blackmer (who was also the builder), and Mark Haskel, at whose house the plans were drawn. He died before the house was completed, and to his widow, Mary Haskel, was given the office of sweeping the meeting-house "once in 15 days or as often as shall be occation for sweeping of it to keep it Deasent."

Minister Arnold's long religious efforts now began to bear fruit, and October 13, 1703, he wrote in the old church book, " It hath pleased our gracious Lord to shine in the dark corner of this wilderness, and visit this dark spot of ground with the dayspring from on high through his tender mercy to settle a church according to the order of the gospel."

Seven Christian men of Rochester, in addition to Mr. Arnold, signed the covenant that day, the names of the signers being Samuel Arnold, Abraham Holmes, Samuel Hammond, Isaac Holmes, Jacob Bumpus, John Benson, Thomas Dexter, Anthony Coomes.

Five years after the church was organized Mr. Arnold died, and was succeeded a few months later by Rev. Timothy Ruggles. Many years afterwards, when Minister Ruggles was asked for some information regarding his predecessor, he wrote of Mr. Arnold that "the neighboring ministers who survived him esteemed him as a worthy minister and approved him as a good Divine, but not so well skilled in church discipline as some others." In contemplating this defect, however, it is well to remember that skill in church discipline counted for more among ministerial qualifications in the eighteenth century than it does at present.

Mr. Arnold left at his death in 1709 a church list of thirty-five members as follows:

Males — Samuel Arnold (unworthy pastor); Abraham Holmes, Deacon; Samuel Hammond, Isaac Holmes, Jacob Bumpus, John Benson, Thomas Dexter, Anthony Coomes, Isaac Spooner, Benjamin Dexter, Samuel Winslow, Samuel White, Thomas Perry, Ebenezer Spooner, Samuel Arnold, Jr., Experience Holmes, John Hammond, — 17.

Females — Elizabeth Arnold, Mrs. Mary Hammond, Mrs. Sarah Arnold, Mary Haskel, Anna Holmes, Alis Spooner, Sarah Bumpus, Elizabet Bumpus, Abigal Holmes, Lidiah Joy, Mercy Winslow, Mary Whitridge, Ruth Perry, Mary Hammond, Sr., Mary Hammond, Jr., Elizabeth Arnold, Sarah Dexter, Mehitable Clark, — 18.

The names on this first church list seem fairly representative of the town territory. The Mattapoisett and Wareham names show that persons from the eastern and western edges of the town were active supporters of the new church, while Abraham and Isaac Holmes, who were brothers, lived near Snow's Pond, and represented the Sniptuit quarter.

After Mr. Arnold's death, Rev. Timothy Ruggles of Roxbury, a young graduate of Harvard, was called to be the town's minister, and was ordained November 22, 1710.

Mr. Ruggles was not made a proprietor as Mr. Arnold had been, but the town gave him a farm of seventy acres, with the use of certain other ministry lands, and an annual salary which was at one time one hundred pounds, though it was often in arrears and subject to adjustments. The town also built him a house, — Mr. Ruggles furnishing the " glasse and nails," and boarded him at Roger Hascol's till the house was done.   Capt. Isaac Holmes, John Hammond, Ensign Edward Winslow, Sergeant Benjamin Dexter, Sergeant John Briggs, Peter Blackmer, and Elisha Andrews were appointed as the building committee, " to set up such a dwelling-house for Mr. Ruggles as he shall give dimensions for."   This house stood on the old road, in the rear of Captain Hathaway's dwelling, that was given up in 1785 when the present road to Marion was built.   The site that the house occupied is still owned by descendants of Minister Ruggles.

The congregation increased rapidly, and in 1714, only eleven years after the church was organized, the meeting-house was voted too small, Some wished to enlarge the building by an addition " at ye backside thereof." But after some delays, in 1717 a new meeting-house was built, which stood for ninety-four years in the grassy triangle opposite the cemetery gate, being used for church purposes about forty-three years.   In 1906 the church and parish at Rochester Center placed a stone in this area to commemorate the two meeting-houses which were built on Rochester Common by the votes and the taxes of all the citizens of Old Rochester.

The new meeting-house of 1717 was " 40 Ft. by 35 Ft. and 20 Ft. between joints."   The pews were " al of a haith and bult workmanlike," and three seats were built

"Nye the pulpit stairs for ancient parsons to sett in." In 1725 there was a "Lock gott for it." Neither of these two first meeting-houses had a chimney or any fire unless in foot-stoves. Nor did the parish meeting-house that in 1760 succeeded the one of 1717 on Rochester Common have a fire until the nineteenth century was well begun, when a chimney was added and two box stoves were introduced.

The meeting-house of 1717 was not long adequate to the needs of the growing town. In 1733 permission was given to certain persons to build pews on the beams above the galleries, — a sort of third-story arrangement to utilize the high roof spaces which belonged to the earliest type of New England meeting-houses. One of these lofty pew builders was Timothy Ruggles, Jr., at that time a young lawyer in the town.

But events were coming that would relieve the congestion in the Rochester meeting-house, and change again the course of town history.

In 1733, the people of Mattapoisett complained that they were "so remote from the Center as to make their Difficulty great in all public Conserns," and asked to be set off into a new precinct. The matter was delayed for a time, during which an effort was made to have Mattapoisett incorporated as a separate town. But this did not meet the general wishes of the people, and in 1735 the Second Precinct of Rochester was finally set off.

With this event, Mattapoisett village began to develop more distinct lines of local interest. Through the keeping of the precinct and church books also its local history began to be put into written form. Yet for more than a hundred and twenty years longer Mattapoisett still held important relations with the other precincts as an integral part of the town of Old Rochester. In 1736 the Second Church of Rochester was organized in Mattapoisett. The interesting history of this old precinct church will be recorded in a later chapter.

With the organization of the Second Precinct, the rest of the town became "The First Precinct or Parish." The first parish was never incorporated by that name, but was always what was left of the town after other parishes had been set off.

With the setting off of Mattapoisett into a separate precinct, the history of the town itself also took a new line of development. Like all other New England towns, Rochester was at first one religious organization in which all householders were taxed for church support. The incorporation of the Second Precinct was the first of a series of events that finally changed the original town into five religious organizations having definite territorial limits, within which all householders (unless personally excused) were subject to taxation for the support of the Congregational Church in that parish. The Ministry Lands of the town were finally divided up among these parishes or precincts. "Minister's Island" at Mattapoisett Neck was perhaps a part of one of these old Ministry Lots.

In 1709, by a vote of the town, those who were "professed Quakers" began to be excused from their ministry dues, and in the latter part of the eighteenth century many Baptists claimed and received such exemption. But it was not until 1836 that the system of church taxation became illegal in Massachusetts and the voluntary system became universal.

The second parish division in Old Rochester took place July 6, 1739, when the town of Wareham was incorporated. The same year a church was established there, consisting of thirty-three members dismissed from the First Church of Rochester.

The Wareham section was not technically a precinct of Rochester, but it was sometimes referred to as the "Wareham Precinct," and it received finally (though not without some controversy) its share of the "Ministry Lands." About 1770 the town of Wareham, with Eben-ezer Briggs as its agent, successfully upheld in the courts the claims of Wareham. After this, Rochester passed a vote stating that "The Precinct of Wareham's part is to the whole as 1103 is to 5728," and that Wareham was therefore entitled to "the Minister's Land lying in their said town and in Horseneck," but added, "It is neverthe-less to be understood that the above proportions are made exclusive of the Friends and Baptists' Societies. We do, therefore consider the Sd Wareham part or proportion made as liable to contribute their part to the Sd Friends & Baptists Societies when the Said Friends and Baptists shall regularly apply for the same according to the Tenor of the Proprietors' vote."

The cutting off of the Wareham district brought a larger change than the separation of Mattapoisett had done, since it divided the people, not only in church interests, but in those of the town as well. It took from Rochester a large piece of the town territory. The vil-lages of Tremont, Tihonet, South Wareham, Wareham Center, and part of The Narrows lie in what was once Old Rochester.

The following account of the formation of the Third or

North Rochester parish is found in an article written by Abraham Holmes in 1821, and published in the Massachusetts Historical Collections, Vol. X, 2d Series:

"During the administration of Mr. Ruggles an unhappy controversy arose between him and Noah Sprague, Esq., which terminated in the erection of a poll parish, taking in the N. W. part of the town and some who lived in the immediate neighborhood of the meetinghouse of the first parish, a part of Middleboro and a part of Freetown. In this parish the Rev. Tho. West was ordained the minister.   Mr. West remained their minister until about the year 1781, though before this time some of the leading members of this church and parish grew disatisfied with this doctrine and some of them went off and joined the Baptist connexion, and at this time his advanced age, & the infirmities incident thereto, induced him to ask a dismission, it was granted.

"The members of this poll parish now found themselves, on account of diminution to be incompetent to settle a minister.   They negotiated with the first parish in the year 1791, and agreed with them for a division line between that precinct and these by which they relinquished a number that belonged to the poll parish and took in a larger number by metes and bounds which had belonged to the first parish.   They then applied to the Legislature and obtained an act of incorporation making a territorial parish, taking in a part of the first and second parishes in Middleboro and a part of Freetown.   More than half of the people who live in this parish are of different denominations of Christians from those who procured the act of incorporation."

After the territorial parish of North Rochester was

organized the First Parish gave them (instead of Ministry Lands) the sum of seventy pounds, six shillings, sixpence, "whether they continue Congregationalists or whether they are Baptists or Friends." They did continue Congregationalists, and the coming of Rev. Calvin Chaddock in 1793 did much to strengthen them in their Congregational faith.

From the historical address of Rev. John P. Trowbridge, the present pastor, given in 1903 on the 150th anniversary of this church, the following account of the church and its early pastors is chiefly compiled:

The first meeting-house in North Rochester stood about a mile westward from the present structure, in the northwest angle of the town. Its frame was raised November 17, 1748, with the sturdy exertion of many men, aided by some West India rum as the custom of the times demanded. It was a poor structure, built hastily because winter was at hand and a place of shelter for the ark of the Lord was sorely needed. Yet it was used for a place of worship a little more than forty years when its timbers were given to the man who would tear them down and carry them away, which lot fell to Mr. Abner Wood and his son Zenas.

In 1791 a second meeting-house was built on the site where a third meeting-house (the present structure) was erected in 1841. At the time of the building of the second meeting-house part of the parish wished it to stand on the lot formerly owned by Luke Perkins, near the Stillwater Furnace, and timber was actually drawn there for the purpose. But others were not pleased with this arrangement and quietly carried the timber down to the present church lot.

The church in North Rochester was organized in 1753, its first pastor being Rev. Thomas West, who was born at the Vineyard in 1708. He was a graduate of Harvard, and labored for some years at the Vineyard as a colleague Missionary before coming to Rochester. He was a good clerical scholar, and fitted several young men for the ministry. He is also described as having "apostolical simplicity of manner," and being "devoted to the prophecies." Two of the sons of Minister West attained distinction in the ministry, one of them, Rev. Samuel West, having been the pastor of the Hollis Street Church, Boston. Rev. Thomas West died in 1790, and was buried in one of the old graveyards of North Rochester, where his epitaph, blurred and broken, reads:

> "Weep ye, my friends, for West is gone,
> His glass of time doth cease to run,
> His active tongue and virtuous heart
> Have ceased to act. They've done their part.
> Although he's gone he yet does live,
> His soul immortal does survive.
> He's now disrobed of earthly clay,
> And shines in one eternal day."

The second minister of North Rochester Precinct, 1791–3, was Rev. David Gurney, of whom the only mention in the church record is found in the following minute:

"Marcus Morton and Polly, son and daughter of Nathaniel and Polly Morton, were baptized Sept. 11, 1791, by Rev. David Gurney." The chief interest in this record, however, lies in the fact that the said Marcus Morton, who was born in the Middleboro part of this precinct, when grown to manhood became the Governor

of Massachusetts, gaining his election by a majority of
one vote.

The third pastor of the North Rochester church was
Rev. Calvin Chaddock, who had studied theology with
Dr. Emmons of Franklin, then at the height of his fame.
The day of Mr. Chaddock's ordination, October 10, 1795,
was an important one in the history of North Rochester.
Dr. Emmons preached the ordination sermon, and in the
words of one who was present, "The Solemnities of the
day were performed." Before the service, the church
met at the house of Mr. Zebulon Haskell (who lived by
Great Quitticus Pond, on the site afterwards known as
"The Roberts Place,") and adopted a new confession of
faith which was "remarkable for its catholicity of spirit
and brevity of statement, considering the habits of thought
of that age."

Mr. Chaddock's pastorate was notable also for an
"Academy" which he established at North Rochester,
the first within the limits of the town territory. It did
good work for a few years and drew some pupils from a
distance, but came to an end at the close of Mr. Chaddock's pastorate in 1805.

After this the North Rochester church went through a
period of irregular preaching with two short pastorates
of Rev. Ichabod Plaisted and Rev. William Utley, —
until the coming of Rev. Isaac Briggs, whose long term of
important service lasted from 1835 to 1857, during which
the present house of worship was built, largely by Mr.
Briggs's efforts in obtaining the funds. As this chapter
deals with the precincts of *Old* Rochester, the shorter
pastorates that have occurred since 1857 are not here
followed.

After the withdrawal of the Mattapoisett, Wareham, and North Rochester members, the people of Rochester Center and Sippican remained together for many years as the First Precinct and First Church of Rochester. Mr. Ruggles continued to be the minister until 1768, when he died after a pastorate of fifty-eight years (his only pastorate), during which 303 members were added to the church.

June 2, 1757, there was a solemn service in the meeting-house called the "Renewal of the Covenant," when Mr. Ruggles was assisted by the ministers of the other precincts, and "16 females and 28 males attended the Solemnity."

Although Mr. Ruggles was a man of peace, his last years were disquieted by a lawsuit, to which he was a party at the solicitation of his people, for the recovering of certain Ministry lands near the church which other persons were "improving," and which it was felt must be recovered "during the lifetime of our present minister." The land does not seem to have been recovered, but several generations later it was given back to the parish by the persons then holding it, and it is known to-day as "The Ministry Lot," lying just north of the church to the west of the North Rochester road.

On a large slate gravestone in the front of Rochester Cemetery one may read:

"In memory of ye Rev'd Timothy Ruggles, pastor of ye church in Rochester, who was an able Divine and a Faithful Minister. Having a peculiar talent at composing Differences and healing Divisions in Churches, he was much imployed in Ecclesiastical Councils and having spent his Days and his strength in the work of his Lord

and Master finished his Course with Joy and departed
this Life October ye 26, 1768, in the 84th year of his age
and the 58th of his Ministry."

Minister Ruggles's successor in the First Church of
Rochester was Rev. Jonathan Moore, ordained in 1768.
He was a graduate of Harvard, and had been librarian of
that college.   Previous to his ordination also, he supplied
for some months the pulpit of Brattle Street Church, Boston, during the illness of Dr. Cooper, who attended his
ordination at Rochester.   His pastorate included the
trying Revolutionary period, and on the alarm of Lexington he joined one of the Rochester Companies as its chaplain.   It is said also that "he shouldered his musket and
marched to Marshfield and also to Wareham during the
Revolution."

The "half-way Covenant," adopted in many New
England churches in the eighteenth century, began to
influence Rochester church during the latter part of
Mr. Ruggles's pastorate and was later supported by
Mr. Moore.   Perhaps this, as well as the religious
decline under the infidel influence of France that was
everywhere prevalent after the Revolution, had something
to do with the disturbances that entered the First Church
of Rochester during the last years of the eighteenth century, although the controversy seems to have been largely
personal in its nature.

Mr. Moore was dismissed in 1792, but refused to recog-
nize such dismissal, and for a while rival services were
held in the meeting-house and in Mr. Moore's own dwelling.   His name was taken from the roll of the church as
well, but before his death in 1814 he was received back
into the full communion of the church.

The anonymous writer of 1815, previously quoted, says of Mr. Moore:

"He was a man of constitutional fearlessness of heart. The face of men in any garb had no terrors for him. — The latter days of Mr. Moore were embittered by disputes and lawsuits with his parish, finally issuing in his dismission. — He continued to preach to a part of the society more than two years in his dwelling-house, but in his closing years, renewed his communion with the church of which he had formerly been pastor. Mutual forgiveness of injuries is a Christian virtue strictly enjoined on all; in a peculiar manner those who make profession of the Christian name. It is proper to state that in 1794 when Mr. M. sued for arrears in salary, the Supreme Judicial Court gave the cause in his favour but the jury returned a verdict otherwise."

It seems probable that Mr. Moore had the technical rights of the case in his controversy with his church. Nevertheless, he was not, like Minister Ruggles, "skilled in the composing of differences." And the frictions of this period had something to do with the setting off of the Fourth Parish of Rochester in 1798.

Yet in the words of Rev. H. L. Brickett, "Mr. Moore was an able fearless and scholarly man." During the first part of his pastorate he did good service for the church in Rochester and his well-written records and other writings have real historic value. He is buried in Rochester Cemetery, and beside him lies Susanna, the wife of his youth. On another stone near by, one may read " In memory of Capt. Jonathan Moore, son of Rev. Jonathan Moore and Susanna his wife. He was master of the ship Newport of Boston and on his pas-

sage to London in Sept. of 1800 the ship foundered in
a storm, when he with all the people on board, being
upwards of 20, perished in the 30th year of his age.

> God does the Raging Sea controul
> 'Tis He that rules the boisterous Deep,
> He makes the Sleeping Billows roll,
> He makes the rolling Billows sleep."

The second wife of Minister Moore was Anna, the
daughter of Polypus Hammond of Mattapoisett, and
some of the descendants of this second marriage are now
there living.

About 1795 the people of Sippican, many of whom
were opposed to Mr. Moore, began to hold preaching
services in that part of the town. In 1798 the Fourth
Precinct of Rochester was set off, and in 1791 a meeting-
house (now the Luce store) was built in the lower village.
One of the ministers who came to Sippican to preach
during this period was Rev. Oliver Cobb, who proved to
be a young man of promise and of power. The people
of Sippican, however, had no desire to separate from the
First Church, nor was either precinct desirous to assume
the full support of a minister at that time. In 1799 the
First Church of Rochester, made up of members of both
precincts, extended a call to Mr. Cobb to be their pastor,
the First Precinct agreeing that the pastor "should preach
in the Fourth Precinct from a fourth to one half of the
time." Practically, services were held alternately in the
two meeting-houses during Mr. Cobb's pastorate. The
call was accepted and Mr. Cobb was ordained and took
up his residence on the road between the two meeting-
houses, though within the limits of the Fourth Precinct.

The account of the forming of the Fourth Precinct is more fully given by Mr. Holmes in 1821, as follows:

"In the first parish a great degree of unanimity prevailed until the year 1788, when an unhappy difficulty arose between the Rev. Mr. Moore the minister, and Major Earl Clapp a leading man in the church and parish. This difficulty though personal in its Commencement, very soon became general, and a more spirited controversy seldom if ever was known. This terminated in the dismissal of Mr. Moore. In Feb. 1799 the Rev. Oliver Cobb was settled as the minister of that parish and of another parish in said town the origin of which will be narrated. —

"In the year 1798 a number of the inhabitants of the S.E. part of the 1st parish living remote from the place of publick worship, having built a meeting-house petitioned the Legislature to be incorporated into a distinct parish, — the first parish accompanying said petition with a certificate that they had no objection to the prayer of said petition. They were accordingly incorporated. These petitioners had no idea of settling a minister by themselves but of joining with the first parish in settling one who should preach alternately in each meetinghouse. They accordingly joined in settling Mr. Cobb, as before mentioned, — but they have a church (*i.e.* a meetinghouse) separately in said parish, and a considerable part of both parishes can attend each meetinghouse, the meetinghouses being only 4 miles distant from each other."

The following description of Rev. Oliver Cobb as well as that of Rev. Leander Cobb, Dr. Cobb's son and successor in the church at Sippican, is taken from an anni-

versary sermon preached by Rev. H. L. Brickett of Marion
in 1903:

"Rev. Oliver Cobb at the time of his coming to Rochester
was 29 years of age, married, well fitted for the ministry
and ready for service. In appearance he was slim, with
a smooth face, medium height, and eyes as blue as the
waters in Sippican Bay. He was a graduate of Brown
University, from which he also received the degree of D.D.
in 1834.

"Two churches, Rehoboth and Rochester, desired his
services and he asked the advice of an Indian as to which
he should accept. The Indian, Yankee-like, replied with
a question, 'What are you going to preach for?' and
added, 'If you are going to preach for money go where
the most money is; if you are going to preach for souls go
where the most devil is.' And he came to Rochester.

"In Mr. Cobb's family was a colored girl named
Dinah, who was fond of Mr. Cobb and could not bear
to hear him criticised. Once when some one had found
fault with him in her hearing she burst forth, 'Anybody
that talks about Dr. Cobb talks about a very wicked thing.'
When Dr. Cobb heard of this he laughed and said, 'Dinah
never spoke truer words.'"

With Mr. Cobb's coming to the First Church of Rochester, it entered on a period of much harmony and prosperity. During this ministry there were three revivals
of marked power, in 1807 and 1808, in 1816 and in 1819,
and many new members came into the church in both
villages.

In 1709 sacramental vessels were bought by the First
Church for the "Harbour Meetinghouse." James Clark
and Timothy Hiller were appointed deacons in that pre-

cinct and thereafter the Communion Services were held alternately in the two villages. Thus by gradual steps there came to be virtually two fully equipped churches in the two parishes, though having the services of one minister in common.

It was the older and larger precinct that first grew tired of this arrangement and desired the entire service of a pastor. In 1827 Rev. Jonathan Bigelow was called to be colleague pastor with Mr. Cobb. The council called to install Mr. Bigelow being asked the question: "Is it expedient that this church be divided?" replied that "It is expedient." So the church roll of members was divided, eighty-three members being assigned to the church in the First Precinct, and fifty-seven to the church in the Fourth Precinct, and Mr. Bigelow was installed as pastor in the First Precinct. Both churches were already fully equipped with officers, and the only change that occurred at this date was that the church at Rochester Center had a new pastor and both congregations now had services each Sabbath instead of on alternate Sabbaths.

Some discussion arose as to the names of the two churches, and some spasmodic and inconsistent attempts were made to call the two churches the Central and South Churches of Rochester, until the incorporation of Marion gave a natural distinction, as, the Congregational churches of Rochester and of Marion.

But in 1861 the following minute was placed on record by the church of the old First Precinct:

"Resolved: — that this church was originally incorporated as the First Congregational Church of Rochester — and that this is our only legal name.

"Resolved: — that the title of the Central Church of

Rochester by which we have sometimes allowed ourselves
to be designated was only temporarily endured in consideration of the peculiar feelings of a former and beloved
pastor now gone to his rest."

When the church of the First Precinct moved into its
new house of worship in 1837, Dr. Oliver Cobb preached
the last sermon in the old meeting-house where he had
ministered for twenty-eight years as pastor, and the
building was then taken down.

It seems entirely natural that Dr. Cobb, whose historic
mind had done much to preserve and record the old church
history of Rochester, ministering as he did to the day of
his death in the same locality where he began his preaching and where his home was located, remembering also
that within this precinct was the spot where the early
settlers of the town first set up their altars of worship,
should have clung to the old church name that for a
whole generation had been applied to the church over
which he ministered.

After all, the truest view of these church relations seems
to be that the old First Church of Rochester, organized
in 1703 on Rochester Green, has found its natural continuance in five ancient sister churches occupying the
five territorial divisions that from the first were the recognized "quarters" of the Old Rochester territory.

Between the years 1837 and 1845 all five of these Congregational churches thus formed out of the old First
Church of Rochester had new houses of worship of similar
architecture, for which Solomon K. Eaton of Mattapoisett
was architect and builder. The one at Wareham was
burned in 1904, and has been replaced by a building of
different architectural style. The other four of these

MEETING-HOUSE OF THE FIRST PARISH

Showing the Academy and Town Hall Building, Rochester Center

meeting-houses are still in use.   They all belong to what
has been called the Third or Christopher Wren style of
New England church architecture, though modified by
the fact that all have square belfries instead of the usual
pointed spire.

After 1827, when the churches in the First and Fourth
Precincts had without reorganization gone on their separate ways, Rev. Oliver Cobb continued with the church
at Sippican as its pastor until his death in 1849.

In 1839 Rev. Leander Cobb became his father's colleague and later his successor.   "He was a man of intellectual attainment and spiritual power, a graduate of
Brown' and of Andover, a gifted sermonizer and faithful
pastor."   Soon after his coming the new house of worship
was begun, and its dedication and Mr. Cobb's installation
occurred the same day, December 1, 1841.   Rev. Leander
Cobb was still the pastor of this parish when the Fourth
Precinct of Old Rochester became the new town of
Marion.

Meanwhile, in the old First Precinct the new pastor,
Rev. Jonathan Bigelow, installed in 1827, also was doing
a noble work for the church and parish.   He served for
many years on the School Committee of the town, and
was perhaps the most influential factor in the establishment of Rochester Academy (opened in 1839), which was
for a generation a most potent educational force in the
town.   He also had much to do with the building opera-
tions that produced within a few years, the church, academy, and parsonage at Rochester Center.   Mr. Bigelow
was a man of intellectual power and held in a marked
degree the affection and respect of his people.   He was
dismissed in 1849 and was succeeded by the Rev. Eli

Harrington, who was pastor in the old First Precinct at the time of the division of the towns.

But the sketch here given of the old precincts of Rochester would be very incomplete unless mention is made of other church organizations that grew up in the various parishes during the century and three quarters that comprised the old town history.

The first form of faith other than that of the legal parishes to find entrance into Rochester was that of the "Friends or Quakers." Meetings for worship among the Friends were begun in Rochester as early as 1702. In 1707 a preparative monthly meeting of Friends was started, this being subordinate to the regular monthly meeting at Apponegansett or Dartmouth. A meeting-house was built which stood for many years close beside the pound in North Marion. The burying-ground opposite the Methodist Church in the same vicinity is still known as the old Quaker burying-ground. About 1740 the relations of this preparative monthly meeting were transferred to the monthly meeting at Sandwich.

In 1790 the rates of church taxes in Rochester by a vote of the towns were remitted to those "of contrery judgment who are professed Quakers." The chief minister or public speaker of this old Friends' Society was Nicholas Davis, who was a man of ability and influence. After 1740 his membership was in the Sandwich monthly meeting. He died in 1755 while on a journey in New York State.

The writer of 1815 previously quoted says of his own era, "The Friends of whom there has ever been some in the place, have a meetinghouse not far from the shore. There may be fifteen families now in the town."

Regarding the conditions of the Friends in Rochester in 1821, Mr. Holmes writes:

" In the N. W'ly part of the town are a number of the denomination of Quakers and attend religious worship in the northerly part of Fair Haven. About 2 miles S. easterly from the center of the town stands an Ancient Friends Meetinghouse [near the Pound, in North Marion]; but the society has for a great number of years been gradually decreasing, and about 5 yrs since their publick speaker died at an advanced age, and it was thought the society would become extinct; but about that time a young gentleman who had recently assumed a religious character embraced their religious sentiments, altered his dialect and dress accordingly; resigned his commissions as a justice of the peace and a captain of the militia, joined their society and became a publick speaker. This event has had a considerable effect on the Society. If it has not increased their numbers, it has called the lukewarm into activity, has brought to the meeting occasionally many of the leading people of that denomination from New Bedford and Fairhaven and has brought to attend meeting some who before that were contented with their private devotions at home and will doubtless be the means of perpetuating the Society."

The society was perpetuated, and now holds meetings in the white meeting-house in Mattapoisett on the road between Mattapoisett village and Marion.

In the latter part of the eighteenth century, the Baptist faith began to spread rapidly in the southeast part of New England, largely through the preaching of Elder Backus of Titicut, who became the historian of the Baptist churches. According to Mr. Backus, a Baptist church

was established in Rochester in 1793. But the organization referred to seems to be the one that now worships in
Long Plain, which had a large Rochester membership in
its earlier years.

The only Baptist society now within the limits of Old
Rochester is in Mattapoisett, at first as a branch of the
church at Long Plain. After a time the members became divided in opinion, and various attempts were
made to start a Freewill Baptist Church, or some other
kind of Baptist organization — but with only temporary
effect. The church was reorganized several years ago
as a "Church of the Christian Connection." Another
"Christian Church" was started about the middle of the
nineteenth century near Cushman's store in Rochester.
But after a few years this was disbanded.

In the article of 1821, Mr. Holmes writes:

"A very considerable part of the inhabitants of this
town are Baptists or Quakers, but Catholicism so far
prevails that no considerable inconvenience arises there-
from. In the election of any kind of officer, no attention
is paid to the particular denomination of Christian to
which the candidate belongs. An incorporated Baptist
Society is in the S. W. part of the town who have a meeting-
house. And a number more in the N.W. part of the town
are incorporated with a Baptist Society in the northerly
part of Fair-Haven. Most of the people of the north-
easterly part of the town belong to a Baptist Society in
Middleboro, and in the S. E'ly part of the town a number
of Baptists have associated together."

About 1841-3 an Adventist movement, known as the
"Miller Excitement," spread through New England, and
had considerable influence in some parts of Rochester,

especially among the Baptists, and a church was formed at Mattapoisett.

During the first half of the nineteenth century two Universalist churches were organized, in Sippican Lower Village and in Mattapoisett.

In 1821 Mr. Holmes writes:

"In the Second Parish some of the Congregational order who had a degree of dislike to their minister's preaching joined with a number of the Baptist denomination and a few Universalians and built the present year a meetinghouse, but a small distance from the parish meetinghouse. This house is not claimed by any particular denomination, but is open to all without exception."

In 1828 the Universalist Church in Sippican was organized. In 1838 the society in Mattapoisett built a new meeting-house at the corner of Church and Barstow streets. Through much of the history of these two churches the same minister has supplied both pulpits.

Some time before 1830 Methodism began to find its way into Rochester. A Protestant Methodist society was formed in North Rochester and built a meeting-house near Sniptuit Pond. Philip Crandon, the pastor of this church, was for some years one of the School Committee of Rochester. During the years of rotation of the town meetings one town meeting was held in this old meeting-house. The building was afterwards converted into Allen's store.

Another old Protestant Methodist society was formed in Sippican, and worshiped for some years in the old disused building on the woodland road that runs between Plymouth road and Wareham road. The society went down many years ago, and has been superseded by the present Methodist Episcopal Church at North Marion.

In 1825 a Union meeting-house was built at about the geographical center of the present town of Rochester, on a lot given by Joseph Purrington. It was dedicated in the fall of 1825, and services began to be held there, Elder Pliny Brett "reading the sermon."

The society has been several times reorganized, being once a Methodist society for some years, but later made a Congregational society. The first building was burned and another built on the same site. Preaching is now held at this meeting-house, being supplied by neighboring pastors.

In East Rochester a Methodist church was established near the middle of the nineteenth century, but it has since been reorganized as a Congregational church. There are no other than Congregational churches in the territory of the present town of Rochester.

Within a few years two Episcopal chapels have been built within the Old Rochester limits, St. Gabriel's Chapel in Marion, and St. Philip's Chapel in Mattapoisett. Both are supported mainly by the summer residents, and hold services only in summer.

CHAPTER VI

THE year 1700 is recognized in the Rochester Records as marking an epoch in the town history. "The Center" was now established; the meeting-house had been built. The general layout of the town was in a good degree determined. It remained for the town to develop its entire territory in accordance with the decisions that had been made.

During the first decade of the eighteenth century the boundaries of the town were again examined and agreed upon. The road system was more definitely developed. The church was organized, plans for schools were entered upon, and some new industries were undertaken.

The ecclesiastical history that began with the founding of the First Church in 1703 has already been told. The other lines of town development during the period when Rochester was under the Province Government form the subject of the present chapter.

In 1695 the bounds with Middleboro were laid out. In 1698 the town settled anew its boundaries with Plymouth; in 1701 with Dartmouth; and in 1702 the bounds on the north were still further fixed with "the tomsons of Middleberry" and others. An important bound and landmark through all the town history has been Peak Rock, which stands on the Long Plain road, and bears

the date 1664, the year when Dartmouth was incorporated.   It became the corner of three towns, Dartmouth,
Freetown, and Rochester, also of Plymouth and Bristol
counties.   By a change of boundary line, however, it is
no longer a corner of Freetown.

One of the most important tasks of the settlers was to
open roads and build bridges, which were often corduroy
roads of pine logs laid over swampy tracts.

Several ancient Indian paths formed the beginning of
the road system.   One of these was the "Old Path" from
Plymouth, which was for generations a part of the stage
road from Plymouth to Dartmouth.

Intersecting the "Old Path," a little northeast of Mary's
Pond, was a long and ancient pathway leading from Sandwich to Dartmouth, passing through Rochester Center in
front of the burying-ground.   It was known in the early
town history as the "Country Road," and very many of
the early roads were laid out as beginning at the "Country
Road."   In Wareham this road was also called "Sandwich Path," and in Rochester, the "Rhode Island Path";
the "Rhode Island Path" being also at a later date a part
of the stage route between Plymouth and New Bedford.

There were other Rhode Island paths leading from
Plymouth besides the one through Rochester.   Weston's
History of Middleboro speaks of a "Rhode Island Path"
through Middleboro and Assonet.   In Massachusetts Historical Collections [1815] we read; "There are two roads
leading from Plymouth to New Bedford, the first thirty-
two miles, by Rochester passing much woods, with but
a few scattered settlements, is yet a pleasant route, except that cross roads in obscure situations may mislead
an entire stranger.   The second, thirty-six miles by

Middleboro, is a more open and obvious route, with continued settlements. These roads diverge about two miles from Plymouth on the summit of 'Sparrow's Hill,' the first being the left hand." Each of the old roads from Plymouth to New Bedford seems to have been constructed on an ancient Indian "Rhode Island Path."

Another old Indian trail came down from Middleboro, passing the site of the Union meeting-house. Its continuation down the west shore of Sippican was called the "Old Bay Path." There was another Old Middleboro Path from the Middleboro Ponds into Mattapoisett, and an ancient pathway in Mattapoisett was also sometimes called the "Bay Path." There was another cross-road or trail connecting the Sandwich Path with· Dartmouth, but lying nearer to the sea than the "Country Road." It may have been over this path that Captain Church traveled on his way westward to meet Queen Awashonks.

Such Indian trails or paths were definite but narrow, and for foot passengers only. Later, they became for the colonists bridle-paths, and on many of them the towns afterwards laid out their wagon roads.

In 1694 several important roads were built in Rochester. In this year a road was definitely built on the "Old Path" beginning at "Middleberry bounds," and following the "Old Path till it came to Boxberry Swamp." In 1739, when Wareham was incorporated, its boundary was to be "Sippican River, as far as Mendell's Bridge, and thence as ye Rhode now Lieth to Plymouth till it meets with the Middleborough line." This ancient road that "lieth to Plymouth" is still the boundary between Rochester and Wareham, so that the village which has grown up on the two sides of the road is a little uncertain as to whether it belongs to East Rochester or West Wareham, and in common parlance it is usually "Pierceville."

Another long and important road laid out in 1694 followed perhaps in general the last of the Indian paths that have been referred to. It is described as beginning on the west side of Mattapoisett River, and after crossing the river and going near Moses Barlow's house, it continued to the long bridge and Joseph Benson's "along the road that lieth to Aaron Barlow's" and then on to the "Sipycan road near John Mendell's," "which is the extent of our Doings."

After the opening of the eighteenth century, a new activity in road-building manifested itself. It is impossible to give an accurate account of the roads as they were successively laid out. The long descriptions, dealing largely with rocks and marked "Oak Trees," would be unintelligible to modern readers. In Town Book No. 10, however (in accordance with a vote of the town in 1824), Abraham Holmes, who was then town clerk, compiled from the older town records an index and abridgment of some of the early town affairs, including a condensed description of the laying out of roads in Rochester after 1700.

From Mr. Holmes's abridgment of the original road records the following still more condensed description has in the main been compiled, and though too brief to be an exact description of the roads, it may yet give some general impression of the development of the highway system, and also show something of the location of the homes of the early settlers.

After the year 1700, the town of Rochester laid out roads as follows:

1704. Towards the Mill (*i.e.*, the Sippican Mill Dam)
touching John White's land and an old bridge,
Anthony Coomb's land, and so to Kenelm Winslow's land.

1704. From the Country Road by Joshua Spooner's and
west end of Kenelm Winslow's land, west to
Arnold's and on to Whitridge's land.

1705-6. A very long highway, beginning east side of
the Ministry Land, "where the Country Road
crosses it," "Nye the meetinghouse," crossing
Joseph Dotey's land, and the bridge near James
Stewart's house, and afterwards dividing into
two roads, towards Charles's Neck and Mattapoisett. (The Dexter and Parlow roads and the
disused woods roads beyond.)

1716. From Common Landing, near Samuel Hammond's
Island to Thomas Clarke's land.

1718. Near George Danforth, by Benjamin Dexter's.

1718. Into Crawmesit Neck.

1718. Beginning at Country Road, on top of a hill near
Isaac Bumpus' field.

1720. Into Great Neck.

1727. (Altered) the road to Cornelius Clarke's Dwelling
House.

1729. Joshua Coggeshall's to Thomas Clark's land, near
Quitticus Ponds.

1734. Quaker Meeting-house to Occoot.

1737. Road by Joshua Cowing's altered.

1739. Occoot to Ephraim Dexter's.

1739. Mattapoisett meeting-house to Josiah Dexter's.

1746. Peaked Rock by John Shearman's, to Quitticus
Brook.

1746. From aforesaid road (by Peaked Rock) by Deacon Elisha Freeman, Peter Crapo, Isaac Freeman, and William Clark.

1747. From Isaac Freeman's by James Lord's to east corner of Thomas Whitridge's land.

1750. From the road between Peaked Rock and Quitticus brook to Freetown line.

1753. John Hammond's to Dartmouth line.

1754. From Elisha Freeman's Corner eastward.

1756. From Seth Snow's into Pine Island.

1757. From John Stetson's to Mattapoisett, through lands of John Steward, William Rotch, and Charles Stetson, and others.

1762. From Winslow's and Rider's gristmill, by Ezra Clarke's.

1772. Sniptuit Neck near Nathaniel Clark's.

1772. Road by the Haunted House (altered).

1774. Middleboro line to Seth Randall's.

1775. Dartmouth line to Isaac Pope's.

1778. Dartmouth line to John Hammett's.

1780. Middleboro line by Stillwater Mills.

1781. From Samuel Rider's across Horse Neck to Aaron Sturtevant's.

1785. Enoch Hammond's to Mattapoisett Neck.

1785. From Mr. Moore's Meeting-house, by Elisha Barrows's, over Muddy Brook, towards the Friends' Meeting-house, giving up two roads already trod, so as to maintain but one bridge (present road from the Center towards Marion).

1786. Road by Mr. Moore's.

1787. From Deacon Whitridge's to the schoolhouse (altered).

1787. Over Rock Bridge by Capt. Joshua Snow's.
1792. Hannah Dotey's to Seth Randall's.
1793. Near John Ellis's.
1793. By Samuel Rider's house.
1799. Highway districts established.
1801. Old Landing to Sippican Wharf.
1801. From Silas Handy's to the wharf.
1805. Over Wolf Island.
1806. At Horse Neck by Moses Mendell's.
1807. From John Crapo's to Nicholas Davis's (widened).
1807. Peaked Rock to Middleboro altered.
1808. Into Mattapoisett Neck from Nathaniel Hammond's.
1810. Near Philip Dexter's.
1810. Into Mattapoisett Neck west of Isaac Barrow's land.
1811. At the Old Landing.
1815. First vote to raise money to clean away snow and mend bridges caused by freshets.
1818. Across Captain Mitchell's land.
1819. By Nicholas Snow's (altered).
1819. From Captain Mitchell's to Nathan Sears, Jr.
1819. At Mattapoisett by Benjamin Barstow's.
1824. From Schoolhouse near A. Mantor's.
1824. At the Old Landing.
1824. Three roads near Rider's Mill.
1825. At Wharf village eastward.
1825. At Horse Neck by Moses Mendell's.
1825. Near Alden Mantor's discontinued.
1827. Streets at Mattapoisett village.
1832. At Mattapoisett village.
1832. On Mattapoisett Neck.

1832. From Eben Holmes's to Wharf village.
1832. Into Charles's Neck by John Clark's.

With the opening of the eighteenth century the industries of the town received new attention.

In 1700 the town voted:

"That Ensign Isaac Holmes repair to Sniptuit Brook and repaire the weare and take the allowance which is to be taken, and he is also appointed to divide the fish 5000 to each family taking those that live nearest the weare first and to have 6d for each thousand so delivered or a peck of corn next fall besides one shilling to be paid down when the fish are delivered."

The herring fishery has always been an important source of food in Rochester as well as of income to the town treasury. In 1821 we are told that the income of the herring fishery was about $400 annually. The so-called herrings of the New England coasts are, strictly speaking, "alewives." The true herring is an ocean fish of somewhat mysterious habits that swims in vast shoals, and is one of the most important kinds of food fish of the world. The alewives much resemble the true herring, but by careful writers in the early days they were always carefully distinguished from the herring to which the colonists had been accustomed on European shores. In local parlance, however, the name, "alewive" was long ago dropped for "herring." At the beginning of Rochester history herrings (or alewives) were seined in the streams of Wareham, and on the setting off of Wareham a weir was reserved for Rochester on the Weweantit River.

The appointment of Isaac Holmes to the charge of the

MATTAPOISETT HERRING WEIR

Sniptuit weare shows that herrings also came abundantly into Sniptuit pond. They came in through the Taunton River, however, and the weir was on the stream now known as North Rochester Brook. An elevation called "Old Weir Hill" is on the Gerrish farm near by, and here may be seen to-day traces of the dwelling once occupied by Experience Holmes, who was a nephew of Isaac Holmes, the first herring inspector of Rochester.

In 1755 an artificial channel from Mattapoisett River led to the yearly passage of vast shoals of herrings into Sniptuit by this route, and since then the Mattapoisett River has been especially the herring river. On this river there are now three weirs, two in Rochester and one in Mattapoisett. At the Mattapoisett weir certain mills are also located that were owned by Old Rochester before the town division and are known as "town mills." Although this mill privilege is not at present highly improved, the mills as well as the fishery are still owned by the three towns in common, and are under the care of the herring inspectors.

February 6, 1699-1700, "Libertie" was given to any of "the proprietors to sett up a mill for Iron Works — if more than eight purchasers do appear to carry on and build sd mill," but it was to be in "Some sutable place where it may be secure from hurting people by cuting choyse timber." No definite record is given as to any mill being "set up," but at an early date there was an iron mill at Leonard's Pond (or Sippican Mills). Also a blast furnace was in early operation at Stillwater Mills in North Rochester.

The iron works at Sippican Mills seem to have been quite extensive, for in 1821 we are told there were a forge, a trip hammer shop and a foundry "all on the Sippican River."

The largest deposit of iron ore was in Lake Quitticus. It was taken from the lake with an instrument resembling tongs, and the industry was attended with some danger. In Middleboro several instances of drowning are recorded in getting ore from "Assawampsett Pond." There was also some ore in Sniptuit Pond, and further south along the streams. In a brook which flows from "the iron country" through Rochester Center, one may to-day find stones showing traces of iron.

In the iron works at Leonard's Pond (or Sippican Mills) there was a trip-hammer by which the iron was converted into "blooms" or masses of iron of oblong shape. These iron "blooms" were then sent to Wareham, where they were rolled out into bars and then cut into small slits to be hammered later into the form of nails.

Of the iron works in North Rochester, Mr. Holmes says: "In the north of the town is a furnace called 'Stillwater Furnace,' on account of the sluggishness of the stream. It stands on Black River, which rises in Middleboro, and only the S. E. end of it is in Rochester. Its operation is confined to the winter season, and then it is very productive." At the Stillwater mills the crude ore was melted in the puddling furnace and iron castings were made.

In 1725, Major Edward Winslow of Sniptuit was empowered to set up an iron mill "on the Mattapoisett River." Rounseville's sawmill in Rochester was formerly known as the Winslow mill, but it is not certain that iron was ever manufactured at this site. At Hartley's mill, however, a little farther north, there are traces of an old iron industry, and this may have been the site of Major Winslow's old iron works.

In 1821 the iron works of Rochester seem to have been in regular operation, though Mr. Holmes records that the usefulness of the forge was cramped by the scarcity of water during the summer season. A few years later the town appointed certain agents to look after the town's deposits of iron ore which had been neglected, and to gather the ore and sell it to some iron works. But no report of these agents is recorded, and it seems probable that the whole iron business was about this time discontinued.

Pasturage was an important source of wealth in Rochester throughout the eighteenth century. About 1732 many pages of records are given to the "distinguishing marks of the Cretures" of various owners, — a crop or half crop "on the nere ear," "two pennies under the ear," holes and crosses, a "flower de luce," "slits cut slantwise," and other marks by which the animals were to be known. Thus in 1778 David Dexter marked his cattle with "2 slits in the end of the left ear," which was the same mark that had been used by his grandfather, Caleb Dexter, many years before.

Much legislation was also needed to keep the "Sheep-rams" within limits, and the swine properly "yoaked and ringed," as they ran at large over the common lands of the proprietary. In 1726 it was specified that a notice of a "Ram or Rames," running at large must be posted, "if in the village called the center at the hous of John Clapp and if in the village called Sipycan at the hous of John Briggs and if in the village called Sniptuit at the hous of Capt. Edward Winslow & if in the fresh meadow village

& Weweantit at Isaac Bumpus his mill & if in Matta-
poyset village at the house of John Hammond."

It is related of Timothy Ruggles, Jr., afterward the
noted Tory leader, that once, for a practical joke, he succeeded in having a law passed that all the men who
owned swine should have their noses ringed; a vote that
later had to be recast so as to make it apply to the animals
rather than the men.

Something of the social and educational condition of
Rochester in the early part of the eighteenth century may
be learned from a diary begun in 1711, by Joseph Prince,
the fifteen-year-old son of Samuel Prince, and continued
at intervals for some years. It is a little book of seventeen leaves, stitched together, and begins with the
heading:

"Joseph Prince, His Book. Anno Domini. Remarks.
        Aug. 4, 1711 Aage 15 years at hom."

Then comes the first laconic daily entry:

        " da 4 Rany, Right, Read."

But most days were not "Rany," and the boy records
his daily work — "drive plow," "mow," "cut sproughts,"
"Rak and Cok Hay." "Reed and Ketch fish," and
various other employments. It was a busy life that was
led by the boys of Rochester in 1711.

But the Prince home was one of education and culture,
and each leisure hour or rainy day gave an opportunity
always improved, to "Reed, Right and Sifer." Something of the books then accessible may be learned from
one entry, "An Accompt of the books that I rede out."
It includes a list of thirty books, headed by "the bibel."
Some of these are general books of history or information,

as "A Discourse Concerning Comets." Others are religious books and include the following titles:

"Time and the End of Time," — "Contemplations on Mortality," — "Now or Never the time to be saved," — "The Joy of Faith," — "The Foly of Sinning," — "The Sincear Convert," — "The poor Doughting Christian drawn to Christ."

The first movement to provide a school in Rochester occurred in 1704, when a rate of ten pounds was voted to be put into Minister Arnold's hands for the support of a schoolmaster, and the next year the selectmen were empowered to "engage some able person to teach children and Youth to Reed and Right," at a wage of two shillings a week with "dyet washing and lodging." Some other references to a school are made about 1705, but exactly what was done is not made clear, nor whether any teacher was really engaged.

September 5, 1711, "mrs. jane masshell" was engaged as teacher, at a salary of twelve pounds a year and her " dyet," but three men of the town, "joseph Benson, john dexter and ichobod burg," entered a protest that she was "not as the law directs." This uncomplimentary remark does not seem to have referred to Mrs. Masshell's moral character, but to her teaching qualifications, for in other years, schoolmasters were examined and duly approved as being "qualified as the law directs." But "jane masshell's" teaching service, if entered on at all, was short, for the following February John Myers was engaged "to sarve in the office of Skollmaster." He held the position for several years, beginning with a salary of twelve pounds and " dyet," which a year later was increased to sixteen pounds, and still later to twenty pounds.

The school was migratory, lots being cast for the order
of the terms, and the town being divided sometimes into
four, but usually into five "quarters" for school purposes.
The villages named as having terms of school include
always Sippican, Mattapoisett, and either "the Center,"
"the Town," or "Whitehall" (the name of Mr. Prince's
residence).   During several years while the Prince family
lived in Rochester, both "Whitehall" and "the Town or
Meetinghouse Quarter" had school terms assigned to
them, but a little later, "Whitehall or the Town" is
named as having one term of school.   In 1711 Pine Island
is named as a school quarter, but this is not continued in
later years.   The earliest schools at Wareham were at
"Fresh Meddows," but later "Weweyantit" is the locality given.   After 1723 Sniptuit becomes one of the
school quarters.

In 1717 Samuel Prince was empowered to provide the
town with a grammar school, and in that year it was
voted that "William Griffeth be schoolmaster for a quarter
of a year, if he will agree on terms."   In 1722-3 Timothy
Ruggles and Samuel White examined Mr. Josiah Masshell
(was this Mrs. jane Masshell's son?), and "did approve
of him as a fitt person Quallified as the Law Directs."
For a considerable number of years Benjamin De La Noy
(Delano) was the town's schoolmaster.   His salary rose
as high as thirty pounds and his "dyet," and he was also
provided with "the use of a horse."

Hon. Abraham Holmes (born in 1754) wrote near the
end of his long life, some "Memoirs," or a chronicle of
events within his memory, in which he speaks of the schools
of his boyhood as follows:

"An old fashioned school was kept in Town of 12

months in a year.   Sometimes a year was missed.   This kept 3 months in each quarter of the Town, kept by men of very limited education.   They generally were tolerable readers and wrote a legible hand — one by the name of Palmer was a fine penman.   They were also possessed of the common rules of arithmetic and some of them understood something of surveying and navigation.   What was taught in these schools was reading writing and the common rules of arithmetic.   Nothing was said about grammar, composition, speaking, geography, or history. The schools were called to spell at night and to say the catechism on Saturday at noon.   Very few books were then.   Most families had a Bible, Testament a Salter and Spelling book, and a man could carry on his back the libraries of the professional men.   Teaching surveying or navigation was not considered as a part of the duty of the schoolmaster, if they taught them they had separate pay.   I believe about half a month's wages."

Writing of himself in the third person, Mr. Holmes says:

"No public school was kept in that part of the town then. . . .   He never had the benefit of a spelling book till after he was a man grown.   However, by the assiduity of his parents and his sisters he was learned to read well, very well.   He then took a fancy to writing, but it was with difficulty he could procure paper for the purpose, but he was indefatigable in attempting the formation of letters when he could obtain paper. . . .   In 1766 Mr. Williams taught a public school in that Quarter of the Town, to that he went, being the first time he was ever in a school. Writing was his object then; he went a fortnight, but made no proficiency."

The school system of Rochester continued to be of the itinerary type for many years. Lots for the order of the terms are recorded as late as 1766. In 1770 a vote was passed about maintaining a grammar school. In 1789 the law of the State allowing towns to divide themselves into school districts was passed, and in 1799 the district system was adopted in Rochester.

An office that was held in much respect in New England during the eighteenth century was that of Justice of the Peace. Justices were appointed for seven years and had jurisdiction over minor claims and offences. Justices' courts were often held in Rochester. A justice had the title Esquire, and was given power to administer oaths and perform marriages. Many of the marriages recorded in Rochester were by Justices of the Peace, although by the middle of the eighteenth century it was becoming common for ministers also to perform this duty. The following Justices are named as performing marriages in Rochester:

Peleg Whitridge, Abraham Holmes, Joseph Meigs, John Martin, Elisha Ruggles, Nathan Willis, Elijah Willis, James Ruggles, Noah Sprague, David Wing, Nathaniel Sprague.

The following persons held the office of town clerk in Old Rochester, several of them serving for many years:

Mark Haskell, Peter Blackmer, Samuel Sprague, Samuel Wing, William Raymond, Noah Sprague, James Foster, Seth Dexter, David Wing, Aaron Norton, Nathan Willis, Micah H. Ruggles, Abra'm Holmes, James Ruggles, Rogers L. Barstow, W. N. Ellis, Nahum Leonard, Jr., Theophilus King.

The names of the selectmen of Rochester before 1697

have not been fully preserved. During 160 years, from 1697 to 1857, the following persons served on the Board of Selectmen for the old town:

Increase Clap, John Hammond, Benjamin Dexter, Aaron Barlow, John Summers, Elisha Wing, Timo Davis, John Randall, Peter Blackmer, Samuel Hammond, John Wing, John Benson, John White, John Briggs, Benjamin Dexter, William Griffeth, Joshua Lawrence, Benjamin Hammond, Edward Winslow, Samuel Sprague, John Dexter, John Cowing, Jeremiah Lout, Roger Haskell, Caleb Blakwell, Elisha Wing, Joseph Blackmer, Nicholas Snow, John Freeman, Samuel Wing, Noah Sprague, James Whitcomb, C—— Briggs, James Foster, Silas Briggs, Elisha Barrows, Elisha Freeman, Barzillai Hammond, Seth Hiller, Antipas Hammond, Seth Dexter, Nathaniel Hammond, David Wing, Nathaniel Ruggles, John Hammond, Samuel Sprague, Enoch Hammond, Samuel Ruggles, John Doty, Jabez Cottle, Melatiah White, John Burges, Stephen Wing, Nathaniel Sprague, Abraham Holmes, Aaron Norton, G. B. Nye, Joseph Gifford, Charles Sturtevant, Nicholas Davis, Harper Delano, —— Bisbe, Nathan Willis, Wilson Barstow, N. Hammond, Gideon Barstow, Caleb Briggs, Timothy Hiller, Timothy Davis, Nathan Jenne, Joshua Pierce, John Church, Stephen Hammond, Stephen Delano, Charles J. Holmes, George King, Benjamin Barstow, Jr., Thomas Bassett, Peleg Whitridge, Philip Crandon, Eben Holmes, Elijah Willis, Noble E. Bates, Butler Wing, Amittai B. Hammond, Theophilus King.

In the early part of the eighteenth century, the question of sending a representative to the General Court of the province seems to have been optional with the towns.

Later, this became a requirement, and in 1773 thirty towns of Massachusetts were fined for neglect of this duty. Rochester from an early date showed a stronger public spirit than some of the other towns in the neighborhood, and usually was represented in the province, though occasionally the vote to send a representative was passed in the negative.

The representatives from Rochester to the General Court before the Revolution include the following names:

Samuel Prince, John Hammond, Thomas Dexter, Joseph Benson, Thomas Turner, Benjamin Hammond, John Freeman, Timothy Ruggles, Jr., Noah Sprague, Elisha Barrows, Samuel Wing, Nathaniel Ruggles, Samuel Sprague.

In 1720, owing to the scarcity of money in New England, the province made a grant of 50,000 pounds to be loaned in the towns. In 1721 Rochester voted to act on the town's part of this loan (which was 365 pounds), John Briggs and Benjamin Dexter being sent as agents to fetch the money into the town. Each person who borrowed money was to give bonds with a personal (not "real") security, and to pay a small interest to the town, and fourpence a pound to the agents for their services. The money could be held for four years, unless the town drew it in. The sum that could be loaned was divided into fifteen parts, and the persons who might draw were decided by lot. The fortunate citizens who drew the lot were Capt. Isaac Holmes, Nathan Hammond, James Steward, John Randall, Samuel Griffith, Samuel Sprague, Moses Barlow, William Raymond, Eben Holmes, Samuel Shearman, Joseph Haskell, John Dexter, Joseph Prince, William Noyes, Thomas Randall.

The "Dexter Elm" and Mill, Mattapoisett

In 1749 the currency of the colony was regulated. Two kinds of paper money had been in circulation, in which a shilling of the new tenor was equal in value to three shillings of the old tenor. Both kinds were now redeemed by the Spanish milled dollar, and after March, 1750, all debts were payable in coined silver under a law which made a shilling a sixth part of the Spanish dollar or sixteen and two thirds cents, so that the colonial pound equalled $3.33⅓ in silver. Money reckonings on this basis continued in use in Massachusetts for several generations. During the Revolution the whole money system became again greatly demoralized.

There is in existence an old tax roll of Rochester, made out in 1776, Nathaniel Hammond, David Wing, and John Doty being the assessors.

This early tax list contains a mysterious set of entries regarding a "faculty tax." Thus in addition to his poll tax and tax for real and personal estate, a man might be called on to pay perhaps five shillings twopence as a "faculty tax." As we read the quaint record, together with the later information that "The tailor was taxed for his faculty," there comes over us an amused sense of shrewdness in these hard-headed old New Englanders in thus levying taxes on the well-known Yankee "faculty" or "knack at doing things." But a moment later, "Webster" takes the force out of this interesting suggestion by informing us that a "faculty" was a "license" or permission giving a "right to act."

Between 1735 and the Revolution, a large number of families from Rochester and some from Dartmouth emigrated to the town of Hardwick in Worcester County.

The father of Minister Ruggles, Samuel Ruggles of

Roxbury, had for some years held proprietary rights in the lands at Hardwick, which was called the Elbows, and was still mostly unsettled.   About 1732, his father having died, Rev. Timothy Ruggles made a visit to the Elbows, and after this undertook to promote its settlement.   The names of Dexter, Sprague, Wing, Foster, Winslow, and Haskell are among the Rochester names that became repre- sented at Hardwick.   Joseph Haskell, the youngest son of Mark Haskell, became an active agent in securing settlers for Hardwick, though he never moved there himself.

In Mr. Ruggles's own large family of twelve children, six of the sons found homes finally in Hardwick. A family of nephews of Mr. Ruggles by the name of Robin- son were also among the Hardwick pilgrims; also a son- in-law, Paul Mendell from Dartmouth, who became prominent in the affairs of the new town.   The best known of these Hardwick emigrants was Timothy Rug- gles, Jr., who, after practising law for some years in Roches- ter, moved in 1753 to Hardwick, the most noted events of his life being subsequent to that period.   He served with distinction in the French War of 1755, attaining the rank of Brigadier-General.   In 1765, Ruggles, Partridge, and Otis were sent as the three delegates from Massa- chusetts to the Stamp Act Congress in New York, Ruggles being chosen President of the body.   But his rulings gave dissatisfaction to the Whigs, and Ruggles was repri- manded publicly.   In 1774 he accepted the office of Mandamus Councillor under direct appointment by the crown.   The members of this Council were held in greater odium than any other class of officers, and their appoint- ment greatly hastened the acts of rebellion in Boston. General Ruggles now became an open Tory.   His countrymen turned against him, his home in Hardwick was mobbed, and in 1776, after the evacuation of Boston, General Ruggles with most of the other Tories of New England moved to Nova Scotia.

The French wars that preceded the Revolution made heavy demands on the towns of the old colony. In 1755 General Winslow of Marshfield was sent with a body of Massachusetts troops to remove the inhabitants of Acadia, Nova Scotia. These people were of French descent, and though they were called "Neutrals" they were suspected of giving secret aid to the French. General Winslow declared that the order was disagreeable to his natural make and temper, and that his principles of implicit obedience as a soldier were put to a severe test, but the order was carried out.

In the rolls of soldiers in this Acadian (or Eastern) expedition, the towns from which the soldiers came are not named, but it seems certain that men from Rochester were in this expedition. On the return of the expedition one thousand of these unhappy French exiles were brought to Massachusetts and parceled out to the different towns, a number being apportioned to Rochester. They were strangers and exiles among people speaking a strange tongue. For some years they were a public charge, and various bills for "Cloath for the french," and for "keeping the old french" appear on the town books. Several petitions for relief on account of the "nutural french" were sent to the General Court. Some of the Acadian people, however, became assimilated later among New Englanders, and some of the family names of French origin that are found in New England to-day may be traced to this Acadian source.

In the later campaigns of the French and Indian War at Crown Point, Ticonderoga, and in Canada, there were many soldiers from Rochester. Captain Bradford's company in Col. Thomas Dotey's regiment in service in Canada, 1758-1760, was composed largely of Rochester men. Captain Pratt's company in the same regiment, and Capt. Abel Keen's company in another regiment, also had some Rochester men. In the hospital records at Crown Point, Rochester names may be found. In Col. Timothy Ruggles's regiment, among many Hardwick names, one may find some that were evidently from Rochester originally. Between 1760 and 1763 also a considerable number of new recruits from Rochester were gathered.

With the fall of Quebec the power of the French in America was broken, and in 1763 a treaty of peace was signed at Paris. The Colonial armies were kept up, however, and continued to contain men enrolled from Rochester for some years longer.

Near the middle of the eighteenth century there were several epidemics of illness that were distressing and fatal. Mr. Holmes makes mention of a "throat distemper," which raged in Rochester in 1754, and proved fatal to almost all who were seized with it. He himself, an infant less than a year old, was attacked, but his father, having heard of a remedy known to an Indian named Nathan Hope, and to three white men, and called by them "Cold water root," procured some for his child, who quickly recovered. In the powdered medicine there was one piece of root which was not pulverized. The father planted it in his garden to see if it would grow. It did so, and developed into a wild herb common to all the region. The remedy thus became known, and from this time forward the "distemper" was no longer to be greatly dreaded.

Minister Le Baron writes: "In 1758 a slow, putrid fever raged in Second Precinct, and proved mortal to thirty in about three months, population 250. It is observable that the inhabitants of a few houses which are situated on the East side of extensive flat swamps have been peculiarly subject to bilious acute diseases and consumptions and sudden deaths have in a remarkable manner been the Lot of those who have indulged themselves in the use of distilled spirituous liquors."

In times of public distress, whether from illness or from drought, fast-days were appointed and services were held in the churches to pray for relief.

Under the head of "Remarkable Providences," the old First Church Book records some signal answers to prayers for rain in this and neighboring parishes, among which are the following:

"August 12th a fast Day was kept at Wareham on account of a great Drought and that Day before night there was a good plentifull rain over the town and none in the next, the very dividing line of the Towns Divided (as it were) the clouds. Also, the next day fast day was kept at Middleborough new precinct and a plentifull rain fell the same night. At which time the Rev'd. Mr. Peter Thatcher of Middleborough gave us an account of two more parishes that kept a fast day on ye account of ye Drought within a fortnight of the time above expressed who had an immediate answer of prayer by rain and it extended only over the parish who kept sd day and no elsewhere."

June 24, 1741, "a fast day was kept at Dartmouth on acct. of the Drought and it was known before, so the Quakers gave out word as they Desired it may not rain next day (tho much needed) for if it Did the ministers and people who attended would say It was owing to sd prayers, but God in his Justice Goodness & mercy was pleased to give a gracious answer & it began to rain before the forenoon service was over & continued till night. It was much the same in Rochester."

In the records of the First Church occurs also the following:

"Rochester, Aug. 9, 1770 Being a day set apart by ye chh for prayer & fasting on account of a severe drought ye chh were stayed after public service & voted that ye Scriptures should be read as part of ye Public worship on Lord's Day."

With the long sermons and prayers that were the rule in the churches, and the length of time it took to sing a Psalm, one need scarcely wonder that Scripture reading had been neglected as a feature of public worship.

The Psalm, "turned into meter," was lined off, or "deaconed" by some appointed person, and when sung to the slow tunes then in vogue, the singing was a work of time. The Bay Psalm Book was everywhere in use in this region at the middle of the eighteenth century. Two generations later, "Watts and Select" had almost the same universal distinction. In the early years only a few church tunes were known, two or three for each meter offering the usual range of choice.

In 1748 the First Parish voted that "Whereas sometimes Deacon Elisha Freeman is absent who is appointed to set the Psalm, it is voted in his absence that Josephus

Hammond do it, and in his absence Mr. Joseph Lovel, and in his Mr. Seth Dexter do it."

During the eighteenth century all over New England a contest arose between the advocates of "singing by rote" and "singing by rule." The feeling of those who opposed "singing by rule" was thus expressed by one writer of the age: "If they sing by rule they will also pray by rule and preach by rule, and then comes popery." But the "singing by rule" party finally triumphed. Near the time of the Revolution many books of tunes were published. Some of them had marked innovations in the style of tunes, and included some tunes with a strong accent and a triple time movement instead of the long uniform notes of the olden tunes. "Fuguing" also came into fashion, though at first strongly discountenanced by persons of sober mind. The New England Singing School became a marked feature of New England village life for two generations. The "taught" singers were also gathered into choirs, and "part singing" was developed.

The emphasis in the music agitations before the beginning of the nineteenth century had shifted to the question of musical instruments in the churches. Pitch pipes were first introduced, then the bass viol, after that the violin, and various other instruments. Among the churches in this vicinity, that of Wareham seems to have been most strongly agitated by the bass viol question; and here a compromise was for a time arranged, giving leave to the bass viol to be "played every other Sunday, and not to Pitch the Tunes on the Sabbath that it don't play." The churches in Rochester did not escape these music dissensions, but the orchestral instruments made their way into use, retaining their place until the advent of the melodeon, followed by that of the church organ, near the middle of the nineteenth century.

During the eighteenth century the tithing-man was a regular parish officer, his duty being to prevent Sabbath desecration, or, as was recorded in the books of the First Parish, to "Inspect the Youth on the Lord's Day to prevent the profanation of the Lord's Day and to bring them to punishment if they don't reform."

In 1748, at the First Precinct, it took ten of these tithing-men to "keep good orders on the Sabbath Day," three for the galleries, three for the body of the house, and four to take their turns in the Intermission of Divine Service."

Tithing-men were on duty in Rochester for many years. From a letter by Henry B. Worth, Esq., of New Bedford, the following paragraph is (in substance) quoted:

"The following advertisement appeared in the New Bedford *Mercury* May 15, 1815.

"'The Tythingmen of Rochester gave notice that they should enforce the law.

JONATHEN KING,	JOHN CLAP,
JOSEPH WHITREDGE,	SETH HASKELL,
WM. SMITH,	JESSE HASKELL,
ALLEN MARSHALL,	NOAH DEXTER,
GEORGE B. NYE,	EZEKIEL CUSHMAN,
SHERMAN LINCOLN,	JONATHAN CHURCH.'

"But one wonders why it was inserted. If aimed at Rochester Sabbath-breakers, the notice might not reach them. Perhaps the warning was intended for young

people who might drive for pleasure from New Bedford
to Rochester, and the purpose was to keep away from the
town an element that might create disorder. In a seafaring community like New Bedford there were many
such spirits, and I have no doubt that the villages of
Sippican were fully as attractive on Sunday in 1815 as
now. Hence, the good Sunday constables were determined to rid the town of a nuisance. But the number
of tithing-men is large for a town of the population of
Rochester, — twelve."

Cases of church discipline were very common, both for
suspected lapses in morals, and also for absenting oneself
from the Sacrament and attending the meetings of the two
chief "heretical" sects of the region, the Quakers and the
"Anabaptists." But with the widening lines of thought
that came in after the Revolution, a larger toleration in
church and religious matters begins to be manifest.

From Mr. Holmes's Chronicle, other glimpses of the town
life at the middle of the eighteenth century may be
gained:

"There was not a wagon of any kind in town, there
were ox-carts and horse-carts, add to these two old riding-
chairs. . . . Such a thing as a chaise was never heard of.
The first that came through Rochester made as much of a
wonderment as a Baloon would have done. . . . No person
could tell what to call it, at last it was concluded that it
was a calash.

"The horses were generally poor creatures. In the
summer they lived on grass, in the winter on hay only,
except when they were going on a journey when on the
evening previous they would have a mess of bran wet. It
was a high priced horse that was valued at $40. A horse

more than nine years old was considered of little value.

"There was no such thing as a clock in town. There were three ministers in Town and each had a watch. I believe there were no others in Rochester.... Not a single pair of silver Buckles were then in Rochester, and an umbrella or a parasol would have made a wonderment.... Very few gloves were worn unless when a man was to be married.

"Good dancing was considered a very important accomplishment. Other diversions among the young people were a number of plays, such as breaking the Pope's neck, the Button, — and among the Quakers who did not allow dancing Blindfold was a very popular amusement.

"As for the Bill of fare at the Table they generally had a boiled dish, the first course was a Bowl of broth then called porridge, generally some beans in it and some dry summer savery sprinkled in. Then came an Indian pudding with sauce with it, then some beef pork and round turnips and a few small potatoes. The quantity of potatoes was very small, three bushels was considered a monstrous crop and these very small. I was a considerable Lad before I ever saw a potato as big as a hen's egg."

From old writings like these, dealing with things that in themselves seem trivial, we get a vivid picture of a phase of human life that is not only interesting in itself (especially to the descendants of the men and women who are described), but it was also important in its effects on American life and history. It was a very human life that was lived by these forbears of ours of a hundred and fifty years ago. There are elements in the picture that seem to us crude and unjustifiable as well as amusing. But underlying the narrow eccentricities we find the rugged and homely virtues that made New England the power that she was in shaping the character and destinies of the American nation.

CHAPTER VII

THE REVOLUTIONARY WAR

WITH the breaking out of the Revolution, the town of Rochester entered on a special phase of history, one that is peculiar to New England. The Middle and Southern Colonies played a large rôle in Revolutionary affairs, but they did not have the *town meeting*. At this period the little town democracy was lifted above the petty anxieties attending its own local affairs and stood face to face with political questions of the largest moment. The story of one town is in a sense the story of all.

In September, 1768, at the request of the Boston Committee, Rochester sent delegates to the Convention at Faneuil Hall, which passed resolutions protesting against the taxing of the colonies. In Plymouth Colony as a whole, there was at first much apathy toward the spirit that was arising in Boston. There were many who took pride in being British-born subjects and felt a good deal of loyalty to the King. James Warren declared to Samuel Adams that Plymouth County towns could not be raised except by a power that would wake the dead. Rochester, however, responded more readily to the appeal of Boston than most of the towns in the neighborhood.

In December, 1772, after another letter of correspondence from Boston, a spirited set of resolutions was passed, endorsing the plans of the Boston Committee.

Samuel Sprague, who had been the town's representative since 1768, was suspected of holding Tory sentiments. So the town voted:

"That if our representative or any other person in this Town that either has or shall hereafter basely Desert the Cause of Liberty for the Sake of being promoted to a Post of Honour or profit or for any other Mean View to Self Intrust shall be looked upon as an Enemy to his Country & be treated with that Neglect & Contempt that he Justly Deserves."

The next year Samuel Sprague was not re-elected. He was succeeded by Ebenezer White, who was afterwards Lieutenant Colonel of a militia regiment. Lieutenant-Colonel White held the office of representative for many years, during the first fourteen of which he was unanimously elected, and during this difficult Revolutionary period the town intrusted him with many important duties.

With the advent of the tea question in 1773, a letter was received from Boston asking the advice of the towns, as to what was to be done. At the town meeting then held the usual moderator was absent, and David Wing, — the careful town clerk, whose copious records in minute printed letters awaken the admiration of the reader — thought it prudent to remain at home. Yet after some delays and embarrassments, the meeting at last became very free and spirited. Energetic resolutions were passed, and "the citizens subscribed a solemn league and covenant to abstain from the use of tea, and to transact no business with those who would not become parties to the Covenant."

During 1774 many town meetings were held. It was

voted "To sign a covenant to break off trade with Great Britain until the Boston Port Bill is repealed." Representative White was enjoined "not to act in conformity with the Act of Parliament altering the Charter." Charles Nye was appointed to examine the town stock. Forty firearms were purchased for the use of the town. Nathan Nye, Jr., was directed to "make up the Town Stock of powder to 400 weight with Lead and Flints Answerable." The Assessors were directed "not to make up the Province Rate," but at a later meeting this vote was reconsidered.

It was also voted "to choose officers to take ye Command of the Military Companies," and that "Every minute man (so-called) in Rochester to the number of One Hundred that shall attend Three Half Days in each week as shall be appointed by their Captain & Twice in a month in one Body to Learn the use of the Fire-Licks from this day to the first Day of April next & be Ready to March when Needed & Equip Himself with a Good Firearm & other acooterments as Recommended by the Provential Congress shall be Entitled to one Shilling ye Week."

September 26, 1774, a company of young men from Rochester made an incursion into Barnstable County in order to prevent the Inferior Court of Common Pleas from holding its regular session. The excuse given was that the method of drawing jurors by the sheriff instead of out of a box in town meeting put in jeopardy the rights of the people. The real aim, however, was, by breaking up the County Court to destroy an avenue through which business could pass to higher courts that were under the King's control. One of this company was young Abraham Holmes, whose zeal for liberty did much to arouse the

Revolutionary spirit of Rochester. As the company passed through Wareham and Sandwich, they were reinforced by others of like spirit, and on reaching Barnstable they succeeded in preventing the session of the Court, and compelling the judges to sign certain pledges. After holding a political meeting at Barnstable, at which it was resolved to boycott British goods and to suppress pedlers who sold Bohea tea, the agitators dispersed.

When the battle of Lexington occurred, April 19, 1775, the rumor reached Rochester April 20, but it was scarcely believed. Abraham Holmes, then twenty-one years of age, was sent to learn the truth of the rumor. On reaching Middleboro, he met a messenger who confirmed the report, and Mr. Holmes records that he returned to Rochester "as gay as a lark" at the joyful news that the struggle for Independence was really begun.

Three companies of militia from Rochester marched to Boston in response to the Lexington call. The "First Company of Minute-men," under Capt. Edward Hammond, a "Second foot Company of Militia," under Capt. Nathaniel Hammond, and a third company under Lieut. Seth Briggs, with which the Rev. Jonathan Moore, pastor of the First Church of Rochester, went as Chaplain. Mr. Holmes records in his diary that because of some misunderstanding in the regiment, formed in the summer of 1775, in Plymouth County, none of the Rochester Militia officers would accept commissions. But this must have been a temporary situation, for there were afterwards many commissioned officers from Rochester.

The three companies that marched from Rochester after the Lexington alarm saw only a few days' service at this time. In August of the same year, Capt. Edward

Hammond's company, with its enrolment much changed, and a company under Capt. Earl Clap were in service at Boston. Gideon Hammond is also mentioned as a captain in the regular army in 1775. Earl Clap rose to the rank of Major in the General Army. He was at the battle of Bunker Hill, and in later life had a pension of $560 a year.

In 1776 a Rochester company was in service under Capt. Samuel Briggs; in 1778 two companies were in service under Capt. Nathaniel Hammond and Capt. Elisha Haskell; and in 1780 there were in service in Rhode Island in the Fourth Plymouth County Regiment, under Lieutenant-Colonel White, four companies from Rochester under Capt. Charles Church, Capt. Nathaniel Hammond, Capt. Barnabas Doty, and Capt. Samuel Briggs. There were also many Rochester men in companies formed in other towns of the State. The person of most note in the military record of Rochester, perhaps, was Major Elnathan Haskell, who became one of Washington's Aids. His portrait in this capacity may be seen in the great painting representing Burgoyne's Surrender, in the dome of the Capitol in Washington. After the War, Major Haskell settled in South Carolina.

It is difficult at present to make a complete list of the Rochester men who did military service in the Revolution, but from various enlistment rolls, — muster rolls, records of "New Levies," of pensions, bounties, and men discharged, a list of some hundreds could be compiled. It was said at the Rochester Bi-Centennial that "it is a historical fact that Rochester furnished more men in proportion to territory and inhabitants than any other town in the Old Colony."

ROCHESTER COMMON

Showing Meeting-house, Academy, Schoolhouse and Town House

It is even more difficult to make an accurate list of those who did naval service. Naval records were less carefully kept than those of the military. Much of the naval service also was by privateering, and this was not officially recorded. But many men of Rochester followed the sea, and were drawn into naval action. Minister Le Baron has recorded the fatalities in this service from Mattapoisett as follows: " In late war a No. lost at Sea out of Mattap't, David Rogers, Captain Rogers, M. Barlow, Joseph Barlow & Reuben, Jo Wing & Wyett Wing — Daniel H. Cowen, Indian Boy, Jo Clarke, Aaron Parker, Lothrop Hamond — Seth Hamond — Micah Hamond, Thos. Williams Jn Cushing, Elisha Toby, Wm. Toby, Sol Young, Ez Hovey, Asa Price, Francis Luce, Eleazer Allen, — Norton, Calvin Hamond — Nie Stevens, Timo Stephens, Jabez Dexter — Jonathan Annable, Sam'l Annable, — Anthony Hamond — Andrew Southw'd."

In 1775 it was voted to hire one hundred pounds to buy war stores, also " two Boats for the use of Capt. Nathaniel Hammond's Company "; also " to send to the West Indies by Capt. Moses Barlow for powder, firearms, molasses and other war supplies."

A climax was now approaching, and the records increase in interest. May 23, 1776, it was " Voted that when the Honourable Congress shall think best to Declare themselves Independant of the Kingdom of Great Brittain that we will Defend them with our Lives & Fortunes."

Soon the link was severed that bound the colonies to the mother country, and now arose new governmental questions. The town government holds on its way, but all else is in a transitional and chaotic state. Each little town by its decisions, made known through its representative, will help to direct the trend of State and national affairs. November 5, 1776, Rochester voted "That the Present General Court of this State agree upon and settle a form of government for the present, to be subject to alteration if need be Hereafter."

But the making of State Constitutions requires time and meanwhile the war-needs continue. Not only must weapons be furnished to the soldiers, but they need the inspiriting influence of music as well. So the town votes the sum of sixty pounds to "purchase guns Drums and Fifes"; also "Voted that the Town draw 50 firearms belonging to the Continant to be returned when called for." New committees are also appointed to take care of the families of the soldiers. Enoch Hammond did much service during the war in the care of soldiers' supplies and soldiers' families, and was called "The Father of the Town."

The draft of the State Constitution being prepared, on May 22, 1777, the town of Rochester took it "into Consideration, and after Mature Deliberation thereon said Town voted said form," but added a list of comments and objections, one of which runs thus:

"The Ninth Article seems to be attended with some Difficulty as To vote for Sennators in the furthest parts of the State when we cannot be acquainted with their Quallifications Said Town think it best that Each District choose their own Senators & no more."

Meanwhile, army reverses had brought a feeling of depression, and a spirit of opposition to the war showed itself which must be suppressed. A committee of inspection was formed in Rochester at an early date to call to account those who uttered Tory sentiments. One of those dealt with had said that he "wished the people of Rochester were in hell for their treatment of Ruggles and Sprague," but on expressing repentance he was duly forgiven.

In 1776, Samuel Sprague, the former town representative, was accused by Isaac Snow, chairman of the Inspection Committee, as unfriendly to the cause of the colonies. It was declared that "he was one of the Addressors of the late Governor Hutchinson (the Tory Governor), that afterwards he had subscribed a declaration manifesting his repentance and retraction of said address, — which confession and retraction was to the general satisfaction of the town, — but that he had since retracted his former confession and repentance and, on the seventh of June last, did declare that he was not convinced of the justice of the Cause of the Colonies, and that he utterly refused to take up arms or be in any way personally active in the defence of the Common Cause of the Colonies."

Exactly what was done about it is not very clear. Sprague did not become an out-and-out Tory. He was probably a man of balanced mind, who recognized some justice on both sides of the great struggle. He sold his home in Rochester soon afterwards, and in the last part of his life was a resident of Fairhaven. He lived to advanced age, and in his closing years was the oldest man living who had served as representative to the General Court. He died in 1825, and left in his will a bequest to his native town from which it still derives benefit, and which is known as the "Sprague Legacy."

Another man in Rochester, whose Tory sympathies were even more pronounced than those of Samuel Sprague, was Nathaniel Sears. He, too, was arraigned by Isaac

Snow of the Committee of Inspection, but there is no
evidence that he was won over to the side of the colonies.
Possibly the zeal of Isaac Snow in the American cause
sometimes outran his discretion.   In 1781 he was dis-
ciplined by the First Church of Rochester because, in a
religious service in which Rev. Thomas West of North
Rochester was the preacher, the said Isaac Snow "spoke
out and called Mr. West an old Tory, while he was preaching."   But the "Committee of Inspection" was held to
be a necessary office, and in 1779 "The town made choice
of Earl Clap to Take evidence against those that are
Enemical to the American States agreeable to a Late Act
of this State."

About this time a rather obscure and complicated
record occurs.   A town meeting was called "To choose
3, 5 or 7 persons who shall be under Oath to prosicute all
Breaches of the Act for preventing Monopoly & Oppression which come to their knowledge or of which they shall
receive information and all Breaches of an Act Intitled
An Act in Addition to and Amending an Act intitled An
Act for preventing Monopoly, etc."

As the weary struggle went on, and the money depre-
ciated in value, the people grew desperate.   Many kinds
of money were in use.   Sometimes in the account of a
single transaction, several kinds of money are named.
We read of money of the "New Emmission" and the
"Old Emmission," of "Hard Money," as well as "Continential Currancy."   These, with English money also in
use, and changing values for all, and various counterfeits
in circulation, made all financial transactions embarrass-
ing.

As an illustration of the state of affairs we read that at

one town meeting Rochester voted one hundred hard dollars as bounty for the soldiers, made an appropriation of "671 £ in Bills of ye new Emission for army beef," and an "assessment of 1860 Continential Dollars upon the town to pay for Constables."

Many futile resolutions were passed in regard to the money situation. May 26, 1779, after certain resolves relating to efforts "to appreciate the Currancy" had been passed, the following malediction was added:

"Whoever shall Directly or Indirectly violate either of Sd resolves made for this important purpose shall be Deemed Infamous & held up to view as an Enemy to ye Indepindence, freedom & happiness of his Country by publishing his name in ye newspapers published in this State, after which publication it shall be Disrespectfull in any Good Citizen to maintain Either Social or Commercial Connections with a wretch so Lost to all publick Virtue as wantonly to Sacrafice the Intrest of his Country to the acquisition of a Little paltery Gain."

It was chiefly the financial troubles which caused the excitements and illegal actions in Massachusetts towns that were focalized in the western counties as "Shay's Rebellion," and made painfully evident the need of a stronger national government that could regulate for all the States their monetary system.

About this time a committee of thirteen was chosen to "Stipulate prices of Labour & of Sundry articles sold to the Town." A few days later, delegates from Rochester attended a Convention at Plympton to discuss the same questions. The prices reported at the Plympton Convention throw some light on the monetary situation. Among them were the following:

	£	s
Labour, Common Labour a Day		42
Mowing		54
Houpwrights a Day	3	
Millwrights a Day	3	12
Masons	3	6
Shiprights a Day	3	12
Tanners Sole Leather, a lb.		18
Shoemakers for making a pair of men's shoes .		42
Women's shoes & finding heels by the shoemaker		42
Making a pair of strong men's shoes and finding all	6	

Prices were also given of "Nails, lumber, pasture, cole, wood, fish, (fresh fish without entrails at ye waterside 1s a pound) etc." Other articles were referred to the committee for further regulation.

August 19, 1779, the town chose Nathaniel Hammond as delegate to a State Convention at Cambridge called to form a New State Constitution. It also appointed a committee of four to prepare instructions for Captain Hammond's guidance in the Convention. This committee presented an elaborate report with many explicit directions to Captain Hammond.

The Constitution proposed by the Cambridge Convention was duly presented to the town for consideration and, in May, 1780, it was voted upon, article by article. Two articles in the Bill of Rights were voted upon adversely, and a number of alterations were proposed, one of them being: "That there be added to the above Frame of Government That there shall no slave be born nor Imported into this Commonwealth."

We are not told whether the Rochester amendments

made any difference in the final form of the State Constitution; but the instrument went into effect duly, and September 4, 1780, the citizens met in town meeting, and voted for State Officers, John Hancock being chosen Governor, with Robert Treat Paine as Lieutenant-Governor.

In December, 1781, a town meeting was called, "To protest against duties laid on Rum wine &c & if thought best to take Lawfull measures to obtain redress of the Grievance." It was voted that "The Act is Disagreeable to the Town," and a committee was chosen to petition for redress. It is plain that the Rochester of that date would not have tolerated either high license or prohibition.

One result of the money troubles was that it became extremely difficult for the town to raise the new "cota of 32 soldiers," called for in 1780 to fill the ranks of the depleted armies. The committee report that they cannot "hire any soldiers in town by reason of Disapointments many soldiers have met with in the depreciation of their wages before they were paid." It was therefore "voted to promise the soldiers that any such Depreciation should be made up by the town"; also a bounty of "12£ & no more," was to be paid to each soldier, "in gold, silver or produce," as he should choose, and soldiers in the field were to have "12£ in Cloathing and other necessaries for self & family." At last by strenuous efforts of the committee, aided by bounties to "3 mos. men," and to "6 mos. men," the "cota" was made up; but in January, 1781, a new committee of eight was appointed to hire "25 soldiers called for by the General Court to serve for three years or during the war." A bounty for these soldiers was also voted, of "One Hundred hard dollars each year in January."

A matter which gave increasing irritation was the requi-sition on the town for beef for the army. It was a never-ceasing need, and became at last a most onerous burden.

December 30, 1782, it was voted "to petition the Great & General Court to receive in all the paper money of both Emissions now in the Town's hands and Give the Town credit for the same." In January, 1787, however, it was reported that the town has "946£ — 10s — 5d of the new Emmission & 49144£ — 8s — 0 of the Old Emmission," though a considerable number of bills of each "ware counterfeit."

Peace was declared in 1783, but it was long before the blessings of peace came to the burdened community. On the contrary, the confusion and dissatisfaction grew ever stronger. The feeling toward the government is shown by the attitude of the town-meeting toward certain grants of the Continental Congress to officers of the army.

February 6, 1784, the town's committee reported the following spirited protest which was adopted:

"To wit that it is the opinion of your Committee that the paying of the Officers of the Continential army 5 years wages after their service is Ended is highly unreasonable & oppressive & will be productive of many bad conse-quencies as one notorious bad presedent. However the power of Congress may be we think the Grant made by them to sd officers was obtained by undue influence & if no Negative to Sd Grant is yet to be admitted (notwith-standing all their Good Service) we shall Esteam them Publick Nusances & Treat them in that Curracter."

Thus the town of Rochester set its own opinion on national affairs above that of Congress, and proposed "to act accordingly."

Peace having been declared, Commerce began to receive attention, and in May, 1785, the town instructed Lieutenant-Colonel White to use his "Influence that a large Impost be laid on all Goods imported in British Bottoms"; also, in 1786, to use his influence, "that there be a Bank of paper money Emitted by the General Court." In August, 1786, Earl Clap, Nathaniel Hammond, and Abraham Holmes were made a committee "to correspond with the other Towns in order to Divise & Adopt" legal measures for a redress of grievances.

Several weeks later, this committee reported, and the town then gave very extended instructions to Colonel White, "which we expect you to follow & by no means depart from them." These instructions, prepared it is said by Abraham Holmes, cover five or six pages of closely written foolscap, and discuss most far-reaching and important principles of government, such as the redemption of the currency, the right of Congress to lay taxes on the State, the Constitutional power of the General Court to place a check on the Acts of Congress, the system of taxation that should be employed, the principle of exempting ministers from taxation, and of making grants to army officers. All of these things are committed to the "utmost endeavors" of Colonel White with the words, "May the great Fountain of Goodness and Knowledge assist you in discharging this Trust with Success."

The preparation of such documents by the country towns shows the magnitude of the intellectual labor by which the state and national governments were developed.

But the effort of small communities to direct the larger affairs of State and nation had its dangers. Disorders were arising, and the excited people in certain towns of Massachusetts overstepped legal bounds in their attempts to regulate abuses. The story of Shay's Rebellion may be read on the pages of the school text-books. It came as a warning to law-abiding persons to pause and see whither things were tending.

February 12, 1787, a town meeting of a very different spirit was held in Rochester, "on account of the Confusions & Disorders in the Commonwealth." A committee of five was chosen to draft a petition and report in one hour. This report expresses the "Attachment of the town of Rochester to the Government of Massachusetts & its poignant regret for the late unhappy disorders." But it adds:

"We humbly pray that the troops under General Lincoln (now the Insurgents are disbursed) may be immediately disbanded. We think this would restore Publick tranquillity if an Act of General Indemnity be passed & we pray your honours patience in praying you to take measures for suitably lowering the Salaries of the Servants of Government & take into your wise Consideration that late act of suspending the privelidge of the writ of Habeas Corpus."

The law adviser of General Lincoln who commanded the State troops during this time of agitation was John Sprague, who was born in Mattapoisett village in 1746, and at this time was the Justice of the Court of Common Pleas for Worcester County.

About this time reports were carried to Boston against Abraham Holmes. It was said that he was a dangerous person, since it was well known that he did not approve of the acts of the Legislature. He went before the Senate in his own defense, declaring that he had done nothing revolutionary. But learning that a state warrant had been issued for his arrest, and fearing that since the act of *Habeas Corpus* was suspended he should be held in jail without a trial, he left Rochester privately during a snow-storm, and remained for a time in Rhode Island. Later he returned to Rochester openly and his fellow-citizens, who had been his firm supporters and indignant defenders during the agitation, gave him an enthusiastic welcome, and the next year sent him as their representative to the General Court.

But the time was at hand when governmental questions were to be settled on a broader basis. Not the little towns, discussing from a local standpoint these matters of national concern, not the several States jealous of their own State rights, nor yet the Continental Congress with its limited powers, could settle finally these tremendous complications. But a broader tribunal was even then constructing the instrument which should marshal the conflicting elements into an organized whole.

December 20, 1787, the town of Rochester "Voted to read the proposed Federal Constitution in Town Meeting, & to send two delegates to the State Convention at Boston," Capt. Nathaniel Hammond and Mr. Abraham Holmes being chosen for this honored service.

So the Federal Constitution began its harmonizing rule, and a year later (December 18, 1788) a town meeting was convened to choose "One Member of the House of Representatives of the united States of America, to be the Representative of Plymouth and Barnstable Counties; also to vote for two persons as electors for President and vice-President of the united States of America."

The Revolution was at last ended, and now the town records change their character, and again glide naturally into the election of local officers and the ever-seasonable regulation of the "Herren fisheries."

CHAPTER VIII

THE Revolution being over, the town of Rochester began again to give attention to its own development. Minister Le Baron writes concerning the town, in 1786:

"Length N. & S. 10, E. & W. 7, — containing two rivers, Mattapoisett and Sipican, on which there are 10 grist mills 13 sawmills, 2 forges and 1 fuling mill; on other less streams 1 foundry, 3 gristmills & 1 sawmill. Agriculture not highly improved. Our Navigation is so much an object of our attention as to be a great disadvantage to our Husbandry. As we have a large proportion of sheep the Inhabitants are enabled to manufacture much the greater part of the thick cloth that is worn & we have about 4 vessels employed in the Whaling fishery, about the principal source of our specie. Ship building & iron are two branches of manufactory not unprofitable."

The fulling mills were used to dress the cloth woven in the homes from wool and flax. Among the many mills that have stood at the Sippican mill site by Leonard's Pond since the beginning of the town history, there was once a fulling mill. Another also stood for a time at the Dexter Dam at Rochester Center.

Around the shore of Mary's Pond, a strip of land two rods wide was owned by the town itself, secure from private ownership, where the flax could be "rotted," so that it might afterwards be "broken" and prepared for manufacture. In the clear waters at the edge of this pond one may to-day see the stones that were used to keep the flax in its place during this preparatory process.

In 1815 there were in town fourteen sawmills and two forges, one having a trip hammer, the other a furnace. At that time also, we are told, "3000 or more sheep are subsisted in Rochester," and "There are farms in the place estimated at $9000."

After the building of the First Parish meeting-house in 1760, the old meeting-house of 1717 became "the town house," though the larger town gatherings seem to have been held usually in the new meeting-house.

In 1773 the town voted to cut the old meeting-house down to one story, and divide it by a partition, also to build a chimney on one end which was to be fitted up for a workhouse, "to promote Industery and set to work those that live Idly and Misspend their time." The other part was to be seated as a town hall. The completion of this work was delayed for some years, as the Revolution occupied the thoughts of the people, but in 1781 provisions and tools were bought for the workhouse, including "2 large wheels, 2 small ones, 2 pair of wool cards, sheep's wool, flax, and a thousand weight of old junk." After this, the "Master of the Workhouse" was a regular town officer for some years, Lot Haskell and Deacon Seth Dexter being two of those who held this position.

In 1792 a new State law was passed, respecting the care of the poor of the towns and State. After this the workhouse was given up, and the poor were boarded in families until 1819, when a poorhouse was provided.

With the giving up of the workhouse, the old meeting-house was again remodeled. The chimney was taken down, the partition removed, and the whole seated as a town house. In 1811 the old building was taken down, and some of the best of its timbers were used in the construction of a new town house, built that year in the middle of the Common. The town house of 1811 was a low, square building, with a pyramidal roof and rising tiers of seats. Old people of to-day recall with interest scenes on town-meeting days, when the "Breadman" from Wareham was always on hand, selling rusk, — a kind of bun with raisins on top, — while the countrymen, coming up, one by one, each shook from his pocket the folds of a clean, red bandanna, and went on his way with one or more of these dainties folded within it.

Near the middle of the nineteenth century, the town house was the scene of some lively town meetings, as questions arose which led, a few years later, to the dismemberment of the town itself.

In 1892, when the new Town and Library building was erected on Rochester Common, the old town house of 1811, with a change of roof, was made into a cranberry house, which stands to-day on the Pratt cranberry bog. When the building was removed, Mr. John S. Ryder found, under one of its timbers, as a supporting block, the capital of an ancient pillar that had been a support for the gallery in the old meeting-house of 1717.

The migratory school seems to have been continued in Rochester for some time after the Revolution. In 1789 a law was passed in Massachusetts, allowing towns to divide themselves into school districts, each having a "prudential committee-man," who should have the care

of the school property and "contract with the teacher."
Horance Mann afterwards declared this district school law
to be one of the most pernicious ever passed. It represented democracy carried to its lowest terms, and was
opposed to a large public spirit. Each district had its
tiny political excitements, and too frequently the passport
to employment as a teacher was relationship to the prudential committee. Yet the old district school had its
redeeming and picturesque features and under a good
teacher excellent work was often done.

In 1799 Rochester voted to adopt the district system,
and divided itself into sixteen school districts, each of
which was entitled to have three months of school once in
two years. The districts were still named as belonging
to the "Four Quarters" of the town. "The Town
Quarter," Sniptuit, Mattapoisett, and Sippican continued to be the town "quarters" until the division of the
towns took place in the middle of the nineteenth century.

In 1820-22 a vigorous effort to improve the schools was
made. The districts were re-divided; twenty-one being
now laid out. It was voted that one half the money for
schools should be divided equally among the districts,
the other half being divided according to the proportion
of scholars. A committee of three (serving without pay),
in addition to the selectmen and the ministers of the
town, was appointed to visit the schools, this committee
consisting of Abraham Holmes, Isaac Thompson and
Philip Crandon.

In 1824 it was voted to "adopt a measure respecting
town schools passed by the legislature," to the effect that
"in any town having less than 5000 inhabitants, and now
required by law to be provided with a Master or Masters

CANNON STREET, MATTAPOISETT, ABOUT 1880

instructed in the Latin and Greek tongues, might instead
be provided with a teacher or teachers well qualified to
instruct youth in orthography, reading, writing, arithmetic, English grammar, geography, and good behavior."

In 1828 a protest was entered against paying the wages
of certain teachers who had been engaged by prudential
committees without requisite certificates as to their qualifications.

In 1832 the appropriation for schools was raised to
$1200, and in 1834 it was voted that the school committee
should consist of three persons only: Jonathan Bigelow,
Charles J. Holmes, and Thomas Robbins being the ones
chosen.   In 1835 an elaborate report on schools was made
and it was voted to increase the appropriation by $200;
one of the arguments presented being that by this means
the town would receive a larger proportion of a State
fund that could be drawn upon for schools.

We know from Dr. Robbins's diary, that during his
service on the school committee he spent much time in
visiting the schools and doing what he could for their
improvement, and the same was doubtless true of the
other ministers of the town who at various times served
on the school committee.

During the continuance of the district system some
private schools were opened to supplement these lower
schools.   The first "Academy" in Rochester was a private school, opened in North Rochester in 1795 by Rev.
Calvin Chaddock, who was an accomplished teacher;
but this came to an end with the close of Mr. Chaddock's
pastorate a few years later.   Through the efforts of Rev.
Jonathan Bigelow, George Bonney and others, an academy
was opened at Rochester Center in 1839, which was for

years an important institution, having among its preceptors Rev. Andrew Bigelow, Rev. Henry M. Dexter, and Mr. Charles P. Rugg, afterwards superintendent of schools in New Bedford. The large boarding-house of this institution, afterwards burned, was kept for years by Mr. Robert C. Randall on the corner opposite the one where the old Dr. Haskell house was burned at a later date.

An academy was also opened at Mattapoisett about 1856, the building of which was afterwards used for the Barstow High School. A school corporation was also formed in Sippican, and a private school was opened, but not definitely organized as an Academy. (Tabor Academy was not opened until 1877.)

In 1850 the district system was still in operation, and no attempts at grading the schools were made until after the town was divided.

The representative from Rochester to the General Court at Boston during the Revolution was Lieut.-Col. Ebenezer White. When the State constitution went into effect in 1780, Colonel White became the first representative under the new frame of government, and continued to hold this office for some years.

During many years the town had two representatives in the State legislature, sometimes three, and once as many as four. The names of those who were Rochester Representatives under the State Constitution before 1857 are as follows:

Ebenezer White, Nathaniel Hammond, Abraham Holmes, Nathaniel Sprague, Nathan Willis, Elisha Ruggles, Gideon Barstow, Jr., Rev. Calvin Chaddock, Caleb Briggs, Jesse Haskell, Thomas Bassett, Elijah Willis, Samuel Winslow, Charles J. Holmes, Joseph

Meigs, Philip Crandon, Wilson Barstow, George King, Eben Holmes, Amittai B. Hammond, Theophilus King, Malachi Ellis, Benjamin Barstow, 2d, Zaccheus M. Barstow, Joseph Hammett, William Sears, James H. Clark, Isaac Smith, Samuel Sturtevant, Jr., James Ruggles, Silas B. Allen, Loring Meigs, George Bonney, Nathan Cannon, Nathan S. Clark, Solomon K. Eaton, John H. Clark, John A. Le Baron, Thomas Ellis, G. B. Blackmer.

A century ago law schools had not been organized in the universities, and young lawyers were prepared for their profession in the office of some older lawyer, an arrangement which in some cases took on the character of a small law school. Such a "Law School" was held for some years at the office of Abraham Holmes, where a considerable number of well-known lawyers were trained. The office stood in "The Flatiron Piece," a grassy triangle in front of Fearing's store (then the Bonney store), and had the sign "A. Holmes, Office." It is related that a wag standing in front of it once read the sign aloud, as follows: "A-hol-mess-of-ice."

One of the students in this law school was Charles J. Holmes, Sr., the son of Abraham Holmes, who became a prominent lawyer, first in Rochester, later in Taunton and Fall River. In the closing years of the nineteenth century Charles J. Holmes, Jr., lawyer and banker, came back from Fall River to spend his closing years in the scenes where his childhood had been passed.

The office of Charles J. Holmes, Sr., in Rochester, was often visited by leading lawyers from other localities, one of these being Daniel Webster. The late Rufus Savery used to recall an incident of his boyhood in which Daniel Webster, driving over from Marshfield, to hold court in

Rochester, met him on the street and stopped to talk with him, giving him some good advice, to the effect that whatever he undertook he must always do it well.

Rochester was then one of the towns in Plymouth County in which Probate Courts were regularly held. There were also many sessions of Justices Courts. A vote of the First Parish in 1806 is on record, however, which refuses to "allow any more Courts to be held in the meetinghouse."

The military interest kindled by the Revolution did not die out when peace was declared. Militia companies continued to exist, and new ones were organized. In 1815 we are told that "Rochester in military affairs is annexed to the fourth regiment, fifth division. It furnished three companies and part of a troop" (i.e., a company of cavalry). Jesse Haskell was at one time a commissioned officer in the cavalry company of Rochester.

The annual muster held on the old Rochester Muster Field was for many years an occasion of great importance. The "Muster Field" was apparently the same lot of land that had been set apart by the town of Rochester in 1697 as a "Training Field." It was a large open lot for many years, but is now occupied in part by the residence of Mr. William Thorpe. The annual "Muster" filled for the community something of the same place that was taken by the county "cattle shows" of the next generation. Here military companies, with smooth-bore guns and improvised uniforms, were gathered from all parts of Old Rochester and the towns around, and performed gyrations to the music of "Yankee Doodle" and "Hail Columbia," while the hucksters in the stalls regaled the crowds of spectators with cider and popcorn.

The War of 1812 was not approved of in Massachusetts, the people not being in sympathy with the governmental actions that led to it, and few chose to enter the general service. But when in June, 1814, two British vessels, the *Superb* and the gun-brig *Nimrod*, appeared in Buzzard's Bay, the people became aroused. The selectmen of New Bedford wrote to the Attorney-General, asking for 560 men to protect the coasts of New Bedford, Dartmouth and Westport, which "had shipping to the value of one and a half million of dollars."

The *Nimrod* came as far as Charles's Neck, and sent some barges to Wareham, whose crews burned a few houses in that village, causing great excitement, in Rochester as well as in Wareham itself. A committee of safety was now appointed, consisting of William LeBaron, Joseph Meigs, Rowland Luce, Timothy Hiller, and Abraham Holmes, and application was made to the Major-General of Militia for 125 soldiers to be drafted for the defense of the town, and for half a company of artillery for the same purpose. It is not clear that this whole force was provided; but two small companies of Rochester men were stationed at the harbors as a coast defense. One of these, called a Sergeant's Guard, consisted of twenty-nine men, commanded by Jonathan Vaughn, Ensign, and Thomas Ashley, Sergeant. It was on duty in June and July. Another company, called on the rolls "Ensign's Guard," had twenty-seven men, with Moses Mendall as Ensign, and was on duty in September and October. Other Rochester men were in two New Bedford companies serving at Fairhaven during the same season.

New military companies continued to be formed in Rochester at various times during the first half of the

nineteenth century. But after the Civil War had taxed
to the utmost the military energies of the people, and
filled their minds with the horror of warfare, the interest
in these local military practices finally died out.

Among the old militia companies was a company of
light infantry organized June 18, 1825, for home safety.

The Fourth Plymouth regiment of militia, when reorganized in 1826, had the following officers from Rochester: David Hathaway, Colonel; Ebenezer Barrows, Lieutenant-Colonel; John H. Clark, Ensign; Dr. Thomas E.
Gage, Adjutant.

In 1842 a company was formed in Mattapoisett called
the Mattapoisett Guards, of which R. L. Barstow and
Loring Meigs were at different times captain. Captain
Barstow was then transferred to the staff of Brigadier-
General Dunham for four years, and the Mattapoisett
Guards were dissolved. Later Captain Barstow was
commander of the Rochester Light Infantry for two years,
and still later was Major of the Ninth Massachusetts
Regiment, having in all a military service of about eighteen
years.

In the exciting political campaign of 1840 (the Log
Cabin and Hard Cider Campaign), Rochester was very
enthusiastic on the Whig side, and a tall flagstaff called a
"Liberty Pole" was erected by the town on Rochester
Common nearly on the site of the present flagstaff. A
few years later it was blown down during a heavy gale.
In Mattapoisett village the enthusiasm was still greater
and a Log Cabin was provided, which stood to the west of
the cooper shop of the late Prince Bolles, on land now
owned by R. L. Barstow. This structure was ninety feet
in length, and was later used for theatrical purposes.

In the closing years of the eighteenth century, Minister Moore of the First Church of Rochester made some notes regarding health conditions in that precinct, which represent probably the general town conditions.

He says:

"During the 30 years of my ministry in Rochester First Church, there have died of all ages and sexes (including those that were killed in the late war, and came to their end by accidents) 376 persons. About a quarter part of sd number died of consumptive ails and these chiefly young women from 16 to 26 yrs of age."

Regarding longevity, Mr. Moore writes:

"Rather more than a fifth part lived to 70 & upwards, — a ninth part to 80, nearly a 50th part to upwards of 90. This precinct has connected to it an average of about 160 families."

In 1801 the town of Rochester voted to provide a hospital for the purpose of "inoculating for and having the small pox." Dr. James Foster was authorized to inoculate for the much-dreaded disease. Certain temporary provisions were made as to houses to be used, but Dr. Foster agreed to build a house for the purpose, which was to be erected on an island in a piece of salt-marsh bought by him. Whether this hospital was really erected is not recorded.

In 1816 a disease called spotted fever broke out in Mattapoisett, and made fearful ravages in that village and in the western part of Rochester. Sixty-one heads of families were stricken. The fever plague stopped in its easterly course about a mile west from Rochester Center, at the home of Charles Sturtevant, who died with it. Dr. Mann of Boston was sent for to aid in controlling the situation, and the measures which he adopted seem to have been finally effective.

A writer in the Massachusetts Historical Collection has said of this epidemic:

"A mortal fever prevailed in Rochester, in the early part of 1816. It spread from Fair Haven, where it appeared in Sept. last.

"Fifty deaths are stated to have occurred in its bills of mortality, since February; but the fever is now abating, in the month of May. Near 200 deaths are stated in the circle of contagion; say Fair Haven, Rochester, east of Freetown and borders, since Sept. 23, 1815, to May 1816."

1832 was the cholera year. The whole country was alarmed and a "colera meeting" was held in Rochester. A committee of twenty-seven was appointed to constitute, with the selectmen, a committee of health, establish quarantine regulations, and provide a place where persons could be taken care of "in case of malignant disease." But cholera did not come to Rochester, and the duties of this committee were probably light.

The winter of 1840–41 was a time of much sickness in Mattapoisett, and it seems probable that the unhealthfulness of the season extended to the other communities as well. The exact nature of the epidemic, which was evidently contagious, is not given. Perhaps the best idea of the conditions of that winter can be gained from Dr. Robbins's diary entries regarding Mattapoisett.

1841

Jan. 2. There are many new cases of the epidemic. Visited many sick and distressed families.

Feb. 14. Spoke on the subject of the late deaths. For three weeks there have been three in each week.

Feb. 28. It is a solemn and distressing time with us. There were seventeen deaths in Mattapoisett in November and December; and in January and February the same number, seventeen.

Mar. 6. There have been four deaths this week.

Mar. 28. At evening had a meeting of prayer and humiliation in the meetinghouse in view of the divine judgments upon us. Oh that we may find help!

Apr. 2. We have new cases. The disease is evidently contagious.

Apr. 10. Two physicians are here from Bedford.

On September 28, 1815, there occurred a great gale, followed by a heavy tide on the Buzzard's Bay shores, which did much damage to all the towns of the region and came to be known as the "September Hurricane." Of this storm it is said:

"The total loss in Rochester is stated at $50,000. The tide there rose fourteen feet above low water mark, and four feet higher than ever known there before; the ordinary tides being about six feet. Vessels floated from the stocks, rope walks, stores and houses were destroyed and a great amount of salt lost."

In Mattapoisett the meeting-house at Hammondtown was partly destroyed, and had to be taken down. The Bethuel Landers house, now occupied as a summer cottage by J. Lewis Stackpole, Jr., was taken from its foundations, turned around in the street, and the occupants were removed in boats.

The damage to the salt industry was far more than was

occasioned by the loss of the salt merely. The works themselves were largely swept away by the tide and the high winds.

Some of the anecdotes relating to this gale that have been preserved are as follows:

" A salt house from Sippican, partly filled with salt, held its position till the tide had risen nearly to the roof, when it was overset and floated across the bay. Its ruins were found in the woods at Wareham."

"Another lot of salt works floated several miles unbroken, but landed on a craggy shore and fell to pieces on the rocks. The salt house, however, settled on some stones that held it in perfect shape, and it was later launched like a vessel and carried back to the original position. The place where it was grounded was about nine feet above the level of common high tides."

" Theophilus Pease, of Rochester, aged seventy-three, having repaired to a small island at Mattapoisett during the gale, to preserve some hay, soon saw his dangerous situation. Having a pitchfork in his hand, and a line in his pocket, he lashed the fork across the limbs of a tree, which he selected, and stood upon it about six hours, partly in the water, until the tide ebbed. There were only three or four trees on the island, all of which were carried away by the flood, but the one he selected; a remarkable instance of preservation."

"A store containing West India goods, situated at Great Neck, was floated entire to Wareham, perhaps a mile, where it remained with its goods in perfect preservation."

From an article in the Massachusetts Historical Collections, by Rev. Ezra S. Goodwin, of Sandwich, some further knowledge of this great storm and its effects may be gathered, as follows:

The injury in Buzzard's Bay was much greater than in Vineyard Sound. The highest water in Buzzards Bay occurred about 11 h. 40 min., three hours later than at Barnstable Bay.

Coasting vessels were scattered about, and mostly driven high on shore. Some of them floated into the forest. One lodged among the trees in an upright position and was later relaunched.

The spray while the tide was rising resembled a driving snowstorm. Grass was entirely killed, not a green blade to be seen. The leaves of the trees appeared as if they had been scorched. Several cedar swamps perished from the salt water. Most of the bushes perished also, but one or two species of laurel, the common bayberry and some swamp whortleberries survived. Winter rye had been sown in August. Rye was resown in some of the fields but the original crop had perished.

The wells and watering places for cattle were filled with sea-water, and fresh water was a thing of price.

Little rain had fallen for some time, and the soil was very dry. Much of the salt water therefore penetrated the earth and saturated it with the salt, which also crystallized along the shore.

Some wells near the sea had formerly risen and fallen with the tide and yet remained fresh. They now changed their habit. The water remained at a fixed height and was also salt. The saltness of the wells continued till November. After the snow of winter dissolved the salt wells became fresh. The freshness came back suddenly.

After a time of dry weather they grew salt again, but not so bad as before. Some did not wholly recover until the spring of 1818.

There was a curious and lasting effect on the land. In 1816 some of the overflowed fields were planted with oats and had a larger crop than ever before. Indian corn also flourished, planted as a spring crop. The salt seems to have acted in some cases like a manure. But in 1817 clover decreased and in 1818 almost disappeared. Mosses also were destroyed, and wild grass came in where the cultivated grass had been. Some good effects of the storm were seen, but not enough to compensate for the property destroyed.

In the middle years of the first half of the nineteenth century temperance matters were prominent all over the United States. A vigorous warfare was made against "New England rum" and other spirituous liquors, which heretofore had been in general use. A temperance crusade known as "The Washingtonian Movement" spread over the country, and total abstinence societies were everywhere formed.

In 1830 the town of Rochester sent a petition to the legislature to make a law authorizing the County Commissioners or the selectmen of the towns to license tavern keepers, giving them all the usual rights and duties of this office, except the right to sell spirituous liquors. A little later a second petition was presented, after an elaborate report (which is duly recorded in the town book) in which the town's committee grew eloquent in regard to "the wife's streaming eyes over her naked and supperless children," and declared that "Banking Corporations, Turnpike Roads, Canals, and even

Railroads sink into insignificance beside this important subject."

It is impossible to describe either the condition or the growth of Old Rochester in the first half of the nineteenth century without entering somewhat fully upon the subject of the maritime industries, which early in the century took on new lines of development in the seaside villages, and (especially in Mattapoisett) gave rapid growth and a new chapter of local history, which had most important consequences in the later town history. The story of these industries, however, and of their historic effects requires a full chapter, to be given later.

In 1840 a book called Massachusetts Historical Collections was published by John Warner Barber, which contains much historic and descriptive matter regarding the Massachusetts towns of that date. Mr. Barber was a personal friend of Dr. Robbins, whom he visited twice while getting the material for his collections. In this book he gives the population of Rochester as 3570 persons, and says that "about 60 sail of merchant and coasting vessels are owned in the town;" that "Mattapoisett village contains about 100 dwelling houses," and is "the principal village of Rochester," and that "the leading business of Sippican is the manufacture of salt."

In 1854 the Fairhaven branch of the Old Colony Railroad was built, which passed through Marion and Mattapoisett, but left the old Town Quarter outside its line of travel;—a fact which has had much to do with the relative growth of the Old Rochester villages since that date.

The discovery of gold in California sent a thrill of excitement over the country. Many persons in Old Rochester were touched with the "gold fever," and joined the

crowds that from all over the world were eagerly pressing
into California.   Some of the Rochester men joined bands
that from New Bedford and Fairhaven were fitting out
vessels to carry the gold seekers on their quest.   And
in Mattapoisett village two vessels, the *Oscar* and the
Mt. Vernon, were equipped and sent around Cape Horn
to the new land of promise.   The first was the brig *Oscar*,
under Captain Dornie, with seventy men from Mattapoisett and the vicinity.   They had a narrow escape
soon after starting, from an encounter with a hurricane,
in which the vessel was blown "on her beam ends."   But
she finally righted herself and the party went on.   Later
the *Mount Vernon* sailed.

Among those now living in Mattapoisett who went in
these expeditions, are Caleb Dexter, Thomas Randall,
and Thomas Luce; also Alden Rounseville, Jr., now a
mill-owner at Rochester.

Six Rochester men also joined the New Bedford Com-
pany that sailed in the *Mayflower:* James F. Dexter, James
Smellie, Freeman B. Howes, Robert C. Randall, Robert
C. Randall, Jr., Dr. Ezra Thompson.

Of these "Forty Niners," as they came to be called,
some returned after some months or years, having attained
a fair degree of success in the undertaking; and now they
delight to tell over to younger listeners tales of these
eventful days of '49.   Those who came back, singly or in
groups, mostly crossed the Isthmus of Panama, with its
dangerous heat and malarial influence.   Some of those
who started home with eager hearts fell victims to those
climatic conditions, and their bones lie buried in that
tropical soil.   Some reached home penniless and with
constitutions ruined for life.   Some elected to stay

in California and never revisited the land of their fathers.

Fifty-eight years have passed since then. Two hundred and twenty-eight years have gone by since the thirty proprietors purchased these lands of the Old Colony Court for the "seating of a township," and to provide a home for themselves and their posterity.

The general features of the region are the same. The contour of the long shore is unaltered, and the larger part of the lands of the interior are still covered with a growth of forest.

The pine groves still give forth their fragrance, yet no one "milks the pine· trees," nor makes tar from their flowing sap. The sawmills keep up a winter activity at various mill-ponds; and a few steam mills have added an all the year round enterprise to the box-board industry in various localities. But the trip-hammer and the puddling furnace of the old iron mills long ago disappeared, and the iron ore that remains is left undisturbed at the bottom of the lake beds.

The "craneberry" is still "a plenteous production" and is sent to-day to even a wider "vicinage" than Boston.

Many of the old stone walls are still standing, in more or less stable condition, "pathetic monuments of vanished men"; although some have been ground up to make the macadam roadways that thread the Old Rochester territory. But the lover of country life will often turn aside from these modern highways into the genuine country roadways, the natural "dirt-roads" of the olden time, with their inconsequent windings and changing blossoming hedgerows,

" Winding as roads will
  Here to a cottage, and there to a mill."

Here or there along these old roadways one will see
some unpainted cottage, with wide chimney and an old
well-sweep, and with lilacs or cinnamon roses about the
door.   Much that is ancient is still left in the Old Rochester territory, and there is folk-lore still to be gathered.
For traditions cling to an old town, and in place of the two
or three haunted houses, which the older generations
named as such, "All houses wherein men have lived
and died are haunted houses."   But the spirit of the
modern age has also touched all parts of the region.   Not
only in the seaside villages, where the beautiful new
homes of summer residents are rapidly multiplying, but
in other parts of the old town new dwellings are erected,
and many of the oldest houses show modern changes that
tell that the life-blood of the community is active and
flowing.

Instead of depending on the old "way-carriage" of
Dr. Robbins's time, the people take the frequent electrics
to New Bedford. The rural delivery carries the mail
to the remotest country farmhouse.   The boys and
girls come to the central schoolhouses on their bicycle
steeds, or by transportation furnished at public expense;
while the village and country matrons "pass the time of
day" with their neighbors through the telephone, and
business men in their country homes keep in touch with
their city offices through the same modern channel.

Wareham has itself become an old town.   The next
generation of its people will be ready to celebrate the
bicentennial of their own township anniversary.   Yet
once in a while the descendants of the Old Rochester

WATER STREET, MATTAPOISETT

settlers in the western villages of Wareham call to mind
the fact that for sixty years they were sharers with these
neighboring towns in the local associations of the older
town that was born in 1679.

In Marion and Mattapoisett something of the old
energy, enthusiasm, and pathos have departed that belonged to the old seafaring days. The windmills are
gone from these shores, and a few crane-beams, laid up
perhaps as a relic in some dry nook, are all that can now
be found of the great salt-works that at many points
were conspicuous objects along the water front. The
village of Sippican began to drop something of its maritime character soon after it laid aside its sibilant old
Indian name. Where it was once agreed that the village
private school "shall hail" as "Sippican Academy," the
modern "Tabor Academy" offers higher education to
the youth of the surrounding community.

The harbors are still the scene of life and activity
but the power-boat, the yacht, the catboat, and other
pleasure craft, have taken the place of the whaleships
and vessels of maritime commerce.

The part of Old Rochester that still bears her name,
having relinquished her claim to the water front and to
the honors of a seaport town, is now, to use the words of
William Root Bliss, the historian of Wareham, "an inland farm, untouched by railway trains." No Probate
Courts are nowadays held on Rochester Green to invite
the visits of distinguished members of the Massachusetts
Bar, or the protests of pious souls against such a secular
use of the parish meeting-house. At the new town hall
on Rochester Common, town business is still transacted,
but the new building does not shelter such a large gather-

ing of voters, nor do its walls ring with such stirring debates as were heard in the low-roofed building of the olden time.

But Rochester of to-day is still "an original corporation of the Old Colony," with a continuous existence reaching back to 1686. It inherits the corporate name and the town records of Rochester of the past. Yet the whole Rochester territory is still, to some extent, united in its local interests. The old precincts that were carved out of this territory are allied in conference relations among their churches, and in other social and religious associations. The automobiles speed daily over the fifteen-mile road that like a connecting cord binds in close proximity the three towns of Rochester, Marion, and Mattapoisett, which for a century and three quarters held equal partnership in the older Rochester. Even the herring fishery is still held in common ownership, and though it is the subject of triple town legislation, it remains a common interest. All have rights also in the clams, the scallops, the quahaugs, and other fish along Old Rochester shores.

July 22, 1879, in Handy's Grove, in Marion, near the Rochester line, the people of the Old Rochester territory joined to celebrate the 200th anniversary of the settlement of all these towns. Six thousand people were in attendance, and under the whispering pines the day was given to history and reminiscence, to feasting and enjoyment. In future anniversaries of this old event the people of these now separate towns will ever feel an equal degree of personal share and interest.

On account of the community of origin something of historic unity must always exist. Similar natural surroundings, a common ancestry, a common past " rich

with the spoils of time," united with the changing conditions and vicissitudes of modern life, are giving, and
must continue to give, to the towns of the Old Rochester
region an inheritance

> " Distinct as the billows yet one as the Sea "

where

> " The Sounding unifies all."

CHAPTER IX

THE DIVISION OF THE TOWN

ROCHESTER TOWN, even after the eastern portion was annexed to Wareham, comprised an extended territory. With the growth of maritime industry the shore villages increased largely in population and wealth, as compared with the agricultural sections of the town. Sippican was not so far from the old town-house at the Center, but Mattapoisett was distant some six miles and North Rochester was about equally far away. The inhabitants around Snippatuit Pond journeyed, as now, by Vaughn's Hill to Rochester Common to participate in the town's business, while those from Mattapoisett traveled the long route back from the shore.

The old Mattapoisett way led up over "Towser's Neck" and came into the "Country Road" above Haskell's mills; but on March 2, 1772, the town had voted, "That the way to mattepoiset from Town be so altered from where it Now Goes by the old Haunted House (so called) as to Continue Dartmouth Road till it Comes Near Great Rock, thence to Turn Southerly on East Side thereof & Continue on a Streight Line till it Enters Mattepoisett way in Such a Place as shall be most Convenient for same to be Laid & to be opened, Continued, & amended without any costs to the Town, till it is Made as Good as the way Used; & all ways to Continue in this place at the

Costs of mr Benja. Hatch, His Heirs & assigns: except that of mending the Way." And thereafter the voters of "Mattapoisett Quarter" went north by the present way through the Church neighborhood, and by the "Wheel of Fortune," to help determine the "town's mind." For a century or more increasing numbers traveled, without open protest, the long route to the town-house.

About the second Sabbath in February, 1837, the citizens found a warrant posted on the "Great Door" of their meeting-houses, issued by Philip Crandon, Amittai B. Hammond, and Earl C. Briggs, as selectmen, to Daniel Hall, constable, calling for a meeting for March 6th, next following: and requesting, in addition to ordinary matters, that action be taken on "Article 12th, To hear the request of the First Parish in said town in regard to moving the town-house, and repairing the same, and to pass any vote the town may see fit in regard to the whole matter." This request of the First Parish apparently started the controversy which only ended by the division into three towns twenty years later.

Some citizens of Mattapoisett, seeing that the condition of the town-house apparently required expenditure, and well knowing that a large minority, at least, of the voters of the town dwelt in that quarter, thought it a fitting time to act; and secured the insertion in the warrant, at its end, after Article 15, an unnumbered article "To decide if the town will hold their town-meetings in Mattapoisett Village for the term of one year from the 20th of March, 1837."

Never before in town had there been a proposition of this sort, and it naturally did not commend itself to the older citizens around Rochester Common. Abraham Holmes, then eighty-three years old, was much stirred

up and joined with James Ruggles and other younger
men of the "Town Quarter" to vigorously oppose any
change from the established order of things. When the
6th of March arrived, as Zebulon H. Thompson, late of
Rochester, states: "The Mattapoisett people surprised
us by arriving very early in barges, all the voters they
could muster," and Esquire Holmes tells that "they had
a flag, which they kept flying from the North side of the
road, opposite Ruggles's store."

The meeting being assembled, and the votes for moderator counted, "Amittai B. Hammond had all the votes but
two that were polled, which was 49 only. He took his
seat, then rose and called the town to order. Elijah
Willis Esqre, Ebenezer Holmes, Nathaniel Haskell, and
John W. Wing were appointed monitors." The first
trial of strength came on the vote for town clerk. Rogers
L. Barstow was re-elected by 275 votes, with 199 for
James Ruggles. A. B. Hammond, Philip Crandon and
Weston Allen were chosen selectmen, and they were instructed "to appoint agents for the taking of the herring,
and inspectors of Mattapoisett river for the year." Then
the meeting voted: "When this meeting be adjourned
it be adjourned to the First Christian Meeting-House in
Mattapoisett Village, and that all the town-meetings be
held in the Village of Mattapoisett for one year from the
20th day of March, 1837." The meeting then took up
Article 12, and voted, "That the First Parish in Rochester have the use of the town-house for public worship
while they are building their new meeting-house." Voted,
"To refer the request of the First Parish in regard to
moving the town-house to the selectmen for them to do
what they think proper." Appointed a committee to

investigate the accounts of the town farm. "James Ruggles Esq. then arose and gave notice that he protested against the vote in regard to holding town-meetings in the Village of Mattapoisett and should call for a reconsideration of that vote at the adjournment of this meeting." Voted to establish the almshouse as a house of industry, and adjourned to meet at Mattapoisett the first Monday in April.

Agreeable to adjournment, April 3, 1837, there was held, in the First Christian Meeting-House, the first town meeting ever assembled within the confines of Mattapoisett. The contingent from the "Town Quarter" was on hand early. Mr. Holmes writes, "After mature deliberation committees were appointed in each school-district to use every lawful measure to get a general turn out. The day arrived, the morning was flattering as to weather, but before noon it became squally. I was obliged to sit in a carriage for more than an hour before the door was opened."

Deacon Hammond finally "called the town to order," the Rev. Thomas Robbins offered prayer, and the moderator then called for the votes for treasurer. Eight monitors were deemed necessary at this meeting, and Lot N. Jones, John Bassett, James Ruggles, George King, Wilson Barstow, David Hathaway, Doctor Haskell, and Philip Crandon were appointed. The people repaired out of the house, except the old men, and gave in their votes as they came in. Seth Haskell had 347 votes and was chosen treasurer. "The town then moved that the vote by which the town-meetings for one year from the 20th day of March last past were ordered to be holden at Mattapoisett be reconsidered, and that when this meeting adjourn it

adjourn to Meet in the Town-House the 17th of April inst
at one of the clock in the afternoon." "The moderator
then rose and said that they should repair out of the house,
except the old men, and all them that were in favor of
reconsidering the vote last past in regard to holding town-
meetings in Mattapoisett should form in a line on the
north side of the street, and them that were not in favor
of reconsiderating the said vote should form on the south
side of said street. After counting the voters it was
found that there was 299 in favor and 296 against reconsidering the said vote, which left 3 majority in favor of
adjourning the meeting, when adjourned, to the town-
house." "Capt. John Atsatt then rose and gave notice
to the town that he should call for a reconsideration at the
adjournment of this meeting." The voters then accepted
the reports of the committees on town farm and in regard
to the surplus revenue, and adjourned "to Monday the
17th of Apr. inst at one of the clock P.M."

Dr. Robbins wrote: "April 3, Attended town-meeting,
the first time, I suppose, ever held in this village. A great
strife for the place. It was adjourned to meet next at
the center of the town by a vote of 299 against 296. I
spoke a little but did not vote. Mr. Bigelow was with me.
It was an unpleasant affair." The day of adjournment,
April 17, "Rode with company to Rochester by the particular desire of my people, and attended town-meeting,
and voted on the question of holding the meeting a part
of the time in this village. The only time I have ever
voted in a town-meeting since I was settled in the ministry."

Dr. Robbins opened the meeting with prayer. The
point in issue was acted on at once. Captain Atsatt
handed in his motion for reconsideration and adjourn-

Town House, Rochester Center, Built in 1811

ment to Mattapoisett. "It was móved that the vote as above, should be taken by Yea and Nay." Mattapoisett was out in force; and Mr. Holmes says, "Our people provided crackers and cheese at the schoolhouse for the benefit of those who lived at a distance, for the intention was that the people should be on the ground before 12 o'clock." "The vote," wrote Mr. Holmes, "could not be taken in the house, it was so crowded, and after various attempts had failed, the doors were shut upon the older men within the house, where ballots were then taken as they came out through the door; while the younger men were sent through the bars into Mr. Bonney's field, and their votes taken as they came out." "The ballots being read and counted, it was found that there were 324 Nays and 278 Yeas, which made a majority of 46 in favor of holding the town-meetings at the town-house." The town then voted, "To take so much of the surplus revenue as will pay for the poor-house farm in full & the Ballance to be invested in Bank Stock;" and adjourned one week to one P.M., April 24th.

"When the day came," writes Mr. Holmes, "before nine o'clock a northeast storm (very cold) commenced, which increased in its fury, and by noon was pretty violent. It was even doubtful if the moderator and town-clerk would come. Very few people from the N. W. part of the town attended, but the people of Mattapoisett had a considerable turn out." Linus Snow, Joseph W. Church, Andrew Southworth, and Joshua Cushing were chosen Assessors, and two ballots were taken for a fifth without choice between Ebenezer Holmes and David Hathaway. "Capt. John Atsatt then rose, and made a motion to adjourn this meeting to the Rev. Thomas Robbins's Meeting-

House in the Village of Mattapoisett, Wednesday the
26th day of April inst., at one of the o'clock in the afternoon, and the above motion was seconded by Elijah
Willis, Esq. The town then called for a vote. After
counting it was found that there were 141 in favor of
adjourning and 125 against. The town then voted to adjourn this meeting to Rev. Thomas Robbins's Meeting-
House. There being 139 in favor of adjourning agreeable
to Capt. J. Atsatt's motion, and 137 against it, which left
a majority of 2 for adjournment."

Upon this, the "Town Quarter" apparently gave up
the contest, and "having only one day to make preparation for repairing to Mattapoisett," they decided, for the
most part, to remain away. So, on April 26th, therefore,
only about 240 voters assembled at the meeting-house
at "the Green" in Mattapoisett, and chose George King
and four of the town's ministers on the School Committee,
— Thomas Robbins, Jonathan Bigelow, Oliver Cobb, and
Theodore K. Taylor. The contest for the fifth assessor
was settled by the absence of the voters from the "Town
Quarter," so Ebenezer Holmes had 238 votes and Col.
David Hathaway had 3. The usual year's business was
performed, and adjournment made to July 10, at the same
place. This appears to have been done simply for the
joy of holding another meeting in Mattapoisett, for being
assembled on that day, and "Deacon Mit" being absent,
they chose Capt. Martin Snow moderator pro-tem;
elected Levi Handy "wood-surveyor for Mattapoisett
Quarter"; and then voted that "the meeting be dissolved."
Thus ended the longest and most strenuous town meeting
recorded in the annals of Rochester.

At the meeting of March, 1838, warned to meet at the

town-house, votes were taken coming in the door, and for moderator, David Hathaway had 264 and Wilson Barstow 145. The "Town-Quarter" also elected its town-clerk; James Ruggles, 264, and Walton N. Ellis, 137. For selectmen, Amittai B. Hammond had 302, Stephen Delano 251, and Joseph Purrington 362. Voted, "To take up Article 8, which they did in the following manner: Voted, that the town choose agents whose duty it shall be to call a meeting in each quarter of the town. These committees chosen by the different quarters shall confer together and make a report on the subject contained in said 8th article at a town meeting called for that purpose only and expressly. The town then proceeded to the choice of said agents and made choice of Chas. J. Holmes, Esq., Wilson Barstow, Esq., Philip Crandon, Esq., and Capt. Jas. Delano." They took action as to herrings, elected school-committee, and adjourned for three weeks.

At the adjournment, March 26, 1838, "A motion was submitted by Elijah Willis, seconded by Ansel Weeks and John Atsatt, to adjourn this meeting to the Universalist Meeting House in Mattapoisett, to Tuesday, the 27th inst, and to divide the house in order to settle the question. The town accordingly repaired out of doors, and those in favor of adjournment paraded the north side of the town house, and those against adjournment took the south side of said house. The moderator then proceeded to count both sides. He counted the south side first and found that there was opposed to the motion 206, in favor of it 147, leaving a majority against the motion of 59 votes. The town then repaired to the house." They voted to proceed to choice of town officers, voted thanks to Philip Crandon, Esq., for his long service to the

town; and that horses, neat cattle and swine be restrained
from running at large on the highways and Common;
and then adjourned.

The meeting "to be only and expressly" for hearing
the report of the committee on Article 8, was warned
for May 17, 1838.   It elected Noah C. Perkins moderator, fixed a bounty on crows' heads; and then voted "that
C. J. Holmes, Esq., read the report of the committee,
which he did accordingly." " *The committee to whom was
referred the subject of future town meetings have considered
the same and submit the following report:* In territorial
extent Rochester is among the largest towns in the commonwealth.   For a century after its settlement agriculture was almost the exclusive pursuit of its inhabitants,
and the population was scattered with great equality
over its surface.   In later times this primitive occupation
has given place to other modes of obtaining subsistence,
and acquiring property.   The fact has been that while
population has remained nearly stationary in many parts
of the town, in others flourishing villages have sprung up,
and population greatly augmented.   This increase has
been principally about the seaboard, and is most strongly
manifested in the southwest division of the town.
Gathered around the harbor of Mattapoisett is an active
and flourishing population numbering probably more
than twelve hundred, a large proportion of whom find
profitable occupation in the shipyards, the workshops,
and other incidental employments of that enterprising
village.   This village is situated six miles from the accus-
tomed place of holding town meetings, with limited means
of conveyance.   This distance of travel to the place of
meeting is an inconvenience deeply felt and submitted to

with reluctance. Propositions have been made to lessen
this cause of dissatisfaction by holding a portion of the
meetings at that village, but it has not been considered
that the relief which would thus be obtained would be
more than counterbalanced by the greatly increased
travel of many who are now as far, or nearly as far, removed from the place of meeting as the citizens of Mattapoisett. The evil complained of might be diminished by
placing the town house nearer the center of travel, and
opening roads for convenient access to it, and if this
measure would be satisfactory as a permanent arrangement, the committee would recommend it to the favorable
consideration of the town; but if it should be deemed
inexpedient to adopt this mode of relief, and the opinion
of those who feel that the existing state of things has so
much more of evil than advantage that its longer continuance may not be endured, and that the only remedy is
by a change of public meetings, then the committee respectfully recommend that measures for a division of the town
be adopted. The committee have not arrived at this con-
clusion but with difficulty and regret. They would not recommend this painful remedy for evils imaginary or unreal,
but to avoid those that seem to be certain, enduring, and
more to be deprecated. A state of things that shall annually
or oftener bring together the citizens, and array them against
each other under local banners, with keenly excited feelings where mutual confidence and respect are made to give
place to jealousy, distrust, crimination and reproach, is
more to be deplored, while it endures, than separation; in
which, in all probability, after many struggles with alienated feelings and lasting enmity, it would terminate. — In
behalf of the committee. David Hathaway, Chairman."

It was then moved by Major Haskell, and his motion seconded by Captain Peckham, to dissolve this meeting, and the town thus voted.

In the warrant of March, 1839, were the following: "Article 12th, To see if the town will re-consider all votes passed in said town at any previous meeting for holding town meetings at any place except the town house. 13th, To see if the town will instruct the selectmen to warn town meeting one third of the time in Mattapoisett Village. 16th: To see if the town will petition the legislature of this session to divide said town of Rochester by setting off Mattapoisett and including or excluding that part known by the name of Sippican, as the town may think proper; if included, the line to run between the old landing, so called, and the lower village, and running westerly across Bartlett's Hill, so called, so in a westerly course to the dwelling house of Jeremiah Randall, thence westerly till you come to the dividing line between Rochester and Fairhaven.

At the meeting March 6th, David Hathaway Esq., had 43 votes, and was unanimously elected moderator. Voted to take up Article 12, and then return to Article 2. On motion of James Ruggles, seconded by Wm. C. Haskell, "The town then voted to reconsider all previous votes that had passed at any meeting held in said town for holding town meetings at any place except at the town house." Dr. Robbins writes, on this date, "Our people sent a remonstrance to the annual town-meeting instead of going"; and the record says, "A protest was then presented by Ansel Weeks against the proceeding of this meeting, signed by several of the local voters of said town, and after he had read the same it was voted to receive it and have it recorded with the records of the town, and here you have it as it reads: 'To the selectmen of the town of Rochester. The legal voters of said town assembled in town meeting under authority of warrant issued by two of the selectmen, under date of the 16th of February, 1839, for a meeting to be held at this time and place, the undersigned legal voters of said town believe, inasmuch as there has been a previous town meeting which instructed the selectmen to issue warrants for town meetings to be held in Mattapoisett Village for one year from Feb. 1839, that this meeting is illegal, antirepublican, unjust and oppressive. We therefore solemnly protest against your proceedings, and that we shall not consider ourselves under any obligation to conform to or comply with any acts or doings of this meeting.'" This protest was apparently somewhat offensive to town clerk Ruggles, and it annoyed him to have to copy into the record the names of the "several local voters" who signed it, for there were 248 besides John T. Atsatt and John Pitcher, and a considerable portion of these were from Sippican.

Taking up Article 13, it was moved by C. J. Holmes, Esq., that the following motion be passed, namely: "In order that the difficulties respecting the place of holding town meetings in the town of Rochester, and other difficulties growing out of the agitation of that subject may be amicably adjusted, we agree that if the town meetings for the year next ensuing, after the close of the present March meeting, including the next annual meeting for the Choice of town officers, be holden at Mattapoisett, and that the town meetings for the two following years shall be holden at the town house, and that at the end of three years the town shall be divided upon fair and equitable terms in all respects. The moderator counted the ayes and nays upon the motion of C. J. Holmes and found that there were in favor of the motion 65, against it 62. So the motion was declared accepted."

The town then passed a vote on motion of Charles J. Holmes, declaring that "the warrant issued by Seth Miller, Jr., Esq., called a meeting of the inhabitants of the town of Rochester to be holden at the Universalist meeting-house at Mattapoisett on the first day of February last past was at the least improvidently issued, as the contingency upon which a Justice of the Peace might issue a warrant did not exist, and that the vote passed at the meeting held under that warrant, respecting the place of holding town meetings in said town for the then ensuing year, imposes no obligation upon the selectmen to warn the meetings in conformity with that vote;" which seems to be a very reasonable proposition. After that the meeting was adjourned to April 1, 1839, at which time Dr. Robbins writes: "Rode to Rochester and attended town-meeting. Presented my school report. All our people were up and appointed two additional selectmen. There seems to be a growing alienation between this and the Town quarter of the town." The selectmen so chosen were Stephen C. Luce and Benjamin Barstow, 2d. Having done that, they adjourned to "Doctor Robbins's Meeting-House, one week from to-day at one of the o'clock:" at which adjournment they simply chose minor officers.

The following year, 1840, it was voted "to warn all meetings in Mattapoisett until the Nov. Meeting, and that thereafter all meetings for one year be at the town-house." Pursuant to that vote, March 24, 1840, a meeting was held at the Congregational meeting-house in Mattapoisett,

under a warrant of two articles, to ballot on an amendment
to the constitution and to fix the price of herring.

In 1841 there was a small gathering of voters at the
town-house, who elected officers and then voted, 61 to 58,
"that the town hold their town meetings in Sippican
Village for one year from the first of March next." Meetings continued to be at Sippican; as when on March 7, 1740,
it was voted "for an Armory for the Mattapoisett Guards,
to pay for Eaton Hall $50, and fitting up the same, which
amounts to sixteen dollars and some cents." July 12th,
there was another meeting at Sippican about the Great
Neck road.

March 13, 1843, met at the town-house, as also in April
and in June. In November, however, there was a meeting
at "the old Congregational meeting-house in Mattapoisett,
which accepted Barstow street from Church to Hammond,
and also "the continuation of Michonicks Street." In
April, 1844, at the same place, when was a spirited contest between Theophilus King and Abner Harlow for
town clerk, resulting on the third ballot, King, 166, and
Harlow, 152. By this time, however, the custom seemed
to be established of holding sessions in the various "Quarters." November, 1844, and April, 1845, at the town-
house, at which latter meeting it was voted "that the town
offers Joseph Meigs $2,500 for the right to the privilege
of the mill at Mattapoisett Weir, except what the town now
owns, and take deed for the same." April, 1846, meeting
at the "old Congregational Meeting-House, Sippican."
November, '46, and April, '47, at the town-house, and
November, '47 and April, '48, at Mattapoisett; then
two meetings at the town-house, and two at Sippican.

At one of the latter, held April 1, 1850, the condition of

the old town-house apparently demanded action, for there were four articles in the warrant; to sell, to build anew, to repair, and "to see what the town would do in regard to the depredations made on the town-house." Only one of these articles was acted on: it was voted to repair. This warrant also called for action on the layout of a road leading from Cannonville corner in Mattapoisett to Neds Point lighthouse. At that meeting also A. B. Hammond was chosen a committee on town map.

November 11, 1850, the citizens met "at the Methodist Meeting-House in North Rochester at 3 P.M.," and after action on other matters, voted unanimously "to hold all future meetings at the town-house in the Center of the Town." Accordingly, on January 20 following, at the town-house, was a special meeting at eleven A.M., the only article being, "To take into consideration the expediency of petitioning the legislature to set off Mattapoisett as a town by itself, also that said Mattapoisett when set off as a town may be annexed to Bristol County, and act thereon." The meeting voted that a committee of three from each quarter of the town be a committee to investigate the whole matter touching the second article of said warrant, and report at a future meeting. Motion made by Wilson Barstow. Voted that John LeBaron, Theo. King, Stephen C. Luce, Wm. Sears, be a committee to nominate the persons for said committee from each quarter of the town who forthwith reported the names of A. B. Hammond, Lemuel LeBaron, John H. Clark, Royal Smith, Thos. Ellis, Walton N. Ellis, Gilbert Hathaway, Jos. S. Luce, Geo. King, Linus Snow, and Josiah Bisbee. Voted that Geo. Bonney be added to the above committee at large.

This committee reported at a meeting, on February 27,

that it was inexpedient to petition the legislature to divide
the town.   Anticipating, perhaps, such a report, various
citizens had in the meantime acted and had petitioned the
General Court: and the town at this meeting was by the
warrant requested to act on both the petition of R. L.
Barstow and others, and of Walton N. Ellis and others.
Abner Harlow submitted a motion "that, in consideration
of the great extent of territory of the town, and the great
inconvenience the citizens in the southern part of the
town are put to in attending town meetings, it is advisable,
and the town believes it expedient, that the town of
Rochester be divided,"—and that the new town or towns
so incorporated should receive proper shares in the town
property; which motion was voted in the affirmative.
Voted against Dr. Ellis's petition, 48 to 96; approved the
Barstow one, 100 to 56; and appointed Col. John H.
Clark to be the town's agent at the legislative hearing.

Three months later, April 7, 1851, the town assembled
and voted, 197 to 127, in favor of the motion of Gilbert
Hathaway.   "Whereas the citizens of Sippican are to
much expense and inconvenience in attending town
meeting, and for other good and sufficient reasons, it is
very desirable and necessary that the southeasterly portion of the town of Rochester be set off and incorporated
into a new town on the basis of the petition of W. N.
Ellis and others now before the legislature, praying for
such new and municipal corporation."

Voted also, on a motion submitted by Wilson Barstow,
"that the town vote to a division of the town agreeably
to the petition of R. L. Barstow and others;" 204 to 93.
And the town was apparently in a hurry, for on motion
of Gilbert Hathaway, it was ordered "that Col. John

H. Clark, our representative to the general court, is hereby instructed to aid by his influence with the members of, and his vote in, the general court, to obtain the enactment of such acts by the present legislature; namely — Incorporating two new towns from Rochester disposing and dividing the present town property and privileges, also the poor and insane, etc., as fully desired by the vote this day taken, a true copy of which together with the vote on the motion, the town clerk will make and attest the same, and see they are forwarded to Col. Clark by Capt. Matthew Mayhew of Mattapoisett, Tuesday morning, to-morrow, and Col. Clark to present the same to the first committee on towns in the afternoon of the same day."

The legislature was not thus to be hurried, for it was the next General Court which, on May 14, 1852, passed an Act (Chapter 225) incorporating the town of Marion, to comprise the territory in the southeastern portion of Rochester, around Sippican Harbor. Why, for a name, the modern Marion was given in place of "soft-sliding sibilant Sippican," is not recorded. Some say the preference of Mrs. Elizabeth Tabor, the founder of Tabor Academy, had an influence. However that may be, Charles Neck, the Great Neck and Little Neck, the Great Hill and Minister's Rock, the Old Landing and Sippican, Rocky Nook and Happy Alley, lie to-day in Marion, the summer town on Buzzards Bay.

By the legislative act town income and property was divided equably, and the new town preserved its interest in the "town mills" and in the alewive fisheries of Mattapoisett River; and the inhabitants of Rochester continued to hold their rights in the shell and scale fish from the shores, flats, and waters of its former territory. To settle

THE OLD LANDING, MARION

matters with Marion, the town of Rochester, June 9, 1852, appointed Rogers L. Barstow, Theophilus King, and Alden Rounseville a committee. Mr. Rounseville desiring to be excused, Wilson Barstow was chosen in his stead. At the same meeting Joseph W. Church was directed to fit up the vestry as an armory.

In the four years from 1851 to 1855 town matters moved along very peacefully. A committee was authorized to sell the almshouse property; Amittai B. Hammond was sent to represent the town at the convention for amending the constitution; and Loring Meigs and Abner Harlow were directed " to meet the county commissioners to show cause why the road should not be built as by them laid out leading from Sippican to Mattapoisett."

On the warrant for town-meeting dated December 27, 1856, there appeared two articles for action toward another division of Old Rochester. Article 6, " To see what action the town will take in regard to a division of said town of Rochester." 7th: " To see what action the town will take in regard to chosing a committee from the north and from the south parts of said town who shall agree on the division line and all other matters pertaining to said division, and also be authorized to petition to the legislature for an act to divide said town;" and also Article 8, " To see what action the town will take in regard to petitioning the legislature to be set off from Plymouth County and annexed to Bristol County."

" Pursuant to the above warrant the town met and the meeting was opened at ten minutes past eleven A.M., the roads being so obstructed with snow the town clerk could not arrive at an earlier hour. The voters had repaired to the vestry under the Academy Hall and had organized

the meeting by choosing Theophilus King Esq. as moderator. On the arrival of the town clerk it was supposed
necessary to reorganize the meeting, whereupon the town
clerk, with a few of the voters, forthwith repaired to the
town hall, read the warrant, and on motion of Jas. Ruggles,
Esq., the meeting was adjourned to the vestry. Mr. King
was then chosen moderator. Mr. King then read the
warrant again. Under Article 6, it was voted to take the
sense of the meeting in regard to a division of the town.
The vote for a division was unanimous. Voted that
voters from the north and south parts of the town arrange
themselves in different parts of the room and agree upon
a committee, three from the north part, and three from
the south part, whose business it should be to agree upon
a division line. Members from the north part reported
on T. King, Geo. Pierce and Thos. Ellis. Members from
the south part reported the names of N. H. Barstow, J. H.
Holmes, Lemuel LeBaron. Voted to accept the above
names as such committee. Mr. King wished to be excused. Voted to excuse him. Voted that Alden Rounseville fill the place of Mr. King. Mr. Rounseville asked
to be excused. Voted not to excuse him. Voted that
if Mr. Barstow should decline on being notified of
his appointment, that the committee be allowed to fill
the vacancy." "Voted to adjourn to one week from
next Saturday at 10 A.M." "NAHUM LEONARD, Town
Clerk."

Saturday, February 7, 1857, the town met, and "Voted
to take up the sixth article." Lemuel LeBaron submitted
a resolution of Mattapoisett citizens. "Voted to divide the
resolution so as to act upon the matter of a line and of the
division of property separately. Voted that the north

line of School District No. 10, as suggested in the Mattapoisett resolution, should be the dividing line. Voted the
last part of the Mattapoisett resolution relating to the division of property according to the valuation be stricken
out, that the property shall be divided justly. Then
voted to lay the Mattapoisett resolution on the table.
6th. Voted to adopt that part of LeBaron's motion
that does not relate to division of property. Voted to
chose a committee of three disinterested persons from out
of town to agree upon conditions of a division. Voted
that the chair appoint a committee to nominate a committee as above. The chair appointed Jas. Ruggles, J. Clark
and J. T. Atsatt. Mr. Atsatt, by request, was excused.
R. L. Barstow was chosen in Atsatt's place, but was excused by request. Voted to reconsider the foregoing
vote. Voted that a division should be effected on these
conditions: The engine should be valued at $1200.00,
town hall and Sprague legacy should be given to the
northern portion, and the remainder of the town property
should be divided according to the valuation. The
meeting thereupon voted to dissolve."

Under a new warrant of March 24, 1857: "To see
what action the town will take in regard to an order of
notice served upon the town by the legislature now in
session, in regard to the division of said town, and to do
anything the town may think proper in relation to said
division or anything they may think proper in regard to
a former vote touching the division thereof or anything in
relation thereto." Meeting was held March 31. "Voted
to chose a committee to consist of three persons from the
north and three from the south part of the town whose duty
it shall be to draft a bill to be presented before the legislative

committee. A committee of nomination selected by the moderator reported the following names as persons suitable to compose this committee, namely: Loring Meigs, R. L. Barstow and Jonathan H. Holmes, Jas. Ruggles, David Lewis and Jos. W. Church. Voted to accept the report. Voted to instruct this committee to be governed by the previous action of the town touching this matter."

Less than two months later, May 20th, the Great and General Court, by Chapter 202 of the Acts of 1857, enacted the division; stipulating, however, that the two sections should continue to vote together at state elections until the next decennial census, or until a new apportionment of representatives. As at the separation of Marion, mill and herring interests and rights to fish and dig shellfish were continued as before. The town's vote that the fire engine be valued at $1200, and be taken by the southern portion; and that the Sprague legacy and the ancient town-house be kept by the part where the building stood, was included in the act. The line of division from Fairhaven across to Marion was defined; and to accommodate Colonel Clark, who desired to retain his citizenship in the northern section, it jogged southerly around his buildings on Wolf Island. Thus Rochester was separated from the sea; and thus was created a new town on the shore of Buzzards Bay, with the old name of Mattapoisett.

CHAPTER X

WRITTEN history within and for the territory now incorporated as the town of Mattapoisett dates from 1736, and begins in two volumes, — "The Chh's Book, or the Records of the Second Chh. in Rochester, Which was first Embodied July 27, 1736," and "The Book of Records for Mattapoisett Precinct in Rochester, December the 9th, 1736." Of these, the volume of Church records is a small book (about 6 x 7¾ inches) bound in full leather, and containing, usually in the handwriting of the pastors, the account of meetings, marriages and baptisms, considerably mixed up through the book, extending down to 1857. Since that date the record is in two volumes, and has, since 1865, been kept by the following clerks: Solomon K. Eaton, 1865–70; Henry Taylor, 1870–80; Noah Hammond, 1880–94; and by the writer since 1894. The first precinct book is a much more pretentious volume of full leather (8 x 12½ inches) of 560 pages. It covers a period of one hundred fifty years, ending 1886. There are many variations of handwriting, of which, with the possible exception of the last entries as made by Noah Hammond, the first forty pages as kept or copied in by Gideon Southworth are by far the best, — as is often the case in ancient records in New England. Many curious forms of spelling appear, both phonetic and otherwise.

The precinct clerks have been: Benjamin Hammond, Jr., 1736; Gideon Southworth, 1737–49; John Hammond, 1749–56; Barzillai Hammond, 1756–57; John Hammond, 1758–71; Enoch Hammond, 1772–78; Benjamin Dexter, 1779–80; Enoch Hammond, 1781–91; Thomas Tobey, 1791–92; Aaron Norton, 1793–94, Thomas Tobey, 1795; Nathaniel Hammond, 1796–1802; Thomas Tobey, 1803–16; Elijah Willis (pro tem), 1817; William LeBaron (pro tem), 1817; Benjamin Barstow, 3d, 1817; Wilber Southworth, 1818–20; Amittai B. Hammond, 1821–26; Wilson Barstow, 1827; Benjamin F. Pope, 1828; Wilson Barstow, 1829; Milton H. Leach, 1830; Allen Dexter, 1831–32; Leonard Hammond, 1833; Moores Rogers, 1834; Abner Harlow, 1835; Allen Dexter, 1836–38; Noah C. Sturtevant, 1839; Calvin C. Cannon, 1840; Leonard Hammond, 1841–42; Noah C. Sturtevant, 1843–44; Allen Dexter, 1845–48; Samuel Sturtevant, Jr., 1849–54; Nathan H. Barstow, 1855–58; Caleb King (pro tem), 1856; Hallet M. Cannon, 1859–67; Solomon K. Eaton, 1868–72; Henry Taylor, 1873–79; Lemuel LeB. Holmes (pro tem), 1874; Weston Howland (pro tem), 1875; Noah Hammond, 1880–94; Lemuel LeB. Dexter, 1894—.

In "The Chh's Book" prior to 1772, there are some lapses; but of the precinct, the record is continuous since Benjamin Hammond, Jr., the noted land surveyor of Bristol and Plymouth county towns, to begin his record as Precinct Clerk, copied in the Order of the General Court of June 9, 1736, whereby "Mr. Jabez Hammond one of the principal inhabitants of the new Precinct at Mattapoisett, in Rochester, was Impowered to assemble and Convene the freeholders and other inhabitants there Lawfully Qualified for Voting, to choose officers to stand

SECOND PRECINCT RELICS

"The Chh's Book," 1758, showing Rev. Mr. Hovey's letter of acceptance. The precinct records, 1736. Old latch and hinge and penny dated 1730, taken from Meeting House Hill and in the possession of Mrs. John Jenney. Pewter communion tankard, given to the Second Church in Rochester by Dr. Lazarus LeBaron, 1772, in the possession of Lemuel LeBaron Dexter.

until their anniversary meeting in March." Since that
entry of the act of incorporation, no year is without its
record, and in two bulky volumes are thus set down in
unbroken succession the business dealings of one of the
few territorial parishes now existing as such within the
Commonwealth.

In 1733 the people at Mattapoisett began to complain
that they were "so remote from the Center as to make
their Difficulty great in all publick Concerns," and they
requested the formation of a separate parish. This was
not arranged, however, until three years later, for the
letter is dated Rochester, July 27, 1736, from "Timothy
Ruggles, Paster in the name & with the Consent of the
Brethren," which certifies "those our Brethren Moses
Barlow, John Hammond, Thomas Dexter, Nathan
Hammond, Thomas Clark, Jabez Hammond, Benjamin
Hammond, Jun'r, Constant Dexter, & Samuel Dexter are
while with us regular members in full communion, and
are recommended as such, and it is hereby signified that
those our Dear Brethren have our free consent that they
form themselves into a Distinct Church according to
Gospel order and we commend them unto God & to the
word of his Grace which is able to build them up and
give them an inheritance among them that are Sanctified.
Desiring their prayers for us, we remain their Brethren
in the faith and fellowship of the Gospel.

"Also the Sisters are Dismissed in like manner, viz.: —
Mary Hammond, Hannah Dexter, Mary Bools, Lydia
Bools, Priscilla Hammond, Allis Clark, Thamsen Tarden."

On July 28 the nine men so dismissed subscribed to a
covenant and thus instituted the "Distinct Church;" and
having set their covenant down in full in "The Church's

Book," none of them deemed it necessary to make further
record, for the next four years, — or perhaps in the
absence of a settled pastor it was no one's duty. They
organized the precinct, however, in December, and on
the last day of the year 1736, the "freeholders and other
Inhabitants," some of them doubtless leaving home by
sunrise, met, as the warrant said, "by eight a clock in·the
forenoon, at the house of Lieut. John Hammond," which
house still stands by the Herring Weir, — "to Consider
and Conclude upon some proper ways and methods in
order to the finishing the meeting-house and to do something Relating to the way that leads from sd Precinct to
the Country Rhode." This last item was evidently a
matter at law, for they voted "to George Danford £3, 7s.
6d. for his trouble in going Down to Plymouth Court
about the way that leads from Parkers Harbour [1] into the
Country Rhode near Mark Haskill's." For officers,
they chose Jabez Dexter, moderator; Benj. Hammond,
Jr., Clerk; and Josiah Dexter, Ebenezer Barlow, and
Benj. Hammond, Jr., as Committee.

They had evidently made a good start on their meeting-
house,[2] before cold weather had come on, so that at this
meeting they were only concerned with its finishing, and
with approving bills already contracted, to meet which
was voted "£7 to Capt. Hammond on an accompt paid
in for framing," "Six Shillings to Jonathan Bools for
Drawing Stones, Thomas Randol 50s. for his timber that

[1] Was this Aucoot Cove?
[2] "These buildings they called meeting-houses. That any of their
posterity should be so regardless of confounding language as to call them
churches is to be regretted." — THOMAS ROBBINS, D.D. *A View of the
First Planters of New England* (p. 261). Hartford, 1843.

was used; also Mr. John Hammonds accompt of £2, 3s.
for boarding the Carpenters while Framing, and £1, 16s.
2d. to Mr. Jabez Hammond for Rum and Sugar provided
for Raising sd House." The precinct met again in June
and approved bills, and on October 13, 1737, the structure
was so far toward completion that they met at the meeting-
house and voted "to build Eleven pews by the Cost and
charge of those that purchase the spots," and making
choice of Gideon Southworth "Vendue Master," they
forthwith bid off said "spots."

This building stood at the fork of the roads, on the top
of "Zion's Hill" as it was later called, which is now cut
into by the town gravel pit, adjoining the present homestead, of John Jenney. The house was, as near as can be
estimated from the size of pews, and the facts shown in
the records, approximately twenty-five feet square, with
the "Great Door," of perhaps five feet width, in the
middle at the south, and the pulpit opposite on the north
side. There was another smaller door about one third
of the way back on the east side. The center space on
the floor was open for seating and was completely enclosed by pews, except where access to the doors or stairs
was necessary, or where the pulpit stood. No pew varied
much from being "Five foot square," and the "spot"
just within the great door at the right was considered the
choicest location, and was secured by Capt. Benj. Hammond for £8, 5s. Near the pulpit was less desired, and
the pew at the west side of and adjoining the pulpit stairs
went to Gideon Southworth: and Israel Hammond for £3.
Josiah Hammond took the northwest corner, and along
the west wall were Joseph Barlow, Thomas Clark, Lieut.
Jabez Hammond; while next, at the left of the south door,

was the pew of Barzillai and Achelaus Hammond. Israel Hammond's was in the southwest corner next the east door, beyond which came Ebenezer Barlow, George Barlow, and then in the northeast corner Nathan Hammond. The gallery appears to have extended around three sides with "mens' stairs" and "womens' stairs," and was apparently open until, in 1744, it was voted "to pew all the front gallery provided they will fetch £30 old tenor, and to divide them into four pews," and other gallery pews were added later. Nathan Tupper, Antipas Hammond, John Hammond, Jr., Gideon Southworth, and Constant Dexter had gallery pews. Out of "money the first pews sold for," Mr. Ebenezer Barlow was instructed "to finish the meeting-house so far as to build a Pulpit and Body of Seats," which was accomplished at a cost of £27, 10s., and here for thirty-five years, on the Sabbath day, the inhabitants gathered for the only religious services in Mattapoisett precinct.

Lest it should pass from our knowledge what territory this precinct included, Enoch Hammond, the clerk of 1788, inscribed on the fly-leaf of the record book:

> "The beginning of the bounds of Mattepoyset Precinct is the bridge of Cedar swamp brook. so called,[1] thence west to Dartmouth town line (now New Bedford). Then beginning at said Bridge and rainging East 200 rods; from thence such a straight line to the sea,[2] as will strike that lot of land which Thomas Winslow's house now stands upon at the most northwesterly part thereof, and so down to the Sea."

The first shepherd of this somewhat scattered flock was Rev. Elisha Tupper, who, on December 31, 1736, ac-

---

[1] Which flows under the Rochester road at the town line.
[2] The present southwesterly line of Marion is the same.

knowledged the receipt "from Capt. Benjamin Hammond, agent, the sum of twenty-five Pounds money, it being for my labor with the people of Mattapoisett precinct for half a year." Mr. Tupper never was settled over this parish, but the question as to whether or not he should be, provoked great feeling. In March, 1737, the precinct voted to pay him all that was due him, but that £70 be raised "to be paid out to the minister or ministers we shall Improve the Insuing year In proportion the sd. minister or ministers finding themselves provision, that the money be Drawed out of the treasury by the Commtt & be paid out to the minister or ministers that the sd precinct Shall Improve the time they are Improved," and that £150 be raised "for a settlement to the first minister that shall be legally & orderly ordained and settled." On May 1, 1738, a meeting was warned to act on a proposed settlement of Mr. Tupper, "but att sd meeting by Reason of some Disorders and Interruption before the Moderator was chosen" the precinct committee "adjourned the meeting forthwith to the dwelling house of Mr. John Hammonds," where the precinct, as the margin reads, "Negatived Tupper," and declined to join with the church in a call. In the church body, two factions appeared each calling itself the "Second Church in Rochester," and both appealed to the First Church for advice, who, — after council held, — through Minister Ruggles, sustained the views of that faction which included most of the charter members and which was opposed to a settlement of Mr. Tupper. This strengthened the position of the precinct, who in 1739 voted when Mr. Tupper "Exhibited an accompt footed £130, 19s. 5d. that the precinct have distinctly considered every article there-

in and find upon the whole that there is but £1, 7s. 3d.
due to Sd Mr. Tupper besides £30, 12s. 6d. already voted
to him." They also voted to "Rev. Mr. Parker of Plymouth and Mr. Samuel Veazie of Duxborough forty
shillings per day for their preaching here last year," for
which service Mr. Veazie received £6. They also chose
Ebenezer Barlow and Jonathan Boles "agents to agree
with Mr. Jedediah Adams for half a year, with what time
he hath been here, and allow him £50 for his services he
finding himself Diet." All parties also subscribed to a
covenant to "Desist all Differences and Indeavour to
cease everything that may bring into Remembrance and
augment the sd Differences but that it shall be buried in
oblivion and all unite for the calling of an orderly Minister." They then voted Mr. Tupper a gift of £8, from
money not required to pay Mr. Adams, and May 10,
1740, chose Mr. Israel Hammond "an agent to look out
and agree with a minister to preach a quarter of a year
after Mr. Adams's Second Quarter is out."

Israel Hammond "looked out" so successfully that
three months later, August 11, 1740, the church desired
the precinct's concurrence in a call to Mr. Ivory Hovey,
"and upon a Deliberate consideration thereof" the vote
was taken, the precinct joined in the call, and voted "to
allow him £100 for his salary the first year, and after that
to raise his salary yearly in proportion as the list and
valuation is raised, which the precinct assessors take to
make the precinct Rates by, until it comes to £150, and
there to stand the money to be equal to bills on this province old tenor" with £200, additional for the settlement.

Mr. Hovey accepted this call with a fervent letter to
the church and congregation, recommending "that every-

thing that is amiss among you be reformed, the renewal
of unhappy Contentions & Controversies be prevented
and an humble, meek, peaceable and forgiving spirit be
revived," and on his part it was by him agreed "to devote
myself to the work of the Gospel Ministry in this place
so long as life and Health shall be continued, a comfortable
support offered and so long as there shall appear a prospect of my best Serving the Interest of Religion thereby."

Ivory Hovey, junior, was born in Topsfield, July 3,
1714.   He joined the Topsfield church when fifteen years
old, "his mind having been seriously aroused by a tremendous earthquake two years before." He entered
Harvard in 1731, and although away nearly a full year
from illness, he graduated in 1735, and received his master's degree in 1739.   In 1737, while teaching in a private
family in Biddeford, he met Olive—the daughter of Captain Samuel Jordan, the well-known Indian Fighter; to
whom he was married February 8, 1739.   He had supplied churches at Tewksbury, Arundel, York, and Biddeford, and appeared at Mattapoisett as a young man of
twenty-six, but recently married, of slight physique, and
of studious and serious mind.   He was ordained and
installed as the first pastor of the Second Church in
Rochester, October 29, 1740.   Eighteen citizens promised about £25 extra toward his settlement, and Jonathan
Boles agreed to give him "2000 great shingles," while
Samuel Look offered four gallons of rum, "if Mr. Hovey
builds a house in said precinct, for raising."

Mr. Hovey started at once organizing his church and
reviving its records.   His first step was naturally to
provide the usual church officers, so "Dec'r 4th 1740.
At a chh meeting the vote was called whither this chh

would chose their Deacons or Persons to stand in the
Room of such & persons to set the Psalm by the major
part of the present voters. Passed in ye affirmative.
Accordingly Mr. George Barlow & Mr. Constant Dexter
were chosen to set the Psalm & Mr. Joseph Barlow and
Mr. Jabez Hammond chosen to stand in the place of
Deacons & perform the work of such until there might
be opportunity for the Chh to proceed into the full observation of the Apostolical Direction — let the Deacons
be first proved, then let them use the office of a Deacon
being found blameless. Also voted at the sd meeting that
the persons chosen to sustain the place of Deacons should
read the Psalm."

These continued on trial until, in 1742, the church met
and "concluded to bring in their Votes for four persons
whom they looked upon best qualified to be invested with
sd office & then refer it to a sacred Lott, which two of
the four God hath chosen unto that office, which affair
was proceeded in with Solemn Prayer unto him who
knew the hearts of all that he would give perfect Lotts,
and the Lotts fell upon Mr. Joseph Barlow and Mr.
Nathan Tupper & they took their place." It was also
voted that "Deacon Barlow should read the Psalm still,
and Deacon Tupper should tune it to the Congregation."
Brother Tupper tried it six weeks and made request to
be relieved, and the "Chh made choice of Mr. George
Barlow as Tuner."

That this church did not escape the controversy as to
music which was general at that time is evidenced by the
record: "April 16, 1744, the Chh met to see whither something might be done to remove the great uneasiness that
had arisen and had been long subsisting among us about

the Rule of Singing in divine worship, or singing by Rule,
and after a considerable debate concerning a Vote or
Agreement or Covenant (as some called it) which was
consented unto by a certain Number of Persons in this
place before there was a church gathered here, viz., that
the new way of Singing (for so they stiled regular singing) should forever be kept out of ye Prect. hereupon
the vote was called whether the Chh did look upon said
act to be but a Vote. Voted in the affirmative; and
hereupon the Vote was called whether this Chh do now
Judge it most proper for ye future to sing by Rule in
ye publick worship of God among us?   Voted in ye
affirmative." In 1751, they further "had discourse
about bringing Dr. Wattses Version of the Psalms [1] into
publick worship, but not very well agreeing in that the
matter was waived for further consideration."

And so the matter rested until ten years later it was
voted "To sing Dr. Watts' Version of the Psalms in Publick" and chose Aaron Barlow "Quorister." Even after
this, Dr. Watts' version was accepted with considerable reluctance, for in 1762 one of the objects of a church council
then called was "to attempt to pacify some of the people
who were dissatisfied with their singing the new version."

Meanwhile, the church life had progressed as was usual
to the times. Mr. Hovey regularly mounted his pulpit
stairs, laid out his sermon (a few of which have been

---

[1] "The version first used by N. E. churches was Ainsworth's after
which they used one called the New England Psalm Book. It was
common for ministers to expound a little on the psalms before singing.
Some congregations sang the psalms in course. The practice of reading
the line was not introduced until many years after the first settlement,
— in Plymouth not until 1681." — THOMAS ROBBINS, D.D. A View
of the First Planters of New England. Hartford, 1843.

preserved, written on twelve pages of paper, four inches wide and six inches long with fifty-three closely written and legible lines to the page) and preached to the occupants of the square pews, the gallery and the "body of seats." Nearly every month, true to Pedobaptist doctrine, some new infant was brought forward for baptism. On a rare occasion some brother arose in the open confessional and expressed sorrow for his indulgence in too much new rum, or some frailer sister "acknowledged her sin in Braking ye Seventh Commandment;" and made their peace with the church. Others needed dealings for absenting themselves from communion. All these matters required the administration of the "needful discipline of the kingdom," and to better perform this branch of the work, the church in 1744, "Mett to Consult something about the Choice of Ruling Elder,[1] distinct from the Teaching Eldr, and after Prayers to God for Direction and some Conference & Debate upon this affair, the Vote was called whither this Chh was Rype for proceeding in the Business; Voted in the affirmative." And after further prayer they put in their votes, and so chose Mr. George Barlow and Deacon Nathan Tupper and instructed them to "look upon the Chh Platform to be a scheme for church Discipline, and to take the same for a rule in their office."

[1] "A ruling elder was held by them to be a proper church officer who was to assist the minister or ministers in the duties of discipline and to take a lead in the church on various occasions which called for their particular deliberations, and in want of a minister to perform the duties of divine service. In some instances the ruling elder was a preacher. Such was Mr. Brewster, the venerable Elder of the church at Plymouth." — THOMAS ROBBINS, D.D. *A View of the First Planters of New England*, p. 252. Hartford, 1843.

Sometimes it was a doctrinal doubt, rather than a moral lapse, which required attention, as that of "our Brother Benj. Hammond whom we had been frequently laboring with to convince of his erroneous principles," and with whom "publickly, the Chh had a conferance, and who freely signified that he had in some measure changed his former Sentiments about Original Sin & the Doctrine of the Divine Decrees, and spake very candidly upon the same to the satisfaction of those in the Chh who had been uneasy about ye matter."

Mr. Hovey especially applied his efforts to restoring the breach caused by the division over Mr. Tupper. Numerous church meetings discussed further means for a reconciliation and settlement of this "Old Diffurance" as they called it. By "mutual agreem'ts & Interchangible Acknowledgm'ts of their Faults," the aggrieved brethren were one by one received back; but some were not easily won over. It was five years after Mr. Hovey's settlement that Lieut. Antipas Hammond, "one of the brethren who for some time had been Dissatisfied with some things that have been laboring in the Chh relating to ye Old Differance now saw light to join with this Chh in full communion, and upon his manifestation of the same the Chh Voted to receive him." The minister who thus recorded this happy restoration little thought that a few years thereafter his precinct would forbid him to preach in their meeting-house, and that his attempts to perform the duties of his pastoral office would stir up more strenuous controversy than ever had arisen over the "Old Difference."

Encouraged perhaps by the offer of great shingles and rum, and expecting doubtless to spend his days with this

parish, Mr. Hovey erected his house (which now, moved
down to the village, stands on the shore near the foot of
Mechanic Street) in the field lying south of the road,
opposite the present dwelling of Nathan B. Denham, —
within easy distance of the meeting-house. Here were
born his six children. The precinct had made him a
liberal settlement, and the people were so glad to have
an "Orderly Paster" duly settled that for some years it
was unnecessary to levy the lawful rates, and his salary
was collected "by way of free Contribution." The
minister, however, could not seem to keep out of debt.
Two years after his arrival, he was granted "£30. old
tenor for to pay his Debts and not as any part of his
salary." Whether the watchful dames considered Mrs.
Hovey to be "Spendfull," or little Dominicus to be too
finely appareled, or too apt to wear his shoes on other
days than Sundays, we know not. But we do know that
it became increasingly difficult to collect the "Gospel
Rates," and harder still for the minister to meet his obligations. Some began to be dissatisfied with his preaching.
Mr. Hovey quit making entries in the church's record
book in 1751, and for the period on to 1772 we can only
learn what occurred from the precinct records, and from
facts set forth by Mr. LeBaron, who, upon taking over
"the Chhs Book," in order as he said "to make the Con-
tents answer in some Measure to ye Title, being Records
of the Chh, etc.," collected from loose papers what he
could find, and set it down in chronological order. As
Mr. LeBaron was on the spot soon after, but was connected with none of the parties involved in Mr. Hovey's
dismission, we cannot do better than to take his version
of the affair.

"June 25, 1765. Mr. Hovey complained to the church that his circumstances were very discouraging, 1,— His Sallary was very low which had occasioned his being involved in Debt; 2, There was growing alienation of the people's affections toward him; 3, His Ministry was attended with little or no success. The Chh. appeared desirous to redress his grievances as far as they were able. They desired a Society Meeting to see if the Society would joyn to redress, etc., which not being done at that meeting of the Society, the Chh. met again and chose a Committee to examine into Mr. Hovey's Circumstances to see what help would be sufficient. The Committee conferred with their Pastor, looked into his affairs and returned to the Chh with the following Report. That if Mr. Hovey could be immediately supplied with a Sum of Money to the Value of about £47 lawf'l Money and have his sallary increased to £60, with his fire wood annually, they and he thought that he would be enabled to discharge his Debts and live well: and Mr. Hovey offered that if they would buy his House and Lot for a Parsonage he would be satisfied with half the 47 Pound. — The society did not comply with the above report, and the Chh could not and so the matter rested. In 1767 the Chh seemed to be too much in Parties and there was a growing Disaffection between the Pastor and several of the members. In 1760 a memorial was drawn up and sent into the Chh containing several things against their Pastor. A council was sent for to adjust matters, and what was their Result I know not, but by what follows it seems that they advised a Dismission, for Mar. 5, 1768 the Revd. Mr. Hovey preached a farewell sermon and after sermon put it to Vote whether the Chh would in Pursuance of the Advice of the Council dismiss him from the Work of the Ministry among them; but one held up his Hand for the Dismission. Mr. Hovey then signified to the people that since the Chh would not Vote his Dismission he looked upon himself obliged to tarry with them and carry on his work as usual.

"1768 — May — Kept a Day of fasting & Prayer, the Ministers that assisted were the Revd. Messrs Conant & Turner of Middleborough and West of Dartmouth. The advice of these Gentlemen was to send for another Council, in which all sides should agree. The Disturbance was at this time at a suprising height. The Chh prepared a Petition to the Society desiring them not to proced as they mention in their Warrant to shut up the Meeting House, but the Petition did not meet with acceptance and the Chh chose a Committee to complain of the Precinct to the Court for shutting up the House etc., but the House being opened prevented their going any further. July, 1768, they agree upon a mutual Council, the Revd. Messrs Williams of Sandwich, Robbins of Plymouth, Conant of Middleborough, Angew of Bridgewater. The Chhs and Ministers sent to, came and formed into a Council on Tuesday Aug. 23 and adjourned from one day to another all that week, hearing all their grievances. What was the result I know not. October 16, 1768, the last Chh Meeting that was moderated by Mr. Hovey was at that time; in which the records of the Chh were delivered to Deacon Clark. I conclude therefore that the Revd. Mr. Hovey was dismissed at this time and I suppose it was agreeable to the result of the last Council."

Mr. Hovey's farewell sermon was printed and a copy is to be found in the Congregational Library, Boston. His text was 2 Cor. xiii. 11. And in his discourse he said: "Lay aside all unchristian resentments toward any whom you may think have been the blameable instruments of the removal of your minister. I repeat it, do not harbor nor indulge in any unbecoming resentments or judge against one another on your own account, or for my sake whom you may think injuriously treated." He also made lengthy remarks especially addressed to "any children or youth who are rejoicing in the thoughts of their minister's Departure in hopes they shall be under less restraint on Sabbath Days and other times."

The correctness of Mr. LeBaron's supposition is also shown by the Precinct record of December 26, 1768, when "a Vote was called & Drafted in the following: — All you that are so minded as to Joyne with ye Church In Compliance with Ye Council's Result to Dismiss Mr. Hovey manifest it. — Voted in ye affirmative." Of the Council's recommendation, as specified in the warrant, that "ye Precinct Pay Mr. Hovey the sum of £70, as a Consideration for ye Damiges he may sustain by his Dismission, & £45, 4s. 6d. for his Ministerial Services from ye first Day of March Last to ye first Day of January next," they made short work; and without discussion "passed the Vote In Ye Negative." This was in full accord with their previous attitude when eighteen months before they had "Maid choice of Ebenezer Magges, Ephr'm Dexter, Zaccheus Meede a Committee to Desier Mr. Hovey to Desist Preeching in our meeting-House & if he Refuses to forbid him," and "also at sd Meeting, voted that the meeting House shall be Loct & fastened & Not be opened but by order from the Ceepers of ye meeting Howse & No other untill we have a minister. And that Enoch Hammond, Sulvenas Gibes, Wilber Southworth should

be an assistant to ye Meeting House Keeper to act against
any who secretly or by open Violence should brake open
said Meeting House." It also accorded with their
vote August, 1769, when, meeting under a warrant "to
Consider the Broken and Distrest circumstances of ye
Precinct Relating to the Minister & to Consider & Act
on proper measurs for handling ye Same," they
directed that "John Clark, Ephream Dexter & Obed
Barlow be a Committee to go to Mr. Ivory Hovey and in
ye Name & Behalf of ye Second Precinct in Rochester to
Inform him that his Preching in our Meeting Howse for
a long time past has bin to our Damige and to ye Preja-
duce of Good Order and the Restoration of Pece amongst
us, and we do as a precinct forbid your entering into sd
Howse to Prech aney more without orders from ye Precinct."

But in finally turning Mr. Hovey away empty, and
terminating his settlement without a penny for his damage,
the precinct evidently let their feelings lead them into
error; for the parson entered his case at Plymouth Court,
and in spite of the efforts of Gideon Southworth, Israel,
Nathaniel, and Enoch Hammond, as agents, and £38,
7s. 5d. spent for attorney's fees and going to Plymouth;
£8, 16s. for horse hire 176 miles, (together with other
charges), Mr. Hovey, his cause having been "Determined in Cort by a Reference," recovered judgment
in 1770 against the precinct for the sum of £130 lawful
money.

Mr. Hovey not only took his cause to Plymouth, but he
moved his family thither, being installed over the "Second
Church of Plymouth," at Manomet, April 18, 1770.
There he preached for twenty-three years, there he died,

and his tombstone there standing reads, "In memory of
Rev. Ivory Hovey who died Nov. 4, 1803 in the 90th year
of his age. —

> By faith he lived, by faith he died,
> Christ was his portion, theme, and guide,
> In precept and example shone.
> With love to God & love to man
> His daily course of action ran,
> Till God his Saviour, called him home."

His funeral sermon was preached by Rev. Mr. Niles of
Abington, from Acts xx. 38, and among other tributes it
was said, "he left behind him as great an example of
meekness, patience, and Christian perseverance as ever
perhaps shown in the character of a finite being," and the
eulogist may have recalled not only his endurance against
ill health at Manomet, but also the fact that he had been
a "good stayer" at Mattapoisett.

He is described as a small man who wore the usual
knee breeches and shoe buckles of the time. His shorthand diary of seven thousand pages has never been trans-
lated. As did others of the educated ministry of his
time, — notably the Rev. Samuel Palmer at Falmouth,
John Tuck at Isles of Shoals, and Michael Wigglesworth
at Malden, — he tended bodily ailments as well as spiritual, and his memoranda which he kept while at Manomet show. accounts for peppermint drops, pills, and
rhubarb, and one man is charged for "bleeding his wife
and physick." When a young man of twenty he set
down some rules for the conduct of life, among which are,
"keep the blood & jueses in due fluidity and nothing will
do this but keeping to a spare, lean, fluid sort of diet.
Frequent purges conduceth much to long life and health.
— I would reccommend could water. Yet I would say

use a little wine for your stomach's sake. But by no
means drink could water or anything else could when
you are hot. For a frequency in the use of liquors which
they call spirits be as afraid of it as you would be of a
familiarity with evil spirits. Chew Myrrh. Smoak little
or no tobacco — if you can help it. It is the observation
of a very discrete man who said he had often got hurt by
eating too much, rarely by eating too little; often got hurt
by wearing too few cloathes, rarely by wearing too many,
got hurt by speaking, rarely by holding his tongue."

Among Mr. Hovey's published sermons are, one on
the "Duty and Privilege of Aged Saints, occasioned by
the death of Lieut. John Hammond of Rochester, Boston,
1749," and a "Farewell Sermon at Mattapoisett, 1769,
2 Cor. xiii. 11, Boston 1770."

During the latter part of Mr. Hovey's pastorate, owing
to variances in the church itself, and in part perhaps to
the inroads of new doctrines, the collection of the rates
caused much worriment in precinct meetings. It was a
thankless job, and with little pay, although obligatory.
In 1769, Samuel Bools and Zaccheus Meed being successively chosen Collector and in turn refusing, Wilber
Southworth was chosen agent to prosecute them both at
the next sessions of the Peace. Sometimes "Raite Bills"
were not turned in for four or five years and suit was
threatened, or often the collector besought that the remainder of his bill might be remitted. In 1770 was
passed the very tolerant vote that "ye Assessors of this
Precinct shall assess all sd Precinct excepting Ebenezer
Magges, Nathaniel Cushman, Baptest; and Barzilla Hammond & all that Goe under ye Denomination of Quakers."

Mr. Joseph Mayhew of Martha's Vineyard was at this

time boarding with Enoch Hammond (whose wife was Drucilla the daughter of the Rev. Thomas West of North Rochester), and "for his Preeching sixteen Saboth days, ten Dolors per Saboth" Mr. Mayhew was voted £9, 12s. Various others probably supplied the pulpit during 1770.

On March 1, 1771, at precinct meeting a vote was "Drafted and put that Doctor Bradford or Nathl. Hammond. or either of them go to Boxford ye last of March Inst & In ye Name & Behalf of this Precinct Desire Mr. Lemuel LeBaron to Return to us & Supply ye place of a minister In our Parish this summer. Voted in the afirmitive." Mr. LeBaron's reply was likewise in the affirmative. June 12, 1771, the church voted "to give Mr. Leml. LeBaron a Call," and appointed Elder Barlow, Antipas Hammond & Deacon Clark to present him with it. On June 25 the precinct joined in the call "by a Vote in the affirmative, unanimous." Preparations for ordination and settlement were made, and Mr. LeBaron was duly installed January 29, 1772. "The Solemnity was introduced by prayer by Rev. Mr. Thatcher of Wareham. A sermon from 1 Tim. 2, last clause of the 4th verse, was preached by Rev. Mr. Robbins of Plymouth,[1] Mr. Hovey made the ordaining Prayer, Mr. Bacon of Plymouth gave the charge. Mr. West of Rochester the right Hand of Fellowship, and Mr. Robbins of Norfolk in Connecticut the concluding Prayer." The Moderator Mr. Parker of Plympton obtained the assent of the people, and thus was auspiciously begun a connection which was severed only by death and that after a period of sixty-five years.

[1] This sermon of Rev. Chandler Robbins was printed, and is to be found in the Congregational Library, Boston.

Rev. Lemuel LeBaron was the grandson of Francis, the first of the name in America, who was the surgeon of a French privateer wrecked in 1644 on a ledge of rocks on the western shore of Sandwich, who was taken to Plymouth a prisoner, and remained there upon request of the selectmen in the practice of his profession until his death in 1704. The mystery of his name and origin has never been solved. His descendants have written lengthy arguments as to whether he was a Huguenot or Catholic, but his grandson, the minister, writing on his eightieth birthday "for the benefit of his posterity," simply says, "He embraced the Protestant faith, but was fond of his crucifix which he wore suspended in his bosom to the day of his death." Lemuel LeBaron was born in Plymouth September 1, 1747. His father was Dr. Lazarus LeBaron, who practised many years in that town, and his mother was Lydia Bradford, a great-granddaughter of the Pilgrim Governor. As he himself expressed it, he received a "Public Education," being graduated from Yale in 1768, receiving his A.M. in due course in 1771. He early united with the church in Norfolk, Connecticut, and not long after went into the study of divinity with Rev. Daniel Brinsmade of Woodbury and preached at sundry places before coming to Mattapoisett.

Although known to the later generation as the "Old Minister," and his house being commonly referred to as the "Old Mansion," it should be remembered that Lemuel LeBaron was less than twenty-four years old when the Second Church of Rochester extended to him its call. Soon thereafter he was required as an executor to settle the estate of his father from whom he received a substantial inheritance. November 24, 1774, he married Eliza-

"THE OLD MANSION"

Built by Reverend Lemuel LeBaron, 1776-7

beth Allen of Martha's Vineyard, and the following spring
he began the construction of his house near the Meeting-
house, — which is now owned by Nathan B. Denham.
Capt. Charles Bryant used to say, and other old people
still have the tradition, that the carpenters left their work
of getting out frame to answer to the Lexington Call, and
that the timbers lay piled together for a year or more of
the war period.   Certain it is that on March 1, 1775, the
precinct voted him his " 10 cds of wood at the place where
his house is to stand," and that on March 1, 1776, when
they "Vandiewd the Giting of the wood to the lowest
Bidder," it was to be delivered "either at Mr. LeBaron's
new seller or at Landing by the harbour side as Mr.
LeBaron chuses."   Also it appears that in the rolls of
Revolutionary soldiers at the State House is the name,
"Rev. Lemuel LeBaron, chaplain, Lexington Alarm Call
— 4 days."   In 1812 he was also commissioned by Gov-
Eldridge Gerry as Chaplain of the Third Regiment.   He
then chose not to qualify, doubtless on account of age,
being then sixty-five years old.

The new minister appears to have early obtained the
confidence of his people.   Imbued with some of his
youthful enthusiasm, contending factions were glad to
unite in the common cause of providing a new and larger
meeting-house.   There were sundry propositions made to
relocate either on land of Israel Hammond or "near
where Ebenezer Barlow's Dwelling-house stood"; but
June 23, 1772, the precinct "mett on the hill where the
Old Meeting House stood," and voted "the new house
should stand on the under pining whare it is began on the
hill."   To defray the cost, pews were sold according to
plan, it being agreed that any deficit should be propor-

tioned, or any surplus distributed. At first it was voted that "sd House be Built Fifty two feete frunt and forty two feete Back," but this was amended to have it "44 Feet & 40 Feet on the Ground & Pew it all round the Wals except two Dors & Eight Pews in the Bodey seets belo, and pew all round the frunt in the Galery and seete all the Remaining room above & below that is proper for seeting." The committee consisting of Moses Barlow, Zaccheus Mead and Enoch Hammond were instructed "to have the House Completed Workman Like, Lathed, Plastered the walls over head and under the Galerys & Handsomly to paint sd house Out sid and Number the Pews on there Dores." In 1795 a few more pews were added on the floor, the next year four more "adjoining the back alley." In 1799 David Dexter was given a spot to build a pew "on the East side of the Broad Alley, adjacent to that Sold to Sherman Lincoln to be the same Bigness of said Lincoln's. He giving the precinct his Pew in the front Galery and two Dollers." In 1805 John A. LeBaron and William Moore purchased at an auction by the moderator, Capt. Moors Rogers, two more lower floor pews for $20 and $24, respectively. After 1772 the spare time of three or four years was spent in "lying the door stones and leveling the Meetinghouse hill," for this was done by the men of the parish, the precinct being divided into four sections each with a director, — of which "Insign Jabez Norton" was one to "oversee and give direction to those persons assessed in his district."

This house stood until it went down before the great "September Gale" of 1815. Wilson Barstow, Esq., in the Plymouth County *Enterprise* (Silas W. Snow's local

publication), November 15, 1879, wrote over the initial
"W" —

> "I remember well how the old church looked; galleries on two
> sides, a small pulpit with a door to shut in the minister, and as
> high or higher than the galleries with a sounding board above it.
> In front of the pulpit were two or three plank seats without any
> backs for old men to sit on. The pews were square, with
> banisters, and seats on three sides, a chair in the middle for
> the old lady to sit in. No cushions and no fire ever built in
> that church, and it was about as open and bleak as an old
> fashioned barn. Very airy. The program of the service was
> to begin at 10.30 A.M. and out at 12, and at 1 and out at 2.30, P.M.
> The service always occupied the time. Mr. LeBaron would
> preach a sermon forty minutes' long from a piece of paper no
> larger than the fly leaf of a primer with a few hieroglyphics on
> it. Most of the people carried a lunch and staid for the after-
> noon. We boys prospected in the orchards during recess."

A few weeks later, Mr. Joseph W. Church, of Rochester,
wrote to the same paper:

> "In your edition of Nov. 15, over the signature of 'W,' I notice
> a description of the Mattapoisett meeting-house which stood on
> the hill. In passing it on a cold, windy day I always seemed to
> feel an additional chill, it looked so cold and dreary. I read
> the reference to that house with a very deep interest, for it
> brought to mind the olden time memories that had receded
> almost beyond my reach.
> "The meeting-house of Mattapoisett was a perfect pattern
> of the old house at Rochester Center; the pews on the lower
> floor, the galleries and the sounding board, how well I remem-
> ber how it looked the first time I ever saw it. All was new to me
> then, and all was interesting; and singular as it may seem, Mr
> LeBaron, that 'W' mentioned so particularly, occupied the
> pulpit for that day, and preached that first sermon that I ever
> heard, though if Henry Ward Beecher had preached the sermon,
> I should have given but little attention to it, as the sounding-board
> took all my thought. What can it be, and what is it there for?
> At last I enquired of someone, and was told that it was to put
> the bad boys in, and if you are not a good boy you will have to

go there; and possibly the fear of being sentenced to go up
there had much to do in making me the good boy that I was."

Mr. LeBaron's long pastorate might well be termed
the "era of good feeling." The attention of the precinct
was largely occupied in arrangements for the minister's
wood; the management of rate bills, the improvement of
the salt meadow, the securing the precinct's right in
ministry lands (by joining in 1773 with Wareham to
defend the action brought by the First Precinct), and
preventing trespass upon them, till their final sale and
exchange about 1789. At that date the precinct thus
obtained the acre called "the Barlow Cemetery" [1] from
Capt. Elihu Sheaman; and the "Hammond cemetery"
of eighty rods, near the meeting-house, from Israel and
Noah Hammond, — the latter tract still being subject to-
day, by the deed, to the right of the heirs of said Hammonds to pasture calves thereon. In 1791, with funds
derived from land sales, the precinct purchased from
Governor John Hancock "what he took by execution from
Elnathan Eldredge," about eighty acres on the Neck,
"for a perpetual parsonage," a portion of which tract the
precinct still holds.

While these were some of the principal concerns in
prudential affairs, there was always, however, the matter
of Mr. LeBaron's salary. This was fixed in 1771 at £70
annually, with ten cords of wood to be delivered at his
dwelling-house; and for a settlement £133, 6s. 8d. to be
given in three equal payments. In accepting this offer

---

[1] This burial-ground in the rear of the late Col. G. M. Barnard, Jr.'s,
house was conveyed to the town in 1886, see vote of the Precinct: Records, Vol. 1, page 555. There had been interments at this location
earlier than 1740.

Mr. LeBaron, in his letter, said: "As to my maintenance I am persuaded that you will be willing to minister unto me in carnal things while I am spending my life in minisiering unto you in spiritual. I shall always endeavor to be as Tender with you in this point as possible." In this he kept his word. When in 1785 some shrewd members of the precinct "thought it reasonable he should abate something in his yearly salary on account of his owning the land in part on which his salary and settlement was levied when first he became minister," "the Rev. Mr. LeBaron came in person to sd meeting, and declared sd precinct might abate five pounds from his stated salary; which was accepted by sd Precinct as a favor, being a greater sum than sd Precinct supposed he ought to abate for the land afore sd," — and his rate so continued for two years. In 1781 he "Generously gave said Precinct £20 of his salary this year." At times of difficulty he accepted notes as cash, consented to "gather his own rates," and agreed to take his wood standing or remit it altogether. In 1779, in the hard times of the Revolution, he "manifested to the precinct that he would be satisfied with one hundred bushels of Indian Corn Delivered him next December in Lu of his sd sallary," and those who furnished corn were allowed £5, 12s. per bushel therefor on their rate. That winter perhaps Mrs. LeBaron, as was said of the wife of another minister who had been partly paid in rye, was obliged "to fire the oven to bake the salary." His only complaint was made in 1780, when being voted a salary of £2100 (currency) the "Gradual as well as the Suding Deprecation of Paper Money is such that it is difficult if not Imposable to assertain its value for one month yet to come," upon his request the Precinct met and voted him, "in Lue of the £100, seventy pounds in Silver Money."

In 1879, "W" in the *Enterprise* wrote:

> "Mr. LeBaron preached sixty years in that old church and the one built after that blew down, without any member of his society ever thinking that the minister could be ousted and a new one put in his place. His salary was $233, and never was increased nor asked to be. One year in the Revolutionary war he received only twenty cents in cash for his salary. He was not only a faithful minister, but equally full of patriotism. He lived a long life without a stain on his moral or Christian character. Would we had more like him. Now, the more a minister knows the more likely he is to be switched off the track."

Mr. LeBaron's catalogue of the eighty-five members[1] at his ordination, in 1772, shows thirty-five men including "Tom, Toby, & Jack, Blacks," and forty-six women of which two were "Negroes." January 1, 1835, he recorded, "the members of the church now living are as follows, viz Males 60, Females 101, total 161." "Scarcely a year passed," wrote Dr. Robbins, "without additions to the church. In 1807, and the year following, there was the greatest revival that has been in this place, about eighty were added to the church. There was also a good work of divine grace in 1820, again in 1824, in 1829 and in 1834." It was at this last-named date that Mrs. Elizabeth Hubbard said she best remembered her grandfather. The "Old Minister" seldom attended the evening services but, being brought out to one, although much affected he took no part until near the close, when, rising, he stretched forth his hands and recited, the tears freely flowing, "Now lettest thou thy servant depart in peace

---

[1] See Extracts from the Records, V, in this book.

according to thy word, for mine eyes have seen thy salvation." A writer in the *American Quarterly Register* of November, 1835, said of Mr. LeBaron: "He is now in the 89th year of his age, yet retaining his mental powers in an uncommon degree. His head bleached with the storms of life, his heavenly mien, his soft and mild voice, and his impressive manner all conspired to speak his worth and give weight and effect to the solemn instructions that fell from the lips of the patriarch."

On the 26th of February, 1836, the "Old Minister" had a paralytic shock, not severe, but rendering him mostly helpless. In November following he was taken with the prevailing influenza, attended with some fever. He died on the 26th of that month. Dr. Robbins chose for the text of his "Uncle LeBaron's" funeral sermon (written, as he says, laboriously and seven hours by candle light the night before), 2 Kings xi. 12, "My father, my father, the chariot of Israel and the horsemen thereof." This was especially fitting from the fact that nearly all of the five of his children who attained maturity had settled and reared their families in the immediate neighborhood, and Dr. Robbins at the funeral said, "He looked upon all his people as his children. He felt that he had lived long seeing one generation after another pass away. No one survives that acted on the subject of his ordination, or that was then a member of the church."

Dr. Robbins further said: "As a preacher Mr. LeBaron was eminently practical and experimental. The great peculiarity of his preaching in which he was distinguished from most others was the Gospel of Love. He possessed a happy talent for addressing children. I think I have not known any person who appeared to have a deeper sense of the importance and privilege of infant baptism than he had. He was a man of great liberality of feeling. Among his people he was a peacemaker. Such was the efficacy of his own example in this respect and the affectionate earnestness of his solicitude that he could hardly fail to prevent contention, or to reconcile such as were alienated. In this connection I would add that he has been greatly improved in Ecclesiastical Councils and highly useful in preventing and healing divisions in churches. In his social character, Mr. LeBaron possessed a very happy talent in conversation; always cheerful he was interesting to every one and his conversasation was seldom other than profitable. In the war of the Revolution he fully shared in the dangers, the toils and privations of his people. His known character abroad was often useful in enabling them to procure necessary supplies. Our lamented friend has been favored with an uncommon degree of health during his long ministry, regularly performing his pastoral duties and seldom absent from home."

A number of the "old minister's" sermons are in the possession of the writer, and they indicate clearly that he was familiar with shorthand, and inserted sections of it everywhere in his sentences. It also appears that paper was a scarce and valuable commodity. One sermon is written on the wide margin of a Thanksgiving proclamation, another on the back of a letter received from Valley Forge; all are of four-page length, the pages averaging about $3\frac{1}{2}$ by $2\frac{3}{4}$ inches in size, with a neat margin at the left in which the text reference and dates of preaching are inserted. From these minute manuscripts, however, the preacher, as Wilson Barstow wrote, "occupied the time," and another of that generation used to say that in his youth he never acquired the proper meaning of the word "finally," for Minister LeBaron having passed by his "fourteenthly" or "fifteenthly" used to then have a "lastly," a "finally," and a "to conclude," and the "to conclude" was longer than all that had gone before.

Of the church during this long pastorate, one generation had passed on and another had become active. Deacons Constant Dexter, Ezekiel Clark, Timothy West, Elihu Shearman, and Thomas Tobey had died; and Isaac Bowles, Nathan Cannon, Amittai B. Hammond, and Nathaniel A. Crosby stood in their places. The community had grown and the church increased in numbers, even after the establishment of other denominations. Those who were carried away by Elder Hix's itinerant preaching had, however, to be reclaimed and dealt with. As early as July 23, 1773, "The Chh met to consider what was dutiful to be done with John Curby, Widow Lydia Bowles, Abigail Southworth, Mary Bowles, and Lydia Cushing, who have for some time absented themselves from our communion, being inclined to the Antipedobaptist sect." and Elder Barlow and sundry brethren were appointed to confer with them. Nathaniel Hammond, who was baptized by Elder Hix the first Sabbath of September, 1793, began in January following to receive delegations of Orthodox brethren, followed by letters of admonition, until in July, 1784, he was cut off from communion "for his Instability in the Christian Profession." Gideon Dexter, Alden Dexter, and Thomas Dexter later became unstable, and in 1809, Philip Atsatt having gone over to the Baptists was considered "a covenant breaker and no longer a member of this church."

Those who sought membership were encouraged, as in 1774 Enoch Hammond and Solomon Young were named to see Theophulus Pease Jun., who " had applyed for admittance but was discouraged by hearing that there would be Objections laid in against him." A certain Mr. and Mrs. Hammond "perpetually were quarrelling, he abusing her shamefully with his tongue," and this domestic affliction had the church's attention for some years. A few cases of unchastity had to be dealt with. Of the "blacks" in the catalogue of members of 1772, Tom, who dwelt with Noah Hammond, was the only one blameless in this respect. In 1782 complaint was brought against one Dexter, "for cruelly scourging a little boy who lived with him, and that on the Lords Day." "The offender condemning his conduct and expressing his sorrow for it, the Chh voted to restore him to former Charity." Nine years later it is recorded: "Voted the acceptance of sd Dexter's confession which he offered to the Chh for his Intemperance, but poor man, 2 Pet. ii. 22." This reference was, from a different appearance of the ink, apparently added later. Perhaps on September 28, 1808, when after much consideration and investigation it being shown that "he still continued to indulge himself in the sin of Drunkunness, voted unanimously that he be unto us as an heathen man and a publican, agreeable to the direction of our Lord Jesus Christ, Mat. 18, 17 and that a coppy of sd Vote be sent to said Dexter. N.B. a coppy was sent." There were other cases of intemperance, but on the whole the instances of discipline are rather few for the long period the records cover.

Meanwhile, successive committees made the rates or solicited funds by way of contribution. Lieut. Dominicus

Hovey and his successors "kept the meeting-house and swept it twelve times the year Insuing, for 15 shilling," or later on, some, as John Lincoln, Wilbur Southworth, Elijah Clark and Nathan Bessey, agreed to "Ceep the House" each three months.   In 1773 the church had "desired Benjamin Hatch, Saml Jenney, Timothy West, Elihu Shearman, Saml. Eldredge & Gideon Hammond to sit in fourth seat in the meeting-house and lead the Church and Congregation in singing Gods praises."   In 1781 the precinct voted "For the accommodation of those that lead in singing the use of the two hind seats in the body seats, on the lower flower, both on the mens and Womans Sides, So long as the present method of Singing by Select numbers shall continue.   And the said singers may erect doors at the entrances of Said Seets at their own Cost, if they think proper, but not to raise the lower flower higher than it now is."

As to music in this old church, "W" commented as follows in the *Enterprise:*

> "No instruments of music were tolerated in church service. Some were opposed to singing except by the saints. Total depravity couldn't sing praises. Seth Barlow, senior, was very pious at that time, having been converted as he said by Elder Hix. (The Elder said it looked like his work.) He, Seth, could bear no instrument of music, not even a pitch pipe to pitch the tune. On hearing the sound of the pipe, which was something like a graduation between a squeak and a schream, Seth left the church in high dudgeon. The next day Seth asked Noah Hammond how he thought they cast out devils in the old times. 'With a pitch pipe,' says Noah."

The great gale of 1815 [1] made some new provision for a

---

[1] "Saturday, Sept. 23rd. — The gale commenced early in the morning and continued with increasing violence until near 12 o'clock.

"At Rochester we are informed the damage done was considerable,

meeting-house necessary, and the growth of "the shore,"
due to whaling and ship-building, made it inadvisable to
restore the structure on the hill. Deacon Bowles, Capt.
Gideon Hammond and Noah Hammond, having been
appointed to provide a temporary place of worship, reported October 30, "They had agreed for the schoolhouse
at the shore for thirty cents per Sabbath when it was
occupied by Mr. LeBaron's People, the Precinct to pre-
pair the Hous for meeting, & the Hous on Monday
mornings to be put in order for Schooles," to which latter
duty Gideon Barstow, Jr., was appointed to find some
person. March 9, 1816, Precinct meeting was warned
to be in this "Olive Branch Schoolhouse" (which is the
present "Goodspeed Memorial," then standing at the
southwest corner of Church and Pearl Streets) and here
the precinct managed its affairs and worshiped until the
new meeting-house at "the green" (now occupied as the
Grange Hall) was ready.

At first it had been voted "to give Deac'n Tobey $25 for
¼ acre and that the meeting-hous should be Sot on the
N. W. Corner of his homestead" (which would have located it near the Lobdell house), and that it "should be
Near the moddle that Thomas Snow presented." Very
soon, however, they reconsidered both the site and the
"moddle," and appointed William Moore, John A.
LeBaron and Joseph Meigs, "to devise a plan for defray-

the salt works belonging to Messrs. Clapp, Nye, Handy, and others with
about 3000 bushels of salt were all destroyed. Several vessels were
driven on the wharves at Sippican Harbour, and at Mattapoisett 3 or 4
large vessels building on the stocks were driven into the street. The
rope walk at that place is all carried away by the tide, the Rev. Mr.
LeBaron's meeting-house unroofed, and several other buildings damaged." — *New Bedford Mercury*, Sept. 29, 1815.

Mattapoisett Academy

Built as the Third Meeting-house of the Second Precinct in 1816
After 1870 the Barstow School

ing the cost, etc." It was arranged by a sale of shares in the meeting-house, and January 31, 1816, agreement was made to purchase the lot of, one third acre, from Joseph Meigs for $50, and February 3rd contract was made with Israel Richmond and Calvin Shaw "to build and finish the house in manner and form to that at Titicut, North Middleborough," (which had been erected in 1808) for $1100. Jonathan Kinney agreed "to lath and plaster for $100, he finding and tending himself." William Bennett (?) of Bedford was to glaze it, "he finding glass at $14 the Box, and to have 3d. a payn for setting," and Abel House had $2 for drawing down four loads of stone from the old meeting-house, which Thomas Snow had previously agreed to take down, saving the stuff in good order and drawing and straightening the nails for $45.

This third meeting-house had a spire and a wide, straight platform across the front. The projection to the south and the existing belfry date from the time it was remodeled for the use of Mattapoisett Academy. Many now living recall the interior with its high pulpit, square pews, and gallery on three sides. It was evidently easier to care for than the old building. The task of keeping it was struck off to the lowest bidder, and George Denham secured the plum for $2.90 per year, agreeing that "the house be swept 6 times in the year." Later John A. LeBaron agreed to sweep it nine times in the year and was paid $3. In 1828 the job included "Keeping the key and making the fires," and Leonard Hammond undertook the task at $2.75. And thus, after ninety-two years of records, is the first mention made of any heat in the meeting-house. This people sat longer in the cold than they had been warmed since.

The "Wretched boys," as some records term them, seemed to have required little attention at Mattapoisett. They are first mentioned when in 1740 Gideon Southworth "was chosen to have the oversight of the youth in the meeting-house on the Sabbath Day," and are not again alluded to until in 1826, when the precinct "Chose Nathaniel Harlow, warden to see to the Boys and girls in the meetinghouse and that there be no behaviour unbecoming the Solemnities of Divine Worship;" and, evidently to give him the best range of observation, directed, "that he have the use of the middle pew in the front gallery next the window."

In 1826 Mr. LeBaron, then in his eightieth year, went to the precinct committee and stated he was "very desirous that a Gospel Minister be settled in the Precinct in his day, and that he would relinquish all demands for pecuniary support being considered the senior pastor of the Church." Amittai B. Hammond, Eliakim Cannon, Abel Hows, Capt. Andrew Southworth, Wilson Barstow, Esq., and Mr. Abisha Rogers "were appointed to provide a candidate, and on December 12th and 13th of that year a council ordained and installed Rev. Asahel Cobb as colleague pastor. He was the son of John and Anna Cobb of Abington. Dr. Robbins says of him: "He continued in the ministry here three years and a half, and his labors were blessed with a pleasing revival of religion." His salary had been fixed at $400, six cords of wood, and the improvement of the salt meadow. In April, 1829, Messrs. Eleazer Waterman, Ebenezer Cannon, and Calvin C. Cannon called on Mr. Cobb to say that his salary thereafter would be $50 less, whereat he gave three months' notice and sought another field for his labors, locating first at Sandwich and later with the First Church of New Bedford at Acushnet. He married May 21, 1834, Helen M. Hamblin, and had seven children.[1] He died in 1876 and is interred at Sandwich.

As to how the pulpit was supplied following Mr. Cobb, the best information is from a scrap of paper found in Minister LeBaron's portfolio. It reads:

"1830, Nov. 9, Mrs. LeBaron died.
1831, Mar. 3, Mr. Clark here.
      May   6, ditto.
      July 6, Wm. (his son) taken sick ague fit.
      Aug. 2, Wm. very sick,
           12, Wm. died — Mr. Clark preacher on the occasion of Wm. death, 1 Cor. v. 55.
      Sept. 10, Mr. Clark leaves us.
           25, Thos. Robbins preached first sermon.
      Oct. 2, Mr. Robbins left us.
           21, Mr. Robbins arrived."

The precinct records simply state that "Mr. Clark would stay for a season for $450 per year." Whence he came or whither he went does not appear.

Thomas Robbins, above mentioned, was the nephew of Minister LeBaron, being the ninth child of Elizabeth the daughter of Dr. Lazarus LeBaron and her husband, Rev. Ammi Ruhamah Robbins, who was settled over the church in Norfolk, Conn., for fifty-two years prior to his death in 1813. There Thomas Robbins was born August 11, 1777. He was fitted for college in his own home and at the age of fifteen was entered at Yale. His father was an early trustee of Williams College, and arranged that his son should take his senior year there and also be graduated at Yale. So that Thomas Robbins has the perhaps

[1] Of whom were Wendell Cobb, Esq., the well-known lawyer, late of New Bedford, and Mr. George A. Cobb, now living at Lunds Corner.

unique distinction of having his name stand as an alumnus on the general catalogues of both colleges, for the year 1796. On January of that year, while at Williams, he began his diary, which he continued up to 1854. He occupied himself prior to 1803 in teaching, in fitting for the ministry, and in preaching in various Connecticut towns. In 1803 he went, in the service of the Connecticut Missionary Society, to the new settlement on the Western Reserve, Ohio. From this service he returned in 1806 seriously broken in health. He began preaching again in 1808 at East Windsor, Conn., continuing there until 1827. For a year and a half he was settled at Stratford, Conn. He accepted a call and continued with the church at Mattapoisett from 1832 to 1844, being sole pastor after Mr. LeBaron's death in 1836.

Mr. Robbins never was married. He was fifty-four years old when, in response to the request of this people, having deferred departure to attend the ΦBK meeting and dinner of Yale, he started from Stratford Saturday, September 17, 1831, for his long ride. He complained that his horse traveled heavily, but the following Thursday he arrived in town, and his "Uncle LeBaron having left his own house to reside with his daughter Meyhew," he put up with family of his cousin William, lately deceased. The following morning he "looked at a fine ship on the stocks," and remarked that the village had increased very much since he was here in 1824. He states in his diary also that "there is a noisy three days' meeting here of the Free Will Baptists." On Sabbath he spoke twice at the meeting-house to a congregation which he thought to be rather small but to appear well, and in the evening preached at a private house. He went back again to Connecticut to prepare his things for removal, returning October 21, in time to see a fine, large ship launched the following morning. He preached the three usual times on the 23d, accepted Capt. Seth Freeman's invitation to board at his house, moved thither on Monday, and on Tuesday rode in the stage to Wareham to meet with the Old Colony Association of Ministers. He took pains to call on the widow of Rev. Noble Everett and returned to Mattapoisett Thursday in time to attend the funeral of a child, who died of the canker rash; thus beginning the record of infant mortality which continued throughout his pastorate. The following week he preached at the ordination of Rev. Samuel Utley at North Rochester. Two weeks later he presided at the ecclesiastical council which ratified the separation of the Pacific (Trinitarian) church from Mr. Holmes's parish in New Bedford, and again six months later he preached the sermon for the dedication of the meeting-house of that new congregation. Like minister LeBaron he was "much improved in ecclesiastical Councils."

February 22, 1832, he was in Boston, where was observed the Centennial celebration of Washington's Birthday. "Great firing and ringing of bells. At the State House heard a good oration of one hundred fifteen minutes. The prayers were poor. Attended a splendid Dinner given in Faneuil Hall to about six hundred guests." He tarried with his cousin Dr. Chandler Robbins, and received, as he says, polite treatment on going into the House of Representatives the following morning. He came home with a new kind of purchase, a "sharp metallic pen." He was in Boston again in May for the Ministerial Convention, and tarrying the night at the stage-house for

an early call, he rode through to Mattapoisett in the day;
"much fatigued," however. He spent some days in
Plymouth, and made another visit back to Connecticut
before his installation which occurred October 17, 1832.
"This day being appointed," wrote Mr. LeBaron in "The
Church's Book," "agreeably to a preceding agreement of
the Church and Precinct for the Instalment of Rev.
Thomas Robbins, the Council consisting of the Ministers
and Delegates of the Churches of the Old Colony Association met at the house of John A. LeBaron,[1] and after
forming themselves into a Council and offering up prayer
to Almighty God for his blessing and assigning to each
one his part in the transaction, proceeded to the meeting-
house where in a very solemn manner Rev. Mr. Robbins
was installed as Minister of the Second Precinct, and
Pastor of the Second Church of Christ in Rochester, and
every part was performed greatly to the acceptance of the
audience and it is believed acceptable to God, and we
most earnestly pray that the blessing of God may accom-
pany the ministry of his servant. N.B. Introductory
prayer by P. G. Seabury, Sermon by S. Holmes, installing
prayer by J. Bigelow, Charge by Oliver Cobb, Right
Hand by Wm. Gould. Address to the People by Samuel
Nott."

The diary entry that day reads: "I was solemnly installed the collegiate pastor of this people. All things
appear favorably. All proceedings have been unanimous. Mr. Holmes preached well on Isa. xxiv. 2. The
meeting-house was very full and the singing fine. At
evening we had a public temperance meeting. Mr.
Gould delivered a good address. Fine weather." Prob-

[1] Being that of the late Col. Geo. M. Barnard, Jr.

ably the bell rope was lustily pulled that day, for it was an important occasion, and the church bell was a new thing and the first in town. Until August, 1832, in Mattapoisett precinct no pealing call had ever broken the stillness of the Sabbath morn. While the clergy had thus been busy at "the Green" with solemn ceremony, launching the new colleague into his work, around the shore, as usual, had re-echoed the sound of the mallet, the hammer and the saw, and just a week later "a fine live oak ship, over 400 tons," was let down off the stocks into the harbor.

Before the month was out, Mr. Robbins moved down from Captain Freeman's with his two wagon-loads of effects to Nathan Crosby's, — which is at present the house of Bruce F. Shaw, on the east side of North Street. He had his chambers on the north side of the house, and here was his home throughout his stay in Mattapoisett. The old minister's grandson, Lemuel, made him a new pine bookcase, which he said was very good work, but not large enough for all his periodicals; and here, having settled his library, which then consisted of well above a thousand volumes, he called in "Uncle LeBaron" and other relatives and friends, who "much admired his chambers, library, etc." He himself said they were "good chambers but difficult to keep comfortable." In his accounts is an item of $3.50 for a new-fashioned warming pan which he very suggestively presented to his landlady. Sometimes even the ink froze in spite of his great stove, with its "duck floor cloth" beneath it, and the plentiful use of wood. To help prepare his fuel, took much of his time. Very often he writes, "Worked at my wood." Sometimes he carried up "thirty armfuls, twenty-five before noon," and we can seem to see the frail figure in knee-breeches, toiling, heavily laden, up the long flight of outside stairs which, until quite recently, connected those chambers of his with the middle of the yard below.

He continued to wear "small clothes" as long as he lived, although the rest of the world had adopted panta-loons a good while before. Most who now remember Dr. Robbins says that he was the only person they ever saw who dressed in knee breeches. Once he wrote after a day of shopping, "I have difficulty in finding necker-chefs such as I wear." For a hat he paid $6, and for "new boots made for me of the best kind $10." Con-sidering that he was particular for nice apparel, his diary contains remarkably few references to clothes. Novem-ber 14 of one year, he writes, "Yesterday put on my flan-nel," and the following June 15, "Took off my flannel;" with nothing recorded as to the time between. One year, on the 26th of May, there is this pathetic entry: "Am not able to get off my flannel."

The good man not only felt that the dignity of his position demanded a good appearance, but he also had a high sense of the respect due to the cloth. Little boys whom he met on the street were expected to remove their caps, and girls to politely curtsey. Having thus shown their good breeding, the children found no one who took more notice of them or who was more heartily interested in their welfare. He laid in especial supplies of figs and sweet crackers in anticipation of their calls to wish him "A Happy Independence." Girls used to help him dust his books, and he loaned to them suitable volumes. One of these girls was Wilson Barstow's daughter, Elizabeth, who later became the wife of Richard Henry Stoddard.

Dr. Robbins says in his diary of June 8, 1833, "Received a present of a valuable box from young Elizabeth Barstow."

It is interesting to quote in this connection what Mr. Stoddard in his "Recollections" says of this early friendship:

> "She had one friend however, a notable man in his way, though he was only the minister of Mattapoisett, where he was considered a queer old fellow. This was the Rev. Thomas Robbins, who was known to antiquarians as the author of "An Historical Survey of the First Planters of New England" and of several sermons preached on special occasions. He took a fancy to Elizabeth Barstow when she was a child, and gave her the range of his library which was a large one for a country minister to have, and which consisted chiefly of the classic works of the eighteenth century.
>
> "She read Addison, Steele, and Dr. Johnson, the Tattler, The Rambler, the Spectator, the delectable writings of Fielding, Richardson, Smollett and Sterne, — 'Tristam Shandy,' 'Peregrine Pickle,' 'Pamela,' and 'Tom Jones.' She read 'Sully's Memoirs' and the comedies of Sheridan, and if the comedies of Vanburgh and Congreve were there (but it is to be hoped not) she read those too. She read hundreds, thousands of volumes in the good doctor's library, which was to her a liberal education, and indeed, the only education she ever had."

Of this library, John Warner Barber, — who on July 2, 1832, had walked about the town with Dr. Robbins, — said in his *Massachusetts Historical Collections:* "Rev. Thomas Robbins, D.D., the successor of Mr. LeBaron, possesses, it is believed, the most valuable private library in the State. It consists of about 3000 volumes, of which more than 300 are folios. The principal subjects on which these volumes treat are theology and history, and many of them are quite ancient. In this collection there are 4000 pamphlets some of which are very rare. Dr. R. has also an extensive collection of coins, manuscripts, etc. The library is carefully arranged in neat and elegant bookcases." Dr. Robbins himself says that he had over 4000 volumes before he left Mattapoisett. May 31, 1839, he looked over his coins and found he had 596, including in the copper a Roman denarius found in England, presented him by Capt. Henry Huttleston of Fairhaven. In May, 1840, he made a "very important addition" to his library — "Walton's Polyglot Bible, purchased of Mrs. Holmes, relict of Dr. Abiel Holmes of Cambridge, eight massive folios in fine order, for $160.00." A little later his cousin, Joseph Battel,[1] sent him from New York "Boyers' splendid edition of Hume's History as a present, — having procured it at my suggestion at auction for $100. Ten large folios, printing, paper, plates, and binding of the richest kind." No wonder when his new carpet came he had to have the help of Waterman and Prentice Crosby to assist him putting the carpet down and the books up.

It seems evident that Stoddard, who, when he was sparking Elizabeth Barstow, was referred to in local doggerel, then privately circulated, as

> "A dude from York, with brains very small,
> Who attended a dance in Eaton Hall,"

even in his later years knew little of this "country minister" other than as was related to his books. Thomas Robbins was probably in ecclesiastical, historical, and educational circles the widest known of any man who ever went in and out before this people. He had already edited the

---

[1] The merchant of New York and of Norfolk, Connecticut, and the giver of Battel Chapel to Yale University.

of con
unged
self s
apois
he h
und
ston
ortu
Bibl
nes
0.00
fro
stor
n s
per
ide
of
ing

as
al

Thomas Robbins.

first and second editions of Mather's "Magnalia," and
had published his "Historical View of the First Planters
of New England." While at Mattapoisett he received
a diploma and gifts from the Rhode Island Historical
Society, before whom he had delivered his lecture on
"The Middle Ages;" was elected a member of the Connecticut Academy of Arts and Sciences, and of the National Institution of Science of Washington. He was in
correspondence with the Royal Society of Northern An-
tiquities of Copenhagen, and John Quincy Adams and
President Josiah Quincy were appointed by the Massachusetts Historical Society to confer with him on a plan
he had proposed for a comprehensive history of the
United States.

He attended the meetings of the Antiquarian Society
with much regularity. For that purpose, October 22,
1834, he took his first ride on a railroad. From Boston
"took the railroad car at two o'clock and rode in seventy-
five minutes to Framingham, twenty-one miles, — the
whole scene is a wonder. Rode in the stage to Worcester." November 2, 1839, returning from Hartford, he
took the cars from Providence for Taunton. "At Mansfield in changing cars, having lost the points of compass
on a cloudy day, I took the wrong one and got ten
miles, perhaps, toward Boston before I found my mis-
take. Went on." Not very amiss after all, for "At
Boston found most unexpectedly a box containing a fine
copy of the Bishop's Bible, a present from the Duke of
Sussex, England, with a good letter from his Royal High-
ness. This was in answer to my application recommended through Mr. Buckingham last winter."

When the Massachusetts State Board of Education was

formed in 1837, with Horace Mann as its chairman, Dr. Robbins was appointed by Governor Edward Everett a member of the board. In that capacity he appeared at examinations of Bridgewater Normal School, or of the "excellent female school" at Norton, or walked in procession with the Legislature (and so with Capt. Zach. Barstow as representative) at the opening of the General Court for 1838. August 28 of the same year his diary reads: "At evening attended our weekly prayer meeting, after which set out on a journey and rode to Bedford. Slept at a tavern. 29th: — Was called early and took the stage at three o'clock and rode to Taunton, took cars and rode to Boston. Rode to Cambridge and went into the Commencement exercises after they had begun. The speaking was good and a very full house. A fine day. In the honorary degrees my name was read most unexpectedly for a D.D. I know not by whose recommendation. I bless God for the favor."

Dr. Robbins, as was his father, was for some years a trustee of Williams College. August, 1843, he was being "very kindly entertained at President Hopkins's. Attended an interesting meeting of the Alumni. I am the senior present. Attended the public services. The president delivered a very good address respecting the college. I delivered mine. Too long — an hour and forty-five minutes, — but kindly heard." At Plymouth, Forefather's Day, 1838, he had done better, — "Delivered my discourse, about sixty-five minutes," and afterwards "made a short extempore address to the Standish Guards to whom the ladies had presented an elegant standard."

He presided often at ecclesiastical councils, laid the corner-stone of Mr. Holmes's new "stone church" in New

Bedford, presided at the ordination of Rev. Homer Barrows at West Middleborough, assisted to dedicate the Naskatucket meeting-house, and the like. Visiting New York in 1844, he found "Wall Street" a "great curiosity." Preached in the Old Tabernacle in Brooklyn, and came home with a special commission to secure a piece of Forefathers' Rock for the projected Church of the Pilgrims. He was very constant in his attendance at the General Ministerial Convention, and regular in his services to the Pastoral Association.

He seldom came back from these journeys abroad without either primers for the Sabbath School, or copies of the "Mountain Miller," the "Dairyman's Daughter," or the "Young Cottager;" and with these tracts he walked to Tripps Mills and made calls (not omitting the aged Mrs. Hovey, the minister's daughter-in-law), or rode to Aucoot or New Boston, or perhaps walked to the Necks for two days of calls, sleeping at Captain Southworth's. When the "fine new ship Joseph Meigs" sailed, he fitted them out with books and tracts, and did the same when Mr. Crosby, with more than fifty other men, sailed for Louisiana to get live oak. Another time he went on a whale brig and supplied the men fully with Bibles. He drove sometimes with "Dr. Southard" in his chaise, and often he ministered to the sick, as when "called in the morning to visit my good neighbor (at William L. R. Gifford's present summer home), Mr. Jonathan Dexter, in a state of great pain and apparently insensible. Hurt by a great blow on the back of his head in the woods." Or again, the mercury standing at 90°, he "walked in the heat up to Solomons and saw sick Mary." Not of strong physique, the heat often made him "languid."

At such times he "slept on a mattress and wore summer dress." August 1, 1837, the thermometer stood at 90° and he felt quite feeble, so he read Sampson Agonistes without leaving his chair, worked at his books and wrote the inscription for his Uncle LeBaron's gravestone.

Other days he read Hudibras, Prescott's Ferdinand and Isabella, Colden's Five Nations, D'Aubigne's Reformation, Lawrence's Natural History of Man, Mrs. Jameson's Female Sovereigns, and once it was a novel, "Miriam Coffin." One very stormy day he "read the Bible and Bony's Court," the scriptures being an antidote for the Harper's Family Library story of "that seat of corruption." Another time it was an account of Philip's War, and of that chief he added: "I think he was not inferior to the early Grecian Heroes." At some periods he had "a scholar;" — as his young cousin Francis LeB. Mayhew. He usually spent considerable time writing and transcribing his sermons, unless, as he put it, he was "hindered by company." Of an evening he "attended the Lyceum," or went to Mr. Sanborn's lecture on Egypt and Babylon. Occasionally he had "polite company," or went over to Bedford, and "called on Mr. James Arnold and had particular conversation with him in his grotto." New Year's Day, '39, he had "many calls from children and others. Dined and took tea at Mr. W. Barstow's. At evening attended a spelling school. Was up late."

There was some slackness in the observance of Fast Day, even as early as 1833, for Dr. Robbins records, "Meetings well attended. A part of the people were off playing ball according to their usual practice here."

Independence day was his especial celebration of the year.

In 1834, he says: "We had a handsome celebration. There has not been one here for many years. The children were all out with their teachers and several soldiers of the Revolution. I delivered my address. A Baptist made the last prayer and a Universalist from Sippican read the Declaration. He did not sit down in the pulpit. Dined out. All appeared to be much pleased." Next year Mr. Bigelow came down from the Center to give the address, and to the six ministers present, Mr. Leonard Hammond (at his tavern, the Plymouth County House) gave a very hospitable dinner. "There was a very handsome procession, military, Sabbath school, — Revolutionary soldiers, etc." With these latter, however, Captain Wallis did not march, for Dr. Robbins had been to New Boston, the day before, to attend his funeral, and his body lay newly buried in the Hammond cemetery.

In 1839, Mr. Bryant (teacher and Baptist preacher) read the Declaration. Mr. Taylor (Universalist) delivered the address. Dr. Robbins prayed and addressed the children, all was concluded by a tea party in a grove; and the "shrubbery" was left in the meeting-house over Sunday. Next year, "the Sabbath schools were out with escort. Mr. Corydon from Bedford delivered a fine address, and we had with our new organ excellent music." Of this instrument, his diary remarks on the previous Sabbath, "Our new organ performed and well. It is certainly a very fine one, made by one of our mechanics, David Cannon," — the doctor's next-door neighbor.

On Fourth of July, 1841, Dr. Robbins, with many, sailed around to Sippican where was a procession and a dinner in a grove. In 1842, he "rode to Bedford and dined with the Washingtonians and Guards of Mattapoisett and Bedford." The next year he spent at home, and "the children called for salutations of Independence, 104 in number." In '44, some youths and older persons came also, so there were about 160, but each one had their cake and fig. Washington's Birthday, 1842, he states: "The new military company formed here, the 'Mattapoisett Guards' called for me and we marched to the meeting house and I delivered my address to a full house. Dined at Esq. Meigs's."

Another company with which Dr. Robbins had relations was the "Cold Water Army," which he organized in 1841, of children between eight and fifteen who had taken a solemn pledge. Two hundred and seventy were mustered in, and when the badges arrived from Boston, he says his army almost overran him. The last mention of this band is August 19, 1842, when "We had our temperance celebration. I received a number of additions to our Cold Water Army. We had a procession with the Military Guards and music, and Mr. Hathaway, of Assonet, a reformed inebriate, gave a good lecture. We went to a grove and had a good collation. At evening we had a lecture from Mr. Colburn, of Salem, late a drunken sailor; pretty ordinary."

At another time he rode to meet with the school committee at Rochester and "attended a Temperance lecture from Mr. Taylor, seamans' preacher at Boston. A sample of eccentricity." Although he stood firm for temperance, his conscience did not forbid him from giving the feeble Mrs. Mayhew a bottle of the best port wine. Apparently he did not object to the circus, — especially if he had a free ticket. "July 14, 1843, there was a famous exhibition here of a caravan of wild beasts.

I attended by invitation. About six hundred persons present." The good doctor could tell a fish story if the occasion required: Diary, April 14, 1843, "This has been a great herring day. The herrings have come suddenly, of good quality and an immense number. A very great blessing to the town. It is said they have taken to-day 70,000."

He did not forget to note other events of general interest in his record. September 21, 1834, "Attended the funeral of Mr. Cannon's child. The first buried in the new burying ground. Endeavored to consecrate the ground in the public service." December 11, same year, "The Universalist meetinghouse has got a clock." March 21, 1838, "Last night our lighthouse was lighted for the first time." He rarely attended town meeting unless "by the particular desire of the people," or some school matter required his presence. He was a hard-working member of the Rochester school committee. Riding or walking he often visited schools in "Orcoot," the Necks, in Sippican, or the Church neighborhood; and sometimes in the village, if it appeared that the teacher there was a "flagellant and whipped rashly." Much of his time was taken in drafting a scheme for a grammar school, in meetings to examine teachers, or in tabulating returns required by the State.

Despite the fact that so much of his effort was expended in public concerns, and in the building up of his library, Dr. Robbins was ever the faithful pastor of his church. He not only ministered to his parish, supplied his pulpit, attended the monthly concert, and worked, as he said, "laboriously" for the Sabbath school (which in 1834 had 154 pupils and in 1840 over 200), but he also held meetings on the Necks, at Cannonville, Pine Islands or Tripps

Mills, and sometimes he preached on a Sunday evening at Isaac Bowles's or at Deacon Amittai Hammond's. Sometimes at the wharf he held service on board a whaleship about to set sail.

Revival seasons occurred in 1834, when simultaneous meetings were held evenings at the Neck and in the vestry (in the east end of the Mattapoisett house), as well as sunrise meetings at Cannonville; in 1840, when extra meetings were held every morning at nine, in which Rev. Mr. Gould, of Fairhaven, and Rev. Leander Cobb, of Sippican assisted, and again in 1842. On Fast Day, 1842, he says: "After meeting I baptized Isaiah Sears by immersion in the harbor. The first time in my life, and I never saw it done but once, in Ohio. It was less unpleasant than I expected. Felt no particular inconvenience." The following Sabbath seventeen persons joined the church, and others in June. In all, during Dr. Robbins's pastorate, seventy-six were added to the church. There was no change of deacons and only one instance of church discipline.

Dr. Robbins was instrumental in procuring the present communion service to replace the one of pewter which had been acquired when Minister LeBaron began his service in 1772, the tankards of which had been presented by Mary Hammond and Dr. Lazarus LeBaron. October 1, 1835, the pastor "suggested to the church the expediency of improving our communion furniture, particularly the cups," and the church appointed Capt. Seth Freeman, Dea. Nathaniel A. Crosby, and Capt. Allen Dexter as committee. The church record states: "The cups were procured Mar. 16, 1836. They were made at New Bedford, nine, the cost $10.35 each. The

charge for making was $4 each. Two were paid for
from the church treasury, seven were given by individuals."

Meanwhile the prudential affairs of the parish proceeded with much regularity. In 1832 the precinct
voted that " we use our influence and exertions to raise by
subscription $450 to be paid to Rev. Mr. Robbins for
his labors with us the ensuing year and that the new subscription paper which shall be drawn shall be deposited
in the store of Capt. Joshua Cushing," who had then
retired from the sea to his home on the east side of Cannon
Street; and whose sword, which he captured in an exciting
struggle from the pirates of the Mediterranean, is now
to be seen in Pilgrim Hall at Plymouth. In a later year
the paper was placed at Harlow & LeBaron's store. Mr.
Robbins's salary continued at the figure named, with the
addition of three or six cords of wood "as it lays on the
Neck," throughout his pastorate.

In 1836, Abner Harlow was chosen to see if the bell
could not be rung for less than $16; and in 1837 it was
decided to have an agent to find seats for strangers,
and James Barstow was appointed. At the same meeting it was voted "not expedient to build new or enlarge the meeting house but to repair the steps, doors,
and windows, and paint the top of the steeple and round
where it was leaded, and move the chimney to the north
end and lead the pipe into the same." But in this
then rapidly growing community this building at "the
Green" was becoming much too small. February 2, 1839,
Benjamin Barstow, as moderator, appointed Andrew
Southworth, John A. LeBaron, Seth Freeman, Wilson
Barstow, and Joshua Cushing a committee on location;

and a month later they reported "a new meeting house cannot go below the hill by the residence of the late Deacon Tobey if there is to be a vestry under it." They advised, however, no action that year, and in 1841 the same committee reported in favor of "a Site or Lot on Universalist Street in back of Capt. Samuel Sturtevant's," and therefore about where the Doctor Sparrow house now stands. In this matter, however, the precinct was not required further to act.

It was decided to build the new house by taking shares and a proprietors' organization was formed. October 9, 1841, Gideon Barstow deeded the present meeting-house lot, for $400, to Ebenezer Cannon, Caleb L. Cannon, Isaac N. Barrows, Benjamin Bacon, Nathan Crosby, Rowland Howland, Edward Buell, Wilson Barstow, Seth Freeman, Leonard Hammond, Arvin Cannon, Samuel Sturtevant, Jr., John A. LeBaron, Jesse Hammond, Jr., Lemuel LeBaron, Solomon K. Eaton, Gideon Barstow, William Merithew, Nathaniel A. Crosby, Henry Barstow, Benjamin Barstow, 2d, Levi Snow, Charles C. Beals, Nathan Cannon, Newton Southworth, Peleg Pierce, Martin Hall, Henry P. Young, James Barstow, Ezra E. Washburn, Nathaniel Clark, Peleg Gifford, James Allen, Thomas C. Hammond, Gideon Hammond, William B. Rogers, Andrew Southworth, Hallet M. Cannon, Mary Leach, Abner Hall, Zaccheus M. Barstow, Matthew Mayhew, Reuben Dexter, Allen Dexter, John Dexter, Rogers L. Barstow, Prentis Crosby, Elnathan H. Cushing, Abner Harlow, Weston Howland, David H. Cannon, Edward H. Willkey, Waterman Crosby, Wyatt Snow, Stephen Snow, Lot. N. Jones, Seth P. Ames, Noah C. Sturtevant, James Coleman, James Cannon,

CONGREGATIONAL MEETING-HOUSE, MATTAPOISETT
The Fourth Meeting-house of the Second Precinct. Erected 1842

Nathan H. Barstow, Richard Mitchell, Amittai B. Hammond, Thomas Nelson, L. N. Jones.

October 28, 1841, the diary states: "Our people have broken ground for a new meeting house." May 10, 1842: "Yesterday the people commenced laying the wall for the new meeting house." May 21: "Afternoon I laid the cornerstone of the fourth meeting house for this people, 1736, 1772, 1816, 1842. Delivered my address. We had a procession, etc. Mr. Cobb (Sippican) was present and assisted." October 31: "Had a meeting in the vestry and in a manner took our leave of that room." November 4: "Observed this as a Humiliation Day in reference to the removal of our place of worship. We had a prayer meeting at sunrise, one at ten o'clock. In the afternoon Mr. Cobb preached very well. We had an evening meeting all in our new lecture room. The first service in the house was prayer — 'Our Father' — etc." Sunday, Nov. 6: "We took our leave of the house of worship where this people have assembled for 26 years." November 9, 1842: "Dedication of our new meeting house to God and his rich grace. Mr. Maltby [1] preached well. I made the dedicatory prayer. Dr. Cobb, Mr. Bigelow, and Mr. Briggs (the ministers of Rochester town) performed parts. The house was very full. Afternoon the pews were sold. The cost of the house and lot ($450) is about $6200, carpetings and lamps included. The lecture room, with the raising the earth, etc, gratuitous about $620. Pews 74, six free, 56 sold including choice money will nearly pay the bills, 12 remain, all wanted.[2]

[1] Rev. Erastus Maltby, a native of Northfield, Conn., a graduate of Yale, 1821, Pastor at Taunton from 1836 until his death in 1883.

[2] A curious deed for one of these pews is dated March 22, 1849, and

The house was much admired. The most of our Association were present. At evening Mr. Barrows preached very well," and on the Saturday following the church bell was removed to the new house.

Dr. Robbins set out many trees in the streets of Mattapoisett. Ash trees seemed to be his favorites. December 16, 1842, he records: "Rode early to the Neck and had two very fine ash trees taken up and brought here and set in front of the meeting house. They are much alike, forty-two feet high and eight inches in diameter. Had good help." For these trees he paid Mr. Gideon Hammond seven dollars. The following summer was exceedingly hot and the good man was worried as to his trees. July 22, he watered them laboriously. Next day, Sunday, "at half past five we had a special season of prayer on account of the drought. Mr. Sullings and the Baptists and the Universalists with us. It was a solemn session." Next day "in the afternoon it pleased God to send us a most greatful shower. It was pretty violent and not long but a great blessing. Our village seems to have been the center of it. I took stage and rode to Wareham. But little rain here."

The doctor's errand at Wareham was to meet with the Association, and on the following day they examined

is that of "John T. Atsatt of Rochester, President of the Mattapoisett and California Mechanical and Mining Company, in consideration of $40 paid by Josiah D. & Noah C. Sturtevant, — a certain pew in the new Cong'l Meeting House with all and singular the furniture of said pew, No. 46, together with a proportionate share of the lot of land on which said house stands; and also one twenty-second of the Riderian School-room under said house, and other privileges in the vestry of said house, with all the privileges and appurtenances thereunto belonging to said pew." — *Plymouth Deeds*, Book 290, page 25.

and licensed Mr. Thacher, of Dartmouth, who, although they then little thought it, would within less than eighteen months sit as a member of that Association, as pastor of the Mattapoisett church, in place of Dr. Robbins.

The bustling village was then growing fast, and was ambitious to be up with the times. It had become less the fashion for a minister to locate with a people for life, and here was settled a little old man who refused to conform his dress to the modern notion, and who when he mounted into the new broad pulpit seemed, in the minds of some of the congregation, to be curiously out of place in the brand new modern meeting-house. His figure was more in keeping with sounding boards, and the square high-backed pews. His thoughts inclined to the past. He was of reputation as an antiquarian. Would not some new licensee better serve this growing maritime parish?

It needed some excuse for a change; but a very little tidbit well twisted on the tongue would perhaps suffice; and being thus minded various of the matrons whose zeal was great in public concerns, and in their neighbors' affairs, proceeded to watch out, and to hold their ears to the ground. Pretty soon they thought they detected a slight concussion, with the center of the disturbance near the Neck. March 25, 1843, Dr. Robbins writes, "Had a piece of unpleasant intelligence." And on the 30th, "My brethren called on me. At evening attended an informal meeting of most of the church, and they voted unanimously on the late slander with which I have been abused, that they received my statement as correct and that they were fully satisfied. They were faithful brethren." He said nothing, however, about the sisters.

December 13, he writes, "My people are in an un-pleasant state;" and later in the month, "Several of my people called on me and presented a petition relative to my removal. — I fear there may be a division among my people." In February, 1844, a meeting was warned "to see if the precinct will continue the Rev. Thomas Robbins their Pastor." The meeting adjourned for four weeks and then without action adjourned *sine die*. But the pastor knew his parish was divided. His intent had been to spend his life with this people in like manner as had his predecessor. He thought on it; he prayed over it, and when his brother Francis, who was over a church in Connecticut, visited in New Bedford, he talked it with him, and his brother thought it best that he leave.

Dr. Robbins had before this had letters from friends and from various institutions, especially Williams College, in regard to the disposal of his library; and at this troubled time came a very alluring proposition through Hon. Henry Barnard, of Hartford, of an arrangement by which the Connecticut Historical Society would eventually come into possession of his books, and Dr. Robbins himself would become the Society's librarian, on a stipulated salary, of nearly double the amount he was then receiving at Matta-poisett, through the remaining years of his active life.

He decided to accept this arrangement and immediately thereafter he requested a precinct meeting and desired that he be given $200 and the expense be paid of removing his library to Connecticut. This was voted unanimously, and the amount raised by the subscriptions of about two-thirds of the congregation. At his request a church council was called, which sat on August 6, and voted dis-mission on the ground of mutual agreement of the parties.

"Many people," he writes, "seem much tried at the prospect of my removal." September 8, 1844, "Preached my farewell sermon on Matthew xvi. 18, in the afternoon to a large assembly. Took a brief review of my ministry in this place. A very pleasant day. Had a solemn meeting. Took notice of the late death of the aged Mr. Jesse Hammond. A very industrious, just and good man."

Monday morning the minister was very busy preparing for his removal. He had engaged a vessel to take his goods around to Hartford, and his library had been packed into over forty great boxes. Tuesday there was "a confused scene" getting things on board. Wednesday morning (11th), "Worked laboriously at my effects and got them on board a vessel which sailed for Hartford in the afternoon." And as the sun drew nearer to the tops of the pines on the ridge at the west, and the shadows lengthened toward Cannonville Hill, we can seem to see the quaint figure of Thomas Robbins, leaning on his cane, out by the end of the wharf, his back to the village and his new meeting-house; watching the little vessel bearing his dearly loved treasure, steer first southeast, and then turn down the bay to head out to the open sea.

When he came up toward the street, caulkers and joiners would have bowed or spoken respectfully. The sailors and captains ashore would have greeted him kindly, for the whalemen felt better to have his Bibles and tracts aboard ship, and when in from the voyage they liked to find his well-known figure as a land mark among the new faces on the streets. They brought him foreign coins, shells and coral; battle-axes and curios from the south seas, and these he cherished with his shot-gourd from the Mayflower, and his piece of Martin Luther's table. It is

said that not long after his departure, one of these whalers
coming in, the captain inquired for the minister, and being
told the recent happenings, broke out in language more
suited to the open ocean than to the printed page and called
down all the anathemas of heaven upon those who had
caused the good man to go away.

September 13, 1844, Dr. Robbins wrote: "Paid Mr.
White, Mr. Baker, Rogers Barstow, and Mr. Crosby.
Balanced all pecuniary accounts. At noon took the stage,
left Mattapoisett and rode to New Bedford. Took cars
and rode to Boston. Much fatigued with many labors.
May God in mercy remember my people now destitute
of a pastor for the first time in more than seventy years."
The Sabbath following he tarried with his brother in
Enfield, finding his surtout lost there on his last journey,
and on the 16th he was in Hartford anxiously awaiting
the arrival of Captain Baker and his vessel. On the 19th
all came safely, and several truck loads of books were
carried up to the Athenæum; where for ten years thereafter
Thomas Robbins filled the office of Librarian.

Dr. Henry R. Stiles wrote in the Round Table of January 6, 1866 (quoted but in part):

> "The old librarian was the last of a line of New England
> Divines. He had been a settled pastor for a good portion of
> his life and was a good writer of sermons. A studious man by
> nature, books were not so much a luxury as a necessity to him.
> It was a pleasant arrangement this by which the books which
> he had spent so great a portion of his life in collecting should
> thus repay his loving care by giving to his old age the little
> comforts which it needed.
>
> "Antiquaries Hall was a rare and fitting shrine for such a
> character. Old portraits, old chairs and chests out of the *May-
> flower*, Captain Miles Standish's dinner pot, Indian relics, worm-
> eaten manuscripts, old battle flags, hacked, haggled and rent,

and scraps of ancient costume were the appropriate surroundings of this old librarian with his small clothes and knee buckles, and his white silk stockings or white top boots with their silken tassels.

"Here old age deepened insensibly the mellow shadows of life, death wooed him so gently that he knew it not, his memory failed, his beloved books alone were able to retain, and then only for a moment, his wandering thoughts. An assistant was procured for him, but the old man scarcely knew the change. He lingered on until September 13, 1856, when he passed peacefully away at the home of his niece Mrs Elizabeth (Robbins) Allen in the town of Colebrook, Connecticut, at the age of 79." [1]

Following the pastorate of Mr. Robbins the history of the Second Precinct in Rochester took on a new aspect. What might be termed the patriarchal system with its lifelong pastorates gave place to the more modern custom of an acting pastor supplying the pulpit for a short term of years. "Dr. Robbins's new meeting house" still stands, and persons now living can review in memory the sixty-three years since this new era began. Its history is not greatly out of the ordinary and need be outlined but briefly.

In November, 1844, Mr. Isaiah Thacher, who was a native of Dartmouth, and who had been graduated from Union College in 1841, having preached two Sabbaths, was invited to supply the pulpit for twelve months at a salary of $600. He accepted and was duly installed by Council, Christmas Day, 1844, and continued as pastor until dismissed in 1849, when he immediately accepted the pastorate of the Central Congregational

[1] The funeral occurred at the Centre Church, Hartford, and the Historical Society, having first listened to a memorial address at its rooms by the Rev. Joel Hawes, attended in a body.

Church, Middleboro, who had that year erected their present house of worship. The precinct seemed to be concerned during this time mainly with the circulating of various kinds of subscription papers. Edward Buell had one to collect "to defray the church's housekeeping," and if you met Rowland Howland, his was for a new stove pipe, to be preferably of copper.

Mr. Thacher is said to have preached good stiff orthodox doctrine, and it appears that members who were "doubtful on the doctrine of total depravity and eternal punishment" were called up to give account. His successor, Mr. Mather, also took a vigorous hold on church discipline, and those who forsook communion, "habitually misrepresented facts," "patronized the ball-room," or kept livery stables open on Sunday, received censure. The last record of church discipline, other than the mere erasure of a name, occurred under Mr. Parsons in 1861.

November, 1850, the precinct had voted to install Rev. Wm. L. Mather, offering a salary of $500, and appointing Alexander Cannon treasurer and collector and Charles C. Beals to solicit money for "contingent expenses:" and these did so well that at the end of the year the balance of $11 was paid to Solomon K. Eaton "for the improvement of singing." In 1855 it was voted "the congregation be requested to sing with the choir the last hymn in the fore and afternoon." The stone posts with chains, which now enclose two sides of the meeting-house lot, were set by William Taylor in the fall of 1851. Mr. Mather dwelt in the house now the home of Mrs. Wealthy A. Cross, and also at Cannonville. He was dismissed by council in 1855, — and in November of that year he and his wife

Amanda were granted letters to the church in Ann Arbor, Mich.

In September Rev. Charles Livingstone was installed pastor, at a salary of $800. He was the son of Neil Livingstone and Agnes Hunter, of Blantyre, in Scotland, and consequently was the younger brother of David Livingstone, the African missionary and explorer. Of Charles, W. G. Blaikie in his Personal Life of David Livingstone, *Harpers*, 1881, page 88, says:

> "In 1839, when David Livingstone was in England, Charles became earnest about religion. A strong desire sprang up in his mind to obtain a liberal education. Not having the means to get this at home he was advised by David to go to America and endeavor to obtain admission to one of the colleges there where the students support themselves by manual labor. To help him in this David sent him five pounds, being the whole of his quarter's allowance in London. On landing in New York, after selling his box and bed, Charles found his whole stock of cash to amount to £2, 13s. 6d. Purchasing a loaf and a piece of cheese as *viaticum*, he started for a college at Oberlin, seven hundred miles off, where Dr. Finney was President. He contrived to get to the college without having ever begged. In the third year he entered on the theological course with a view to becoming a missionary. He did not wish, and never could agree as a missionary, to hold an appointment from an American Society on account of the relation of the American Churches to slavery; therefore he applied to the London Missionary Society. The Directors declined to appoint Charles Livingstone without a personal visit, which he could not afford to make. This circumstance led him to accept a pastorate in New England, where he remained until 1857, when he came to this country and joined his brother in the Zambesi Expedition. Afterwards he was appointed H. M. Consul at Fernando Po, but being always delicate, he succumbed to the climate of the country and died a few months after his brother, on his way home in October, 1873."

He appears as joint author with his brother in an account

of the Zambesi expedition: on which journey Dr. Livingstone took his party twenty miles off their regular route that they might see the grand Victoria Falls, and "Charles Livingstone, who had seen Niagara, gives the preference to Mosi-oa-tunya." And it is evident that, at that time, he was the only person in the world able to make that comparison. He had left Mattapoisett abruptly, and sent back but little information of his plans or movements either to his parish or his family. Various committees waited on Mrs. Livingstone, but she could give them no news; official inquiries remained unanswered. So the precinct voted, July 13, 1857, "To instruct the committee to write Mr. Livingstone, that as the time having expired for which he asked leave of absence, and having no intimation from him when he may return, if at all, and being destitute of a minister we have decided to invite a supply of the pulpit without reference to his return."

The position was then offered to a Rev. Mr. Wheeler, but Dr. Bartlett reported he could not be obtained. Others declined. Rev. William L. Parsons, D.D., accepted at a salary of $900, and preached for six years. He was duly installed, in which service Rev. Mr. Thacher and Rev. Asahel Cobb had parts. This church participated in the general revival season of 1857 and '58, and on May 9, 1858, seventy-seven were admitted to membership upon confession of faith. In July and September following were others, among whom was John Smith, the son of Solomon, a free negro, who until his death was seldom absent a Sunday from his northeast corner pew, and who in his later years, in the absence of a deacon, at times officiated at communion.

Mr. Parsons was the first minister to occupy the parsonage, the land for which was deeded on July 19, 1860 (for so long as thus used), by Capt. Franklin Cross, to the precinct; the official title of which was changed by the Act of March 5, 1860, to "The First Precinct in Mattapoisett."

Mr. Parsons continued as pastor until the fall of 1864, when on account of his health he left to become the instructor in mental and moral science at Ingraham University, LeRoy, N. Y., where he died December 23, 1877. He preached his farewell sermon at Mattapoisett, on September 4, 1864, and at the same time set apart to the office of Deacons, Solomon K. Eaton and Noah Hammond, both of whom were men of value to the community as well as the church. Mr. Eaton as an architect and the builder of his own and four or more other meeting-houses within the limits of old Rochester territory; the first Lieutenant of Company I, 3d Regiment, M.V.M., in the Civil War; and as organist or choirmaster for fifteen or twenty years he maintained a standard of church music seldom attained in a small community. Esquire Hammond had an extensive practice in probate court, and as a conveyancer and surveyor. He completed the town map begun by the data of Ansel Weeks. For an extended period he was the chairman of the selectmen, and died in 1893 while serving as representative to the General Court. Mr. Parsons while at Mattapoisett published a religious work entitled "Satan's Devices."

The minister who presided at the council which installed Mr. Parsons was the Rev. John P. Cleveland, of the Appleton Street Church, Lowell. The precinct requested Mr. Parsons, when he left, to seek the services of this friend of his in their behalf. As a result Dr. Cleveland was acting pastor at Mattapoisett from October, 1864, to June, 1867. He was a graduate of Bowdoin in 1821 and studied theology with Rev. C. Upham at Rochester, N. H. He had been dismissed from Lowell in 1862 to accept the chaplaincy of the 35th Massachusetts Regiment, which served at Ship Island and New Orleans. His vigorous sermon at Mattapoisett on the occasion of the assassination of Lincoln is often referred to by those who heard it.

A speaker at anniversary services of the Lowell church said of Dr. Cleveland: "He loved the doctrines and often preached them with great point and power. He had logic and keen wit. He studied men as well as books. An earnest advocate of temperance and a true patriot. He was a thoroughly consecrated minister of the gospel. His spirit was balmy, buoyant, kind and sweet. His face beamed with goodness." He had other pastorates at Salem, Detroit, Cincinnati, Northampton, and Providence. He died March 7, 1873, being seventy-three years of age.

In the decade following 1867 there were three short pastorates. Rev. Benj. F. Manwell was called in May, 1868, and continued as installed pastor until the spring of 1870. He was a man of literary attainment and was leader in the organization of the local "Philistorian Society." Rev. Edward G. Smith was installed in April, 1871, and dismissed in June, 1875; and Rev. Nathaniel Larselle served as acting pastor from May, 1876, to July, 1878. He came to Mattapoisett from Amesbury, being a graduate of Bowdoin and a man who read much, especially of unusual literature. He had held prominent pastorates, and by those who recall him he is said to have been the ablest and most eloquent preacher among the later ministers of this church.

In the interim following Mr. Larselle the precinct voted "to continue to have while we are candidating two services, and meeting in the evening, but when we get a permanent supply the A.M. service is to be omitted." The candidate who became this permanent supply was Rev. Augustus H. Fuller, who was ordained at Lynn in October, 1878, and came at once to Mattapoisett for his first charge. He was a graduate of Brown University and Bangor Theological Seminary. He continued with this church until May, 1886, and held pastorates in Massachusetts, at West Medway, Billerica, and Easton, before his present service at Ballardvale, Andover.

Mr. Fuller's successor was a young man of twenty-five who had been preaching at Woods Hole. Rev. Frank L. Goodspeed was ordained and installed at Mattapoisett, June 29, 1887. He continued his studies during his pastorate, taking degrees from Harvard College of A.B. and Ph.D., and was also a graduate of Boston University School of Theology, and later received an honorary D.D. Leaving Mattapoisett in 1890 he held successive pastorates at Hingham and Amherst, and for the last thirteen years has been settled over the old First Church of Springfield, one of the largest in the Congregational denomination.

He was followed at Mattapoisett by a more elderly man, the Rev. Charles H. Phelps, who had been born in 1835 upon the frontier of Pennsylvania, his paternal ancestor, William Phelps, having participated in the emigration led by Thomas Hooker, one of the founders of the town of Windsor and of the Connecticut Colony. Before coming to Mattapoisett, Mr. Phelps had been in mercantile business, had taught at Tabor Academy, Marion; and had served through the Civil War as private and hospital steward, and had preached in Smithfield, Pa., Greenwich, Marblehead, and Kelley's Island, in Ohio. Mr. Phelps resigned, from ill health, at Mattapoisett, in Sepember, 1893, since which time he has lived at his childhood home farm at Milan, Pa.

The two ministers who have completed their service at Mattapoisett since 1893 were both natives of London, in England, and both had served with their wives in the foreign mission field. Rev. Charles A. Ratcliffe came to this church from pastorates at Buxton, West Scarboro, Baldwin, and Madison in Maine. From 1885 to 1888 he had served under Bishop William Taylor in the African mission at St. Paul de Loanda. His early education was obtained at Bancroft's Hospital, London, and he had drilled in soldierly tactics in the broad moat and yard of the old Tower of London. He had also taken a course of study at the Kortegarn Institute, Bonn, Germany; and while at Mattapoisett he continued the study of theology, at Boston University. He accepted a call to North Attleboro in June, 1896, and has been pastor at Norton since April, 1901.

Mr. Ratcliffe's successor in Mattapoisett was Rev. Robert Humphrey, who came to this country from Ontario in 1883, having left England in 1881. He had acquired his education in the public and science schools in the old country, in part in Canada, and in part at Oberlin College. He was graduated in 1886 from Oberlin Seminary, and took special post-graduate work under Professor Moore at Andover.   Besides pastorates at Rye, N. H., Saugatuck, Mich., and Randolph, N. Y., he and Mrs. Humphrey were connected for two years with the Madura mission in South India, and for three years just prior to their coming to Mattapoisett they were in the work of the A.M.A., and founded and taught in the High School at Whittier, N. C. Mr. Humphrey continued at Mattapoisett for nine years until March, 1905, and held a short pastorate at Hooksett, N. H., before accepting a call to Dighton early in 1907.

The present minister, Rev. C. Julian Tuthill, began his service as acting pastor August 11, 1905. He is a native of Belchertown, a graduate of Boston University and Andover Theological Seminary; and had previous pastorates at Saylesville, R. I., Sanford, Me., and Georgetown, Mass. Mr. Tuthill is a member of various fraternal orders, and recently won a large prize for the preparation of the ritual now in use in the A.O.U.W.

In February, 1891, the meeting-house was struck by lightning and damaged to the extent of about $1000. by the resulting fire. William L. Hubbard and George H. Dexter acted in behalf of the precinct in the adjustment of this matter, and the structure was renovated under the direction of Dr. William E. Sparrow, Nathan S. Mendell, Mary F. Dexter, Elizabeth R. Winston, and Harriet W. Dexter. The large enclosed pulpit had previously been taken out and the principal change then made was the building of an arch on the plain north wall, and the removal of certain pews at the front and rear. The bell brought down from the third meeting-house had been replaced prior to 1870. This second bell cracked in January, 1880, and the present one, of about

fourteen cwt., was secured by Noah Hammond, Joseph
R. Taber, and Elbridge G. Caswell, committee, at a cost
of $453.

Various members of the precinct have in recent years
left bequests for the general expenses of this parish.
Among these are, Alice Meigs, Susannah P. Dexter,
Lemuel LeBaron, William B. Rogers, Nathan H. and
Mary Barstow, Francis LeB. Mayhew, and Stephen
Randall. The deacons of the church chosen since 1864
have been Arvin Cannon, 1868–85; James Cannon,
1885–87; William B. Rogers, 1887–94; Elliot R. Snow,
1894–; J. Charles F. Atsatt, 1894–1905; Thomas L. Ames,
1904–06; Nathan Smith, 1905–; Dr. David H. Cannon,
1906–. This church, January 1, 1907, had seventy-three
members. Sarah E. C. Hathaway has for some time
been treasurer, and Elliot R. Snow, Dr. Walter E.
Blaine, and Dr. Irving Niles Tilden, are the Precinct
Committee in 1907.

Not quite ten years after minister LeBaron was installed at Mattapoisett, a young man of twenty-six was
called and settled over the Baptist church in Dartmouth.
His name was Daniel Hix, and the region about his meeting-house soon became known as Hixville. His father was
Elder John Hix, of Rehoboth, and at his house there,
three quarters of a mile south of Oak Swamp Meeting-
house, Daniel was born, November 30, 1755. As a boy he
was a leader in mischief; as a youth a minute-man for
Lexington alarm; and as a man, Elder Goff, in the "Herald
of Gospel Liberty," said of him: "Father Hix was one of
the most popular Baptist ministers in Massachusetts.
The evidence, aside from the unanimous verdict of his

contemporaries, exists in the following facts, — first, large congregations, including many of his orthodox neighbors, everywhere waited on his ministry. Second, he collected in a rural and sparsely settled community a church of more than five hundred members. Third, his interposition to settle difficulties. And fourth, when seven or eight years later he left the Baptists and united with the Christians, his whole church accompanied him. He had then been submitted to inquisitorial examination and pronounced heterodox. This only increased his popularity."

His sermons are said to have been long, often two or three hours, and although not carefully prepared, so remarkable for strength and originality of thought, so practical and full of the Holy Spirit, that his hearers never tired. Elder George N. Kelton remembered Elder Hix, and said: "I was at a conference of ministers at Swansey, in September, 1830. The impressive services of the day were about to close, a feeling of deep interest pervaded the audience, when an aged man, of medium height, compact muscular build, broad chest and shoulders, short neck, bushy iron gray hair, heavy beetle brows and broad swarthy features, slowly arose in the pulpit, ejaculating, 'When the lion roars the weaker beasts tremble, eh? The Lion of the Tribe of Judah has roared to-day, and there is an awful trembling in the camp.' In the man I saw a lion type, and in his words heard Judah's lion in princely right and dignity." [1]

Elder Hix especially excelled as an organizer of churches.

[1] A Sketch of Elder Daniel Hix, with a History of the First Christian Church in Dartmouth, by S. M. Andrews, New Bedford, 1880. Page 22.

He was installed at Dartmouth, October 10, 1781, with at first no stated salary; he working at his trade and his wife at her loom, while various of his parishioners tilled his farm or contributed from their crops toward his support. He traveled extensively, preaching in all this region and at times upon the Cape. Various congregations in Fairhaven, Long Plain, Berkeley, and Freetown were gathered separately, or as branches of the mother church at Hixville; and in addition to these was this church at Rochester, which originated from Elder Hix's itinerant preaching. In the list of churches of 1795 in Backus's History of the Baptists (page 391), Rochester is not mentioned, its membership being included in the Dartmouth church which was reported with 347 members.

William T. Faunce, in whose possession are the early Baptist records, makes the following statement: "The original Baptist church in Mattapoisett was founded in the year 1789. It appears, however, that there was no real organization effected at that time. In 1792 there was a general revival of religious interest. As the outcome, a meeting-house was erected in that year; a statement of which is given in this wise: 'A number of inhabitants of Mattapoisett and New Bedford joined and built a meeting-house for public worship, being often visited by Elder Hix and other Baptist preachers, meetings being held at the meeting-house on Lord's Day.' In 1794, in the latter part of the year, there was a revival of religion; Elders Lawrence and Bolles labored with us. On January 18, 1795, at a meeting held for the purpose, after imploring divine blessing and assistance, Elder Hix and some brethren in the church being present, the persons whose names are hereinafter written covenanted together to walk in all

the ordnances and commands of the Lord and Saviour
Jesus Christ, as the Gospel teaches; under the pastoral
care of Elder Daniel Hix, and to be as a branch of his
church.

Abner Howard.	Jesse Ellis.
Joseph Leavit.	Nathaniel Hammond.
Joshua Besse.	Jedidah Robinson.
Charles Tinkham.	Elizabeth Besse.
Malaki Ellis.	Hulda Howard.
Ephram Tinkham.	Phebe Mireck.
Daniel Randall.	Experience Ellis.
Jethro Randall.	

At this meeting Nathaniel Hammond was chosen clerk."

The meeting-house mentioned as built in 1792 is the
same referred to in the Massachusetts Historical Collections in 1815 as being "on the confines of Fairhaven,
but within this place." It in fact stood on substantially
the same spot as does the present chapel at Tinkhamtown.
It had long windows, the usual high pulpit and square
pews, and continued to be used occasionally until destroyed by fire, perhaps soon after 1850.

Extracts from Elder Hix's journal, as published in his
biography, indicate his activities with his branch church
in Rochester. He writes: "The first Sabbath in Sep-
tember (1793) were baptized Nathaniel Hammond and
Thos. Spooner. In Rochester meeting-house, Jan. 23,
1795, had a solemn session and baptized Thomas Ellis,
David Randolph, Jesse Tripp, Eph. Tinkham, and Mariah
Tripp. Mar. 15, baptized Mary Parlor, Anna Robenson,
Lydia Dexter, Bathsheba Tripp. A day of rejoicing.
May 17, baptized Unice Ellis, Lydia Westgate, Waty
Stephens, and Deliverance Ames. Nov. 15, in Rochester,
Unice Tinkham.

In 1806, July 27, baptized in Rochester, Thos Sherman. 1807, Micah Winslow, Hannah Winslow, Deborah Shearman. In Rochester, 11th August, at the Shore, a precious season, Medad Cannon, Thos. Kinney, Mary Studson, Susannah Frasher, Penney Beck and Eliz. Dunham were baptized. Aug. 20, Joseph Whitridge. At Mattapoisett Harbour, a glorious Day, Aug. 25th, Anna Weston, Betsey Briggs, Polly Green, Mary Dexter, Arty Besse, Amelia Haskell, Abigail Briggs and Thankful Shearman were baptized. This was a time to be remembered. The next morning at the same place the Glory of God was evident, and four others were baptized, Seth Ames, Timo. Ellis, Edmund Beck (Buck?) and Mollie Ellis. Sept. 9, at Rochester Shore, Thos. Ames, Asa Dunham, Ebenezer Fuller, Joseph Hammond, Betsey Haskell, Mary Dunham, Joa Hammond, Rocksa Haskell, Thankful Higgins, Joa Bowles, Lois Atsel (Atsatt?) and Dolly Snow were baptized. A glorious work in this place, the Lord reigns marvelously, saints rejoice and sinners mourn. At Rochester Shore, Oct. 6th, the Lord leadeth and his people follow, — Nancy Hammond, Seney Hammond, Prudence Wilbur, Abigail Kinney, Joanna Dexter, Holder Gelatte were baptized. Also in Rochester soon after, Jos. Edwards, Benj. Perkins, Judah Perkins, Lucy Haskell, Polly Haskell, and Abigail Skiff.

In 1808, May 25, in Rochester, James Blankenship aged 86, James Blankenship Jr., Chas. Chandler, Rebecca Chandler. June 28, — Ellis Mendall, Abigail Whitridge, Sarah Jenny. On Rochester Great Neck, 29th, Ruth Blankenship and Betsey Allen. Rochester Shore, Aug. 16th, Abr. Harrison, Danl Shearman, Wm Shearman, Luke Dexter, Vira Paine. Sept. 27, in Rochester, Deborah

Hall & Eliz. Hall. Rochester Shore, Nov. 3, Eliz. Cannon and Nancy Paine. 1809, Apr. 18, Philip Atsetts. In Rochester, Nov. 2, John Cole, Rebecca C. Cole. 1811, baptized in Rochester, Ezekiel Cushman and Wid. Rider. July 18th, two persons named Miggs. Aug. 13, Andrew Randall, Ebenezer Keene, Jr., Abigail Wilbur and Eliz. Wilcox, a good work in this place. In Rochester, June 18, 1812, Lydia Randall and Susanna Howard. 19th, Richard Randall and Keziah Randall. July 10, Caleb and Maria Mendell.

Elder Hix doubtless continued to minister as opportunity afforded to this branch of his church as long as health permitted. The records of Mattapoisett church are missing — presumably lost — from 1823 to 1858. We know that Elder Hix was active at the revival time of 1829, but that after 1833 he preached but little, being afflicted with kidney disease. His death occurred March 22, 1838, at the age of eighty-two years, and he was buried near his meeting-house in Hixville.

In the Mattapoisett town meeting of April, 1883, there was a discussion as to the advisability of a change of the name of Pearl Street to School Street; the argument being that "here the ancient schoolhouse stands," and that no pearls ever had been found in that vicinity. Thomas Nelson then took the floor and said that if the change be made, to be consistent, the name of Baptist Street should be changed to Christian Street, for there were no real Baptists to be found in that locality. The correctness of this statement is shown by the church record of March, 1807, which reads: "The church at Dartmouth, Elder Daniel Hix, pastor, of which this church is a branch, agreed to come out from the Baptist denomination into the name and order of the New Testament, taking on themselves the name Christians." And because of this action the Hixville church and its branches were dropped out of fellowship from the Baptist Conference at East Greenwich, R. I., June 19, 1811, although Mattapoisett Church has continued to be locally called the "Baptist Church."

Discipline was required and practised much as in all other church organizations of that time. Some member left to enter other denominations. February, 1808, the church voted, "To withdraw fellowship from Zephaniah Shearman and his wife, whose name on the book stands Weighty Stevens, for withdrawing from the church and joining the Methodists."

In 1814, William Ellis was clerk, and it may have been he who, in 1816, made reference in the records to the prevailing epidemic. "March, — A church meeting attended by Elder Whitin. At this time it is more than common sickly with an epidemic fever, perhaps one hundred persons or more have been sick during the winter, one half of whom, perhaps, have died in this town and Fairhaven, but no member of this church has died that I know of." In April, 1816, "Elder Whiting moved away."

The growth of "the Shore" even in Elder Hix's time seemed to demand a new meeting-house in that locality. The matter was discussed October 28, 1820, and November 3, following, meeting was held at the house of Philip Atsatt, with Wilbur Southworth as moderator, when a committee was chosen consisting of John Atsatt, Malachi Ellis, and Luke Dexter. A month later it was reported that a subscription for thirty-nine shares had been made, to build a structure "42x32 with a projection 3x24, said house to be one story high with 14 foot posts, a small gallery in

FIRST CHRISTIAN MEETING-HOUSE, MATTAPOISETT

front, a decent pulpit and 39 pews; the floor to arch overhead and to be handsomely finished. To stand on the
lot lately purchased in the village of Mattapoisett of
Thomas Tobey." Which lot is said to have been procured from the orthodox deacon by creating in his mind
the impression that it was likely to be used as a site for a
blacksmith shop. "Uncle Philip" took three shares and
the following had shares or fractional interests: John
Atsatt, James Hammond, William Shaw, Wilber South-
worth, George Shaw, Ebenezer Barrows, Josiah Holmes,
Malachi Ellis, James Purrington, James Curtis, Luke
Dexter, James Luce, Jno. Kinney, Elijah Willis, Samuel
Purrington, Seth Ames, Andrew Dunham, Joseph Snow,
Nathaniel Hammond, Thomas Holmes, Elisha Dexter,
Clement Randall, James Coleman, Lewis Randall, Jr.,
Christopher Hammond, Joshua Bates, Theodore C. Ames,
Benjamin Hammond, Nathan Briggs, Samuel Bowles,
John H. Randall.

Samuel Purrington was the first clerk of the proprietors,
and later Dennis Boodry was clerk for some years. The
mason work was given to Jonathan Kinney at $75, Wilber
Southworth contracting to dig the trench for $6. The
contract for carpenter work went to James Purrington for
$1075, he agreeing "to find all material for completing
even to locks, keys, latches, and hinges." March 7, 1822,
John Atsatt, Seth Ames, Philip Atsatt, Malachi Ellis,
and Samuel Snow deeded the lot to the proprietors,[1]
bounding it on the east "nine rods by the ropewalk."
Such was the origin of the most ancient religious building
in present use in Mattapoisett.

The high fence around the lot on the street sides con-

[1] Plymouth Deeds, Book 178, page 93.

tinued to stand until after 1890; and the interior including the old high pulpit remained unchanged until William T. Faunce began his alterations in 1906; at which time the corner projections in front were added.

The pews below remain as always, some of the short-backed square pews in the gallery having, however, lately been removed.

In the end gallery sat the choir, which for years always contained a good number of natural singers who performed their part of the service, not grudgingly, but with a will which on a still summer's night carried the notes of Gospel Hymns to the remotest sections of the village. The editor of the *Enterprise* perhaps associated in mind this musical activity with the shape of the building, when he continued to refer to this meeting-house as "the Bee-Hive."

The pews in the side galleries for a number of generations had been the choice of location for the somewhat irresponsible youth who attended evening meetings. The low seats around the little square boxes tended to sociability, and even Elder Faunce occasionally had to pause and announce "Now we'll take three minutes to laugh and everybody finish up." The congregation below probably looked less serious when seen vertically, and if "Uncle Calvin's" cap which he spread over his bald head looked all proper below, it certainly read "best salt" from above. Once a group of young people were standing outside the big gate "finishing up" their laugh, when Miss Marchant, coming along, halted before them. They paused expectantly. Said she, "The spirit of the Lord must have been present to-night or the devil wouldn't have been so uneasy;" and off she went. But in spite of all, in the later generations at least, when Elder Faunce was in charge, the young people all liked the Elder and respected much the good old man.

In days long gone, it is said, the older people did not always set the best example of conduct to the young. By the original subscription this house had been built to "be free for any respectable preacher who might come," and the exponents of differing doctrines often sought the use of the house at the same time. The Universalists at their start used it for a short period. Their records of March, 1835, show that Seth Mendall, Joseph Meigs, and Elijah Willis were appointed "to wait on the other committee and see if they can agree for the house a part of the time on the best terms they can." Earlier than that, very soon after the meeting-house was built, there had been a division and the "come-outers" withdrew to worship in the building later used as the engine-house, and then, for some unexplained reason, dubbed "The Little Belt." This building at that time had pillars in front, pulpit at the north, and a small gallery. The Millerite agitation in the '40s caused another schism, and resulted in the organization of the Advent Church.

In the period from 1823 to 1860 there were various preachers in the old house. The records of October 14, 1823, state that "Bro. Hervey Sullings has the summer past attended meetings about half of the time." From the recollection of older people it appears that Elder Briggs preached for two or three years about 1830. Elder Israel Wood from 1832 to 1841, and Dr. Robbins acted with him occasionally at funerals. Rev. William Bryant, whose adherents were locally known as the "Bryantites,"

preached to a part of the congregation about 1838 to
1840. Rev. Alexander M. Averill came to Mattapoisett
at the age of nineteen. Dr. Robbins attended his ordination February 4, 1841, joined with him in revival services in
March, 1842; and December 14 of the same year, the diary
states: "Mr. Averill preached another farewell sermon.
His people here are much divided about the Second
Advent." He is reputed to have been a good student
and an able preacher, and to have gone to Cambridge-
port.

Soon after, the stalwart Burnham brothers came to
town. Edwin preached for the Adventists at the "Little
Belt," and Hezekiah dwelt in Capt. Isaiah Purrington's
(now Dennis Mahoney's) chambers, and preached in the
Baptist meeting-house. April 23, 1844, Dr. Robbins
"heard a temperance lecture from my neighbor Burnham," — presumably public. Rev. Mr. Taylor, Rev. Mr.
Eldredge, and Elder Henry F. Carpenter also preached
here sometime between 1845 and 1855. About 1857
Rev. Benjamin S. Bachelor, then a young man of zeal
and ability, commenced a most acceptable ministry, coming over from New Bedford each Sabbath. His labors
were very effectual in upbuilding and uniting the church.

In 1864, Mr. Bachelor was succeeded by Rev. William
Faunce, who came hither from the mother church in Hixville. Mr. Andrews in his history [1] states: "The Church
at Hix's Meeting-House April 16, 1857, elected Elder
William Faunce as successor of Elder Howard Tripp.
He was a native of Plymouth, and being in the prime of
life he entered upon his work with a zeal that made suc-

[1] Sketch of Elder Daniel Hix, etc., S. M. Andrews, New Bedford,
1880. Page 169.

INTERIOR OF FIRST CHRISTIAN MEETING-HOUSE, MATTAPOISETT, 1905

cess sure. Like most of our older preachers, Elder Faunce had to struggle with many difficulties in early life, but possessing a good voice and natural preaching talent, with the blessing of God his labors were crowned with success. He preached also at North Westport each Sabbath afternoon and organized the church there in November, 1857. Many joined there in 1858 and were baptized at the Narrows in Watuppa Pond. The church and society re-elected Elder Faunce pastor in 1864, but finding obstacles to his success increasing he resigned after a short time, leaving the pulpit to be supplied until fall by Elder Frederick P. Snow, who was born in Rochester in 1812. He learned cabinet-making and upholstery. His privileges of early education were limited. He was ordained in New Bedford December 28, 1845, and was pastor at Hixville one and a half years."

Rev. William Faunce was born in July, 1813, being a descendant of the venerable Elder Thomas Faunce. He began preaching while very young at Chiltonville, and also was with the Union church at Long Pond, Plymouth, before going to Hixville. He lived first in Mattapoisett at Pine Islands, and at the John A. LeBaron house; he at one time owned the Lot N. Jones (Goddard) place; for many years he dwelt in the old house which stood on the site of his son William T. Faunce's house; and his descendants are numerous in the town.

For thirty-four years he continued as the pastor of this church; faithful unto death; which occurred in April, 1898. It might well be said of him, as one wrote of Elder Hix, "He preached not by constraint, but willingly; not for filthy lucre, but of a ready mind." He especially excelled in prayer. In his old age, when able, he loved, at

intervals, to gather those who remained, to hold service
in the old meeting-house. After his death the house was
opened but occasionally, until in 1905, following the revival
season under Rev. David L. Martin, of Boston, when
many were baptized at "the Shore," the church was reorganized, and Rev. Frank S. Jones of New Bedford has
served as pastor until July, 1907.

As already stated, the Advent Christian Church in Mattapoisett was formed by a division of those who worshiped in the old Baptist meeting-house. Services were
held in the "Little Belt," and for a time in the old "Vestry," now a part of the Mattapoisett House. Elder
Macomber for a while held meetings near the Herring
Weir. When Elisha Dexter built his new shop, just south
of his house, he fitted up the upper floor for services; and
later when the cabinet shop was brought up from Water
Street, somewhere about 1870, and converted into the
Advent Chapel, he provided the lot where it stands. Soon
thereafter it was decided to complete a church organization; and Theodore Ames, Bruce F. Shaw, Charles H.
Buck, William E. Bolles, Elisha Dexter, James B. Ransom and Joseph E. Smith, having addressed a petition to
Noah Hammond, Esq., "to issue a warrant for a meeting
in our chapel," March 28, 1872, the society was organized. Others then interested were John A. Shaw, Russell
E. Snow, Hiram Hammond, Stephen Merrihew, Nathaniel
H. Denham, and Humphrey Taber. The only regular
minister shown by the records was Frederick W. Blackmer,
of Springfield, who was ordained here April 13, 1882,
Elder E. A. Stockman preaching the sermon. He resigned July 20, 1884. Meetings have not been regularly

held by this society for some years and most of the members have joined other churches.

Some independent meetings have in recent years existed in this town. The two Union Chapels now standing were erected sometime after 1880; the one on the site of the old Aucoot schoolhouse being sustained largely by Mrs. Bruce F. Shaw and some of the Marion Congregational church. Meetings are still held in the chapel at Tinkhamtown, and it is one of the regular meeting places for the "Neighborhood Convention." Roman Catholic services have sometimes, in summer, been held in the town hall.

Many who have summer homes in Mattapoisett have been adherents of the Church of England. These, for several seasons, after 1874, held services in the Congregational meeting-house. Then land was given from the lot of Thomas Parsons, on which "St. Philip's Church" was erected and was consecrated by Bishop Benjamin H. Paddock, July 11, 1884. A clergyman comes for the summer, and service is regularly held for about three months in each year.

From 1884 through 1890, Rev. Dr. Andrew Oliver of the New York Theological Seminary, was the clergyman in charge; Rev. A. W. Seabrease, 1891–'92; Rev. Henry Cunningham 1893; Rev. Charles Lewis Slatery, 1894–'96; Rev. Charles Mason, 1896–'97; Rev. C. H. W. Stocking, 1897; Rev. Percy Browne, 1898–1900; Rev. Edward Drown, 1900–'02; Rev. M. Kellner, 1903; various clergymen during 1904; Rev. H. W. Perkins, 1905–'06. Rev. W. A. Holbrook, Rev. T. D. Martin, and Rev. Jas. L. Tryon have preached the present year although Rev. William H. Falkner, of Louisville, Ky., is in charge for

most of the season of 1907.   Bishop Lawrence has
twice visited this church.   It is under the care of Venerable Archdeacon Samuel J. Babcock, of Eastern Massachusetts.

The original trustees were Rev. Andrew Oliver, D.D.,
Dr. Fitch, Edward Oliver, Thomas Parsons, Charles J.
Whittemore, Henry Warren, Causten Browne, and Dexter
Tiffany: and the present board consists of Causten
Browne, Theophilus Parsons, Charles A. King, J. Lewis
Stackpole, Jr., Charles S. Hamlin, and George O. G. Coale.

As in the rest of New England at that time, liberal
doctrines began to have an influence in Rochester in the
earlier part of the nineteenth century.   On the 5th of
February, 1828, Wilber Southworth, Elijah Willis, Ansel
Weeks, Thomas Dexter, Newton Southworth, George
Purrington, James Purrington, Warren Weeks, Alden
Dexter, and Wyatt Snow addressed a petition to Joseph
Meigs, Esq., of Rochester, "one of the Justices appointed
to keep the Peace," that he might by his warrant call a
meeting of all concerned in the First Universalist Society
in Rochester, at the house of Elisha Ruggles, Esq., on the
first day of March at two o'clock.   At which time organization was had by the choice of Jesse Martin, moderator;
Newton Southworth, clerk; Noble E. Bates, treasurer;
and Seth Mendell, Jesse Martin and John Clark, 2d, "a
committee to govern the affairs of the society."   Incorporation was voted, and the committee instructed "to
treat with some one of the Universalist ministers and
request him to come and preach one or more sermons in
the several quarters of the town;" and Wilber Southworth was directed "to prepare the minits of the present

meeting that they be sent for publication in the Universalist Magazine and Christian Telescope."

Dr. Southworth, later in the record, says: "The Rev. Mr. Robert Hillam commenced preaching here about the first of ———— ,1829. Mr. Pickering, I think, was the first person to preach the doctrine of universal salvation on Sabbath in this town, I think in June, 1828." The annual meeting of March, 1829, was warned to be held in "Mr. Young's meeting-house," and in 1831 it occurred in "the First Baptist Meeting House."

In May, 1830, the following names, the record states, "were handed to the Clerk of the Second Precinct in Rochester" as members of this poll-parish:

Elijah Willis.	Aldin Dexter.
Wilbur Southworth.	James Purrington.
Noble E. Bates.	Edward Shearman.
John Washburn.	Newton Southworth.
Ansel Wicks.	Wiatt Snow.
Stephen Nye.	Albert Daggett.
Christian Konkeal.	Prince Snow Jr.
Joseph Snow.	Wilson Snow.
Joseph R. Taber.	John E. Ross.
Thomas Dexter.	Ebenezer R. Hammond.
Bezald S. Hammond.	Larnet Hall.
George Purrington.	Dennis Snow.
Ebenezer Coleman.	Jesse Martin.
Warren Wicks.	Barnabas Hiller.
John Clark 2d.	William Clark.
Thomas Bassett Jr.	Lewis Russel.
Seth Mendell.	William Ellis.
Seth Cowing.	Seth Burgess.

And the following soon after subscribed to the "Uniting Compact":

Jabez Goodspeed	Job Jenney.
Benj'n F. Barstow.	John W. Hammond.

Alpheus Barrows.	Ivory Snow 2nd.
Thomas Shearman.	Lothrop Foster.
Joseph Jenney Junr.	Joseph Meigs.
James Snow 2nd.	John H. Randall.
Jabez Waterman.	Albert Bates.
John C. Cannon.	Joseph Hudson.
Ezra Burbank.	Roger W. Hammond.
Rogers L. Barstow.	Oakes R. Howes.
William T. Boyd.	Joshua T. T. Bates.
Samuel Mendell.	Ebenezer Barrows.
Charles Dexter.	Hosea Reed.

There is no record of any regular minister for these first few years. July 10, 1830, it was voted "to choose a committee to correspond with the Universalist societies in the towns of New Bedford, Fairhaven, and Wareham, in order to ascertain what they will do respecting procuring a minister to preach jointly in the above named towns and in the society in this town."

March 18, 1835, a request was made to Rev. Theodore K. Taylor to preach for the year ensuing; and Mr. Taylor's service continued until October, 1840. Dr. Robbins at first did not fancy Mr. Taylor's tactics. May 10, 1835, he said: "At five o'clock the Universalist Taylor had a meeting and preached on the same text that I have lately, Ezek. xiii. 22. Tuesday morning received a note from Dr. Southworth requesting me to attend and assist at the meeting. Yesterday I wrote to him and declined." By December, 1837, however, the two ministers were going about together visiting schools; and in 1839 Mr. Taylor delivered the address, and the Orthodox minister spoke to the children, on Fourth of July. September 27, 1840, Dr. Robbins noted: "Mr. Taylor, our Universalist, preached his farewell sermon and is going to the Cape." During his pastorate the society had

increased in numbers and in strength; and a proprietors' organization had, in 1836, erected the meeting-house now standing, which was dedicated December 21st of that year.

At that time Rogers L. Barstow was clerk of the society, and he was succeeded in 1839 by Woodbridge R. Howes. In his record it is written, — "We have had the Rev. H. W. Morse to dispense the Word of Everlasting Life since the departure of Br. Taylor." August 18, 1841, the committee were instructed to engage Rev. Henry C. Vose to preach the ensuing year, and for some years thereafter he continued to preach at Mattapoisett and at Sippican. Rev. Thomas Borden was pastor in October, 1851, and was dismissed September 18, 1853, "on account of ill health."

Apparently there was no regular minister for some years, for March 2, 1858, a committee was chosen "to procure if possible a suitable Pasture." There was a reorganization in February, 1859, and in March, Rev. Joseph Crehore became pastor. He lived with his family in the upper portion of the house of James W. Dexter. In 1861 he was succeeded by Rev. J. E. Davenport. A new uniting compact was adopted May 22, 1876; the Rev. Frank A. Bisbee having taken charge of the parish in January previous. Dr. Bisbee preached later in Philadelphia and for some years has been at Boston as editor of the *Universalist Leader*.

Rev. Charles R. Tenney came to Mattapoisett in May, 1877, was settled as a regular pastor in September, and continued here for about five years. He was born in Glover, Vermont, was a graduate of Tufts, and has held pastorates at Stoughton, and Grove Hall, Dorchester, before his present charge at Auburn, Me. During Mr. Tenney's pastorate, in the fall of 1879, an addition was made to the west end of the meeting-house to accommodate a large new organ, the gift of George Purrington, Jr.

In May, 1882, Rev. Edward F. Temple became pastor. He had rooms at Charles B. Barstow's and organized a very popular boys' club, for the study of natural science, known as the "Antelope Guild." After 1885, Rev. Benton Smith occupied the pulpit, living meanwhile in the house he had purchased from the estate of Arvin Cannon, now owned by James T. Jones. He resigned on account of ill health, March 29, 1887, and died in Mattapoisett October 16, 1896. In November, 1887, Rev. George F. Jenks began his pastorate, which continued for three years. In 1890 and 1891 various students and preachers occupied the pulpit. May 1, 1891, it was voted "to unite with the parish at Marion for one year," and this union has since continued, except that during 1895–96 Rev. William F. Potter, of New Bedford, preached regularly in the afternoon at Mattapoisett.

Rev. John Eills from Tufts served the united parishes from 1896 to 1898, when he went to Foxboro and Mansfield. Rev. Edward F. Temple, who, since his pastorate in 1885, had been in the ministry at Oneonta, N. Y., and at Trenton, N. J., again preached to these societies for a few months before his death, which occurred in Marion, January 30, 1899. In March following, Rev. Henry B. Taylor began his service, which continued until he accepted a call to St. Paul, Minn., in November, 1901. His successor, Rev. William G. Schoppe, was a native of Maine, and as a Congregationalist minister had preached at Helena, Mont., and Ashland, O. This was his first Universalist charge. He resigned September, 1904, and until June, 1907, was at Webster, Mass.

During Dr. Schoppe's pastorate Mrs. Ebenezer Jones purchased the west-district school-building, moved it to the meeting-house lot, and gave it to the Ladies' Society as a church home for this parish, to be known as the Goodspeed Memorial in memory of her parents Jabez and Melintha Goodspeed. Rev. J. Frank Rhodes, who had preached at Fairfield, Me., in Chicago, and elsewhere, was pastor, 1904–06, when after a remarkable record of thirty or forty years of continuous service in the pulpit he died at Norwell, July 29, 1907. Rev. James W. Peardon, a graduate of Tufts in 1901, now occupies the parsonage in Marion, having begun his service to these parishes in 1907.

James D. Forbes and William Loring Taber were at different times deacon of this church at Mattapoisett, and Isaiah P. Atsatt and Charles H. Nye at present hold that office. Ellis Mendell is clerk of the parish and Walter C. Dexter of the church.

The Friends began to hold meetings in Rochester about the beginning of the eighteenth century. In the records of the Dartmouth Monthly Meeting [1] there is a reference, September 17, 1705, to "Rochester or Sippican Meeting," which on July 18, 1709, signified a desire to meet weekly, and to have the meeting then kept at John Somers' thereafter at John Wings. By 1712 the Rochester Meeting desired assistance in the "settlement and security of their meeting-house land," and the adjustment of the title thereto required action extending over a long period.

[1] The writer is indebted to Dr. Edward T. Tucker, Recorder of New Bedford Meeting, and to his indices of the Dartmouth Meeting records for aid in securing the data here given.

July 15, 1717, the Dartmouth Meeting advised that "the land be made over to particular Friends, and named Savery Clifton, Stephen Wing, Nicholas Davis, and Thomas Hathaway. In February, 1796, Stephen Tripp and Ezekiel Braley were appointed to "examine and get deed," and have it run to Richard Davis, Stephen Tripp, and William Wing. Another committee was appointed in 1816 in regard to the title of the land, the house, and the burial-ground. The meeting-house referred to by a writer in the Massachusetts Historical Collections of 1815 as being "not far from the sea-shore," is the old meeting-house at Happy Alley, which by that time was becoming out of repair, and was somewhat remote from many who there worshiped.

In January, 1818, meetings having, for a while previously, been held "at a school-house in the neighborhood where Friends principally reside;" it was decided to make only temporary repairs to the meeting-house, to put in a stove for that winter; and hold meetings "on First Days at the meeting-house, and on Fourth Days at the school-house near David Hiller's, or at his house, which had been offered." June 23, 1825, it was recommended that a new meeting-house be built "near where the meeting is now held." Later, it was advised that it "be 32 x 25, with 10 foot posts, to be built on the land offered, to cost $450." April 6, 1826, the Quarterly Meeting granted liberty to make sale of the old house, and on June 28, 1827, the committee reported the acceptance of the deed for the new lot, and the completion of the new meeting-house at Aucoot. David Hiller who had been so interested in the plans for this new building died before its completion, but the committee reported that $100 towards its cost had been received from his bequest: $149.25 was received from the "old house," and the remainder of the cost, which was "rising $470," was raised by subscription.

Such was the origin of the neat "Quaker Meeting-House" standing on the height of the ridge between "Pine Islands" and "Aucoot;" and here, on First Day gathered the Hillers and the Cowens, and their neighbors. Josiah Holmes became a member of Friends from the Baptists, and his son Josiah Holmes, Jr., grew to be prominent in the meeting; and even after he became a leading minister in New Bedford he used often to drive over, sometimes alone and sometimes with Edward Dillingham, either to sit in silence, or to speak with eloquence and power of the joys of the simple faith. On the 26th of July, 1904, the little house was filled, and many stood without, by the windows, listening to the Friends from neighboring meetings who spoke as they were moved, of Captain Joshua L. Macomber, who after many years of service to this Meeting was to be laid at rest in its burial-ground.

Mattapoisett Meeting has never been large in numbers and it has been the custom of New Bedford Friends to maintain a committee for its assistance. From 1730 to 1795 the Rochester Meeting was allied to Sandwich; but in all its recent history in Mattapoisett it has been a member of Long Plain Preparative Meeting and so of the New Bedford Monthly Meeting.

Such have been the religious activities of this Massachusetts town. To one who carries in mind the picture of a Quebec village, with its single glistening spire rising far above the clustering housetops; or recalls the thatched

cottages grouped around some venerable parish church
in England; it may have seemed, in following the story
here presented, that this small town is burdened by its
heritage from the past, and that the effectiveness of its
moral forces and of its religious influences is likely to be
dissipated in the maintenance of these various organizations. However that may be, if, as was written of the
Pilgrims at Plymouth, —

> "They shook the depths of the desert gloom
> With their hymns of lofty cheer;
> Amidst the storm they sang,
> And the stars heard, and the sea!
> And the sounding aisles of the dim woods rang
> To the anthem of the free!"

these records of the inhabitants of the "plantacion of
Mattapoyst" give ample proof that their descendants
here

> "Have left unstained what there they found, —
> Freedom to worship God!"

CHAPTER XI

MARITIME AND OTHER INDUSTRIES

ONE thing may well be claimed for the people who founded old Rochester, they were industrious — like all the settlers of the old colony; hard continuous work was the portion of the men and women. In many places primeval forests covered the land and concealed the rocky soil beneath. The amount of work involved in creating the farms of the town may be appreciated if the matter of rock clearing alone is considered, which being removed from the soil were disposed of in building the fences for the farms. Hundreds of miles of these walls, laid up with infinite toil, existed in the Mattapoisett portion of Old Rochester, some of them still to be traced in places now covered by heavy growth of forest.

But farming, while it furnished the essential of food, could not, in a community where every one farmed, procure things needed which were produced elsewhere; the settlers must themselves with something besides farming crops, for the purposes of exchange.

Fortunately for them, the settlers of Rochester were not all originally farmers, many came from Kent in old England, noted for its ship-building. Among the first comers to Rochester, most were from Scituate and Marshfield, where ship-building had been pursued for thirty years, and while they began here as farmers and food

raisers, not a few were capable mechanics and skilled in
other trades.   Farming was harder work then than to-
day, and men who could do other things were anxious
to do them; then, too, the roads were rough and poor,
transportation over them was slow and laborious, while
the sea, which touched the town, offered a quicker and
easier means of communication with the outside world.
About the middle of the seventeenth century the colony
had had constructed somewhere in Buzzard's Bay a vessel
with which to trade with the Dutch in New York.

All these conditions made it natural and inevitable that
the building of vessels should be entered upon in Rochester
at an early date, and so it proved.   Boats were first built
for freight and passage, small at the start but growing
larger.

The early building was on the co-operative plan; the
vessel, when produced, was the joint property of a number
of persons who had contributed to the enterprise.   Some
had done the mechanical work of constructing, some had
furnished timber, some iron work, some sails and rigging,
and other money; the work would be going on in the
winter when the farmer-mechanic could best spare the
time.

The late Wilson Barstow, who lived to be over ninety
and died in 1891, said in a communication to the press
about thirty years ago, that "vessels were built here as
early as 1740 or 1750, sloops and small schooners.
There was no science, they were built by sight of the eye
and good judgment;" that is, there was no preliminary
drafting.   The keel would be laid and the stem and stern
affixed, then the midship frame or rib set up and fastened to the keel, and a few more ribs between the mid-

ship frame and the ends of the vessel; after that, ribbands or thin strips of boards would be run from the bow to the stern at various heights from the keel outside of the few frames so set up, and the remaining frames made to fit the lines so produced by the ribbands.   There were no models.

Queer results were sometimes produced by this method. "Mr. Hastings," says Wilson Barstow, "was put in a towering passion by being told that his starboard bow was all on one side, and one sloop was nicknamed *Bowline* because she was so crooked." The old whaler *Trident*, of 448 tons, built in 1828, was so much out of true that she carried one hundred and fifty barrels more oil on one side of the keel than the other. The sailors said she was "logy on one tack, but sailed like the mischief on the other."

In the early days of building, the sloop or schooner constructed during the winter would be sold to Nantucket or New Bedford (then Dartmouth), and the money divided among those entitled; this contributed substantially to the prosperity of the whole town. Not all the vessels so built were sold away; by the use of the same co-operative plan they were sailed for joint account. A sloop called the *Planter* was built and so run as a freighter from Rochester, before the Revolution. And at the same early date, Rochester also had whaling vessels of the small type then used. The sloop *Defiance*, which departed on a voyage in 1771, was one such Rochester vessel. Without doubt there were a number of others, but the difficulty of tracing them arises from the fact that Rochester was not then a port: by which is meant a place from which merchandise could lawfully leave or enter the country, where records of vessels sailing and arriving would be kept, and proper papers to evidence the nationality and regularity of the vessel's business supplied, to be carried on the voyage, to protect the vessel as a regular British craft. New Bedford (then Dartmouth) was not a port, and Rochester and Dartmouth vessels, therefore, had to clear from Nantucket, or Newport, which were ports. Whaling vessels generally cleared from Nantucket because that was on the way to the whaling grounds at the Straits of Belle Isle, around Newfoundland and on the Grand Banks.

Many of these Rochester whaling sloops could, perhaps, be traced in the Nantucket records from the names of their captains, and also of their agents, by one familiar with Rochester names.

As evidence that whalers were built for Nantucket before the Revolution, there is the record of the sailing from Nantucket, June, 1774, of the sloop *Rochester* owned by Nathaniel Macy of Nantucket. Her name sufficiently shows her origin. The *Rochester* on this voyage met with misfortune; she struck Great Point Rip and was lost. This calls attention to the fact that the mortality of these small whaling sloops was great. From gales, uncharted bays, lack of lighthouses and buoys, and the activity of French and Spanish privateers, fully twenty per cent of their number were lost yearly — but the business was still profitable, and so, in a way, the losses were the ship-builders' pecuniary gain.

Gideon Barstow, Sr., born in 1738, died 1826, came here about 1765 from Hanover, where he had been building ships. He was the great grandson of William, who came to Hanover, 1649, and was practically the first to build ships in the old colony. The coming of Gideon Barstow to Mattapoisett gave a new start to the industry and

SHIP NIGER
Built in Mattapoisett in 1844

ships of the largest size began to be launched from his yard.

Abner Pease was an old builder, but of a smaller class of vessels. His yard was in the extreme eastern portion of the town, just north of Pease's Point, in Aucoot.

Ebenezer Cannon, born about 1750, the great-grandfather of Dr. David H. Cannon, was another old builder. His yard was at Cannonville, so named from him.

Washington Gifford, another of the old builders, built on the Mattapoisett River. These four were all building before 1800.

Ship-building continued as an industry in Mattapoisett for nearly a century and a half, the last vessel to be built leaving the ways in 1878. It has been estimated that between four hundred and five hundred vessels, in all, were built during this century and a half. This amounted to more than one hundred thousand tons, and of a value, at the quite regular rate that prevailed of forty dollars per ton. Whether expressed in United States money or in Massachusetts pounds, shillings, and pence this would amount to $4,000,000.

There were eight yards located in the Mattapoisett section of Rochester — possibly nine, viz.:

1. On the east bank of the Mattapoisett River, just south of the herring weir.
2. At Pease's Point, in Aucoot Cove, at the extreme east section of the present town of Mattapoisett.
3. Barstow's yard, at the bend of Main and Water streets, opposite the summer home of Miss Martha H. Munro.

4. Holmes's yard, just east of Long Wharf, at the south of the post-office.
5. The Hammond yard, south of the old County House, opposite the residence of Thomas Luce.
6. A yard opposite the east end of the Mattapoisett House, south of Water Street.
7. The Meigs yard, south of Mrs. Sophia Means's house.
8. The Cannonville yard of Benjamin Barstow, located west of Miss Mary W. Barnard's summer residence; this, as a separate yard, had a brief existence.
9. The Cannonville yard of Ebenezer Cannon, north of Ship street; which Benjamin Barstow later acquired.

Vessels were built in strange places. Libni Rogers built a sloop in the yard of the premises where Edgar Silva now lives, and she was launched into the creek at Goodspeed's Island. Prince Ames built a schooner at the house north of and adjoining the Cushing Cemetery; she was taken to the shore and launched from Rogers L. Barstow's wharf; and afterwards went up into the Great Lakes. A few vessels were built at a yard near the present residence of Charles A. King, and a ferry-boat to run between New Bedford and Fairhaven was built near Mrs. Stackpole's house.

Mr. Leon M. Huggins, in the New Bedford *Standard* of January 9, 1904, contributed a very valuable and interesting sketch of Mattapoisett ship-building, from which many facts have been obtained in writing this chapter.

The Mattapoisett River yard, as already seen, was early in operation. It is quite possible a number of separate yards may have existed up and down the river, at which small vessels, wood-barges, sloops, and little schooners were built; for instance, there was the sloop *Rochester*, engaged in whaling in 1774, and the sloop *Defiance*, which sailed from there in 1771. These have already been alluded to and were doubtless built on the river, but the Revolution and the British guardships put a stop to such enterprises.

The first record we now have of a vessel built on the river was the brig *Nile*, built in 1800 by Washington Gifford. The last vessel built on the river was the brig *Brutus*, of 200 tons; she required six weeks of continuous labor to float her down the river, and doubtless satisfied her builders that the river yard was no longer practicable.

It seems quite probable that Gideon Barstow's ship-yard was located where his son and grandson afterward carried on ship-building, which, as we have said, was opposite Miss Munro's summer residence. From this yard the greatest number of Mattapoisett vessels were launched; more than 150 in all, it is said, and here the *George Lee*, 650 tons, the largest Mattapoisett vessel, was built. Two launching-ways were located on it, and building carried on there for nearly one hundred years. It is to be regretted no record now exists of the total number. As many as four ships a year are known to have been constructed there; this was the case in 1832, and in the years 1838, 1841, and 1852 three ships were launched from this yard. They were mainly of large tonnage.

Abner Pease, an old ship-builder at whose yard many of the Mattapoisett mechanics learned their trade, built, as we have seen, in Aucoot Cove. No record of his vessels exists. They were mainly small crafts, schooners, and sloops. He must have been building at the time of the Revolution: afterwards he moved to Fairhaven.

Benjamin Barstow, a relative of Gideon Barstow, had his yard at Cannonville, first, as we have seen, west of what is at present Miss Barnard's house, which then was Mr. Barstow's; afterwards he came to occupy the Ebenezer Cannon yard, just north of Ship Street.

Ebenezer Cannon, his sons and grandsons, were noted ship-builders, and many of the finest vessels were due to their skill. His grandsons, James and Arvin Cannon, ran the Cannonville yard for some years. Arvin was at one time master builder in Meigs & Pratt's yard. Watson Cannon, another grandson of Ebenezer, held the same position in Wilson Barstow's yard. No traces of the vessels built by Ebenezer Cannon exist, but they were numerous.

Benjamin Barstow in 1832 built the first live-oak ship in town, the *William C. Nye*, 389 tons. He relinquished his yard in his latter days to his two sons, Nathan H. and Henry. This yard was the first of the prominent yards to go out of business.

Loring Meigs and David Pratt, his brother-in-law, had a yard on what are now the premises of Mrs. Sophia Means, at the foot of Mechanic Street; Arvin Cannon, as already stated, being at one time the master builder. The last vessel built in that yard was launched about 1860.

There was also a yard in front of the easterly end of the Mattapoisett House. This was carried on by the Cannons for a number of years.

Farther to the west, and just beyond Thomas Luce's barn, Leonard Hammond had a yard. The last ship

THE OLD BARSTOW HOUSE, WATER STREET, MATTAPOISETT
Wilson Barstow in the foreground

built from this yard was the *Clara Bell*, in 1852, by George Crandall, of Newport.

Adjoining Hammond's yard on the west came the Holmes ship-yard, established about 1800 by Josiah Holmes, Sr. This was next in importance to the Gideon Barstow yard. Mr. Holmes, Sr., learned his trade of Abner Pease. He carried on ship-building alone for about forty years; then with his son Josiah, and afterwards, about 1846, he relinquished the business to his two sons, Josiah and Jonathan H. Holmes (the latter the father of the late Reuben F. Holmes, and of Judge Lemuel LeB. Holmes). The sons carried on the business as the firm of Josiah Holmes, Jr., and Brother, until 1868; the Civil War interrupting for some six years, during which there was no building.

After 1868 Jonathan H. Holmes built a schooner and two whale-ships. The last Mattapoisett vessel, the *Wanderer*, was built at this yard in 1878. Thus closed the story of one of the most famous ship-building ports of the country.

In the busiest period two hundred and seventy-five workmen came up from the yards and workshops, when the six o'clock bell rang at the foot of Mechanic Street; the little bell which afterward summoned the scholars from the East District schoolhouse.

The panic of 1857, which ruined the business men of the village, the Civil War which disarranged everything, and finally, and most potent of all, the discovery of petroleum in Pennsylvania, sounded the knell of the whale fishery, and left the little village stranded and without an industry.

But a splendid business this building of ships had been! Each yard striving to produce the best ship, and under this competition turning out the finest vessels of their class to be found in the world. The workmen were skilled and intelligent; their work was continuous. The young men were not obliged to seek employment elsewhere, home offered better than most localities. Under these conditions the village enjoyed, for a century, a continually increasing prosperity. Its social condition was the typical and almost ideal one that existed so generally in this Commonwealth up to half a century ago and then began to disappear. There were no large fortunes and consequently no caste to cause envy and disquiet. There was social equality and a sturdiness of character which such conditions produce. It was fitting that the prominent device on the seal of Mattapoisett should be a vessel on the stocks.

So far as possible with the aid of Mr. Huggins's article in the *Standard* and Starbuck's "American Whale Fishery," we have made up the following list of vessels built in Mattapoisett, and their builders. It comprises some 138 vessels. A study of this list satisfies one that probably not a third of the vessels have been obtained. Mattapoisett built whalers for Nantucket, New Bedford, for towns in Bristol County, Rhode Island and Connecticut; she built coasters, merchantmen, steamers, and a variety of craft. The list, therefore, must only be regarded as a partial one. It shows the date of building, name of vessel, rig, tonnage, and in many cases the builder, written in this order:

1800. *Nile*, brig, Washington Gifford.
1802. *John Jay*, ship.
1811. *President*, ship, 293 tons.
1812. *John Adams*, ship, 296 tons.
1819. *Alexander Barclay*, ship, 301 tons.

1820. *Ontario*, ship, 354 tons; *Cicero*, ship, 252 tons, B. Barstow & Josiah Holmes, Sr.

1821. *Phenix*, ship, 323 tons; *Spartan*, ship, 333 tons.

1823. *Rose*, ship, 350 tons; *Congress*, ship, 239 tons.

1826. *Omega*, brig, 363 tons; *Frances*, ship, 347 tons. G. Barstow & Son; *Swift*, brig, 456 tons.

1827. *Aurora*, ship, 340 tons, W. Barstow; *Zone*, schooner, 365 tons.

1828. *Meridian*, ship, 381 tons.

1829. *Rambler*, ship, 318 tons: *Richard Mitchell*, ship, 386 tons, W. Barstow.

1830. *Mary Anne*, ship, 240 tons, W. Barstow; *Clarkson*, ship, 380 tons, W. Barstow.

1831. *Mary Mitchell*, ship, 369 tons.

1832. *Catharine*, ship, 384 tons, W. Barstow; *Mt. Vernon*, ship, 384 tons, Holmes; *Hobomok*, ship, 412 tons; *Wm. C. Nye*, ship, 389 tons, B. Barstow & Co.; *Mariner*, ship, 349 tons, W. Barstow; *Young Eagle*, ship, 377 tons, W. Barstow; *Gideon Barstow*, ship, 379 tons, W. Barstow.

1833. *Levi Starbuck*, ship, 376 tons, Holmes; *Ohio*, ship, 381 tons; *Champion*, ship, 390 tons, W. Barstow.

1834. *Alfa*, ship, 345 tons, Cannon; *Christopher Mitchell*, ship, 387 tons, Holmes; *Elizabeth Mitchell*, ship, 381 tons, Holmes.

1835. *Gold Hunter*, brig, 202 tons; *Splendid*, ship, 392 tons; *Nile*, ship, 321 tons, B. Barstow.

1836. *Catawba*, ship, 335 tons, Cannon; *Sarah*, ship, 370 tons, Meigs; *Caduceus*, brig, 109 tons, W. Barstow; *Henry*, ship, 346 tons, Holmes; *Annawan*, brig, 148 tons, Holmes; *Young Phœnix*, ship, 377 tons, Holmes; *Sarah*, brig, 171 tons, Meigs.

1837. *Sarah*, bark, 179 tons; *LeBaron*, brig, 170 tons,

W. Barstow; *LaGrange*, bark, 170 tons, W. Barstow; *James Loper*, ship, 348 tons, Holmes.

1838. *Napoleon*, ship, 360 tons, W. Barstow; *Daniel Webster*, ship, 336 tons, W. Barstow; *Solon*, brig, 129 tons, Holmes; *Young Hero*, ship, 339 tons, W. Barstow; *Willis*, bark, 164 tons, E. Cannon.

1839. *Henry Clay*, ship, 385 tons, Holmes; *Richard Henry*, bark, 173 tons, W. Barstow; *Chase*, brig, 153 tons, W. Barstow; *Volant*, bark, 210 tons, Holmes.

1841. *Edward Cary*, ship, 353 tons, W. Barstow; *Harrison*, ship, 371 tons, W. Barstow; *Elizabeth Starbuck*, ship, 388 tons, Holmes; *Montecello*, ship, 358 tons, W. Barstow; *Elizabeth*, bark, 219 tons; *Potomac*, ship, 356 tons, Holmes; *Massachusetts*, ship, 360 tons, Holmes; *Narragansett*, ship, 398 tons, Holmes; *Annawan*, brig, 159 tons, B. Barstow.

1842. *Callao*, ship, 324 tons, Meigs; *James*, ship, 321 tons, Holmes; *Joseph Meigs*, ship, 338 tons, Meigs.

1843. *Empire*, ship, 403 tons, Holmes.

1844. *Niger*, ship, 437 tons, Holmes; *Isaac Walton*, ship, 440 tons, W. Barstow; *Union*, bark, 124 tons, Holmes.

1845. *Cachelot*, ship, 230 tons, W. Barstow.

1846. *Dunbarton*, bark, 199 tons, W. Barstow.

1847. *Cleone*, ship, 373 tons, B. Barstow; *Platina*, bark, 266 tons; *Osceola II*, bark, 197 tons, Holmes.

1848. *Nauticon*, ship, 372 tons, Holmes.

1849. *Mattapoisett*, brig, 150 tons, Meigs; *President*, bark, 180 tons.

1850. *Ontario*, ship, 368 tons, Holmes; *Arctic*, ship, 431 tons, W. Barstow.

1851. *Elisha Dunbar*, bark, 257 tons, Holmes; *Europa*, ship, 380 tons, W. Barstow; *Northern Light*, ship, 513 tons,

W. Barstow; *Sea Queen*, bark, 195 tons, Holmes; *Sea Fox*, bark, 166 tons; *R. L. Barstow*, bark, 208 tons, Hammond; *Alice Mandell*, ship, 425 tons, Holmes.

1852. *Daniel Wood*, ship, 345 tons, Holmes; *Gay Head*, ship, 389 tons, W. Barstow; *John A. Parker*, bark, 342 tons, W. Barstow; *Polar Star*, ship, 475 tons, Holmes; *Clara Belle*, bark, 295 tons, Hammond; *Vigilant*, bark, 282 tons, Holmes; *Daniel Flanders*; *Gazelle*, ship, W. Barstow; *Wm. Upham*; *James Arnold*, ship, 393 tons, B. Barstow.

1853. *Lapwing*, ship, 432 tons; *Petrel*, ship, 350 tons, Holmes; *Reindeer*, ship, 450 tons, Holmes; *Siren Queen*, ship, 461 tons, Meigs.

1854. *Matthew Luce*, bark, 410 tons, Holmes; *Onward*, ship, 461 tons, Holmes.

1855. *Plover*, ship, 330 tons, Holmes.

1856. *Contest*, ship, 441 tons, W. Barstow; *Eliza*, bark, 360 tons, Meigs; *Huntress*, bark, 383 tons, Holmes; *Merlin*, bark, 348 tons, Holmes; *Brewster*, ship, 225 tons, Holmes; *Sunbeam*, bark, 360 tons, Holmes; *Thomas Pope*, ship, 327 tons, W. Barstow; *South Seaman*, ship, 497 tons, Meigs; *Sea Ranger*, bark, 370 tons, Holmes.

1858. *Two Brothers*, bark, 288 tons, N. H. & H. Barstow.

1859. *Ocean Rover*, of Nantucket, ship, 314 tons, Holmes.

1860. *Ocean Rover*, of Mattapoisett, bark, 417 tons, Holmes.

1865. *Active*, tugboat, Holmes.

1867. *Alaska*, bark, 346 tons, Holmes.

1868. *Concordia*, bark, Holmes.

1869. *Laura Robinson*, schooner, Holmes.

1877. *Gay Head*, bark, Holmes.

1878. *Wanderer*, bark, Holmes.

Other vessels known to have been built in Mattapoisett, but in what year is not known, are:

George C. Gibbs, W. Barstow; *Brutus*, brig, 200 tons, built on Herring River; *George Lee*, ship, 650 tons, W. Barstow; *Watkins*, bark, W. Barstow; *Lamartine*, schooner, W. Barstow; *Ormus*, brig, B. Barstow; *Sarah*, schooner, B. Barstow; *Laura Jane*, schooner, Holmes; *John Milton*, ship, W. Barstow; *Lydia*, ship, Meigs; *Eliza*, schooner, N. H. Barstow; *Elizabeth*, bark, 219 tons, Cannon; *Polly Hall*, Cannon; *Almira*.

Mattapoisett built whalers for other ports, but she also built for herself and carried on a considerable whaling business for nearly a century. As early as 1771 we find that the sloop *Defiance*, hailing from Rochester, sailed on a whaling voyage, and between that date and 1865, when the *Willis*, the last whaler, was sold, some fifty different vessels sailed from the port. It does not seem to have been a prosperous business for the village, nor for Marion, which had about half as many whalers. The voyages were generally short, and three hundred or four hundred barrels were thought to be good catches. Perhaps they were outfitted too well; the supplies may have cost more because they were to be eaten by the men and boys of the village, of whom the crews were largely composed, and who would have to be faced by the owners when the voyage was ended. The voyages were alluded to by the New Bedford and Nantucket people as "Plum Pudding Voyages;" whether this was because of their lavish food supplies or for some other reason is uncertain.

The list of these whaling vessels is likewise imperfect.

The year when each vessel first appears is given, together with her name and who were first her agents, the agents afterwards changed in most instances.

1771. Sloop *Defiance.*

1816. *Sally*, a schooner.

1820. *Orion*, a brig.

1822. *Pocohontas*, a brig.

1826. *Magnolia*, schooner, 90 tons.

1827. *Sophronia*, schooner.

1830. *Franklin*, bark, 250 tons, G. Barstow & Son, Agents; *Lexington*, schooner.

1831. *Dryade*, bark, 263 tons, G. Barstow & Son, Agents; *Laurel*, schooner, G. Barstow & Son, Agents.

1832. *Gideon Barstow*, ship, 379 tons, G. Barstow & Son, Agents.

1833. *Shylock*, ship, 277 tons.

1836. *Annawan*, brig, 148 tons, G. Barstow & Son, Agents; *Caduceus*, brig, 109 tons, Joseph Meigs, Agent; *Mattapoisett*, brig, 150 tons, G. Barstow & Son, Agents; *Sarah*, brig, 171 tons, G. Barstow & Son, Agents; *Orion*, brig, 99 tons, Elijah Willis, Agent.

1837. *Lagrange*, brig, 170 tons, Elijah Willis, Agent; *LeBaron*, brig, 170 tons, G. Barstow & Son, Agents.

1839. *Chase*, brig, 153 tons, G. Barstow & Son, Agents; *Richard Henry*, bark, 173 tons, G. Barstow & Son, Agents; *Willis*, brig, 164 tons, R. L. Barstow, Agent.

1841. *Edward*, brig, 133 tons, Wilson Barstow, Agent; *Elizabeth*, bark, 219 tons, R. L. Barstow, Agent.

1842. *Joseph Meigs*, ship, 338 tons, Joseph Meigs, Agent.

1845. *Cachelot*, ship, 230 tons, Wilson Barstow, Agent.

1846. *Dunbarton*, bark, 169 tons, Wilson Barstow, Agent. *Sarah*, ship, 370 tons, Joseph Meigs, Agent.

1847. *Helen*, brig, 120 tons, R. L. Barstow, Agent.

1850. *Samuel & Thomas*, bark, 191 tons, R. L. Barstow, Agent; *America*, brig, 148 tons, R. L. Barstow, Agent.

1851. *R. L. Barstow*, bark, 208 tons, R. L. Barstow, Agent; *Massasoit*, bark, 206 tons, Caleb King, Jr., Agent; *Oscar*, bark, 369 tons, S. K. Eaton, Agent; *Sun*, bark, 183 tons, R. L. Barstow, Agent.

1852. *Clara Bell*, bark, 295 tons, R. L. Barstow, Agent; *Excellent*, brig, 70 tons, John T. Atsatt, Agent.

1853. *March*, brig, 89 tons, R. L. Barstow, Agent.

1856. *Amelia*, brig, 127 tons, L. Meigs & Co., Agents; *Elvira*, brig, 131 tons, L. Meigs & Co., Agents; *Palmyra*, schooner, 100 tons, L. Meigs & Co., Agents.

1857. *Brewster*, ship, 225 tons, J. Holmes, Jr. & Bro., Agents; *Union*, bark, 124 tons, R. L. Barstow, Agent.

1859. *Ocean Rover*, ship, 314 tons, J. Holmes, Jr. & Bro., Agents.

Agents of Whaling Vessels.

Gideon Barstow, probably before 1800, and down to 1830; Gideon Barstow & Son (Wilson Barstow), 1830–1844; Wilson Barstow, 1841–1850; Elijah Willis, 1836–1847; Rogers L. Barstow, 1839–1860; Seth Freeman, 1841–1854; Leonard Hammond, 1841–1844; Samuel Sturtevant, Jr., 1847–1849; Loring Meigs, 1851–1860; John T. Atsatt, 1852–1854; Atsatt & Sturtevant, 1854–1858; Josiah Holmes, Jr., 1854–; Josiah Holmes, Jr. & Brother, 1854–1862; Solomon K. Eaton, 1851–1854; Caleb King, Jr.,

BARK SUNBEAM
Built in Mattapoisett in 1856

1852–1854; N. H. Barstow, 1861–1863; J. R. & W. L. Taber, 1861–1864.

But if the owners of Mattapoisett whalers did not prosper, the master, officers, and crew did; many acquired a competency in the business, and Mattapoisett whalemen were quite famous. To Archelus Hammond, born 1759, died 1830, a noted whaleman, belongs the credit of striking the first whale ever struck in the Pacific, and of introducing whaling into that ocean.[1] Mattapoisett whaling masters were recognized as good business managers of voyages, as navigators, and skilful whalemen.

An excellent account of the life on one of these vessels has been written in "On Board a Whaler," by Thomas West Hammond, M.D., a native of Mattapoisett, now a member of the bar in Tacoma, Washington.

The following extracts show what Dr. Robbins noted in his diary in regard to shipping while he was in Mattapoisett:

1831

Oct. 22. A large fine ship was launched here this morning. 360 ton. It did not go off well.

1832

June 28. Toward evening two fine ships were launched here, and a third was attempted and failed.

June 29. At evening the other large ship was launched.

Aug. 11. Went on board the new ship Gideon Barstow, which is to sail soon.

Sept. 23. A ship was launched here in the evening, unnecessarily I think, and a good deal of work done during the day.

Oct. 15. Looked at a fine new ship of live-oak, built in four months.

Oct. 22. The schooner Laurel, anxiously expected came in with 230 barrels of sperm oil.

[1] Ship-building on North River, Briggs, page 167.

Oct. 24. In the morning attended the launch of a fine live-oak ship, over 400 tons. It did not go clear.

1833

Feb. 11. We have a painful account that the captain and a boat's crew of a whaleship belong here is lost.

Mar. 26. Two promising young men of this place have been lost at sea from a whaleship. Visited one of the families.

May 2. Looked at a new ship, which was well launched toward evening.

May 23. Attended the launching of the finest ship, probably, that ever was built here. It did not float actively.

June 18. Another ship was launched here successfully. All whalers.

Nov. 13. A schooner belonging here came in from whaling, having made a very profitable voyage.

1834

May 20. Saw the launch of a fine ship — the first from Mr. Cannon's new yard. It went very well.

May 21. Saw another ship launched in fine state from Mr. Cannon's yard.

June 30. Rode to Bedford and procured some tracts to give to the ship Dryad.

1835

Sept. 22. Attended the launching of a good ship.

Sept. 25. Yesterday saw a fine ship launched here.

Oct. 23. A ship launched in the morning.

Dec. 9. The ship G. Barstow, mostly owned here, came into the harbor, after a voyage to the Pacific of more than three years, with a moderate cargo of 2100 bbls. They had hoped for 3000. The first Cape Horn ship loaded that has entered this harbor.

1836

Apr. 4. A new brig owned here was launched Saturday evening.

May 30. Attended the launching of a ship.

1837

Apr. 21. At evening saw the launching of a ship.

May 22. A good ship was launched here Saturday evening.

Sept. 24. Afternoon preached the sermon on Ps. XCVII: 1, 2, on the loss of the brig Cadmeus (Caduceus?) which sailed from here Apr. 28, 1836, and was spoken at sea, bound home, Nov. 28, and had not been heard of since. Their crew were fifteen; eleven from this town.

1838

Mar. 26. A fine ship was launched here this morning.
July 10. A ship was launched here this morning.

1839

Apr. 4. News came that the brig Annawan of this place, coming home with a valuable cargo, was wrecked near Bermuda, and the men are reported missing. Several families are much distressed.

Apr. 15. Painful news received here this morning from the brig Annawan, wrecked. Of 21 of the crew, 14, including the captain and mates, are lost; 7 are saved, 7 from this place; 4 lost. The cargo worth about $20,000.

Apr. 26. Saw a seaman Chase, who was wrecked in the Annawan. His story is very affecting. Four promising youths of this place were lost.

May 10. A whale brig came in here that has done well.
May 17. Yesterday a whale brig came in with 600 barrels of sperm oil.

June 12. Wrote a letter to Capt. Samuel Mitchell of Bangor, who took our seamen from the late wreck.

Aug. 9. A ship from this place with 2000 barrels of oil has been lost in the Indian Ocean; men saved. A severe loss.

Aug. 21. A whale brig sailed from here.
Aug. 27. A fine ship was launched here this morning.

Oct. 7. It is supposed we have lost a schooner from this place; a good vessel with its crew, on their passage from Philadelphia to Boston, in the disastrous storm of Aug. 30.

Nov. 7. A whale brig came in here last night after a very prosperous voyage.

1840

July 27. We had a very fine launch of a good ship.
Sept. 15. A bark whaler sailed from here. Gave bibles and tracts.
Oct. 2. Whale brig sailed.
Oct. 12. In the morning a fine new ship went off with fine launch.
Oct. 13. Whale brig sailed.
Oct. 28. Whale brig came in from a good voyage.

1841

Apr. 6. A whale brig sailed this morning. One went last week.

Apr. 11. A whale brig sailed yesterday.

May 31. Five ships and a brig on the stocks.

June 11. There are six ships and one brig on the stocks in our ship yards.

June 15. Mr. Crosby and his company launched a fine brig.

June 19. Last evening a fine ship was launched here. Another large whale ship was launched this evening.

July 8. A new whale brig sailed from here this morning.

Aug. 16. Two fine ships were launched within a few minutes of each other.

Sept. 16. Two fine ships were launched here this morning.

Dec. 22. A whale brig sailed from here this morning.

1842

Apr. 17. A whale brig came in this morning with a good cargo, but oil is very low and has a dull sale.

Aug. 6. Saw the launch of a ship.

Aug. 13. A barque ship sailed from here for whaling.

Sept. 6. Two good ships were launched here this morning near together. A whale brig came in.

Oct. 8. The fine new ship Jos. Meigs sailed from here this morning.

Oct. 12. A whale brig came in.

Nov. 25. A whale brig came in.

1843

Apr. 28. Two whale brigs sailed from here this morning.

June 10. A ship of 400 tons was launched here.

Oct. 19. A whale brig sailed from here.

1844

Apr. 4. A whale brig came in.

May 30. A whale brig came in.

May 31. Two large ships were launched at our yards within a few minutes of each other.

June 17. A whale brig sailed from here.

Aug. 24. A fine live oak ship was launched here yesterday, built it twelve weeks.

Sept. 3. A whale brig, gone three months and twenty-three days, came in with 450 barrels, sperm oil. A great voyage.

Early in the nineteenth century, salt-making became an important industry in the shore villages of Rochester.

It attained a higher development at Sippican than Matta-poisett; yet the industry was largely developed in the latter village also, and is a part of the history of Rochester town. Abraham Holmes writing in 1821, says:

"The principal manufacture of this town is salt. This business is carried on on an extensive scale and it is believed that more salt is manufactured in this town than in any other town in the Commonwealth, and it is the most productive of any business here practised."

During the Revolution salt had been in great demand, and some was obtained along the Buzzards Bay shores by the process of boiling sea-water. In 1806 a more important salt industry was established in Rochester as well as in neighboring towns. The direct occasion of this was the Embargo Act, shutting out the salt from the West Indies, which had been the chief source of supply.

The process used was one of simple evaporation, but required considerable machinery and equipment. The water was pumped from the sea by windmills, and carried through pipes (or tunneled logs) to shallow vats twelve or fifteen feet square, from which the water was evaporated by sun exposure, being carried from vat to vat at different stages of the process. There was a salt-house to receive the completed product, and at night and in rainy weather, great covers (or roofs), moved by heavy "crane-beams," were placed over the vats to protect the drying salt. One "crane" of salt-works usually included four of these evaporating vats.

People used to come in their wagons to the salt-works to purchase their home supply of salt, and much was also exported. It is said that in the days of the early boiling process, one enterprising salt-maker, made each year an ox-wagon-load of salt which he carried to Vermont. There he sold his oxen, returning with a fresh yoke of animals and a return freight of butter and cheese for the home market.

In the days of the sun-evaporating process, much larger quantities were obtained. At the height of this industry twenty thousand bushels of salt were sometimes produced in the town during a single year.

The largest salt-works of Sippican were those of Ebenezer Holmes in the lower village near Nye's wharf, below the Sippican House. He lived to be a very old man, and continued to look after his salt-making through his closing years. There were many other salt-works, at Great Neck, Little Neck, along the shore of the upper village, and between the two villages. It is said that salt-works were "all over Sippican" and the windmills of these salt-works were a distinctive feature of the village landscape. The works of Captain Hammett were at the upper village; the Delano salt-works were at several localities, at one of which medicinal salts were manufactured.

In Mattapoisett also, salt-works were carried on, at Aucoot Cove, at Goodspeed's Island, in a large field in the rear of the Baptist Church, and in other places. The last salt-maker was Isaac Hiller, who continued in this industry at Aucoot Cove until about the time of the Civil War.

About 1812 the First Parish of Rochester, having attempted, without great success, to raise the minister's salary by voluntary subscription instead of by taxation, a movement was started to obtain a fund for church support by carrying on some parish salt-works. In 1815 six cranes of salt-works were built at Briggs's Neck, and others were added afterwards at different points on Sippican harbor. They did not prove financially profitable, however, and about 1838 these parish salt-works were sold.

The September gale of 1815 was very damaging to the salt industry, not only spoiling the salt already made, but sweeping away the works themselves, which however, were afterwards rebuilt.

CHAPTER XII

WHEN the news arrived of the firing on Fort Sumter, April 13, 1861, the same patriotic feeling that surged up and down through all the Northern States filled the breasts of our people, and the records of the town for the years 1861–65 show that Mattapoisett was not behind in its realization of the duty it owed to our common country.

This being a seaport town, and the whaling industry being at its height, it was natural that the Navy should claim a large number of enlistments among the seafaring men, as was evidenced by the fact that out of one hundred and fifty men apportioned as our quota, sixty-five entered the Navy.

During the year 1861 the town in its corporate capacity took no action in relation to the war, but during the year thirty-nine men entered the Army and Navy. On July 18, 1862, however, the town voted to pay a bounty of one hundred dollars to each volunteer, to the number of twenty, "who shall enlist within the next sixty days for three years or the war." The treasurer, with the consent of the selectmen, was authorized to borrow money to pay the same; the interest and ten per cent of the capital to be paid annually until the debt should be discharged.

August 7, 1862: Voted to increase the bounty for three

years' volunteers, fifty dollars, and fifty dollars additional to those who would enlist before the 15th of the month. August 30, 1862, voted to pay a bounty of one hundred and twenty-five dollars to each volunteer for nine months' service, to fill the quota of the town. December 15, 1862: Voted to pay a bounty of one hundred and fifty dollars to volunteers who enlist for three years and are credited to the quota of the town.

In that year Thomas Nelson was appointed special recruiting agent for the town, and one of his grandsons has in his possession a poster which he, as agent, then put out, calling for volunteers.

During 1863–64 the authorities continued to recruit men and pay bounties, but no special action appears to have been taken by the town in its corporate capacity except to appropriate money when necessary.

In 1865, in the warrant for the annual town meeting in April, was an article "to see if the town will authorize the selectmen to borrow money to pay bounties to keep the quota of the town filled." During the proceedings of the meeting information was received from the South, and the clerk noted the fact on the town record in these words, written in large letters: "NEWS of THE CAPTURE OF RICHMOND RECEIVED." In consequence of which no appropriation was made to pay bounties to volunteers, for the war was practically ended.

Schouler, in his "Massachusetts in the Rebellion," says that "Mattapoisett furnished one hundred and fifty men for the military service, which was a surplus of eight over and above all demands." A careful count on the records shows that this town furnished one hundred and eighty men for the Army and Navy. The whole amount of money appropriated and expended by the town on account of the war was $7110.

The following are the names of the men from Mattapoisett who gave up their lives in the great struggle:

EDWARD F. BARLOW, Co. E., 18th Mass. Reg., died September 3, 1864, while a prisoner at Andersonville prison, Georgia.

JOHN T. BARSTOW, Co. K., 1st Mass. Reg., died at Ascension Hospital, Washington, D. C., December 20, 1862.

JOHN BATES, U.S.N., was killed March 22, 1862, at Mosquito Inlet, Fla., while on a boat expedition.

Acting Master JOHN S. DENNIS, U.S.N., died February 27, 1865, at New Madrid, Mo., while in command of U.S.S. *Huntress*.

WILLIAM C. DEXTER, Co. E., 58th Mass. Reg., died in hospital at Fortress Monroe, August 4, 1864.

FRANKLIN A. LOBRE, Co. I., 3d Mass. Reg., was taken prisoner December 10, 1862, at Plymouth, N. C., and died at Petersburg, Va., January 19, 1863.

ELIJAH W. RANDALL, U.S.N., died on board U.S.S. *Housatonic*, April 19, 1863.

EDWARD F. SNOW, Co. D., 18th Mass. Reg., died at home, September 6, 1864, only four days after his discharge from the service.

GEORGE D. SNOW, Co. D., 18th Mass. Reg., was killed in action at Fredericksburg, Va., December 13, 1862.

WILLIAM HENRY TABER, Co. C., 17th Penn. Cavalry, died March 18, 1862, in hospital at Mumfordsville, Ky.

CHARLES H. TINKHAM, Co. D., 3d Mass. Reg., died at Newbern, N. C., November 30, 1862.

EBENEZER TRIPP, Co. G., 20th Mass. Reg., was killed in action at Ball's Bluff, Va., October 24, 1861.

GEORGE W. WILCOX, Co. D., 18th Mass. Reg., died August 23, 1862, in hospital at Philadelphia.

WILLIAM S. WILCOX, 5th Batt. Lt. Art., died November 28, 1862, in hospital at Falmouth, Va.

The names of Amittai B. Hammond, Joseph E. Smith, Jarvis Ellis, Nathan H. Barstow, Thomas P. Hammond, Josiah Holmes, Jr., Wilson Barstow, and Franklin Cross should ever be held in grateful remembrance by the people of Mattapoisett, for it was these men who, as selectmen during the years 1861–65, piloted the town through the serious turmoil of war.

The name of Thomas Nelson should also be gratefully remembered, for it was he, as Town Clerk, through the same years, who kept a most careful record of the service of every man who enlisted from the town, and as recruiting agent, and in service to the families of men at the front, he in many ways endeared himself to the people.

Too much credit also cannot be awarded to the women of the town for their zeal in working faithfully for the soldiers and sailors, while in the field, in the hospital, or on board the ships of the Navy. There are no records to show how much was thus done, but if there were, Mattapoisett, we are sure, would be proud of their service there shown.

During the Civil War a number of vessels from these ports were taken by Confederate cruisers. One of these was the bark *Ocean Rover*, the last whaler built and fitted in Mattapoisett before the war. She carried four Mattapoisett men, James M. Clark, Captain; William Harlow, second mate; Marshall Keith, fourth mate; and Charles B.

Hammond, boat steerer; of whom Mr. Hammond is the only survivor. On the 8th of September, 1862, while lying in almost a dead calm about fifteen miles off the island of Flores, the *Ocean Rover* was overtaken by the Confederate cruiser *Alabama*. Seeing that capture was inevitable, Captain Clark ordered the stars and stripes set and helpless in the calm summer evening the whaler awaited her fate. The officers and crew received very courteous treatment from the Confederates. Having signed the parole of honor, they were sent with their personal effects to Ponta Delgada, Flores, and on the following day the *Ocean Rover* was burned. Another was the *Altamaha*, from Marion, commanded by Captain Gray, with Capt. Judah Hathaway, of Rochester, as mate and part owner, and James R. Blankinship, of Mattapoisett, second mate. The *Altamaha* was captured by the *Alabama* and burned, and the officers and men sent to Fayal. In later years the owners and crews of these vessels gained some restitution in the form of "Alabama Claims."

It took Mattapoisett a number of years to recover from the financial drain of this four years' war, chiefly on account of the decline of the ship-building and whaling industries, the proceeds of which had been its mainstay. Conditions to-day are very different than they were in 1861–65, but if called upon again, as in those years, we feel sure that this town would respond as generously as before.

October 22, 1904, a fine monument, as a memorial to the men of Mattapoisett who gave their lives in the service of their country, was appropriately dedicated by visiting posts of the G.A.R., Naval Veterans, Sons of Veterans,

BARSTOW STREET, MATTAPOISETT

Showing Monument and Library Building

and the school children. This monument was the gift
of George Purrington, Jr., and stands on a lot on Barstow
Street purchased with a special fund which had been held
by the town for several years.

There is in town an organization known as the Army
and Navy Memorial Association, composed of veterans
and their wives, and several others, formed for the purpose of perpetuating the proper observance of Memorial
Day.

List of men who served in the Civil War from Mattapoisett:

Ames, Loring T.

Bannon, Alexander, Co. K., 58th Mass. Reg.

Barlow, Edward F., Co. E., 18th Mass. Reg.

Barlow, Gideon B., Co. B., 3d Reg. H.A.

Barrows, Alpheus, Co. I., 3d Mass. Reg., also Co. F.,
53d Mass. H.A.

Barrows, Andrew J., Co. F., 3d Mass. H.A.

Barrows, George, Co. L., 3d Mass. Reg.

Barstow, Elijah W., 1st Lieut., Co. —, 3d Mass. H.A.,
also 1st Lieut., Co. H., 5th U.S. Art.

Barstow, John T., Co. K., 1st Mass. Reg.

Barstow, Josiah M., U.S.N.

Barstow, Solomon, Master's Mate, U.S.N.

Barstow, Wilson, Jr., 37th Reg. New York Vols., Ensign
Capt., Lt. Col., Col., and Brevet Brig. Gen.

Barstow, Zaccheus M., Co. D., 23d Mass. Reg.

Bates, John, U.S.N.

Bolles, Charles E., U.S.N.

Bourne, Edmund L., Acting Ensign, U.S.N.

Bourne, George W., Acting Master, U.S.N.

Bowman, Ebenezer H., U.S.N.
Buck, Charles H., Acting Ensign, U.S.N.
Burbank, Charles M., Co. D., 18th Mass. Reg.
Butts, Joseph A., Co. I., 3d Mass. Reg.

Cannon, Fred J., Co. B., 3d Mass. Reg. H.A.
Cannon, Thomes J., Acting Ensign, U.S.N.
Carpenter, Wright, Co. D., 23d Mass. Reg.
Carr, John P., Acting Master, U.S.N.
Caswell, Elbridge G., Master's Mate, U.S.N.
Clark, Elijah W., Acting Ensign, U.S.N.
Clark, Freeman, Co. E., 18th Mass. Reg.
Covert, Eugene S., Co. E., 18th Mass. Reg.
Cowell, William G., Acting Ensign, U.S.A.
Crosby, E. Frank, Co. I., 3d Mass. Reg.
Crosby, William K., Co. C., 8th Vermont Reg., also
    1st Lieut., 1st Louisiana Reg.
Cushing, Edward L., U.S.N.

Davis, Lemuel LeB., U.S.N.
Davis, Thomas R., U.S.N.
Dennis, John, S., Acting Master, U.S.N.
Dexter, Albert M., Co. I., 3d Mass. Reg.
Dexter, Benjamin 2d, U.S.N.
Dexter, Elisha L., Co. I., 3d Mass. Reg.
Dexter, Francis E., U.S.N.
Dexter, George, Co. K., 8th California Reg.
Dexter, George H., Master's Mate, U.S.N.
Dexter, Horace, U.S.N.
Dexter, James W., Co. I., 3d Mass. Reg.
Dexter, Thomas D., Co. E., 3d Mass. Reg.
Dexter, William C., Co. E., 58th Mass. Reg.

Eaton, Solomon K., 1st Lieut., Co. I., 3d Mass. Reg.

Ellis, Albert, U.S.N., also Co. F., 3d Reg. Mass. H.A.

Ellis, Daniel S., Co. I., 3d Mass. Reg., also 23d Unattached Co., Mass. Vols.

Gallon, James, Co. E., 18th Mass. Reg.

Gifford, Charles P., U.S.N.

Gifford, Jesse C., Co. D., 18th Mass. Reg.

Gifford, John L., Acting Vol. Lieut., U.S.N.

Gifford, Robinson, U.S.N.

Gifford, William C., Co. I., 3d Mass. Reg., also Co. F., 3d Mass. Reg. H.A.

Goodspeed, Oliver J., Co. B., 3d Mass. Reg. H.A., also U.S.N.

Gorham, Albert H., U.S.N.

Graham, William H., Musician, 9th Mass. Reg.

Hammond, B. Frank, 23d Unattached Co. Mass. Vols.

Hammond, George F., Acting Master, U.S.N.

Hammond, James A., 23d Unattached Co. Mass. Vols.

Hammond, John W., Co. I., 3d Mass. Reg.

Hammond, Larnet H., Co. D., 18th Mass. Reg.

Hammond, Roland, Co. I., 3d Mass. Reg.

Harris, William Jr., Co. B., 15th New Hampshire Reg.

Hayden, Benjamin F., Co. D., 18th Mass. Vols.

Hayden, Charles H., Co. C., 29th Mass. Reg.

Hiller, Alpheus B., Co. D., 18th Mass. Reg., also Co. E., 32d Mass. Reg.

Hiller, Ebenezer R., Co. I., 3d Mass. Reg.

Holmes, Heman G., Co. I., 3d Mass. Reg., also Master's Mate, U.S.N.

Howes, Woodbridge R., 1st Lieut., Co. D., 18th Mass. Reg., also Asst. Surgeon, 3d Mass. Reg.

Johnson, Thomas W., Acting Master, U.S.N.
Jordan, Samuel R., 5th Battery, Light Art.

Keith, Albert, Acting Master, U.S.N.
Keith, Charles F., Acting Master, U.S.N.
King, James W., Co. D., 18th Mass. Reg., also 2d Lieut., Co. C., 32d Mass. Reg.
Kinney, Jireh, Jr., Co., E., 1st Rhode Island Reg.; 2d Serg. Co. I., 3d Mass. Reg.; 2d Lieut., 23d Unattached Co. Mass. Vols.
Kinney, William H., U.S.N.

Lawson, Elias, Acting Ensign, U.S.N.
Leavitt, Robert E., U.S.N., also Co. I., 3d Mass. Reg.
LeBaron, Frederick L., Master's Mate, U.S.N.
LeBaron, John A., Co. C., 71st Pennsylvania Reg.
LeBaron, William H., U.S.N.
Leonard, Nahum Jr., Capt., 58th Mass. Reg.
Lobré, Franklin A., Co. I., 3d Mass. Reg.
Look, Gilbert A., Co. E., 2d Heavy Art.
Luce, Shubael K., Acting Master, U.S.N.

Merrithew, Alexander C., U.S.N.
Morse, Edward A., Master's Mate, U.S.N.
Morse, Frederick L., 23d Unattached Co., Mass. Vols.
Morse, George F., Acting Ensign, U.S.N.
Morse, Theodore S., Master's Mate, U.S.N.

Nye, Charles H., Boatswain's Mate, U.S.N.

Nye, Mavro C., Master's Mate, U.S.N.

O'Connor, Daniel, Co. D., 58th Mass. Reg.

Paine, Francis M., Acting Master, U.S.N.

Peck, George G., Co. D., 7th Mass. Reg.

Peckham, William F., Co. F., 18th Mass. Reg., also
Co. D., 1st Battery H.A.

Perchard, Clement H., Acting Ensign, U.S.N., also
Co. A., 50th Mass. Reg.

Phelan, John E., 23d Unattached Co. Mass. Vols.

Pierce, George, Co. F., 29th Mass. Reg.

Purrington, Francis M., Co. E., 18th Mass. Reg., also
Co. H., 32d Mass. Reg.

Purrington, Henry J., Musician, 19th Mass. Reg.

Purrington, John A., Musician, 19th Mass. Reg., also
Co. I., 3d Mass. Reg.

Randall, Charles H., Co. G., 2d N. H. Reg.

Randall, Elijah W., U.S.N.

Randall, Fayette E., Co. I., 3d Mass. Reg.

Randall, George W., Co. I., 3d Mass. Reg.

Ransom, Sidney, U.S.N.

Ransom, Theodore S., Master's Mate, U.S.N.

Richmond, William L., Co. F., 19th Mass. Reg., also
U.S.N.

Robinson, Benjamin F., Co. I., 3d Mass. Reg., also
Master's Mate, U.S.N.

Rounseville, Job P., Acting Master, U.S.N.

Rounseville, William H., Co. K., 3d Mass. Reg.

Sherman, Noah, Hospital Nurse.

Shurtleff, Henry A., 23d Unattached Co. Mass. Vols.

Simpson, Oscar, U.S.N.

Smith, James, A., Co. I., 13th Mass. Reg., also Co. H., 58th Mass. Reg.

Smith, John, U.S.N.

Snow, Allen W., Acting Ensign, U.S.N.

Snow, Charles F., Co. D., 22d Mass. Reg., also Co. L., 32d Mass. Reg.

Snow, Edward F., Co. D., 18th Mass. Reg.

Snow, Elisha, U.S.N.

Snow, George D., Co. D., 18th Mass. Reg.

Snow, Henry L., U.S.N., also Co. B., 3d Mass. H.A.

Snow, Silas W., Co. B., 3d Mass. Reg. H.A.

Sparrow, William E., Volunteer Surgeon.

Stone, Richard, U.S.N.

Sweat, William W., Volunteer Surgeon.

Tinkham, Charles H., Co. I., 3d Mass. Reg.

Tripp, Charles A., U.S.N.

Tripp, Ebenezer, Co. G., 20th Mass. Reg.

Tripp, Job. P., Co. D., 47th Mass. Reg.

Washburn, John M., Co. A., 60th Mass. Reg.

Waterman, Sylvanus D., Co. I., 3d Mass. Reg.

Weston, Lewis S., Co. E., 18th Mass. Reg.

Wilbur, John E., Co. B., 3d Mass. Reg.

Wilcox, George W., Co. D., 18th Mass. Reg.

Wilcox, William S., 5th Battery Light Art.

Wright, Henry M., 23d Unattached Co. Mass. Vols.

CHAPTER XIII

THERE came a time when the inconvenience of administering the affairs of a large territory with two centers of population grew serious. It was felt most keenly when some three hundred or four hundred voters had to travel eight or nine miles either to the Town Hall in Rochester Center, or to Minister Robbins' meeting-house near the sea, to attend town meeting; and it gradually became a bitter fight of section against section as to where these meetings should be held. So there was little opposition when in 1857 the adherents of the "meeting house," secured incorporation as a separate body. The name which the new town should bear was already long settled. As early as 1640, certain parties were granted lands in "Mattapoyst," and in 1674 the vicinity of the present village had become well known as "Mattapoisett." According to a survey of Ansel Weeks, in September, 1857, the division line began at a stone post in the Fairhaven line, "thence E. 5° S. to road of Ellis's Mill, to the brook from Ellis's Mill to the Wolf Island Road, to Mattapoisett River, by the river to a stone post. From the post to Rock Bridge course E. 2° S., to Cedar Swamp, across the swamp to upland, to the Boat Rock road, to the Bear Swamp, across the Swamp to Towsers Neck, across Towsers Neck to Haskells Mill Swamp, across this Swamp to the Eben Snow old town road, to the Bonney road, to road from four corners to Anthony lot, to the Marion line."

The youthful town started on its new career under the most favorable auspices. In the first meeting the utmost harmony prevailed. The assembly was called by the warrant of Amittai B. Hammond, Justice of the Peace, directed to Rogers L. Barstow, a "principal citizen." It met in Purrington Hall, then recently erected on the former site of Eaton Hall, on Saturday, June 20, 1857, and proceeded to elect officers to conduct its affairs.

There were gathered within "Mattapoisett" a population of about seventeen hundred sturdy, industrious people. Farming was on the increase, but the whaling industry, with ship-building and the necessary accompanying trades, was the principal occupation of the town. For a few years no busier community could be found. The apparent prosperity was, however, but transient; a cloud appeared on the horizon, and the spirit of civil war was soon hovering over even the peaceful village by the sea. At the same time there became evident the sure and rapid decline of "whaling," which was in a few years to sound the knell of the entire mechanical industry of the town.

The rather serious-mindedness, but deep religious faith of the early settlers in this crisis is well shown by this paragraph from the report of the school committee in 1861:

"We would suggest that the present gloomy aspect of our political, commercial, and industrial affairs should impress our minds with the importance of a faithful discharge of duty to our children. If, then, the hope of transmitting to them political blessings is overcast, — if the

wish to bequeath affluence seems doomed to disappoint-
ment, — we should solicitously endeavor to prepare them
for the future, by storing their minds with that true wisdom
which holds 'length of days in her right hand, and in her
left hand riches and honor.'"

At the opening of the war, nearly fifty vessels engaged
in the whale fishery were owned in whole or in part in
Mattapoisett. The ravages of the Confederate cruisers
only hastened the inevitable, and vacant wharves, unused
ship-yards, and empty houses were the signs of a prosperity that had departed.

Industrially the town never recovered from the blow.
A few attempts were made to regain the lost ground. In
1880 the town voted "to exempt from taxation for five
or ten years any parties who will start some manufacturing
business in our town that will give employment to our
citizens." And the next year the selectmen were authorized "to expend not exceeding $75 in advertising the
business facilities of the town, and exemption from taxation." And the citizens contributed liberally from their
private resources to erect and furnish a factory building.
No permanent business, however, could be obtained.

The advent of the "summer resident" in the "seven-
ties" was the beginning of a new era. The accompanying
increase in the real and personal property brought the
valuation of the town, which had shrunk from $800,000,
to $480,000 in 1865, to its highest mark in 1876. The tax
rate, however, has always remained nearly stationary,
ranging from $6 to $9.50 on $1000. During the height
of ship-building some seventy-five yoke of cattle might
have been seen engaged in the laborious work of moving
heavy timber, spars, and other materials, and in 1861

there were taxed fifty-five yoke of oxen and fifty-seven sheep.

Mattapoisett has been a good example of a true democracy, a real government "by the people." Its town meetings have always been well attended and the fullest discussion of affairs has been the rule. And as always results from such interest, her finances and affairs have been ably managed.

The town meetings, up to the time of the building of the Town Hall, were held in Purrington Hall, with a few exceptions such as the case when in 1863 "the meeting met in front of Barstow Hall, and not being able to find the key to the hall organized upon the sidewalks and adjourned to the store formerly occupied by L. Meigs & Co.," and again when in 1867 the meeting met in front of Purrington Hall and, for a similar reason, adjourned to the "sail loft," or an occasional meeting in the "Engine House." Barstow Hall was in the second story at the east end of what is now the "Mattapoisett House." Loring Meigs's store was burned and the town now owns its site, by purchase with the wharf property. The sail loft was in the storehouse building still standing at the head of Long Wharf, while the old engine house, which formerly stood on part of the present town hall lot, has, after serving as a church, engine house, town hall, and shop, become a tenement house on Baptist Street.

Perhaps the most memorable town meeting was that of April 3, 1865, when, just after acting on the eleventh article in the warrant, this entry appears on the clerk's records: "NEWS OF THE CAPTURE OF RICHMOND RECEIVED." At the same meeting, the fourteenth article, which related to "keeping full the town's proportion of the quota of volunteers called for from the Commonwealth," was passed, on account of the "*news from Richmond.*"

In addition to furnishing volunteers, the town, in 1862, offered to open a hospital for sick and disabled soldiers, but it was not needed.

Amid the serious discussion of municipal affairs there was always present a sense of humor — on one occasion under an article "to see if the town will prohibit playing ball or passing, throwing and catching balls or kicking footballs within the following limits, viz.: from the house of the late Wilson Barstow on Main Street, within the limits of said Main Street to Mechanic Street," the vote was to make the limits "from Jarvis Ellis' to Wm. Richmonds" (the extreme north and south ends of the town).

How the voters should be notified was settled by directing, in 1867, that a copy of the articles in the warrant should be posted "upon the oak tree on the corner near Abraham Tinkhams (still used for the purpose), at the Town Mills, Cowins Mills, and at the Post Office."

Out of the twenty-one district schools in Rochester in 1857, ten came within the limits of the new town of Mattapoisett. There were at the time "academies" in the town, "second, we believe, to none in this Commonwealth." But the defective district school system was a constant source of trouble. Each district, through its "Prudential Committee," provided its schoolhouses and expended the money appropriated by the town for the support of the school as it saw fit. The office of the Prudential Committee, including as it did the power of hiring teachers, having charge of the schoolhouse and the running of the

school, carried with it considerable patronage, and was
the cause of fierce, if limited, political struggles. As one
committee on investigation remarked, "the chief quali-
fication of a member of a Prudential Committee seems
to have been not to have served the preceding year."

That the district schools did their work as thoroughly
as they did, has been the wonder of later times. Perhaps
the secret may be found in this statement from the school
committee's report in 1857: "But few branches of study
should be prosecuted at a given time. Not the quantity,
but the quality of learning should be considered. Better
to learn a little thoroughly, assuredly, than a great deal
superficially and doubtfully."

The village districts were, in 1857, at once combined,
and in the first school committee's report, the districts
were defined as:

District No. 1. Mattapoisett Neck, where in that year
there was no summer term, but for three months in the
winter, fifteen scholars were taught by Mr. John W.
Hammond, who "proved a competent teacher," so that
the committee thought the school "would compare favorably with most any other district school in the town." It
occupied rented quarters, having the year before been
taught by Mrs. E. R. Beetle at her residence, and in 1855
in the "Upper Chamber" a building erected or used for
a corn granary, and "illy adapted" for school purposes.

District No. 2. Hammondtown, with E. G. Caswell,
Sr., Prudential Committee, had six months of "school."
In the summer Miss Almira E. Denham taught eighteen
scholars, and in the winter Noah Hammond had thirty-
two. It was the first school either had taught, but was

WEST DISTRICT SCHOOLHOUSE, CHURCH STREET, MATTAPOISETT

Formerly "The Olive Branch Schoolhouse"

satisfactory to the committee, "and we think to the district."

Districts Nos. 3 *and* 4 were united and comprised the village west of Barstow Street. About fifty pupils had school for seven and one-half months with Miss Buretta W. Hammond as principal and Miss Olivia H. Freeman, assistant, in the summer; and Miss Abby P. LeBaron and Miss Mary E. Davis in charge in the winter. "The school, though a large one, was very quiet."

Districts Nos. 5, 6, *and* 7 were also consolidated and included the easterly portion of the village and as far east as "Thomas Dexter's corner." This was in the summer divided into an "Intermediate Department" in charge of Miss Olivia R. Look; and a "Primary School" taught by Miss Mary E. Davis, "whose demeanor was characterized by mildness and affability." For the winter term, "Mr. Henry Taylor gave his whole attention to the school, and gave general satisfaction."

District No. 8, "Pine Islands," maintained less than six months of school. Miss Mary Hammond taught twenty-four pupils in the summer, and Mr. George Cushman had forty-two for the winter term.

District No. 9, "Aucoot," with Isaac Hiller, Prudential Committee, and Miss Salome E. Bates and Miss Priscilla Sparrow, teachers, had five and one-half months of school, with nine scholars in the summer and seventeen in the winter.

District No. 10, "Tinkhamtown" and "Randalltown," included all north of Captain Hoxie's and James Purrington's, and with Thomas Randall, Prudential Committee, had six and one-half months of school for twenty-eight scholars, with Miss Mary K. Clark as teacher. "In No.

10," the committee reported, "although there are two places where children go to school, at neither is there anything that resembles a decent schoolhouse. . . . The citizens of this district understand economy too well to repair these old buildings, and there being no immediate prospect of agreeing on the location of a new one, it seems a most auspicious time to unite with number 2, — although this district has evidently the next poorest schoolhouse in the town."

The faults lay with the system, for as the committee reported, the town that year appropriated $1524, "which is all that the most zealous friends of common schools can ask so far as money is concerned." They complain that "the town committee have not been heretofore considered of much consequence in connection with the schools," and congratulate the town that "schools have been kept two terms in all the districts but one, which has not been the case for many years."

In 1862 another consolidation was brought about by joining districts 3, 4, 5, 6, 7, thus bringing together all the village districts, and in 1867 the town, after repeated attempts, voted to abolish school districts. The income of a bequest of Abner Pease, in favor of districts Nos. 8 and 9, enabled a school to be kept for an additional seven weeks in schoolhouse No. 3 in 1869.

From this time the common schools of Mattapoisett passed through only the customary evolution, until in 1899 the new building, a gift of Mr. Henry H. Rogers (who received a part of his early education in the private school, kept by Mr. Woodbridge Howes, in Eaton Hall) was opened, and all grades above the sixth were brought under its roof.

As a result of a desire of those inhabitants of Rochester, living within the limits of Mattapoisett, to secure for their children the benefits of a higher education than could be obtained in the district schools, some public-spirited parties secured control of a large interest in the old Congregational meeting-house. And in 1854, James Barstow, B. F. Hammond, A. B. Hammond, Seth Freeman, Wm. B. Rogers, John Atsatt, Loring Meigs, Arvin Cannon, Leonard Hammond, Matthew Mayhew, Nathan Crosby, Andrew Southworth, Benjamin Barstow, Nathan'l A. Crosby, John A. Le Baron, Cynthia Dexter, Nathan'l Clark, Alice Sparrow, Deborah F. Howes, W. Barstow, Bethuel Landers, Jabez Goodspeed, Judith C. Rogers, H. M. Cannon, Martha O. Young, Priscilla A. Southworth, Priscilla N. Hammond, Peleg Pearce, Isaiah Sears, Benjamin Bacon, Leonard Dexter, all of Mattapoisett in the Town of Rochester; and Lazarus LeBaron, of North Turner, County of Oxford, State of Maine, Yeomen, "In consideration of our desire to promote the cause of education," conveyed unto Loring Meigs, Henry Barstow, and Abner Harlow, "who have been appointed a committee by the subscribers of the Stock in the property hereinafter, conveyed to receive the title to the same," all their interest in and to the Old Congregational Meeting-House, so called; "It is hereby understood that said Meeting-House shall be fitted up in a manner suitable to be occupied as a place where instruction may be given to youth, and said building shall be used for such purposes."

The building was promptly fitted up and a private school successfully opened. In 1857 the "Mattapoisett Academy," then conducted by Mr. and Mrs. Orange H. Spoor and Miss Lucy B. Washburn, had enrolled 133 pupils, including 36 from other towns and 7 from other states. Its catalogue showed English, Classical, and Teachers' Departments, with special courses in "Music, Pencilling and Crayoning, Monochromatic and other ornamental branches." It was "partially supplied with chemical and philosophical apparatus," and had "a spacious gallery fitted up for the especial accommodation of visitors, who can call at any time without interrupting the school." The trustees then were Loring Meigs, Maj. Rogers L. Barstow, and Capt. Samuel Sturtevant, Jr. Arvin Cannon was treasurer, and Solomon K. Eaton secretary.

In 1860, in order to straighten out the title, the property was conveyed to John T. Atsatt, by Loring Meigs, Henry Barstow, Abner Harlow, Rowland Howland, Arvin Cannon, James LeBaron, Solomon K. Eaton, Matthew Mayhew, Samuel Sturtevant, Jr., Wilson Barstow, executor to estate of Z. M. Barstow, Joseph Hudson, Samuel Sturtevant, Jr., Rogers L. Barstow, Cynthia Dexter, Josiah Holmes, Jr., Jonathan H. Holmes, Dennis S. Boodry, Nathan'l A. Crosby, John Dexter, Nathan Crosby, James Cannon, Martin Hall, Lemuel LeBaron, Wm. L. Bourne, Ebenezer Jones, Barton Taber, and George Purrington, Jr., "in consideration of $1725." In this deed the property is described as "a certain lot of land with the buildings thereon, and also the fixtures therein, consisting of Pieoano, Seets, Desks, Bell, Philosophical Aparatus, etc., and known as the Mattapoisett Academy."

The private institution was successfully maintained until the stress of war times came on, and its then instructor, George G. Harriman, took charge in 1862 of the village Grammar School. Capt. Zaccheus M. Barstow, having left property to the town valued at nearly $9000, and provided that upon the winding up of the Lyceum that the income of his gift "be applied to the purposes of education in higher branches than are taught in primary English Schools," his trustees purchased from the proprietors the Academy building for $1450 out of the income, and in 1872 it was turned over to the town, "in trust as a part of the Barstow School Trust Fund." The Barstow School was opened (as a result of the legacy above referred to) in December, 1871, and Mr. Charles Smith, "with a registry of forty-six scholars, successfully operated during a term of three months."

The town the next year made an appropriation in aid of the "Barstow School," and has continued to do so to the present time. The school was transferred in 1899 to the new village building, and beginning with this year (1906–07) its scholars have the privilege of attending, without cost, the new High School in Fairhaven.

The year 1881 witnessed the birth of the "Free Public Library" in Mattapoisett. The beginning was certainly humble. At the annual meeting that year, the town voted that the "dog fund" should go to its aid, but this amount of $56.96 did not become available until the close of the year. Isaiah P. Atsatt at the same meeting, agreed to furnish a room and librarian for two years, and "Capt. Charles Bryant kindly volunteered a lecture on Alaska," the net proceeds of which, $7.20, were the only "available assets" of the first trustees. The Selectmen's office over "Atsatt's store" was used for a short time. Then an unused room in the upper story of the "Primary" schoolhouse was fitted with a few shelves and a high desk in a section railed off. "Col. Geo. M. Barnard, Jr., presented a large quantity of periodicals, some of them in bound volumes. With this kind donation, together with about twenty-five volumes, contributed in town in answer to printed solicitations," the library was opened to the public, and on Saturday afternoons sturdy children tugging homeward ancient half-year volumes of the *Illustrated London News* were often met. Monday evening, after seven o'clock, was "Library night," and was usually so popular that one had to draw a number for his turn, and the assistant in charge (on a salary of $18 per annum) frequently required the active aid of one or two of the trustees. On some week in the winter, books were called in, the library closed for the "annual examination," when the trustees assembled in solemn session, verified the count and inspected the condition of all the books. In two years the library had accumulated 728 volumes and a catalogue was issued. "Young ladies entertainments" are credited as adding to the funds and "Johnnie Morgan" and "Sunflower choruses" helped secure additional books. Steadily increasing rows of manilla covered book-backs, yellowed and soiled by constant wear, crept around the sides of the room and filled the available wall space. In 1892 the library was moved to a vacant store on the northeast corner of Main and Cannon streets, and thereafter was opened four times a week. In 1897 the town made an extra appropriation of $100 to fit up a connecting reading-room, and that year the library was opened for one afternoon and six evenings in the week.

A most happy event was the offer of Mr. George Purrington, Jr., in the town meeting of 1902, of $10,000 for a building. As a result of this gift the present building was erected upon a lot given by Mr. Samuel D. Warren. Money from the estate of William B. Rogers, in the hands of J. Chas. F. Atsatt, furnished book stacks and an acetylene plant. In the meantime the trustees had secured the re-cataloguing of the 4600 volumes then on hand; and in 1904 the "free public library" stood well housed and equipped to influence the future intellectual life of the town.

The list of trustees is as follows: Rev. Augustus H. Fuller, 1881-86; George H. Dexter, 1881-1905; William B. Nelson, 1881-93; Isaiah P. Atsatt, 1881-90; J. Chas. F. Atsatt, 1881-90, and 1893-95; William E. Sparrow, Jr., 1889-91; Sarah H. Crosby, 1892-93; Lemuel LeB. Dexter, 1894 —; Nathan Smith, 1905 —; Dr. Irving N. Tilden, 1905 —.

Despite the pranks of mischievous youth, of which Mattapoisett has had its full share, its local history has been essentially peaceful.

Illustrating the seriousness of offenses which have at times disturbed the serenity of the town, it appears that at one time the Selectmen were authorized "to provide a place to detain truants," and the question naturally arises, — were they to be detained *from school?* Also in 1868 it was voted "to instruct the Selectmen to offer a reward of $20 for such information as shall lead to the conviction of any man, woman, boy or girl, breaking glass in town." History does not relate whether any women or girls were convicted.

The problem of providing a place in which to maintain its poor had early attracted the attention of the town. In 1865 the selectmen were authorized to purchase "the Barstow House," now the "Mattapoisett

House," and the "Harris House" later the Gammons house near J. L. Stackpole's cottage, which at present is the Nye house on Baptist street, was also proposed; but no action was taken until in 1866 the "Joseph Hiller Farm" was purchased and fitted up as an almshouse. After a few years however, the number of inmates began to decrease and the "poor house" is now hardly more than a name. The Rebellion forced the dependent relatives of many soldiers and sailors to seek aid toward their support, and in 1866 the town paid from the treasury the largest sum ever required for its poor. Of late years these expenses have been rapidly growing less. Additional purchases of land have added to the almshouse farm, and it is now a very valuable property, with its shore frontage on Aucoot Cove.

The village of Mattapoisett was equipped with fire apparatus before the separation from Rochester. The act of incorporation provided that "Mattapoisett shall pay to Rochester their proportion of twelve hundred dollars for the interest they have in the fire department; and Rochester shall relinquish all right and claim in said fire department to Mattapoisett." The next year the town voted "to accept Engine No. 1, with a company not exceeding 20 members to draw pay," and proceeded to purchase an engine house and fixtures for $396.49. And in 1859 it was reported, "the town now owns 1 Engine House and Lot, 2 Fire Engines, 12 leather and 11 wooden buckets, 25 feet suction hose, 600 feet leading hose, 2 torches, 1 lantern, 2 stoves and pipe, 4 fire hooks, 4 ladders about 100 feet, all in good condition for the relief of any portion of community that may be invaded by the calamity of fire." Engine No. 1 was kept in a shed in company

THE OLD ENGINE HOUSE
Formerly "The Little Belt," Church Street, Mattapoisett

with the "hearse," on the premises of Prince Bolles on North Street.

One very disastrous fire took place shortly before the incorporation of the town. It burned the "County House," as was called the hotel run by Leonard Hammond; the large stable with adjoining sheds belonging to the hotel, Eaton Hall, a boat-shop, Hammond's store then run by George Purrington, Jr., a "nine pin alley," and Jonathan H. Holmes's house. The fire swept towards the west, and after an unsuccessful attempt to blow up Eaton Hall, Jonathan H. Holmes's house was blown up and the flames stopped. It was during one of the coldest winter nights ever known in the town, and was the worst experience the town has ever had from fire. The stable stood where Thomas Luce's stable now stands; County House where the cellar hole may still be seen, just to the east of Purrington Block; Eaton Hall occupied the present location of Purrington Hall, and Jonathan Holmes's house was where Mendell's drug store now stands; the horse chestnut tree, which stood in Holmes's front yard, though injured, survived the fire and still stands. In 1857 S. K. Eaton was paid for "a plan of burnt district," and "James Ruggles's Vigilence Committee" received a large sum for investigating the causes of the fire. Another unusual fire was that of June 27, 1846, when the whaleship, *Joseph Meigs*, which had just arrived here from a voyage with a full cargo and was anchored just inside Mattapoisett Light, waiting for an opportunity to reach Long Wharf, was burned to the water's edge. The fire was late at night and the burning oil made a brilliant spectacle. It is interesting that the hulk was towed ashore, the upper works rebuilt, and the ship again sailed.

Other fires might be mentioned, but in general the fire
department has ably coped with the "invader," and
Mattapoisett has been spared since 1857 a serious
"calamity of fire."

Its herring or alewife fishery has always been a matter
of considerable value, as well as of annual interest to the
town.   The fish formed no small part of the food of many
a family and the receipts from the sales were at times quite
large.   How valuable the "run" was, is shown by the
numerous acts of legislature obtained to "preserve the
fish called Alewives in Mattapoisett River."   In 1788 a
forfeiture of ten pounds was provided for any one who
should set a net in the harbor "between the southwesterly
end of the island, owned by Rev. Mr. La Barron, and from
thence to the mouth of the creek which runs out of Barlow's Pond"; and in 1811 the excluded limits were made
"northward of a line running directly from the most
southerly part of Capt. Job Haskell's farm on the westerly
side of the harbor, to the most southerly part of Joseph
Edward's land (now Ned's Point), on the easterly side
of said harbor."   The same protection was in 1830
extended to shad.

In the very first year we find a payment to Noah
Spooner of $185.89, the "expense of petitioning for a new
herring river."

In 1860 it was voted "to divide the income of the herring
stream on the polls."   Apparently the legality of the vote
was questioned, as J. B. Ransom and James LeBaron
were appointed a committee to get legal advice on the
subject of division "and pay their own expenses."   As a
matter of fact, the Supreme Court afterwards decided
that such a division could not be made.

Not satisfied with the run of herring in Mattapoisett River, in 1865 the town voted to establish a herring fishery in the creek or outlet leading from the Eel or Barlow's Pond to the harbor. An act of the legislature was obtained under which an abutment was built along the east side of the creek, and an attempt was made to induce an annual run of herring, but it was never very successful. An attempt had previously been made by a company of individuals, incorporated as the "Mattapoisett Oyster Co.," to plant and raise oysters in this pond and creek, but while partially successful, both herring and oysters seemed to prefer the deeper waters of Mattapoisett River.

Among the early attempts of the town at improvement was the securing of authority from the legislature to provide a public common, and in 1874 the town voted to accept the act. Public sentiment, however, turned against the project and the work was undone.

The subject of laying out and discontinuing roads occupied much of the town's time and of its records, which from 1857 to 1880 show: The discontinuance in 1858 of the "Old town road leading eastward from North Street near the house of James LeBaron;" the widening and straightening in 1861 of the highway from the "house of John Bowlin, now of George Fox," to Cedar Swamp Brook, "provided Solomon E. Bolles shall fill the slough of said road with stone and give the gravel from his barn cellar which he contemplates making and also one week's work on said road;" in 1868 the acceptance of Pearl Street, north of Church Street, "as now opened;" in 1874 the acceptance of the road known as "Freeman Street," leading by the houses of Charles

Smith and James H. Tinkham; also that year the acceptance of a way from Main Street to Barnard's Island as a private way; the next year the action of the County Commissioners in widening and straightening North Street "from highwater mark northerly to the Rochester line," and that of the town in accepting the road known as Foster Street leading from Macy Bowman's to N. C. Ransom's. In 1876 the County Commissioners relocating, widening, and straightening Main Street, "from a point on Cannonville Hill, at the former residence of Prince A. Snow, to the Barstow Schoolhouse;" also that same year, the acceptance of Mechanic Street, "from Church Street to Sturtevant Street," as laid out; and of Oakland Street, "as laid out;" in 1877 the County Commissioners' altering of the highway between the house of J. L. Stackpole and the store of P. G. Munro; and in 1879 the acceptance of the report of the Selectmen widening and straightening the road from the house of Isaac D. Tinkham to the town line of Acushnet. In general, the streets have kept their original names, but "Willis" and "Jerusalem" streets are names of the past.

Practically the whole water front of Mattapoisett Village was a public common until after the close of the ship-building days, so that it was not until 1884 that the town, realizing the need of access to the harbor, secured the "Leonard Hammond ship-yard lot," the "Durfee Beach lot" in 1886, and still later the wharf property of the Mattapoisett Wharf Company.

Another piece of land devoted to quite a different purpose came into the possession of the town in 1889, when Lemuel LeBaron, Weston Howland, and Wm. B. Nelson, the Precinct Committee of the First Precinct in Mattapoisett, conveyed to the town the interest of the Precinct in "the Barlow Burying place, and being the same land conveyed to said Precinct and to the inhabitants thereof, by Elihu Sherman, by deed dated June 8, 1789."

The first steam train passed through the town on the 4th of July, 1854. It consisted of an engine and a number of flat cars which were trimmed with birches, and a free ride to Fairhaven was provided for all. Later years have brought the daily "Dude" train, for the accommodation of summer residents, and a high-grade electric street car service.

As early as 1876 the town began to experiment on watering its streets, and that year is found a payment to the Mattapoisett Wharf Company for "water from their dock."

The original mode of keeping the ways in repair by a labor tax was soon changed to making money appropriations which were expended from time to time by different officials as the town changed its systems; the price allowed for labor on the highways advancing from ten cents to twelve and a half cents an hour in 1859, and it was voted that "all who pay their highway tax before the 4th of July, either in money or labor have a discount of 20 per cent." The first substantial advance was made when the first macadam road was built in 1893 by William L. Hubbard, Ephraim A. Dexter, and Joseph R. Jenney, Road Commissioners, under the supervision of Captain Jenney. A piece, 4900 feet long, was built at a cost of $1400, and attracted considerable attention outside the town. It lasted for many years and led to the adoption of this method of road construction. There are at the present time fourteen or fifteen miles of stone road in the town, more is built each year, and its shore and woodland drives cannot be surpassed.

Joseph E. Smith was the first and only "Pound Keeper" elected by the town, and in 1882 the town pound was conveyed to him for the sum of $40. The next year $10 of this amount was refunded to him, presumably because the pound was missed less than was expected. The pound stood on the south side of the Fairhaven Road in the northeast corner of the house lot now owned by Nathan Smith.

The conscientious service of its officers has been frequently recognized by the town.

In 1874 the town passed a vote of thanks to Thomas Nelson, Town Clerk, for his long and faithful services. Ten years later a similar vote was given Capt. Franklin Cross, who had served twenty-one years as a Selectman. Henry A. Shurtleff, Town Clerk, and Wilson Barstow, Selectman for twenty-seven years, were honored in a similar manner in 1891; and in 1894 resolutions were adopted on the death of Noah Hammond, Selectman for twenty-one years, setting forth the town's obligations to him.

While perhaps not unusual in Massachusetts, the Puritan strain of ancestry of the early settlers of Mattapoisett is shown by many given names appearing on the town's records, such as "Fear, Content, Justice, Hope, Wealthy, Thankful, Hope, Prudence, Patience, Charity, Mercy, Faith, Experience, Desire, Remember, Ransom, Resolved."

Even to the present time, the whole history of Mattapoisett may be read in the annals of "whaling." Even now it is rare to find on her streets a man of fifty years who has not shipped for at least one "cruise," and "Capens" are as common as were ever "Kurnels" in the South, after war time.

Most of the well-to-do families owe their prosperity directly to "oil" and "bone;" and curiosities from the sea, or relics from foreign lands the world over, are treasured in every household.

It will be many a year before the influences born of arduous toil and exciting adventure in every sea shall cease to bear fruit.

Some day, as the wheel of time slowly turns, again the noise and strife of busy commercial enterprises may fill the streets and throng the wharves; till then, as one of her sons has written:

> "The wanderer o'er the troubled sea of life,
> Come safe to port here after all the strife,
> May think himself, aye, more than three times blest,
> At harbor in this quiet *place of rest*."

LIST OF TOWN OFFICERS

The following persons have served the town as indicated:

Selectmen, Assessors and Overseers of the Poor from 1857 to 1907:

Amittai B. Hammond, 1857–61, inclusive.

Joseph E. Smith, 1857–62.

Jarvis Ellis, 1857–61.

Nathan H. Barstow, 1862.

Thomas P. Hammond, 1862.

Josiah Holmes, Jr., 1863–69.

Franklin Cross, 1863–83.

Wilson Barstow, 1863–68, 1870–90.

Isaac Hiller, 1868.

Bruce F. Shaw, 1869–73.

Noah Hammond, 1874–94.

Joseph L. Cole, 1884–1900.

Reuben F. Holmes, 1888.

Ephraim A. Dexter, 1888.

Jonathan H. Holmes, 1891–93.

Allen D. Hammond, 1894–95.

James F. Hammond, 1894–96.

Thomas D. Dexter, 1895–97.

Nathan S. Mendell, 1897–1902.

Abner Harlow, 1899–1901.

Lester W. Jenney, 1901—

Horace F. Field, 1902—

Isaiah P. Atsatt, 1903–04.

Everett C. Stetson, 1905—

Treasurers and Collectors, 1857–1907

Samuel Sturtevant, Jr., 1857–60, inclusive.

Benjamin W. Shearman, 1860–66.

Henry Taylor, 1867–68.

A. S. LeBaron, 1869.

Isaiah P. Atsatt, 1870–82.

Reuben F. Holmes, 1883–87.

Benjamin L. Boodry, 1888.

Freeman C. Keene, 1888–99.

Elwood B. Hiller, 1900—

Town Clerks, 1857–1907

Thomas Nelson, 1857–74.

Lemuel LeB. Holmes, 1874–76.

Reuben F. Holmes, 1876.

Henry A. Shurtleff, 1876–91.

William B. Nelson, 1891–93.

George H. Dexter, 1893–1905.

William N. Johnson, 1905—

School Committee, 1857–1907

Josiah Holmes, Jr., 1857–61, 1866–69.

Weston Howland, 1857–60, 1872–76.

Wm. E. Sparrow, 1857–59, 1867–72.

Woodbridge R. Howes, 1859–61.

Wilson Barstow, 1860–66.

Noah Shearman, 1861–62, 1870–71.

Henry Barstow, 1861–65, 1870–71.

Thos. Nelson, 1862–67.

Noah C. Sturtevant, 1865–68.

Jonathan H. Holmes, 1868–70.

Herbert Shurtleff, 1869–70.

William Weaver, 1871–74.

Jarvis Ellis, 1871–74.

Joshua L. Macomber, 1872–78, 1879–82, 1887–96.

Joseph L. Cole, 1872–75, 1876–86.

Geo. Purrington, Jr., 1874–76.

William E. Sparrow, Jr., 1875–76, 1885–87.

Nancy M. Caswell, 1876–79.

William B. Nelson, 1878–81.

Edward B. Hiller, 1882–85.

Mary F. Dexter, 1882–87.

Alonzo W. Westgate, 1886–87.

Charles Bryant, 1887–90.

David H. Cannon, 1887–92, 1894–97.

Pliny A. Allen, 1890–91.

Charles H. Johnson, 1891–94.

Joseph L. Meigs, 1892–97.

Robert L. Dexter, 1896–97.

Charles H. Tinkham, 1897–1900.

Clara L. Hammond, 1897–98.

Lemuel LeBaron Dexter, 1897 —

Elizabeth E. Shaw, 1898.

Heman G. Holmes, 1898—

James S. Burbank, 1900–03.

Mary W. Wood, 1903–

Among members of the professions from Mattapoisett since its incorporation are:

Lawyers. — John Eddy, John W. Hammond, Nahum

Leonard, Jr., Lemuel LeBaron Holmes, Thomas W. Hammond, Hollen M. Barstow, Alvah E. Snow, Frank M. Sparrow, Lester W. Jenney, J. E. Norton Shaw, Lemuel LeBaron Dexter, and Jonathan H. Holmes.

Doctors. — William E. Sparrow, William W. Sweat, Dr. Bartlett, Dr. Bass, Woodbridge R. Howes, Charles E. Bolles (D.D.S.), Roland Hammond, Herbert Shurtleff, Thomas W. Hammond, David H. Cannon, Clarence L. Howes, John C. Shaw, Henry A. Shurtleff, William F. Holmes,

Ministers. — Pliny A. Allen, Jr.

CHAPTER XIV

MATTAPOISETT OF THE PRESENT

DURING the fifty years of independent town history there have been two eras. Mattapoisett was once a busy seaport; it is now a summer resort.

After the ship-yards were abandoned, and the sound of the hammers — which yet lingers with such charm in the memories of the older people — was stilled, a kind of decadence set in. It was no longer the inevitable thing for the young men to make their "first voyage;" and, if good sailors, to continue following the sea, or if not, to settle down at ship-building or farming. Instead, they went West, or to the large cities, and so established their homes where they could find employment. The young women, having no longer their traditional amusement of watching for ships to come in, and of writing six months' news to absent sailor boys, caught the new spirit of independence and also went away to seek their fortunes. The older people and the easy-going remained, and the times were very dull indeed. One finds in a town report of the period a pessimistic page on which Mattapoisett is contrasted most unfavorably with "brisk and flourishing interior towns," and a prayer is offered that "some business may be instituted in which we can all participate." An old sea captain, whom most can yet remember, used to sum up the situation with less elegance, and say with a thump of his cane: "The town is getting a cant."

The ministers could no longer pray with the old-time weekly fervor for "those that go down to the sea in ships, that do business in the great waters," nor could the villagers throng the wharves on a summer's evening to watch a vessel slide off the ways. Long Wharf Middle Wharf and Short Wharf no more were covered with great casks of oil and the piled-up paraphernalia of whaling enterprise. Ned's Point light house still threw its nightly beam across the harbor, but no whaleman, returning from an Arctic voyage, had a lookout aloft, scanning anxiously the distance to catch the first gleam of its welcoming light. No merchant ships were eagerly waited by sailors' wives in Mattapoisett, and new stones were rarely set up in the village burying-grounds to the memory of sons or husbands lost at sea. The shipping in the harbor was reduced to a few schooners in the fall that brought, perhaps, a cargo of coal; and departed, laden with box-boards, for Philadelphia or some other home port.

But as the village waited, and the years passed by, a time came when the popularity of summer seaside homes was established among the wealthy people of the cities, and the south shore of Massachusetts began to be "discovered." Mattapoisett was too charming in location and natural beauty to be passed unnoticed. The first to perceive its possibilities, and to make for themselves a place of summer rest, were Mr. and Mrs. George M. Barnard, of Boston, who came in the fall of 1869, and soon bought up much of the shore and inland property, and continued as summer residents of Mattapoisett as long as they lived. Their home, the old Benjamin Barstow

house, now owned by their granddaughter, Miss Mary W.
Barnard, has an unbroken exposure to the sea, a beautiful
view of the harbor, and has — although much enlarged —
been kept in its simple old-style character, with the picturesque weather-beaten trees around it.

The Barnards were soon followed by other families,
who built new cottages or made over old houses all along
the shore, many of whom have continued to come summer
after summer, growing more and more attached with
the associations of years.   Among these early summer
visitors were Dr. Oliver Wendell Holmes and his son, Mr.
Justice O. W. Holmes, Jr.   The latter owned and occupied for many seasons — but has lately sold it — the
old Cowen place on the eastern shore of the town just
back of the "Cedars," — a rocky elevation of the beach
crowned with those hardy trees.   Hon. George O. Shat-
tuck built on the Edwards' land next the lighthouse,
which place is now the summer home of Hon. Charles S.
Hamlin.   Another Boston lawyer, J. Lewis Stackpole,
converted the Hall blacksmith shop, west of the "company ship-yard," into a summer home on the sea sands,
swept always by the sea winds.   Thomas Parsons, of
Boston, whose place just east of the village includes in
its former bounds the lot of St. Philip's Episcopal Church; and Francis E. Bacon, the Boston merchant,
whose charming house and garden are in "Cannonville,"
were among the earlier summer residents, and their families
are to-day still welcomed back with each return of the
vacation season.   So also is the family of Edward Atkinson, the scholar and social economist, who, until his death,
came regularly to his quiet home, which nestles in the
woods with an outlook toward the sea.   On the grounds

Mattapoisett Village from Neds Point

is the big boulder, — "the Great Rock," — around which generations of Mattapoisett children have picnicked and played, and have wished it could tell them of its long-ago journey in the ice age, and of when and how it was broken in two.

Some were drawn back to Mattapoisett by family ties. Mrs. Elizabeth Barstow Stoddard was often a visitor in her native town, and Rogers L. Barstow, the Boston banker, and Mrs. Seavey, Mrs. Battelle, and Miss Munroe, the granddaughters of old "Squire Willis, . . ." have many interests and associations with the past, to attach them to their summer homes. William T. Faunce, the Boston shoe man, son of the kindly remembered old Baptist minister, has enlarged and improved his old homestead; and James T. Jones has returned to his native town and converted the William LeBaron place into a summer residence. Within recent years rows of smaller cottages have been built along Pico and Crescent beaches, and at various points on the Necks, either for personal occupancy or for rental, and for these the demand increases.

Of course the chief attraction to visitors, and the particular pride of the inhabitants, is the harbor. The land seems to stretch out long, guarding arms on either side. On one is Ned's Point, with the lighthouse, and on the other is the Neck, named long ago by the Indians, "Antassawamuck Neck." This harbor is always beautiful under sunny or cloudy skies, or by moonlight; and the fresh southwest breeze tempers the hottest midsummer day. The opportunities for boating, fishing and bathing are good, and the public bathing beach, so wisely acquired by the town some years ago, is more and more used, both by the village people and by the transient visitors. Of

these latter there are many each summer, two
hotels are often crowded, and more would doubtless come
if accommodation were more easily obtained.

Around the town are many beautiful drives. The
macadam roads run not only along the shore, but stretch
back into the fragrant pines which abound in all the Old
Rochester territory. One can take visitors first down
the Neck road for the pretty view of the village and the
curving line of shore stretching to the lighthouse, with
the gay-colored roofs piled high on "Cannonville Hill,"
and beyond the light "Strawberry" and "Angelica,"
stretching out toward the Falmouth shore. On the west
neck there is the winding, woodsy, Brandt Island road
ending over across the bridge on the island itself. Another circuit back from the water, to the northern limit
of the town, leads through alternate pieces of pine woodland and cultivated farms, "around Wolf Island." The
island is not evident, but it is there, formed by the Mattapoisett River dividing and uniting again, and between
two little narrow bridges the road crosses the lower corner
of it. There is still less evidence of the "wolf," which,
according to one tradition, roamed there once. According to another it was only a man named Wolfe from whom
the place was called.

To those who delight to explore old roads and cart paths
leading into the woods, this part of the town is very attractive, especially when the laurel is in bloom. The great
fluffy masses of white flowers seem to catch all the sun-
beams, and to lighten up the dim vistas of the shady
paths. The swamp apple blossoms, which have about
the same season, are less beautiful, but the air is made
sweet by their fragrance. If one is interested in geological

curiosities there is in this neighborhood the impression in
the stone called the "Devil's foot," and also the "Dumpling
Rock," which a man can move with one hand, but which
many stout young men together have vainly tried to roll
off its rocky base.

For longer drives there is the fifteen-mile circuit through
Marion and Rochester, or the still longer courses around
the Lakeville ponds, or around Long Plain and Fairhaven. Skirting the bay the macadam is unbroken from
New Bedford to Sandwich and is a trunk route for automobiles. By trolley and steam train or boat, Plymouth
and the Cape, Martha's Vineyard and even Newport, and
all the resorts of Narragansett Bay, are within easy reach
for single-day excursions. If one prefers to seek solitude,
there are attractive old woods roads leading by the "Boat
Rock," or to Solomon's, and even through to the neighboring towns, upon which one can tramp for miles without
view of any dwelling.

The Mattapoisett River flows along, in the inconsequent
way of rivers, from Snippituit to the sea. It is beautiful
when seen from the highway, but still more beautiful in
the dark places where the trees and tangled vines inter-
lace overhead, and the cardinal flowers in August make
vivid spots of color all along the banks. It was the
Indians' course to the seashore, and if their shades any-
where revisit the glimpses of the moon it must be beside
this stream. One wonders if they seek the nearly vanished
spring where, by tradition, on their return from the shore,
they made the first clambakes, naming the spot the
"place of rest," and thus giving a name for the river and
the town. Where the river begins to widen out is the
romantic spot known as "Lovers' Bridge," a rustic

log foot-way has long existed across the stream,
and according to the legend it was the trysting place for
an Indian maiden and her lover from the North who came
down the river in his canoe to meet her.   From the bridge
winding paths lead to open fields, from which more shady
lanes can be followed further in various directions to the
highways.   One path, leading through thickets of sweet
briar roses, follows the course of the river for some distance.

Of the public buildings none has more interesting
associations than the old "Barstow High School," once
the Congregational meeting-house, and later the Academy.
Its churchly architecture made it rather a unique schoolhouse, and gave it a certain dignity and sanctity.   It had
been separated into two stories, and the upper one included a small hall used as a lodge-room by the Sons of
Temperance.   This room was always securely locked
and was as interesting and mysterious as Bluebeard's
chamber to the children; but the rest of the building they
could generally overrun.   At times they were even allowed
to climb the dusty, creaking stairs to the belfry steeple
and to eat their lunches there on a summer's day, with the
village all below and the distant sparkling waves melting
away into the blue sky at the horizon line, — which line
was plainly circular, therefore the world must be round as
the geography said.   Now that the new and spacious
school building on Church Street has been given by Mr.
H. H. Rogers, the former Barstow schoolhouse has become the Grange Hall.   The old Grammar schoolhouse,
considerably more than a hundred years old, which stood
formerly on the corner of Church and Pearl streets, has
been purchased for the Universalist society and fitted up

LOVERS' BRIDGE, MATTAPOISETT RIVER

for a church home. It now stands on the south side of Church Street, facing the new brick schoolhouse, — an interesting example of the contrasts of time. The town hall now occupies the corner where once stood Ezra Brownell's house and the engine house. This last named building had a career of varied usefulness as workshop, store, and "Little Belt" meeting-house, and is now a dwelling on Baptist Street. On Barstow Street is the new Public Library and the Soldiers' Monument, the gift of George Purrington, Jr., to the town.

A summer visitor once said that he could not imagine Mattapoisett in the winter. To think of it without the life and color, the yachts in the harbor, the summer verdure, and the summer girls, was quite impossible. Like the old enchanted city, Germelshausen, which had one day in a hundred years and then sank under the bogs and the marshes, it seemed to him that Mattapoisett must vanish from one season to another. Occasionally on a winter's evening the streets may appear so utterly deserted that one might almost imagine that to be the case. But the enchanted sleep effect is only out of doors; within, one finds warmth and cheer; and his meeting, club, society, or class, very much awake and alive, and ready to settle all questions temporal and spiritual. For the social activities of the town are largely in the line of societies. Of course the people entertain each other more or less, but weekly, fortnightly, and monthly meetings abound. There are the numerous auxiliary societies of the churches, the Lodge of the Sons of Temperance, and the W. C. T. U.; the Grange, the Memorial Association, — a social organization mostly of Grand Army men and their families; dancing classes, whist clubs, reading circles, and study classes to suit all tastes. As a needed change one man recently proposed to organize a "home rest" club, each member pledging himself to spend one evening a week at his own fireside, but that has not yet been organized.

The Village Improvement Association was started in 1904, mainly through the efforts and influence of Mr. and Mrs. Charles S. Hamlin. Since its inception, Mrs. Hamlin has continued its president, and under her leadership there has been enthusiastic support from every one. Many improvements have been made, materially benefiting and beautifying the town, and the society will increase in usefulness in the future. Could the old sea captain, previously quoted, return to us, and should he discern any deviation from the perpendicular now, he would but need to point it out to the Improvement Association to have it instantly taken in hand and righted up.

A year ago some benevolent citizens organized a society to maintain a summer home for convalescing or tired out people who need rest and change, but cannot afford the usual rates of board at the seashore. The successful first year of this home seems to justify a continuance of the work.

For the last twenty years Mattapoisett has increased steadily in population and in valuation. In supplying the needs of the vacation spenders many hands find employment in varied ways. The trolley has placed the village within the suburban radius from New Bedford, and the lately established steamship line to that port from the Western Islands has tended to stimulate the immigration of the Portuguese into the villages and farms of all

MATTAPOISETT HARBOR

the Old Rochester territory, and one wonders what changes their influence will make in the future upon this town which has always followed the old New England ideals.

So Mattapoisett sits to-day on her beautiful open harbor; the waters of Buzzards Bay roll in as blue as ever; the alewives still go up the river each April; there is still good fishing in the bay and shell fish on the shore. The catboats ride at their moorings around the buoy, or their sails glisten in the sun far out toward the Falmouth shore. The old family names are on the narrow elm-shaded streets, and many of the ancient houses look out upon them still. The town is full of pleasure-seekers who play tennis or golf, drive, sail, or fish, or dance at the Casino; but there is always the sense of rest and quiet, the salt air full of ozone, the fragrant breath of the pines, and the respite from city noise and dust.

And all along the shore from Aucoot Cove to the Fairhaven line, each year sees new homes built for those who seek their rest in close touch with nature and old ocean. Vacation and holiday are a part of the world's true needs, and in lending its own quiet charms to these forms of human demand, this seaside village has entered into a new and worthy role, more harmonious, perhaps, than were the activities of the past, with the musical name that it carries, — Mattapoisett, — the place of rest.

We can look with hope into the future for the increasing prosperity and attractiveness of the town, and we know that those who will be in our places then will linger

with the same interest over our present as we do over the
past which in this volume has been reviewed, for

"The present time is like a nearer sail,
    Fretted and torn and soiled by stormy tears;
Anchored far out beyond recalling hail,
    All sails look white across the sea of years."

THE BAY PATH'S END

The snake-like trail, o'er hill, through dale,
  Winds to a mound beside the sea
O'er which the white-winged Gods shall sail
  From their far land of mystery.

. . . .

Here clustered wigwams thinly smoked
  'Mid fields of undulating maize;
And here the arrow-maker chipped,
  In those last neolithic days,
The flakes of milk-white quartz to shape
  Keen-edged, or barbed, for chase or fight, —
To stain with Narragansett blood,
  Or stop the wild-goose in its flight.
Here Wampanoag wampum strung,
  Carved from the blue-eyed quahog shell,
Or framed the birch-bark's graceful curves
  To cleave the broad Atlantic swell.
The warrior bent the tough oak bow
  With tight-stretched vibrant deerskin string,
Or decked the scalp-lock with the plumes
  Far-borrowed from the eagle's wing.
With harsh-hued war-paint on the face,
  Dug from the shore-side beds of clay,
A wild, fierce silhouette he made
  Upon the headlands of the Bay.
Here Massasoit saw unmoved
  The Pale-face paddle to his shore;
Here met the Little Captain bold,
  And smoked the peace-pipe o'er and o'er.
Here, where still from the white sand floor
  The crystal waters bubbling burst,
The hunted Philip knelt one day
  Within the wood to quench his thirst.

. . . .

To-day no signal rends the ear
  In fish-hawk's cry or night-owl's screech;
The Red-man's spirit stalks unseen
  In moonlight eves beside the beach.

. . . .

Long sleep to warrior and long dreams,
    A Happy Hunting in the West,
A swift canoe o'er pleasant streams,
    And here a peaceful Place of Rest.

                     CHARLES ELMER JENNEY.

EXTRACTS FROM THE RECORDS

I

ROCHESTER SOLDIERS AND SAILORS IN EARLY WARS

These lists are necessarily imperfect. They have been compiled by Mrs. James L. Hammond from various sources, such as assessors' tables, etc., and especially from lists made by Miss Mary H. Leonard and others from the rolls in the State archives. Future research will undoubtedly add many names. The list for the Revolutionary War has been compared with the official record as far as that has been published, and is therefore correct for the names given.

FRENCH AND INDIAN WARS

1748
In Col. Doty's Regiment
Joseph Dexter

1755-6
In Col. Doty's Regiment

Nath. Holmes	Ab'm Ashley
Constant Dexter	John Foster
William Comes	Daniel Dexter

1756
Joshua Hammond

1760

Barnabas Hammond	John Coltran (?)
Jeduthan Hammond	Avery Parker
Paul Sears	Stephen Bennett
William Griffith	David Perry
Joseph Edwards	Nathan Bassett
Joseph Bumpass	William (Negro)

1762

Officers in First Plymouth Regiment

Capt. Nathaniel Ruggles   Ensign George King

Lieut. John Winslow

Rochester men, Col. Doty's Regiment, in hospital at Crown Point

Abm. Ashley   Nathaniel Holmes

Constant Dexter   C—— Ashley

—— Delano

Joseph Doty   *Dead*

—— Doty   Constant Dexter

Zenas Delano   Joseph Robinson

Joshua Hammond

Muster Rolls, Capt. Bradford's Company under Col. Tho. Doty, 1758–60.

Service in Canada

Dominicus Hovey   Paul Sears

Jonathan Crapo   Jabez Dexter

Lot Cowen(?)   Ebenezer Dexter

Barnabas Freeman   Charles Sturtevant

John Brigs   John Mags

Amasa White   Isaac Handy

Ishmael Trip   William Southworth

Isaac Job   Robert Clarke

David Sers   Nehemiah Bosworth, Jr.

Joseph Barlow

Service in Canada

Col. Doty's Regiment, 1758–60

Micah Griffin   Samuel Hastings

Silas Burgis   Luke Tobey

Elihugh Eldridge   Pollypus Hammond

Joseph Snow   Edward Doty

Joseph Moss   Samuel Steward

Aquilla Benson   Earl Clap

Samuel Brigs

Micah Sprague, Recruiting Officer

Recruits from Rochester 1760

Elhanan Cowing (?)
Stephen Bassett
David Perry
Samuel Burgis
Nathaniel Besse

Gideon Bennet
Nathan Bassett
William (Negro)
James Wing

In Bradford's Company, Doty's Regiment, were the following Rochester men:

Benjamin Hovey
Joseph Barlow
John Meigs
Jacob Allen(?)
Luther Arnold
Eph'm Doty
Asa Robinson
Marcus (?) Robinson

Constant Southward
Thomas Southard
Josiah Freeman
John Meigs
Joseph Barlow
Clark Foster
Joseph Barlow

In Capt. Pratt's Company

Thomas Combs
Zebulon Haskel
Solomon Doty
John Bennett
Ebenezer Barrows
John Barlow

Elna —— Barlow
Elnathan Combs
Samuel Joy
Gideon Cobb (?)
Galens Sparrow

Muster Roll of Capt. Bartlett's (Plymouth) Company

Stafford Hammond
Joseph Look
William Doty
E—— Doty
Joseph Bessy

Zibedy (?) Delano
Nath. Winslow
Joseph Dexter
Constant Southward
Gamaliel Arnold

Pay Roll, Abel Keen's Company

Solomon Young

In Stephen Holmes' Company

Nathan Forster

In Abel Keen's Company

Nathan Foster   Joshua Morse

REVOLUTIONARY WAR

In the official printed record of service, "Massachusetts Soldiers and Sailors of the Revolutionary War," many of the following names appear several times under various spellings, which variations are there noted under the commonly accepted form of each name.

Joshua Allen
William Annible
Charles Anthony
Kennedy (also given Canada) Asher
Abiel Atwood
Abner Baker
Joseph Bailey
Stephen Barden
Amittai Barlow
Ebenezer Barlow
Joseph Barlow
Obed Barlow
William Barlow
Joseph Bassett
Melatiah Basset
Newcomb Bassett
Rufus Bassett
Silas Bassett
Stephen Basset
Thomas Bassett
Willam Basset, Jr.
David Bates
Elijah Bates
Moses Bates
Sylvester Bates
—— Beats
Aquilla Benson
John Benson
Nathaniel Bessey
Seth Blackwill
Charles Blankinship

George Blankinship
William Blankinship
Lot Bly
William Bly
Amos Boals
Asa Boles
Ebenezer Bowles
Hosea Bolles
Joshua Boalls
Asa Bomp
Nehemiah Bosworth
John Bozworth
John Bozozard
Arnold Briggs
Elihu Briggs
Elisha Briggs
Elisha Briggs
Elisha Briggs, Jr.
Isaac Briggs
John Briggs
John Briggs, Jr.
Joseph Brigs
Nathan Briggs
Nathaniel Briggs
Samuel Briggs
Seth Briggs
James Brown
Charles Budget
Stephen Burdin
Bangs Burgess
Ebenezer Burges
Ichabod Burgess

John Burggs
Samuel Burges
William Cammel
Ebenezer Cannon
Lemuel Casvel
John Caswall
Elijah Caswell, Jr.
Thomas Caswell
John Chilson
Charles Church
Jonathan Church
Thomas Church
Silvanus Churchil
Thomas Churchill
Benjamin Clapp
Earl Clap
Ichabod Clap
Increase Clap
Kenelm (?) Clap
Seth Clap
Barnabas Clark
Ebenezer Clark
George Clark
John Clark
John Clark, 3rd.
Jonathan Clark
Joseph Clark
Joshua Clark
Josiah Clark
Melatiah Clark
Nathaniel Clark
Roger Clark
Weston Clark
William Clark
Elemuel Clarke
Caleb Combs
Ebenezer Cornell
Jabez Cottle
William Cowen
Asahel Cowing
William Cowing
Elnathan Crapo

Jeremiah Crapo
William Crapo
Daniel Croxford
Nathaniel Cushing
Manuel Dagget
John Daley
Benjamin Davis
Joseph Davis
Harper Delino
Jabez Dileno
Nathan Delano
Benjamin Dexter
Caleb Dexter
Constant Dexter
David Dexter
Ephraim Dexter
Isaiah Dexter
Jabez Dexter
Joshua Dextor
Noah Dexter
Silas Dexter
Thomas Dexter
Emanuel Doggett
Barnabas Doty
John Doty
Thomas Doty
David Edwards
Jonathan Edwards
Samuel Eldred
Ebenezer Ellis
George Ellis
Joel Ellis
Joshua Ellis
Nathan Ellis
Rowel Foot
Ebenezer Foster
Tilly Foster
Alden Freeman
John Gallt
Dodavah Garland
Jonathan Garland
Thomas Gould

John Gray
Samuel Green
Benjamin Gurney
George Gurney
Levi Gurney
Josiah Haket
Seth Hall
Reuben Hamlin
John Hammett
Anthony Hammond
Barzillai Hammond
Benjamin Hammond
Daniel Hammond
Ebenezer Hammond
Edward Hammond
Elijah Hammond
Elnathan Hammond
George Hammond
Gideon Hammond
Gideon Hammond, 2nd.
Hunne'l (Hunnewell) Hammond
James Hamon
John Hammond
John Hammond
John Hammond
Joseph Hammond
Josiah Hammond
Nathaniel Hammond
Noah Hammond
Phineas Hammond
Polypus Hammond
Seth Hammond
Shubael Hammond
Stafford Hammond
Stephen Hammond
Edward Handy
Elisha Handy
James Handy
Jonathan Handy
Silas Handy
Zaccheus Handy, Jr.
Aaron Harlow

Barnabas Haskel
David Haskell
Elias Haskel
Elnathan Haskell
Elnathan Haskell, Jr.
James Haskell
Job Haskell
Joseph Haskel
Joseph Haskell, 2nd
Micah Haskel
Nat Haskel
Timothy Haskel
Jonathan Haskell
Moses Haskell
Nathan Haskell
Zebulon Haskell
Benjamin Haskins
John Haskins
Nathaniel Haskins
Thomas Haskins
Benjamin Hatch
Jonah Hatch
Joseph Hatch
Jonathan Hatch
Sylvanus Hatch
Ichabod Hartheway
Savory Hathaway
Seth Hathaway
Simon Hathaway
Solomon Hayward
John Hazeltine
John Hiller
Timothy Hiller
Israel Holmes
William Hopper
Abel House
Ezra Hovey
Israel Hovey
Solomon Howard
James Howland
Nathan Jenne, Jr.
Samuel (?) Jenne

John Keen
Consider King
Ebenezer King
Ichabod King
Jonathan King
Nathaniel King
Lemuel LeBaron
Barzilla Livingston
Sherman Lincoln
Adam Look
Samuel Look
Francis Luce
Samuel Lombard
Caleb Lumber
Josiah Lumbard
William Maxwell
John Meiggs
Church Mendall
Daniel Mendall
Samuel Mendall
Seth Mendall
John Millard
Rev. Jona. Moore
Ebenezer Morse
John Morse
Benjamin Morton
John Muxam
Barzillai Nickerson
William Nicoll
Robert Noulton
Ezekiel Nye
Ichabod Nye
Nathan Nye
William Nye
John Oliver
Russell Oliver
John Omey
Philip Omey
William Paddy
Ephraim Painee
Abner Pane
Ebenezer Parker

Joseph Parker
Thomas Parlow
Cuff Perry
James Perry
William Poddy
Dr. John Pitcher
Theophilus Pitcher
Ebenezer Pope
Elnathan Pope
Isaac Pope
Seth Pope
Caleb Randall
Constant Randall
David Randal
Elisha Randel
Hathaway Randol
Jethro Randel
John Randall
Lemuel Randel
Micah Randall
Moses Randall
Nehemiah Randel
Seth Randel
William Randall
Christopher Ricks
Nathaniel Rider
Robert Rider
Roland Rider
Israel Roach
Prince Rodman
Elisha Ruggles
Nathaniel Ruggles
Timothy Ruggles
Jeffrey Sachamus
Samuel Samson
Nathan Savery
Allen Sears
David Sears
Judah Sears
Nathan Sears
Nathaniel Sears
Silas Sears

Jeffrey (also given Jephthah) Sechamin
Christopher (also given Crispan) Shaw
Isaiah Shaw
Isaac Sherman
William Shermand
John Short
Joshua Shermon
Godfrey Shreve
John Simmons
Nathaniel (also given Nathan) Smith
Richard Smith
William Smith
Borman Snow
David Snow
Ebenezer Snow
Edmund Snow
Isaac Snow
Ivory Snow
James Snow
Mark Snow
Nicholas Snow
Paul Snow
Richard Snow

Samuel Snow
Thomas Snow
Andrew Sothworth
Daniel Southward
David Southworth
John Southworth
Stephen Southworth
Joshua Spooner
Samuel Sprague
John Stephens
Nye Stephenson
John Stevens
Nathaniel Stevens
Nye Stevens
Charles Stetson
Peleg Stewart
Samuel Stoder (?)
James Stuart
Charles Sturtevant
John Sturtevant
Zadok Sturtevant
Thomas Tabb
John Tanner
Hezekiah Tinkham
Thomas Tobey

The official record of the following has not yet been published, and the remainder of this list is therefore unverified.

Ruben Tripp
John Wallis
John Warren
Richard Warren, Sergt.
Calvin Washburn
Ephraim Washburn
Isaac Washburn
Thomas Weeden
Eliphalet Weeks
Joseph Wellen
Francis West
Joseph Whellen

Cornelius White
Justis White
Mel'a White
Thomas Whiteridge, Corp.
Richard Whittemore
Benjamin Wilbor, Corp.
James Wilkens
Thomas Wilkens
Thomas Wilkey
Samuel Wilomen (?)
William Wiltshire
—— Wing, Jr.

Benjamin Wing
David Wing
James Wing
John Wing
Joseph Wing
Joseph Wing, Sergt.
Jonathan Wing
Philip Wing
Shubael Wing
Stephen Wing
Asa Winslow

Edward Winslow
John Winslow
Kenelm Winslow
Lemuel Winslow, Sergt.
Nathan Winslow
Stephen Winslow
Tisdale Winslow
Howland Yong (?)
Henry Yong, Corp.
Solom Yong, Lieut.

The following names appear in the official record, but without residence given. They were undoubtedly Rochester men.

Oliver Allen
Weston Allen
Jonathan Annable
Samuel Arnold
John Baker
Aaron Barlow
Seth Barlow
Gideon Bester ⎫
Gideon Besto ⎬ (Barstow)
Gideon Bestow ⎭
Hopestill Bisbce
Dennis Blackwell
Job Blankinship
Amaziah Bolles
Benjamin Bolles
David Bolles
John Bolles
Peter Bosworth
—— Briggs
Benjamin Brown
Elisha Brown
Seth Bumpus
Ebenezer Burge
Elijah (also given Elisha) Burge
Seth Burges
Thomas Carter
Earl Church

Jeremiah Clap
John Clap
Isaac Clark
Lemuel Clark
William Conant
James Cowing
Barnice Crain
Edward Croell
Stephen Cushing
Cephas Cushman
Samuel Daggott
Sanford Davis
Stephen Delano
David Dexter, Jr.
Elijah Dexter
Elisha Dexter
Jonathan Dexter
Joseph Dexter
Jerathmeel Doty
Joseph Edwards
John Ellis
Malachi Ellis
Thomas Ellis
Robert Foote
Job Gibbs
Aaron Hammond
Enoch Hammond

"Iturael" (Israel?) Hammond
John Hammond, 3rd.
John Hammond, 4th
Roger Hammond
Ebenezer Haskell
Lot Haskell
Peter Haskell
Timothy Haskell
Thomas Hiller
Abner Hillman
Dominicus Hovey
Nathaniel Jenne
Joseph Levitt
George Lincoln
Barnabas Luce
Stephen Luce
Jesse Lumbart
John Macomber
Alden Manter
Zaccheus Mead
Ebenezer Meads
Ebenezer Meigs
Nathaniel Meigs
John Miller
John Muxcomb
John Muxham, 2nd
George B. Nye
Peter Oliver
Aaron Parker
Asa Pease

Joseph Perry
Jonathan Pope
Asaph Price
Joseph Prince
Amos Randal
William Raymond
John Rider
David Rogers
Dr. —— Samson
Jabez Shearman
Abishai Sherman
Cornelius Sherman
Elisha Sherman
Joshua Sherman
Micah (also given Micajah) Sherman
Nathaniel Shearman
Richard Sherman
Stephen Sherman
Joseph Snow
Joshua Snow
Nathaniel Snow
Josiah Sole
George Taylor
William Tanner
James Swift
Job Sturtevant
John Spence
Andrew Sturtevant
Wilbr (Wilber) Southworth

WAR OF 1812

Ten thousand militia were called out in Massachusetts for the service of the War of 1812. No militia company is accredited to Rochester on the regular rolls.

Jesse Haskell, Serg't   Thomas Ellis, Corp.

Capt. Stall's Company of Artillery, under Gen. Goodwin, in service at New Bedford from June 16 to August 1, 1814.

Jona. Kinney   Seth Mitchell

A Company in service in New Bedford and Fairhaven, Col. Lincoln's Reg't, June 30 to July 14, 1814.

Sergeant's Guard at Rochester under General Goodwin, June and July, 1814.

Jonathan Vaughn, En.
Thomas Ashley, Sergt.
Tillotson Dunham, Sergt.

Joseph Doty, Corp.
Azel Bryant, Corp.

Privates

Philip Avery
Elijah Briggs
Briggs Crapo
Peleg Clark
Joseph Bennett
Joseph Bishop
Barnabas N. Douglas
John Sears
Jesse Pratt
Richard Corsing (?)
Jonathan King
John Cornwell

Benjamin Rider
Samuel Cowing
Joseph Lombard
Charles P. Hammond
Moses Bates
Solomon Hitchman
Micah Blackwell
William Stetson
Eph'm Snow
Peleg Hathaway
Mich Stevens
John Shearman

Ensign's Guard at Rochester, under General Goodwin, from September to October, 1814.

Moses Mendall Ensign
Dennis Prince, Sergt.
Israel Hammond, Sergt.

Perez Bassett, Corp.
Jared Blankinship, Corp.

Privates

Samuel Mendall
Eph'm Snow
Benjamin Snow
Gideon Dexter
Luke Dexter
James Snow
Caleb L. Cannon
Jonathan Dexter
Geo. Boston (Barstow?) Jr.
Nathaniel Cushing
Jabez Handy

Francis Hillis
Lemuel W. Lain
Paddock Bates
George Blankinship
James Blankinship, Jr.
William Crapo
Briggs Crapo
Josiah Cobb
James Freeman
Eph'm Tinkham
Benjamin Cushing

II

A RATE BILL OF THE INHABITANTS
OF ROCHESTER, 1776

From the original in the possession of Lemuel LeBaron Dexter Mattapoisett.

The figures show the total tax levied, including Polls, Real, Personal, and Faculty taxes. Polls were assessed 5s. 5d.

Oliver Allen, £1
Ephm Annible, 5s. 10d.
Saml Annible, 5s. 5d.
Eleazer Allen, 5s. 5d.
Jeremiah Austin, £2 7s. 10d.
Nathan Briggs, 9s. 0d. 2q.
Ebenr Barlow, 5s. 10d.
Nathl Bessey, 6s. 8d. 2q.
Willm Barlow, 7s. 10d. 2q.
Thos Bolles, 16s. 9d. 2q.
Seth Blackwell, £1 3s. 4d.
Saml Bolles, 17s. 2d. 2q.
Joseph Barlow, 6s. 10d.
Moses Barlow, 11s. 4d. 2q.
Aaron Barlow, 17s. 8d.
Silas Briggs, 11s. 4d. 2q.
Saml Briggs 2nd, £1 2s. 2d. 2q.
Silas Briggs Junr, 7s. 9d.
Obed Barlow, 15s. 9d.
Amittai Barlow, 15s. 9d.
George Barlow, 6s. 3d. 2q.
Benja Bolles, 11s. 6d.
Benja Bolles Jnr 5s. 5d.
Seth Barlow, 7s. 5d.
David Bolles, 15s. 4d.
Gideon Bestow, 17s. 2d. 2q.
Seth Bestow, 8s. 10d.
Wyat Barlow, 8s. 11d.
Ebenr Bolles, 5s. 5d.
Hosea Bolles, 5s. 5d.

Amesiah Bolles, 8s. 2d.
Thos Carter, 5s. 5d.
Robert Clark, 14s.
Joseph Cannon, 7s. 8d. 2q.
Thos Dexter, 5s. 5d.
Silas Cross, 5s. 5d.
Lot Cowing, 8s. 9d.
Nathl Cushing, 17s. 1d.
Stephen Cushing, 6s. 10d. 2q.
Earl Clap, £1 0s. 5d.
Ebenr Cannon, 7s. 3d. 2q.
Ezekiel Clark, 11s. 10d.
Cephas Cushman, 9s. 2d. 2q.
John Clark, 1s. 5d.
John Clark 4th, 5s. 5d.
John Clark 3rd, 15s. 11d.
Joshua Cowing, 15s.
Zebeth Cowing, 7s.
Zadock Cowing, 6s. 7d.
Asael Cowing, 6s. 7d.
Seth Cowing, 11s. 8d.
John Curby, 14s. 8d. 2q.
Charles Church, 12s. 1d.
Richard Church Jnr, £1 2s. 0d. 2q.
wd. Bathiah Church, 19s. 11d. 2q.
Lemuel Church, 5s. 5d.
Gideon Cornall, 7s.
James Clark, 5s. 5d.
Seth Dexter, 19s. 8d. 2q.
Elijah Dexter, 7s. 9d.

wd Mary Dexter, £1 2s.
Jsiah Dexter, 6s. 1d. 2q.
Jabez Dexter, 7s.
Ephm Dexter, 11s. 11d. 2q.
Caleb Dexter, 11s. 11d. 2q.
Benja Dexter Junr, 15s. 3d. 2q.
Jonathan Dexter, 9s. 2d. 2q.
David Dexter, 9s. 2d. 2q.
John Dexter, 17s. 9d. 2q.
John Dexter Junr, 5s. 5d.
Silas Dexter, 5s. 5d.
Edward Dexter, 8s. 9d.
Benja Dexter, 17s. 1d. 2q.
Saml Eldredg, 5s. 5d.
John Ellis, £1 0s. 3d. 2q.
Joshua Ellis, 5s. 5d.
John Ellis Junr, £1 1s.
Joseph Edwards, 5s. 5d.
Elnathan Eldredge, 19s. 1d. 2q.
Joel Ellis, £1 3s. 4d. 2q.
David Edwards, 8s.
Chillingsworth Forster, 5s. 5d.
Silvenas Gibbs, 12s. 6d. 2q.
Abel House, 5s. 5d.
Henry Headley, 8s. 5d. 2q.
James Headley, 8s. 0d. 2q.
John Haskell Junr, 15s. 4d. 2q.
Elijah Hammd, 7s. 5d. 2q.
Jabez Hammd, Junr 10d. 2q.
wd Abigail Hammd, 19s. 13d. 0q.
Barzillai Hammd, 6s. 3d.
Honeywell Hammd, 6s. 7d.
Josiah Hammd, £1 1s. 3d. 2q.
Elnathan Hammd, 5s. 5d.
James Hammd, £1 0s. 3d. 2q.
Israel Hammd, 15s.
John Hammd 2nd, 5s. 5d.
John Hammd 3rd, 5s. 5d.
Gideon Hammd, 7s. 9d.
Nathan Hammd, 12s. 11d. 2q.
Enoch Hammd Esqr, £1 4s. 11d. 2q.

Elisha Hammd, 1£ 7s. 1d. 2q.
Ebenr Hammd, 7s. 3d. 2q.
wd Mehittable Haskell, £1 1s. 8d. 2q.
Elias Haskell, 5s. 5d.
Barnibas Haskell, 5s. 5d.
wd Anna Haskell £1 12s. 9d. 2q.
David Hammd, 5s. 5d.
Dominicus Hovey, 6s. 7d.
Saml Hovey, 5s. 5d.
Thos Haskell, 6s. 6d. 2q.
wd Abiah Haskell, 9s. 11d.
Zebulon Haskell, 5s. 5d.
Job. Haskell, 6s. 3d. 2q.
Seth Hiller, £1 10s. 11d.
Ebenr Holmes, 6s. 10d. 2q.
Isaac Handy, 7s. 3d. 2q.
Jonathan Handy, 5s. 10d.
Silas Handy, 5s. 5d.
Moses Hiller, 19s. 3d.
Isaac Hiller, 14s. 8d.
Solomon Howard, 5s. 5d.
wd Rebecca Hiller, 16s. 4d.
Silvenas Hammd, 1s. 9d.
Nathl Hammd, 15s. 2d.
John Hammd, £2 6s. 6d. 2q.
Timo Hammd, 18s. 6d.
Zoath Hammd, 5s. 10d.
Ebenr Haskell, 5s. 5d.
Benja Hatch, 11s. 6d. 2q.
Lurey (?) Hatch, 1s. 2d.
Willm Irish, 16s. 5d. 2q.
Noah Hammd, 5s. 5d.
Saml Jenne, 7s. 9d.
John Keen, 6s. 5d.
Josiah Lumbard, 5s. 5d.
Stephen Landers, 5s. 10d.
George Lincoln, 5s. 5d.
Zacchs Mead, £1 4s. 1d.
John Marshell, £1 11s. 2d. 2q.
John Meggs, 7s.
Nathl Meegs, 10s.

Jabez Norton, 12s. 10d.

Ichabod Norton, 6s. 3d.

Matthew Norton, 5s. 5d.

Elijah Norton, 7s.

Jonathan Nye, 11s. 11d. 2q.

George Bonum Nye, 17s. 4d. 2q.

Nathan Nye Junr, £1 4s. 3d.

Willm Nye, 5s. 10d.

Asa Price, 7s. 7d.

Theophilus Pease, 4s. 9d. 2q.

Theophilus Pease Junr, 11s. 4d. 2q.

Doct John Pitcher, 11s. 11d.

Isaac Pope, 7s. 10d. 2q.

Isaac Pope Junr, 11s. 10d.

Stephen Perry, £2 10s. 4d.

James Randol, £1 2s. 5d. 2q.

Nathl Ruggles Esqr, £1 9s. 2d. 2q.

John Randol, 8s. 11d.

David Randol, 8s. 0d. 2q.

Simeon Randol, £1 0s. 7d.

Amos Randol, 8s. 0d. 2q.

John Randol Junr, 5s. 5d.

Lemuel Randol, 7s. 10d. 2q.

Wd Mary Read, 18s. 8d.

Lemuel Randol Junr, 5s. 5d.

Thos Southworth, £1 4s. 6d. 2q.

Daniel Southworth, 5s. 5d.

Joseph Snow, 6s. 3d. 2q.

Seth Snow, 15s. 7d. 2q.

Nye Stevens, 5s. 5d.

Boreman Snow, 5s. 5d.

John Shearman 2nd, 18s. 6d. 2q.

Willm Shearman 4th, 6s.

Willm Shearman 2nd, £1 2s. 11d.

Jabez Shearman, 5s. 5d.

Saml Shearman, 16s. 2d. 2q.

Nathl Sears, 16s. 4d.

Ebenr Sears, 6s.

Andrew Stevens, 11s. 5d.

Timo Stevens Junr, 10s. 10d.

Prince Stevens, 6s. 10d. 2q.

Charles Sturtevant, £1 13s.

Charles Sturtevant Jun, 5s. 5d.

Charles Stetson, 14s. 4d.

Ezra Stetson, 15s. 11d.

Wilber Southworth, 15s. 11d.

John Simonds, 6s.

Zadock Sturtevant, 19s. 10d.

Micah Sturtevant, 5s. 5d.

Jonathan Sturtevant, 8s.

James Stuart, 2s. 4d.

James Stuart Junr, 7s. 5d. 2q.

Anthony Savory, 7s. 3d.

Ichabod Smith, 11s. 2d. 2q.

Joshua Snow, 7s. 2d.

Timo Snow, 5s. 5d.

Willm Shaw, Dart, 1s. 9d.

Consider Sampson, 11s. 3d.

Joshua Studley, 6s.

Saml Sampson, 8s. 4d.

Abisha Shearman, 15s. 9d. 2q.

Elihue Shearman, 15s. 7d. 2q.

Jesse Trip, 13s. 7d.

Saml Trip, Dart, 5s. 10d.

Jonathan Trip, 5s. 5d.

John Terry, 11s. 8d.

Majr Zacchs Tobey, Dart, 3s. 1d. 2q.

Peter Tinkham, 7s. 3d. 2q.

Charles Tinkham, 5s. 5d.

Ephm Tinkham, 5s. 5d.

Isaac Vinsent, Dart, 4s. 4d. 2q.

Willm Wiltshire, 7s. 9d.

John Winslow, £1 10s. 6d.

wd Bethiah Winslow, 17s. 8d.

Nathan Winslow, 5s. 5d.

wd Margaret Wing, 1s. 9d.

Jonathan Wing, 6s. 5d.

Charles Wing, 5s. 5d.

Capt Edward Winslow, £1 4s.

Tisdale Winslow, 7s. 3d.

John Wallise, 5s. 5d.

Timo West, 13s.

Jonathan Wing Junr, 10s.

Solomon Young, 17*s.* 8*d.*
Solomon Young Junr, 5*s.* 5*d.*
Thos Tobey, 5*s.* 5*d.*
Asa Winslow, 5*s.* 5*d.*
Ebenr Bishop, 5*s.* 5*d.*
Benja Wilbour, 5*s.* 5*d.*

Willm Nichols, 7*s.* 7*d.*
Daniel Croxford, 5*s.* 5*d.*
—— Whittemore, 5*s.* 5*d.*
—— Beard, 5*s.* 5*d.*
Abraham Devill, 10*s.* 4*d,* 2*q.*

This Rate bill of the Inhabitants of the Town of Rochester Containing the Sum of £132: 8: 2 in the Sum Total Compleated by us Janr 25: 1776.

> NATHL HAMD
> DAVID WING } *Assessors of Rochester.*
> JOHN DOTY

In the above rate bill the following persons were assessed for a *faculty tax* of the amount indicated: —

Jeremiah Austin, 10*d.*
Gideon Bestow, 1*s.* 5*d.* 2*q.*
Stephen Cushing, 7*d.*
Earl Clap, 7*d.*
Wid Bathiah Church, 10*d.* 2*q.*
John Hamm^d, 1*s,* 5*d,* 2*q.*
Benja. Hatch, 7*d.*

Nathan Nye Junr. 1*s.* 2*d.*
Doct, John Pitcher, 10*s.* 2*d.*
Wilm Shearman 4th, 7*d.*
Zadock Sturtevant, 7*d.*
Abisha Shearman, 10*d.* 2*q.*
Elihue Shearman, 10*d,* 2*q.*

Another rate bill of even date, for the sum of £101: 1: 2: 2, was made by the same assessors and contains the same names.

III

A LIST OF MAXIMUM PRICES; ROCHESTER, 1777

"In obedience to a law of Massachusetts Bay, entitled, 'An Act to Prevent Monopolies and Oppression;' we the selectmen & Committee in the Town of Rochester, in the said state, have proceeded to a Statement of the several articles enumerated in their act, & others as directed by the said law to be stated, as shall not be sold in the said Town of Rochester, anytime hereafter for more than the prices affixed to the said article, as hereunder enumerated:"

Reaping & Mowing, not to exceed 4*s.* per day.
Other common Labour from the first day of Apr. to the first day of Oct. not to exceed 2*s.* 6*d.* per day, and the other six months not to exceed 2*s.* per day.

House-carpenters, Wheel-wrights, and Joyners, not to exceed 4s. per day in the summer season, & in the winter not to exceed 3s. per day.

For one pair of oxen a day 2s. 6d.; for a cart a day 1s.

For a Plow one day, 1s.

Bloomery iron by the Cwt. not to exceed 30s.

Maple coal not to exceed 4d. by the Bushell.

Pine Do. not to exceed 3d. by the bushell.

Horse-shoeing, all around, with toe and heel corks, not to exceed 6s.

Good narrow axes not to exceed 8s.

Good scythes not to exceed 8s.

Good hoes not to exceed 4s.

Iron work by the Cwt., or the single lb. not to exceed 3d. the lb.

Good board nails by the M. not to exceed 15s.; and in ye like proportion for a smaller quantity.

Good double tens by ye M. not to exceed 28s.

Shingle nails by ye M. not to exceed 7s.

Clapboard nails by ye M. not to exceed 11s.

Raw hides not to exceed 3d. per lb.

Raw calves skins not to exceed 6d. per lb.

Good tanned leather by ye lb. not to exceed 1s. 4d.

Curried Do. in proportion.

For good shoes for men made of neats leather, best sort, not to exceed 8s. 8d.; and others of that kind in proportion.

Good women's calve skin shoes of the best sort not to exceed 7s.; and others in proportion.

For making one pair of men's shoes, workmanlike, not to exceed 3s.; for makeing others in proportion, as usual.

Weaving all wool, ell wide, not to exceed 6s. and other weaving in proportion according to former usage.

Good summer wheat by the bushell not to exceed 6s. 6d.

Good rye not to exceed 5s.

Good Indian corn not to exceed 4s.

Good merchantable sheeps wool not to exceed 2s. per lb.

Pork, well fatted and of good quality not to exceed 4½d. by ye lb.

Salt pork in the usual proportion, according to the price of salt.

Beef, well fatted, grass fed, not to exceed 3d. per lb.

Good imported salt, not to exceed 10s. per ye bushell.

Salt, in town, manufactured from sea water, not to exceed 13s. per bushell.

Good West India rum by the gallon not to exceed 7s. 8d.; and by the quart not to exceed 2s.

Good phlip or Toddy by the mugg or the Bole with one-half pint of West India rum in the same, not to exceed 1s.

For a Common Dinner, at Tavern, not to exceed 1s.

Other meals in proportion.

For horse keeping by the night or twenty-four hours, by hay, not to exceed 1s. 6d.

A night's lodging at a Tavern, 4d.

Horse keeping by grass at night or twenty-four hours not to exceed 1s.

New England rum by the gallon not to exceed 4s. 8d.; or by the Quart not to exceed 1s. 3d.

Best Muscovado Sugar by the Cwt. not to exceed £3, and the same for half or half-quarter by the hundred, and by the single lb. not to exceed 8d.

Molasses, the best sort, by ye hogshead, not to exceed 3s. 4d. by the gallon; by the barrel not to exceed 3s. 8d. a gallon; by the single gallon not to exceed 4s.

Chocolate by ye lb. not to exceed 1s. 8d.; cheap not to exceed 6d. per lb.

Butter by the single lb. not to exceed 10d.; by the firkin not to exceed 9d.

Pease by the bushell, not to exceed 8s.

Beens, by the bushell, not to exceed 6s.

Spanish potatoes by ye bushell not to exceed 1s. 6d.

Good yarn Storkins, best sort, not to exceed 6s.

Salt-Pork, 220 lbs. in a Barril, not to exceed £5.

Salt-Beef by the Barril, 240 lb. in a barril, not to exceed £3, 14s. 6d.

Good Cotten wool by ye lb. not to exceed 3s. 8d.

Good oats, by the bushell, not to exceed 2s.

Good flax, well dressed, by the lb., not to exceed 1s.

Good coffee, by the lb., not to exceed 1s. 4d.

Tryed Tallow by the lb. not to exceed 7½d.

Good yard wide Toe Cloth by ye yard not to exceed 2s. 4d.

Course Linen & toe Cloth of Different widths in proportion.

Good striped flannel, yard wide, of a Good quality, not to exceed 3s. 6d. per yd.

Flannel, Chect or Striped, Suitable for Shirting, not to exceed 4s. and other cloth in proportion, according to former usage.

Oak wood at the shore not to exceed 13s. per cord.

Split pine Do. at ye shore, not to exceed 9s. per cord.

Homespun, yard wide, cotton and linnen cloth of the Common sort not to exceed 4s. by ye yd.; and other widths and qualities of linnen cloth in like proportion.

Mutton & Veal not to exceed 4d. per lb.

Flower from the Southern States not to exceed 24s. by the Cwt.

Teaming work, To cart a ton one mile, not to exceed 1*s*. 6*d*.; and in proportion for a greater distance, referring to journeying with a team.

Turkies, Dunghill Fowls, and Ducks, not to exceed 5*d*. per lb.

Grease not to exceed 4*d*. per lb.

Milk by the quart not to exceed 2½ *d*.

English Hay, in the winter and Spring, not to exceed 3*s*. 8*d*. per Cwt.; English hay in the meadow, before stacked, not to exceed £2. 14*s*. per ton.

Salt hay in the marsh, before stacked, not to exceed 36*s*. per ton.

Do. in the Winter and Spring, not to exceed 2*s*. 5*d*. per Cwt.

Good merchantable white-pine boards, at the landing, not to exceed £3, by the M.

Oats by the pottle, not to exceed 4*d*.

Horse hire for Journeying not to exceed 4*d*. per mile.

Ship carpenters, at old work, not to exceed 4*s*. 8*d*. per day if boarded.

Corkers not to exceed 5*s*. 4*d*. per day if boarded.

Cedar rails, not to exceed 28*s*., by the swampside, merchantable.

Good merchantable cedar shingle not to exceed 22*s*. per M. at the Landing.

Turnips, old sort, not to exceed 1*s*. 10*d*. by the bushell.

Turnips, Called french, Do., not to exceed 2*s*. 2*d*. by the bushell.

Best Tobacco, leaf-stalked and pig tail role, not to exceed 8*d*. per lb.

Common Do. not to exceed 5*d*. per lb.

The best of men Taylors at journey work not to exceed 2*s*. 8*d*. per day.

Records of the Town of Rochester, Vol. III, page 224,

IV

ASSESSORS' LIST, 1740

A LIST OF PERSONS ASSESSED IN MATTAPOISETT IN 1740

"This List and Valuation taken by the assessors of Mattapoisett Precinct in Rochester, in the year 1740, as followeth:

MEN'S NAMES	POLES	REAL		PARSON^L	
		£	*s.*	£	*s.*
Joseph Alliver	1	6	0	10	8
Joseph Bools	2	4	0	7	18
Jonathan Bools	1	8	0	9	8
Samuel Bools	1	6	0	12	13

MEN'S NAMES	POLES	REAL		PARSON[L]	
		£	s.	£	s.
Joseph Barlow	1	18	0	21	10
Ebenezer Barlow	1	18	0	26	0
George Barlow	1	12	0	17	8
Thomas Clark	1	29	0	24	4
Benjamin Bools	1	0	0	0	0
John Clark	1	0	0	0	0
Caleb Clark	1	0	0	0	0
Thomas Dexter	1	20	0	16	8
Josiah Dexter	1	6	0	8	14
Constant Dexter	1	18	0	5	19
Jabez Dexter	2	6	0	9	0
George Danford	1	2	0	9	14
Stephen Dewolf	1	0	0	1	18
Daniel Dexter	1	0	0	0	0
Ephraim Dexter	1	12	0	13	2
Samuel Dexter	1	0	0	5	18
John Danford	1	0	0	0	0
Capt Benja. Hammond	2	20	0	26	8
Lieut John Hammond	1	21	0	23	13
Lieut Jabez Hammond	1	18	0	17	9
Lieut Antipas Hammond	1	11	0	15	11
Thomas Winslow	1	7	0	15	13
Barzillai Hammond	1	9	0	18	6
Rowland Hammond	0	0	0	8	17
Matthew Howard .. :	1	3	0	6	4
Barnabas Hammond	2	9	0	23	2
Benja. Hammond Junr.	1	10	0	19	2
Israel Hammond	1	11	10	18	14
Nathan Hammond, 2nd	1	12	0	17	0
Archelaus Hammond	1	1	10	16	6
Josiah Hammond	1	9	0	12	6
John Hammond, Junr.	1	0	0	0	0
Samuel Hix	0	4	0	0	0
Mark Haskell, Tanner	0	9	0	0	0
Ephraim Haskell	0	9	0	0	0
Jonathan Johnson	1	0	0	7	18
Miles Parker	1	2	10	4	0
Thomas Randoll	2	10	0	12	0
Lazarus Randoll	1	2	0	5	0

MEN'S NAMES	POLES	REAL		PARSON[L]	
		£	s.	£	s.
Simeon Randoll 1		0	0	1	10
William Raymond...........................1		10	0	4	0
Jonathan Tobey 1		12	0	13	0
Zaccheus Tobey 1		3	0	0	0
Joseph Turner 2		3	0	6	0
Elisha Tupper 0		6	0	0	0
Meded Tupper 1		0	0	0	0
Nathan Tupper 1		3	0	8	10
William White 1		0	0	0	0

This List and Valuation Consisting of £878 19s 0d Estates and 52 Poles being Mattapoisett Precinct State bill for this Present year made and compleated this 23 Day of June one thousand Seven Hundred and forty.

Pr. { GIDEON SOUTHWORTH
BENJA HAMMOND JUNR. } Assessors.
ISRAEL HAMMOND

"Recorded pr me GIDEON SOUTHWORTH Prect Clerk."

A true copy; Records of the Second Precinct in Rochester, Vol. I, page 34.

LEMUEL LeBARON DEXTER, Precinct Clerk.

V

LIST OF MEMBERS, 1772

THE SECOND CHURCH IN ROCHESTER; MATTAPOISETT PRECINCT

" A Catalogue of the Members of the Chh when Mr LeBaron was Ordained: January 29, 1772."

MEN	WOMEN
Dn Clarke.	Abigl Wife of Antipas Hammond.
Dn Barlow.	Pheba, Wife of Nathl Hammond.
Eldr Barlow.	Abigl, Wife of Jabez Hammond.
John Hannable.	Mary, Wife of Josiah Hammond.
Zacheus Mead.	Hannah, Wife of James Hammond.
Josiah Hammond.	Hannah, Wife of Dn Clarke.
Aaron Barlow	Drusillah, Wife of Enoch Hammond.

MEN	WOMEN
Joshua Snow.	Mary, Wife of John Hammond.
Antiphs Hammond.	Abigl, Wife of Thos Southworth.
Nathl Hammond.	Mary, Wife of Seth Dexter.
Jabez Hammond.	Mary, Wife of Jonathn Bowles.
Enoch Hammond.	Ann, Wife of Thos Bowles.
John Hammond.	Mary, Wife of Saml Bowles
Jonathn Bowles.	Desiah, Wife of Seth Snow.
Thoms Bowles.	Epiphania, Wife of John Clark.
John Danford	Experience, Wife of Ebenezr Cannon.
John Curby.	Merriam, Wife of Saml Jenny.
Ephm Dexter.	Ann, Wife, of Luke Tobey.
John Clark.	Jane, Wife of Gideon Barstow.
Edward Dexter.	Bathsheba, Wife of Charles Studson.
Ebenr Cannon	Sarah, Wife of Zacheus Mead.
Saml Jenny.	Ruth, Wife of George Barlow.
Luke Tobey.	Abigl, Wife of Dn Barlow.
Gideon Barstow.	Huldah, Wife of Abner Hammond.
Saml Look.	Elizabeth, Wife of John Annable.
Nehemiah Randall.	Elizabeth, Wife of Archelaus Hammond.
Benjamin Bowles.	Mary, Wife of Jed: Hammond.
Zacheus Hatch.	Mary, Wife of Zachs Hatch.
Timothy Stephens.	Lydia, Wife of Nathl Cushing.
Amaziah Hammond.	Susannah, Wife of John Bowles.
Nathl Hammond.	Hannah, Wife of Ben: Bowles.
Archelaus Hammond.	Deborah, Wife of James Peckum.
Tom. ⎤	Elizabeth, Wife of the Revd Bezl Shaw.
Toby. ⎬ Blacks.	Dinah, Wife of Thos Mitchell.
Jack. ⎦	Elizabeth, Wife of John Clarke.
	Widow Else Clark.
	Widow Charity Hammond.
	Widow Lydia Bowles.
	Widow Mary Dexter.
	Widow Abigl Dexter.
	Widow Bath: Hammond.
	Abigl Clarke.
	Rose Hammond.
	Widow Cowen.
	Judah ⎤ Negroes.
	Phal. ⎦

A List of 81 Members, — 35 Men; 46 Women.

VI

INFANT BAPTISMS AND MARRIAGES

*From the Records of the Second Church in Rochester, Mattapoisett
Precinct*

1. BAPTISMS

The record books of the Congregational Church show the following
baptisms between the years 1740 and 1857.   Compiled from lists
furnished by Lemuel LeBaron Dexter, Church Clerk.   Where several
children were baptized at one time, they appear under the name of the
first child mentioned in the record.   The following list of pastors indicate what minister officiated: —

Rev. Ivory Hovey	1740–1768
Rev. Lemuel LeBaron	1772–1836
or Rev. Asahel Cobb, (Colleague)	1826–1830
or Rev. Thomas Robbins, (Colleague)	1832–1836
Rev. Thomas Robbins	1836–1844
Rev. Isaiah C. Thacher	1844–1849
Rev. William L. Mather	1851–1855
Rev. Charles Livingstone	1856–1857
Rev. William L. Parsons	1858–1864

ALLEN, Abigail Smith, Child of Perkins & Abigail, Nov. 8, 1776.
  Benjn the Chield of Barnibas by his wife ———— was baptized on
    her account, Feb. 2, 1755.
  Betty, Jesse, Elisha, Loice, Children of Ebenr & Mary, Sept. 1778.
ANNABLE (ANNIBLE), Elisha, William, Benjamin, Childr of Wilm
    & Taba (Hannable), Dec. 6, 1772.
  Elizabath the Chield of John, July 18, 1747.
  Ephraim Son to John by his wife, Nov. 24, 1744.
  John, Elizabeth, twins of William and Tabitha, Dec. 1777.
  John, Son of Tabitha & Wm, Oct., 1780.
  Jonathan, Ann, Samuel, Children of Wilm & Tabitha, Apr. 12, 1772.
  Leonard, Child of William & Tabitha, Dec. 11, 1774.
  Saml, Chield to John, Aug., 1749.

BACON, Benjamin James, son of Benjamin Aug. 27, 1837.
  Eliza Ann, 1817.
  Nathan Crosby, Child of Benjn & Patience, Aug. 10, 1829.
  Sarah Allen, Child of Benjn & Sophia, 1823.

Sophia, Child of Benjamin & Sophia, Nov. 2, 1825.
Sophia Allen, dau. of Benjamin, Sept. 21, 1834.
William Francis, son of Benjamin, Aug. 11, 1839.
BAKER, Hunneman, adult, June 12, 1842.
BARLOW, Abigail Daughter of Deacon Joseph by his wife Abigail, July 29, 1744.
Benjn the Chield of Aaron by his wife Mary, Jan. 20, 1765.
Ebenezer, the Son of Joseph, March 25, 1750.
George, the Son of George by his wife Ruth, July 26, 1741.
Hannah, Daughter of Obed & Rebekah, March, 1776.
Mary, Child of Aaron & Marah his Wife, Oct. 23, 1774.
Mary, the Daughter of Joseph by his wife Abigail, Oct. 25, 1747.
Nathaniel the son of Aaron by his wife Mary, April 5, 1767.
Rebekah, Child of Obed & Rebekah, Aug., 1784.
Ruben, Enoch, Children of Obed, July 10, 1774.
Ruth, Daughter of Aaron & wife Mary, Jan. 31, 1773.
Ruth, the Daughter of George by his wife Ruth, May 19, 1745.
Sarah, Child of Obed & Rebekah, 1782.
Timothy, Son to Aaron & Mary his wife, Jan. 5, 1764.
William & Wiate the Twins of Joseph by his wife Abigail, July 18, 1742.
William, Thomas, Jirah, Lewis, Childr of William & Content, July, 1780.
BARROWS, Almira, Child of Thomas & ———, 1807.
Branch, son of Isaac and Lydia B., Aug. 31, 1845.
Lucy Clark, Child of Branch, Nov., 1819.
Mary Clark, dau. of Isaac N. & Lydia B. April 6, 1854.
Samuel, Clarissa, George, Alpheus, & Bethiah, Childr; of Thomas & ———, 1807.
——— Child of Branch & ———, 1813.
BARSTOW, [see also BESTER and BESTOW].
Altol Olmner, son of Wilson, June 19, 1836.
Anna, Child of Gideon Junr & Anna his wife, Jan., 1796.
Benjamin Franklin, Edwin, Nathan Hammond, Childr of Benj & Rebecca, 1807.
Betsy Drew, Child of Wilson & Betsy, 1824.
Caleb, Child of Gideon Jun & Anna, 1796.
Carolina, Child of James & Sarah, 1825.
Deborah Loring, dau. of James, Oct. 30, 1832.
Elizabeth Penn, Child of Benjamin & Rebecca, Oct. 1815.
George Wales, Child of George & Sally, 1802.
Gideon, Son of Wilson, Aug. 26, 1838.

Gideon, Jenny, Children of Gideon & Anna Junr. July, 1787.

Helen, Caroline, and Elizabeth Penn, daughters of Nathan H., July 5, 1835.

Henry, Child of Benjamin & Rebecca, 1817.

James Munro, Child of James & his Wife, 1820.

Jane Wilson, Chd of Wilson & Eliz.: Aug. 6, 1827.

Mary, dau. of James, Oct. 21, 1829.

Jonathan Moore, Henry Wilson, Children of Wilson & Susanh, 1799.

Joseph Chield of Aaron by his wife Mary, March 27, 1763.

Lucy, Daughter of Gideon & Jenny, May 17, 1772.

Lucy, Child of Wilson & Susannah, May, 1798.

Mary, Child of Gideon & Anna, 1793.

Mary Tobey, dau. of Nathan H., June 19, 1836.

Mary Tobey, dau. of Nathan H., at home, sick, Nov. 26, 1840.

Sarah Munro, Child of James & ———, Aug., 1822.

Samuel, son of Wilson & Betsy, Aug. 15, 1829.

Samuel Wilson, Child of Wilson & Betsy, Aug., 1825.

Susan Congdon, Child of Benjamin & Rebecka, Oct., 1820.

Susannah Parkman, Caleb, children of Wilson & Susanh, 1746.

William Parkman, Child of Wilson & Susanh, 1803.

Wilson, Child of Gideon & Anna, June, 1798.

Wilson, Child of Wilson & Eliza, 1831.

Zacheus Mead, Son of Gideon & Anna, 1789.

Zaccheus Mead, son of Wilson, May 3, 1835.

BEALLS, Mary Bealls, adult, April 7, 1839.

BERRY, Nathan the Son of Ebenzer by his Wife Abigail, Nov. 10, 1751.

BESSEY, Elizabeth, Child of Nathan & Elizabeth, 1810.

James, Son of Nathl & Susanh, Sept. 20, 1772.

Lovina, Daughter of Nathl & Susannah, June 15, 1777.

Martha, Child of Nathl & Susanh, July, 1782.

Nathan, Joshua, Benjamin, Nathaniel, Children of Natl & Susannah his Wife, June 7, 1772.

Susana Hammond, Lydia Gifford, Almira, Childr of Nathan & Eliza, June 28, 1807.

BESTER, Benjn the Chield of Gideon by his wife Jinne, Sept. 27, 1767.

Giddeon, Mary & Wilson the Children of Gideon by his wife Jinne, Aug. 11, 1766.

BESTOW, Marah, Daughter of Seth & Ruth, May 5, 1776.

Sarah, Caleb, Children of Gideon & Jenny, Aug. 9, 1772.

Sarah, Child of Gideon & Jane, Dec. 1777.

BEWEL, [see also BUELL,]

Marietta & Edward Franklin, children of Edward & Clarrissa, Oct., 1829.

BISBER, Molly, Aurelia, Benjamin, Robert, Ezra, Joseph, Children of Benjamin & Hannah, Jan. 1775.

BLACKWELL, John, Seth, Loice, Children of Seth & Loice, July, 1808.

BOLLS, Unice the Chield of Saml by his wife Mary, July 1, 1764.
Lydia the Chield of Saml Junr by his wife Mary, April 3, 1763.

BOOLS, Asa the Chield of Thoms by his wife Anne, June 27, 1756.
Benjn the Chield of Benjn by his wife Hannah, Feb. 17, 1751.
Deborah Ye Chield of Benjn by his wife Hannah, March 26, 1758.
Ebenezer the Chield of Hozea, Mar. — June, 1851.
Joannah the Chield of Samuel Junr by his wife Mary, July 5, 1767.
Joseph the Chield of Samuel by his wife Mary, Aug. 21, 1768.
Joshua the Chield of Saml Junr by his wife Mary, April 19, 1761.
Mary the Chield of Benjamn by his wife Hannah, Augt. 3 1755.
Paul the Chield of Thms by his wife Ann, Aug. 30, 1761.
Prince the Chield of Benjn by his wife Hannah, Novr. 28, 1762.
Rhoda the Chield of Thoms by his wife Anne, July 24, 1763.
Ruben the Chield of Thoms by his wife Ann, March 6, 1766.
Samuel the Chield of Samuel Junr by his wife Mary, Novr. 17, 1765.
Sarah the Chield of Thoms by his wife Anne, May 13, 1759.
Sarai Ye Daughter of Thoms by his wife Anne, March 25, 1753.
Hozea the Chield of Ye Widow Mehitible, April 28, 1754.
Thankful the Daughter of Thoms by his wife Anne, March 30, 1755.

BOOLES, Joanna the Chield of Benjn by his wife Hannah, July 22, 1753.
John Jonathan & Experience the younger Children of the above Jonathan, Jan. 24, 1742.

BOWLES, Ann Tobey, Child of Isaac & Catharine, Oct. 1825.
Ezra, Mary, Children of Saml & Mary, May 7, 1777.
Isaac, Son of Isaac & Catharine, Aug., 1821.
John, Child of Isaac & Catharine, 1811.
Joshua Wolden, Child of Asa & Keziah, 1796.
Justus White, Child of Isaac & Catharine, Oct., 1816.
Loice, Nathan, Children of Saml & Molly, July 7, 1772.
Ophelia Butler, dau. of Isaac & Sarah, June 7, 1846.
Resolved White, Child of Isaac & Catharine, 1823.
Silvanus Tobey, Child of Isaac & Catharine, Sept., 1814.
Sophia Wing, dau. of Isaac Jr., June 30, 1844.
Stephen Wing, Child of Isaac & Katharine, Feb. 1813.
Thomas, Jamima, Anna, Reuben, John, Childr of Asa & Keziah, 1795.

BRIGGS, Anna, Sarah, Mary, Nathan, Hannah, Childr of Nathan & Mary, March, 1786.

Andrew Southworth, son of George, at home, sick, Feb. 5, 1841.

Elisha, Chield of Nathan & Mary, 1795.

Elizabeth, Child of Nathan & Mary, July, 1786.

Lois, adult, June 7, 1840.

Lucy, the Child of Clement & Hannah, 1809.

Silvanus & Abigail, Children of Nathan & Mary, Oct., 1792.

Thomas Barrows, Child of Clem. & Hannah, Oct., 1815.

BUELL, Edward Watson, son of Edward, June 14, 1835.

Edward, son of Edward & Clarissa, June 26, 1853.

Eliza LeBaron, dau. of Edward, June 17, 1838.

Laura Josephine, dau. of Edward & Clarissa, Jan. 4, 1846.

Reuben Dexter, son of Edward, Dec. 2, 1841.

CANNON, Arvin, son of Watson, Aug. 4, 1839.

Caleb Leonard, Child of Ebenezer Jun & ———— his wife, 1796.

Clara Meigs, dau. of Watson & Deborah, Nov. 16, 1845.

David Howland, son of James Cannon, June 30, 1844.

Ebenezr the Chield of Ebenez by his wife Experience, July 19, 1767.

Ebenezr, Henry, Lincoln, Children of Eben & Eliza his Wife, July, 1824.

Eliakim, Son of Eben & Experience, Nov., 1780.

Eliakim, Child of Eben & Elizabeth, Nov. 2, 1825.

Elsa Howland, Dau of Watson, Aug. 21, 1842.

George Harrison, Child of Deacon Nathan & Eunice, Aug., 1825.

Hallet Mitchell, Abigail Haskell, Martha, Joseph, Childr of Dn Nathan & Eunice, 1824.

James, Child of Eliakim & Mary, 1808.

Joseph, son of Ebenezer, Jr., Sept. 24, 1837.

Martin Luther and Samuel Thomas, children of Ebenezer Jr., Oct. 12, 1834.

Mary & Martha the Children of Ebenezr by his wife Experience, May 12, 1765.

Mary Howland, dau. of David H. & Susan C., June 26, 1853.

Medad the Son of Ebenezer by his wife Experience, by Ye Revd Mr. Moore, Rochester, Aug. 10, 1770.

Melinda Crosby, child of Calvin & Melinda, Jan. 6, 1829.

Molly, Child of Ebenezer & Experience, Dec. 25, 1774.

Nathan H. Barstow, son of David & Susan, Nov. 2, 1856.

Nathan Son of Ebenezer & Experience his Wife, June 20, 1772.

Priscilla Cushman, dau. of Calvin, Oct. 30, 1832.

Priscilla Cushman, daughter of Calvin, Sept. 27, 1835.

Ruth Briggs, Child of Eben, 1804.

Ruth Briggs, Child of Ebenr & Silence, 1805.

Silence Brigs, Child of Eben & H. ———— Cannon, 1814.

CARVER, Chandler, Zadock, Sarah, Lydia, Lucy, Children of Thos &
———, 1807.

CATHEWAY, Helen Marr and Mercy Ann, daughters of William &
Sarah, March 2, 1850.

CHADWICK, Sarah Emily, dau. of John & A. M. D., June 26, 1853.

CHURCH, Abigail the Chield of Calib, May 10, 1761.

Alice Daughter of Caleb by his wife Mercy. Pr Revd Mr. Parker,
Dec. 9, 1770.

CLAGGON, Hannah the Chield of Joseph, Oct., 1743.

Hannah the Chield of Joseph, July 22, 1750.

Joseph the Chield of Joseph by his wife ————, April 23, 1759.

Nathan the Chield of Joseph by his wife Hannah, April 10, 1763.

Prince the Son of Joseph, May 4, 1752.

Saml the Son of Joseph, at home, being sick, July 17, 1747.

———— the Chield of Joseph by his wife, July 7, 1754.

CLARK, Abigail the Chield of Deacn by his wife Abigail, May 10, 1760.

Abby Ann, dau. of Watson & Drusilla, June 20, 1847.

Allis Daughter to ye Widow Deborah, Jan. 13, 1744–5.

Arelia Child of Elijah & Cynthia, & Hannah, of the same, 1796.

Deborah Mead, dau. of Nathaniel & ————, Aug. 23, 1829.

Elijah the Chield of Deacn Ezekiel by his wife Hannah, June 14, 1767.

Elizabeth, Child of Elijah & Cinthia, 1799.

Elizabath the Chield of John by his wife Elizabath, June 13, 1756.

Eunice, Daughter to John by his Wife Epiphena, Sept. 10, 1749.

Ezekiel, Child of Elijah & Cynthia, 1805.

Ezekiel the Chield of Deacn Ezekiel by his wife Agibail, April 23, 1759.

Harriet Deane, dau. of Nathaniel, at home, sick, Feb. 2, 1841.

Helen Maria, dau. of Nathaniel, June 30, 1844.

John Ye Son of John by his wife Epiphena, July 29, 1753.

Joseph The Chield of Deacn Ezekiel by his wife Abigail May 8, 1757.

Judith, daughter to Ezekiel by his wife Mary, 1749.

Mary, Child of Elijah & Cynthia, 1807.

Mary Ann, Child of Nathanl & Debo his wife, 1827.

Mercy Daughter to Caleb by his wife Deborah by the Revd Mr. Peirce
of Dartmouth in ye Pasters Absence, July, 1743.

Moses the Chield of Deacn Ezekiel by his wife Hannah, June, 2, 1769.

Nathaniel Dean, son of Nathaniel & Susan, Aug. 31, 1845.

Nathaniel, son of Nathaniel & Susan, June 26, 1853.

Parker the Chield of Deacn Ezekiel by his wife Hannah, May 26, 1765.

Susanna the Chield of John Clark by his wife Elizabath, Nov. 10, 1754.

Susannah Child of Elijah & Cinthia, June, 1798.

Temperance the Chield of Ezekiel by his wife Abigail, Oct. 20, 1754.

Thomas son of Ezekiel by his wife Hannah, Pr Revd Mr. Shaw, Nantucket, Sept. 22, 1771.

Thomas Parker, Child of Elijah & Cinthia, 1811.

Unice the Daughter of Ezekiel by his wife Abigail Oct. 19, 1755.

Walter, Child of Cornelius & Hannah of the First Chh in Rochester, Dec. 1793.

William the Chield of John by his wife Elizabath, June 11, 1758.

CLARKE, Elijah Mead, son of Nathaniel, Sept. 9, 1838.

COHOON, Elizabath the Chield of William by his wife Elizabath, July 22, 1759.

COTTLE, John, Son of Abisha & Katharine, 1780.

COWEN, John the Chield of Midean by his wife Sarah, Jan. 8, 1754.

William the Chield of Midean by his wife Sarah, May 9, 1756.

COWING, Mary, Israel, Jonathan, Patience, Experience, Children of Seth & Penelope, July 10, 1774.

Penelope Cowing, Wife to Seth, March 6, 1774.

Penelope, Daughter of Penelope & Seth, April, 1779.

Ruth, Child of Seth & Penelope His Wife, Aug., 1776.

———— Child of Seth & Penelope, July, 1782.

CROSBY, Stephen Amos (?), son of Waterman, July 5, 1829.

Eliza Ann, Child of Deacon & Eliza his Wife, Nov. 13, 1831.

Elizabeth Sears, Alfred Kendrick, Franklin Kendrick, children of David, Oct. 6, 1839.

Frederic Allen and Mary Ann, children of Prentiss, Sept. 6, 1835.

Joseph Allen, son of N. A. and Louisa, July 6, 1856.

Louisa, dau. of Uberto and Mary, July 9, 1848.

Lurane Lovel, Child of Wat. & Susan, Aug. 11, 1829.

Mary Eliza, dau. of Uberto & Mary, May 4, 1847.

Nathaniel Allen son of Dea. Nathaniel, July 12, 1840.

Uberto Crocker, Child of Mr., June, 1819.

Thomas Kempton, son of Prentiss, Sept. 10, 1837.

A child, dau. of Dea. (Nathaniel A.) at home, sick, Jan. 25, 1832.

Uberto Crocker, son of Uberto C. & Mary, Dec. 28, 1845.

CROSBY, William, son of Dea. N. Crosby, Dec. 2, 1841.

CUSHING, Alice, Child of Alice & Nathl, 1817.

Asa Pease, Child of N. & Phebe, Dec., 1792.

Elizabeth, Child of Stephen & Rachel, July, 1782.

Elizabeth West, Child of Nathanl. & Alice, 1820.

Elnathan Hammond, Child of Nathl & Alice, 1811.

Eunice Hammond, Child of Nat. & Eliz., 1809.

John the Chield of Nathal by his wife Lydia, June 14, 1761.

Martha, Child of Natl & Phebe & Sarah Child of the same, 1797.

Mary Ann, Child of Nathl & Alice, 1822.

Mooly the Chield of Nathaniel by his wife Lydia, Sept. 14, 1766.

Nathaniel, Benjamin, Anna Turner, Joshua, Phebe, Childr of Nathl & Phebe, 1790.

Oliff the Chield of Zattue by his wife Bethiah, Jan. 26, 1766.

Sarah the Chield of Nathll by his wife Lydia, July 1, 1764.

Thomas, Child of Stephen & Rachel, March, 1786.

William, Jane, Stephen, Milton Foster, Children of Stephen & Rachel, May, 1781.

Zattue the Chield of Bethiah Widw, Oct. 16, 1768.

Zattue the Chield of Nathaniel by his wife Lydia, July 17, 1768.

CUSHMAN, Henry Milton, Son of Alerton & ———, July 3, 1829.

Philander, Alerton, Gardener, Sally, Laura, Childr of Alerton Cushman, June, 1820.

DEAN, Rachel Tyler, Child of Noah & ———, Newbedford, 1809.

DE MARANVEL, Mary the Chield of Mary, April 4, 1756.

DEXTER, Abigail Child of Ephraim by his wife Martha, May 5, 1746.

Abigail, dau. of Jonathan, Mar. 6, 1833.

Allis the Daughter of Josiah, Septembr 22, 1751.

Anna, Child of Reuben & Polly, 1799.

Anna, Child of Edward & Mary, Apr., 1779.

Anne the Child of Edward at their own House by reason of its mother's Confinement by Sickness, Feb. 27, 1758.

Benjn the Chield of Ebenezr by his wife Lydia, April 23, 1758.

Benjamin, Son of Benjamin & ———, June, 1783.

Benjn & Phillip Children to Josiah by his wife Abigail, Augt. 3, 1746.

Benjamin Potter, Son of David & Sally, 1799.

Caleb the Son of Ephraim, June 16, 1751.

Caleb, Child of Caleb & Hannah, 1793.

Caroline, Child of Reuben & Mary, Nov.. 1813.

Charles Robinson, Child of Eben & ———, 1821.

———, Chield to Josiah, 1749.

Drucilla Child of Eb. & Desire, 1815.

Eben Allen, Child of David & Sarah, July, 1786.

Edward the Chield of Edward by his wife, Jan. 11, 1767.

Elias Son to Seth & Mary his Wife, June 7, 1772.

Elisha, the Chield of Peleg by his Wife Catharine, July 11, 1747.

Elisha the Chield of Seth by his wife Mary, April 28, 1765.

Elizabath the Chield of Seth by his wife Mary, Oct. 2, 1768.

Elizabeth Rogers, dau. of John, May 13, 1838.

Elnathan the Chield of Elnathan by his wife Mary, at his own house a Lecture being preached at Ye same time, Decr. 13, 1758.

Ephraim the Child of Ephraim by his wife Martha, July 18, 1742.

Freeman & ——————— Children of Alden, 1814.

Gideon the Son of Constant by his wife Meribah, Augt. 19, 1750.

Hannah the Chield of Ebenezr by his wife Lydia, Oct. 31, 1756.

Hannah daughter to Josiah by his wife Abigail, Jan. 31, 1747–8.

Hannah Jane, adult, Dec. 1, 1839.

Harvey, Child of David & Sarah His Wife, 1790.

Hope, Child of Thankfull & Hannah, 1791.

Isaac Son to Constant by his wife Meribah, July 22, 1744.

Isaiah the Chield of Seth by his wife Mary, April 14, 1754.

Jabez The Chield of Seth by his wife Mary, Octobr. 1, 1758.

James Son to Edward and Mary His Wife, Feb. 16, 1772.

Jane Chield to ye Widow Epiphena, Oct., 1745.

Jesse the Son of Peleg, July 15, 1750.

John the Son of Peleg by his wife Catherine, July 14, 1745.

Jonathan the Chield of Josiah by his wife Abigail, Septr. 30, 1753.

Jonathan Kelly, Child of Jno & Mary, 1812.

Loess, Chield to Ephraim by his wife Martha, March 19, 1749.

Lucy Alden, Child of Alden & Lucy, Oct., 1816.

Martha Mayhew, dau of Allen, Sept. 10, 1837.

Mary the Chield of Seth by his wife Mary, June 27, 1762.

Mary, Child of Edw & Mary, July, 1782.

Mary Jane, dau. of John & Mary, Aug. 13, 1848.

Meriah, Snow, Child of Jno & Mary, June 20, 1819.

Meribah, Thomas, Ebenezer, Betty, Childr of Thomas & Hannah, March, 1780.

Moores Rogers, son of John, Jan. 3, 1836.

Nathan the Child of Constant by his wife Meribah, April 4, 1742.

Nathan, son of Reuben & Mary, 1800.

Pamela, Child of Jona. & Mary, Oct., 1816.

Rebeckah, Child of Caleb & Hanh, 1790.

Ruth and Ellis the children of Ephraim by his wife Martha, Aug. 9, 1741.

Saml, Child of Edward & Mary his Wife, March 13, 1774.

Samuel Studly, Child of Jonathan & Mary his Wife, June, 1824.

Sarah the Daughter of Seth by his wife Mary, Oct. 12, 1755.

Stephen the Son of Constant by his Wife Meribah, April 24, 1748.

Stephen Delano, son of Allen, June 14, 1840.

Susan Parkman, Child of Reuben & Mary, 1803.

Thankful the Chield of Josiah by his wife Abigail, May 30, 1756.

Thankfull, Child of Joshua & Thankful, Sept. 30, 1787.

Thoms Son to Constant by his wife Meribah, March 5, 1745-6.

Thomas, Son of Eben & Desiah, 1807.

Unice the Chield of Edward by his wife Mary, Dec. 4, 1768.

DILINO (DILLINO, DELINO), Harper, the Chield of Jabez, April 21, 1748.

Nathan & Jabez Children of Jabez at his own House, Aug. 5, 1761.

Stephen, the Son of Jabez, March 13, 1751.

DUNHAM, Margaret Albertson Child of George & Mary, 1810.

Mary Albert, Child of George & Mary, Aug., 1808.

Mary, Sophronia, Childr of George & Mary, Nov., 1815.

Rufus Albertson, Martha Ann, Children of George & Mary, June 1820.

EATON, Maria Rogers, dau. of Solomon & Maria, April 12, 1846.

. Martha Ann, dau. of Solomon Eaton, at home, sick, May 3, 1842.

ELLIS, Ebenezer & Thankful the Children of Joel by his wife Elizabath, at their own House, Aug. 27, 1765.

George the Son of Joel by his wife Elizabath, April 1, 1753.

Mary, Child of Wm., Aug. 1780.

FOSTER, Jerusha, Child of Elnathan & Thankfull, 1790.

Polly, Elnathan Pope, Childr of Elnathan & Thankfull, July 16, 1787.

FISH, Edwin Francis, son of Mr. & Mrs. Abiah, Jan. 1, 1851.

GIBBS, Lucy LeBaron Child of A. & L., living in Fairhaven, Feb., 1813.

GODFREY, Sarah & Mary the Children of Mehittibel wife to Joseph, Aug. 19, 1759.

HALL, Abner Leonard, son to Abner, Aug. 21, 1856.

Emily Francis and Nathan Dexter, children of Abner, Aug. 24, 1834.

Martha Gibbs & Lucy Clarke, children of Abner & Anna, Aug. 30, 1829.

HAMLIN, Andrew Thomas, Lydia Weeks, Mercy Swift, children of Alpheus, June 12, 1842.

HAMMOND, Abia Moore, Child of Leonard & Acenath, 1820.

Abigail the Chield of Elisha by his wife Elizabath, Aug. 31, 1760.

Abigail the Chield of Captn Jabez by his wife Abigail, July 25, 1762.

Abigail, Daughter of Jabez & Priscilla, July 29, 1774.

Abigail, Matilda, Nancy, Antipas, Childr of Joseph & Rachel, Aug. 25, 1780.

Abner, Son of Abner & Huldah, Aug., 1776.

Amitti Barlow, Child of Noah & Lydia, 1788.

Ann Eliza, Child of Leonard & Acenath, June 15, 1829.

Anna the Daughter of Rogr. Nov. 12, 1748.

Anne the Chield of Jedediah by his wife Mary, June 11, 1758.

Ansel, Son of Wyat & Mary, July 7, 1822.

Anstus the Chield of Elisha by his wife Elizabath, April 23, 1758.

Archelaus & Ruth the children of Amaziah at his House, Feb. 22, 1764.

Benjamin the Chield of Antipas by his wife Abigail, May 9, 1756.

Benjamin the Chield of Enoch by his wife Druzillai, Sept. 4, 1763.

Benjn the Chield of John by his wife Mary, April 2, 1759.

Benjn the Chield of Rogr, July 26, 1752.

Benjamin Franklin and Georgianna Kendrick, children of Franklin and Lurania, June 26, 1853.

Betty, Moses, Stephen, Abel, Mehitable, Mercy, Childr of Moses & Mehitb., Aug. 1, 1773.

Caleb, Son of Jabez & Priscilla, Aug. 16, 1776.

Calib the Child of Captn Jabez by his wife Abigail, Jan. 9, 1757.

Calvin Son of Jabez, Feb. 9, 1745-6.

Cary the Chield of Josiah by his wife Rebeccah, May 6, 1764.

Charity Daughter of Abner by his wife Huldah, Pr. Revd Mr. Moore, Oct. 28, 1770.

Charles the Son of Arculaus, May 17, 1752.

Deborah daughter of Rogr by his wife Charity, Nov., 1746.

Deborah & Susannah Ruggles, Childr of Wo Debo, Aug., 1784.

Dulcina, Deborah, Children of James & Deborah, 1807.

Edwin, son of James, Dec. 4, 1838.

Elisha the Chield of Elisha by his wife Elizabath, June 19, 1763.

Elizabeth Daughter of Abner & Huldah, Apr. 19, 1772.

Elizabath the Chield of Antipas by his wife Abigail, March 8, 1752.

Elizabeth Pitson (?), Micah, Children of Micah & Eliz. she being a Member of a Chh. in Boston, 1782.

Elizabeth Pope adult, June 12, 1842.

Elnathan Son to John by his wife Mary, July 27, 1746.

Elnathan, Anstriss, & Richard, Children of Josiah by his wife Rebecca, Sept. 5, 1756.

Enoch, Child of Nathl & Lucy, Oct., 1798.

Gardnr the Chield of Ameziah by his wife, Aug. 15, 1757.

George the Son of Captn Jabez by his wife Abigail, Sept. 22, 1754.

George Augustus, child of Leonard & Acenath, June, 10, 1825.

Hannah Daughter to Benjn Junr by his wife Priscilla, Dec. 25, 1743.

Hannah the Chield of Elisha by his wife Elizabath, July 13, 1755.

Hannah Chield of John by his wife Mary, March 26, 1763.

Israel the Child of Israel by his wife Elizabath at their own House being Dangerously Sick, July 21, 1745.

Israel, a man of 92 years of Age, 1799.

James, an Adult, March 28, 1773.

James, Child of Gideon & Mary, 1796.

James the son of James by his wife Hannah, Aug. 21, 1763.

Jabez, the Son of Jabez by his wife Abigail, July 5, 1741.

Jane Leonard, dau. of Leonard, Oct. 5, 1834.

Jedediah the Chield of Jedediah by his wife Mary at a Lecture at Mr. Jonathan Bool's publickly notified, Sept. 23, 1767.

Jesse the Chield of James by his wife Hannah, May 26, 1765.

Jirah, Son of Faunce & Mary, Oct. 1778.

John the Son of Capt. Jabez, March 11, 1750.

John ye Son of John by his wife Mary, July 22, 1783.

John the Chield of John by his wife Mary, Nov. 7, 1756.

John Son of Israil by his Wife Elizebath, Jan. 22, 1748–9.

John Clapp, son of Dea. A. B. & Lucinda his Wife, July 15, 1829.

Joanna and Susannah Children of Elisha by his wife Elizabath, April 19, 1748.

Jonathan the Chield of Abner by his Wife Huldah, Jan. 9, 1763.

Joseph Son of Antips, Oct. 11, 1747.

Joseph, Jenny, Adeline, Amelia, Loring, Frederic, Mary Blossom, Childr of Gideon & Rebecka, 1824.

Joseph Franklin, Child of Leonard & Acenath, 1817..

Josiah was Baptized & all his Children Nathan Charity Deborah Peckum Josiah Bethiah Hannah Abner & Mary at his own house, Nov. 19, 1741.

Judah the Chield of Archelaus by his wife Elizabath, Oct. 9, 1753.

Lemuel Son to Saml by his wife Elizabath, Nov. 22, 1741.

Lothrop the Chield of Josiah by his wife Rebecca, June 6, 1762.

Lucy Daughter to Saml by his wife Elizabath, Aug. 5, 1744.

Lucy, Hannah, Sophia, Sukey, Marah, Childr of Jesse & Sukey, 1806.

Luther, the Son of Faunce & Mary, June 10, 1781.

Luther Son of Jabez by his wife Abigail, April 12, 1744.

Mary of Barzillai by his wife Anne by Revd Mr. Brown of Little Comptn, Sept. 21, 1755.

Mary the Daughter of John by his wife Mary, Feb. 25, 1749–50.

Mary the Chield of Pollipus by his wife Barsheba, Oct. 3, 1756.

Mary Elizabeth, dau. of James, March 26, 1842.

Mehitable wife of Moses, Nov. 29, 1772.

Moses, June 13, 1773.

Nathan the Chield of Josiah by his Wife Rebeccah, June 29, 1766.

Nathan an Adult of 80 Yrs. (recorded in proprio loco), 1779.

Nathaniel, Stephen, Ruth, Sally, Jabez Holmes, Children of Faunce & Mary, March 27, 1774.

Noah, Son of Noah & Lydia, Sept. 1787.

Olive the Daughter of Rogr by his wife Charity, July 14, 1745.

Parnal the Chield of Jedediah by his wife Mary, May 25, 1760.

Priscilla the Daughter of Benj. Junr. by his wife Priscilla, April 12, 1741.

Priscilla, Child of Natl & Lucy, 1796.

Priscillai the Chield of Josiah by his wife Rebecca, March 23, 1760.

Rebekah daughter of Jabez & Priscilla, April 12, 1772.

Rebekah, Elizabeth, Priscilla, Childr of Noah & Eunice, Sept. 26, 1784.

Rhode Daughter to Jabez, Dec. 27, 1747.

Rogr the Chield of Abner by his wife Huldah, May 3, 1761.

Rogr the Chield of Rogr by his wife Charity, June 15, 1757.

Roger Wing, Child of Jessee & Susan, 1807.

Rose the Daughter of Samuel by his wife Elizabeth, May 15, 1748.

Rufus, Son of Nathl & Lucy, 1799.

Ruth, Child of Abner & Huldah, July 3, 1774.

Ruth the Chield of Enoch by his wife Drewzillar, April 14, 1765.

Ruth the Chield of Captn Jabez by his wife Abigail, Oct. 7, 1759.

Sarah the Daughter of Israel by his wife Elizabath, at their House, being Dangerously Sick, Novr. 11, 1741.

Sarah, Meribah, Mary & Ellis the Children of Barnabas by his wife Susanna, July 11, 1742.

Sarah Shaw, Child of Jesse & Susan, 1809.

Sarah Winslow, child of Joseph & Sophia, July 6, 1851.

Seth & Barnabas Children of Saml by his wife Elizabath, Sept. 29, 1745.

Susannah the Chield of James by his Wife Hannah, Oct. 1, 1758.

Susan, Joseph, Jesse, Sarah Winslow, Childr of Jesse, 1825.

Sylvia Russell, dau. of Gideon 2nd, April 24, 1834.

Sympson the Chield of Jedediah by his Wife Mary, Oct. 14, 1750.

Thankful the Chield of Roger by his wife Charity, Sept. 22, 1754.

Thankful & Hannah the Children of Abner by his wife Huldah, July 31, 1768.

Thoms the Chield of Enoch by his wife Drewzillar, Aug. 31, 1766.

Thomas C. son of Franklin & Lurana, Nov. 2, 1856.

Thomas Cushman, Child of Leonard & Acenath, Aug., 1823.

Thomas Faunce, Son of Faunce & Mary, Jan. 30, 1784.

Timothy Son to John Junr by his wife Mary, March 11, 1743–4.

Unice the Chield of Josiah Junr by his wife Rebecca, April 9, 1758.

Waty, Child of Gideon & Mary, 1801.

William George Cowell and John Mayo sons of James and of his wife, Jan. 9, 1838.

William LeBaron, Mary Allen, Childr of Wyatt & Mary, June 18, 1820.

———— Chield to Jedediah by his Wife Mary, 1749.

———— the Chield of Jedediah, July 5, 1752.

———— the Chield of Jedediah by his Wife Mary, July 27, 1755.

———— the Chield of Jedediah by his wife Mary Oct. 16, 1763.

HARLOW, Abner Wood and Mary Stanton, children of Abner Harlow, at the funeral of their mother, May 20, 1839.

Sarah, Daughter Nathanal, July 27, 1829.

HASKIL, Ephraim, Jabez & Barnibas Children to Ephraim of Ye other Parish, Feb. 1, 1748–9.

HATCH, Ann Folgar, Child of Benjn & ————, 1799.

Martha the Chield of Obed by his wife Ruth, Nov. 14, 1762.

Samuel The Chield of Obid by his wife Ruth, July 6, 1760.

———— the Daughter of Timothy, July 19, 1752.

HIGGINS, Hannah, Elizabeth, Jonathan, Wilson, Childr of Heman, 1799.

HITCH, Frederic Augustus, Child of H. Living in Fairhaven, Feb., 1813.

HOLMES, Alsy, Child of Ebnr & Desire, July 5, 1807.

Mary, Child of Eben & Keziah, 1809.

HOODLY, Ann Allen, Daughter of Joshua & Amy, June 4, 1775.

HOSKINS, Bethiah the Chield of Samuel by his wife Elizabath, March 10, 1766.

HOUSE, Abel, Son of Abel & Bethiah, Oct., 1781.

HOWARD, Phebe the wife of Mathew, Nov. 1, 1741.

HOWLAND, Delia Eldredge, dau. of Rowland and Grace, Jan. 3, 1847.

Eldredge, dau. of Rowland, Sept. 28, 1834.

Edward Payson, son of Rowland, July 8, 1838.

Grace Ellen, dau. of Rowland & Grace, Sept. 1, 1850.

HOVEY, Anne the Chield of Ivory Hovey by his wife Olive, Nov. 10, 1754.

Ivory the Child of Ivory by his wife Olive, July 18, 1742.

Ivory 2nd, the Son of Revd Ivory by his wife Olive, Jan. 8, 1748–9.

Olive Daughter of ye Revd Ivory by his wife Olive, Aug. 10, 1746.

Samuel the Chield of Ye Revd. Ivory, Dec. 23, 1750.

JACKSON, Jemimah, the Child of Samuel by his wife Elizabath, Dec. 20, 1742.

JENNY, [see also JINNE.]

    Joshua Cushman, Benjn Cushman Childr of Ansel & Phebe, 1807.

JINNE, Abner the Son of Jabez, Sept. 13, 1747.

    Anne Ye Chield of Saml by his wife Mary Anne, Oct. 15, 1758.

    Benjamin the Chield of Samuel by his wife Mary Anne, July 29, 1764.

    Caleb Ye Son of Caleb, April 11, 1750.

    Elizabath the Child of Jabez by his wife Ruth, March 2, 1745-6.

    Hannah, Chield to Jabez, Aug. 20, 1749.

    Ingatius the Chield of Samuel by his wife Mary Anne, Nov. 1, 1761.

JOHNSON, John, Child of John, Living in Fairhaven, Feb., 1813.

    Jonathan at his own house being by the Consent of this Chh & in the Presence of Some of the Brethren, Nov. 2, 1741.

JONES, Mary Angeline, dau. of Lot N., Sept. 10, 1837.

    Lettice the Chield of Samll by his wife Mary Anne, Aug. 16, 1767.

    Levy and ———— children of Cornelius of Dartmouth at his own House, April 11, 1750.

    Mary, Chield to Lettice, at Dartmouth, June 22, 1749.

    Nathaniel Ye Chield of Samuel by his wife Mary Anne, March 11, 1759.

    Patience Hall the Chield of Saml of Dartmouth by his wife, Oct. 19, 1760.

    Zilpha Daughter of Jabez, March 24, 1745.

    ———— the Chield of Jabez by his wife at the House of Mr. Ignacious Jinne's at a Lecture, June 14, 1763.

LANDERS, Elizabeth, dau. of Bethuel, at home, sick, Dec. 20, 1840.

    Mary Alice, daughter of Bethuel, Feb. 7, 1841.

    Washington I, son of Thomas & Nancy, July 29, 1849.

LeBARON, Ann, Child of Leml & Elizabeth, Dec., 1777.

    Charles Henry, Child of Wm & Eliz: Dec., 1823.

    Elizabeth, Child of Leml & Elizabeth, 1784.

    Elizabeth the Child of Wm & Elizabeth, July, 1816.

    Elizabeth Allen, Child of Lazarus & Priscilla LeBaron, Nov. 6, 1813.

    Enoch Hammond, Jane Barstow, Children of Lazarus & Priscilla, Aug. 7, 1824.

    James, Child of Leml & Elizabeth, 1794.

    John Allen, Son of Lemuel & Elizabeth, May 26, 1782.

    Lazarus, Child of Leml & Eliz: 1788.

Lemuel, Son of Leml & Elizabeth LeBaron, Feb., 1780.

Lemuel, Son of Leml & Elizabeth, Sept. 7, 1775.

Lemuel, James, Horatio Gates, Childr of Jn A. & Abigail his wife, Deceased, 1816.

Sally Alden, a Child of Leml & Eliza: 1791.

Sarah Ann, Child of Wm & Elizabeth, May 26, 1811.

Thomas Kitredge, Child of Leml & Martha, Roxbury, June, 1820.

Thomas Robbins, Child of William & Eliza, June 20, 1819.

William, Child of Lemuel & Eliza: 1786.

William Bradford, Child of Wm & Eliza, Nov., 1814.

LEWIS, Almira Lewis, adult, June 7, 1840.

LOOK, Adam, Joseph, John, Ruth, Rebecca, Margaret, the Children of Samuel by his wife Ruth, at his own House, Jan. 12, 1742.

Ellis the Child of Samuel by his wife Ruth, Sept. 19, 1742.

LUMBERT, Abisha Hammond, son of Capt Thomas & Mary, April 26, 1846.

MAYHEW, Elizabeth Child of Matthew & Sally, July 11, 1819.

Elizabeth, Child of Matthew & Sally, March 31, 1831.

Elizabeth Allen, dau. of Matthew, Mar. 31, 1833.

Francis LeBaron, Son of Matthew & Sally, June, 1822.

John Allen, Son of Math. & S., July 20, 1829.

Thomas, Child of Matthew & Sally, 1824.

MEAD, Anna, Child of Eben & Priscilla, 1790.

Anne ye Chield of Zecheus by his wife Sarah, Nov. 19, 1758.

Debby, Daughter of Eben & Priscilla Mead, 1799.

Ebenezer the Chield of Zechaus by his wife Sarah, Aug. 31, 1760.

Elijah Son of Eben & Priscilla, Dec., 1792.

Elizabeth Child of Eben & Priscilla, 1794.

Mary, the Child of Ebenr & Priscilla, June, 1803.

Rachel the Chield of Zacheus by his wife Sarah, Aug. 1, 1762.

Rachel, Child of Eben & Prissy, May, 1788.

Samuel the Chield of Zecheus by his wife Sarah, May 8, 1765.

Sarah, Child of Eben & Prissy, Sept. 30, 1787.

MEIGGS, Abigail, Sarah, Ephraim, Mary, Joseph, Childs of Ephm & N., 1807.

MEGGS, Caleb & Joseph, Childr of John & Elsa, Aug, 1780.

Mary, Nathaniel, & Rebecca Children of Ebenezer April 20, 1750.

MERRITHEW, Henry Davis, William Warner, Calvin Cannon, Alexander Coffin, Eugene Bradbury, children of widow Silence, Jan. 31, 1852.

Samuel Nye, son of William, Aug. 30, 1835.

William, son of William, July 1, 1838.

NEALL, Josiah Nathan, Abigail, Nathaniel Hammond, Childr of Mary & Job, Aug., 1792.

Mary, Daughter of Job & Mary, 1794.

NICKERSON, Nathaniel the Cheild of Samuel, Feb. 24, 1751.

NORTON, Aaron, Child of Aaron & Abigail, June, 1780.

Adoniram, Child of Aaron & Rhoda, June, 1786.

Betty, Child of Aaron & Abigail, May 26, 1782.

Jabez, Son of Aaron & his Wife Marthar, Sept. 15, 1777.

Mary the Cheild of Jabez by his wife Elizabeth, June 11, 1758.

Matthew, Son of Aaron & Abigail, June, 1784.

Priscillai the Cheild of Jabez by his wife ———, May 25, 1760.

PARKER, Hannah, wife to Jesse and was received into full communion, Mar. 28, 1756.

Bethiah & Moses Children of Jesse by his wife Hannah, Apr. 4, 1756.

Aaron the Cheild of Jesse by his Wife Anna, Feb. 26, 1758.

PEASE, Asenath, Daughter of Theophilus & Ruth, July 18, 1773.

Cornelius, Child of Cornelius & Phebe, July, 1782.

Eunice, Theophilus, Onesiphorous, Joanna, Abner, Childr of Theoph & Ruth, Oct. 18, 1772.

John Merchant, Son of Cornelius & Phebe, Aug. 1785.

Lydia, Daughter of Cornelius & Phebe, Dec. 30, 1780.

Phebe, Polly, Nabby, Ruth, Childr of Cornelius & Phebe, June, 1780.

PECKUM, Susanna & Isaiah Children of James of Dartmouth by his wife Deborah, Apr. 10, 1743.

PELL, John Son to Edward by his wife Jerusha, Oct. 10, 1744.

PHELPS, Edward Phelps, an Adult a Black, & Afterward Sarah his wife, 1784.

Jane, Alvin, John, Sarah, Childr of Edw & Sarah, Nov. 1785

POPE, Joanna, Cheild to Thomas of Dartmouth, July 22, 1749.

PRICE, Lydia Child of Asa & Thankfull, May 9, 1773.

Sarah, John, Chadwick, Children of Asa & Thankfull, June 20, 1772.

Thankfull, Child of Asa & Thankfull, 1778.

AIMOND, Deborah Child to Willm by his wife Hannah, July 28, 1745.

Hannah the Cheild of William by his wife Hannah, Dec. 26, 1756.

Nathan the Cheild of William by his wife Hannah, June 16, 1754.

Thankful the Daughter of William, Oct. 13, 1751.

William the Child of William, March 27, 1743.

Zilpha, the Daughter of William by his Wife Hannah, Nov. 22, 1747.

RANDAL, Bashebah the Chield of Nehemiah by his wife Hopestill, Aug. 26, 1764.

Elizabath the Chield of Micah by his wife May 27, 1764.

Moses & Ann, William & Hannah the Children of Micah by his wife Elizebath at their own house, Oct. 20, 1762.

Nehemiah the Chield of Nehemiah by his wife Hopestill, May 25, 1760.

RANDOL, Clement, Child of David & Priscilla, July, 1782.

Peace, an Adult, May 30, 1781.

REVES, Joseph Fontain, Child of Abiel & ————, 1809.

RICHMAN, Lucy, the Chield of Perez of Dartmouth in Coxit, May, 1752.

ROGERS, Clarissa Moores, Child of Moores & Mary, 1803.

Elizabeth, Child of Widow, June, 1783.

Ezra Cushman, Child of Abisha & Judith, Aug., 1808.

Isaiah, Child of ———— & Isaiah, 1807.

Judith Cushman, Child of Mary & Moores, 1811.

Judith Cushman, Child of Abisha & Judith Rogers, Nov. 1813.

Martha Ann, Child of Abish & Judith, Oct. 1825.

Mary Soul, Child of Moores & Mary, 1809.

Meriah Sanford Child of Abisha & Judith, 1811.

Moores Allen, Child of Moores & Mary, 1807.

Rachel Rogers, adult, Feb. 7, 1841.

Rebekah, Moors, Sarah, Children of Wido Alice (?), July, 1782.

William Barrows, Child of Moores & Polly, Nov., 1813.

William Loyd, son of William B. & Sarah, June 26, 1853.

RUSSELL, Frederick Leonard, son of Frederick & Caroline, Nov. 3, 1850.

Sarah, dau. of Frederick & Caroline, July 29, 1849.

SANDERS, Edward, Child of A. & ————, 1823.

Lydia the Child of Henry by his wife Mary, July 21, 1745.

SEARS, Isaiah, adult, by immersion, Fast Day, April 1, 1842.

Rebeccah, Child of Nathn & ————, July, 1782.

Thankful Josephine, adult, Aug. 4, 1830.

SIMMONS, Mary Ye Daughter of Peleg by his wife Mary, July 5, 1747.

————, Chield to Peleg, Aug. 30, 1740.

SHERMEN, Asa, Child of Deacon Elihu & Eliza His Wife, Dec. 1791.

Elihu, Child of Elihu & Elizabeth, Dec. 1777.

Elihu An Adult, June 4, 1775. (recorded in proprio loco.)

James, Son of Elihu & Eliz., May 6, 1781.

Jedediah, Elizabeth, Childr of Elihu & Elizabeth, Aug. 4, 1775.

Melintha, Daughter of Elihu & Elizabeth, May 5, 1776.

SMITH, Jeremiah, Joseph, William, Anna, Mary, Childr of Sol & Zilph, June, 1807.

Lucy, John, Children of Solomon & Zilpha, 1811.

Mary the Child of Thos & Cassandra, Nov., 1815.

SNOW, Charles Dunbar and Harrison, sons of Stephen and Eunice, Sept. 8, 1844.

Ebenezer the Child of Seth By his wife Desire, May 16, 1756.

Ebenezer Son of Eben & Eleanor, 1800.

Edward Francis, Joseph Cannon, Susan Amanda, Abigail Haskell, — children of Stephen, Oct. 5, 1834.

Eleanor Young, Child of Eben & Eleanor, 1796.

Henry Hudson, Child of Thomas, Nov., 1813.

Ivory the Chield of Joshua by his wife Ruth, Aug. 1, 1762.

James the Chield of Seth by his wife Desire, April 23, 1758.

James & Mary Children of Joshua & Ruth, May 24, 1772.

James, Susanah, Chloe, Maryan Snow, Mary Eliza. Childr of Eben & Desire, 1807.

Jane, Child of Prince & Martha, July, 1816.

Joanna, Child of Ebenr & Eleanor, 1790.

Joseph, Child of Joseph & Rachel his wife, Oct. 10, 1773.

Joshua the Chield of Joshua by his wife Ruth, May 5, 1765.

Levi Morton, son of Levi, at home, sick, Dec. 1841.

Lidia the Daughter of Joshua by his wife Ruth, May 11, 1735.

Lucy, Child of Freeman & his Wife, 1788.

Nancy, James, Betsey Prince, Stephen, Harvey, Avery, Rachel, Children of Prince & Martha, 1808.

Nancy, John, Children of Thmas, 1807.

Nancy & John, Children of Thos, July 26, 1807.

Phebee Daughter to Joshua by his wife Joanna, June 12, 1757.

Rachel & Elizabeth, Children of Eben: May, 1788.

Rebekah, Child of Joshua & Ruth, Sept. 4, 1774.

Rebekah West, Child of Eben & Eleanor, 1793.

Richard the Chield of Seth by his wife Desire, May 26, 1754.

Ruth the Chield of Joshua by his wife Ruth, July 12, 1767.

Saml & Nicholas Children of Nathaniel of the other Parish, Jan. 14, 1745–6.

Sarah the Chield of Seth by his wife Desire, Oct. 5, 1760.

Seth Boardman, Desire West & Benjamin, Children of Seth by his wife Desire, April 20, 1750.

Susan Willis Child of Thomas & Nancy, 1811.

Thomas, Son of Joseph & Rachel, Sept, 1776.

Timothy the Chield of Joshua by his Wife Ruth, April 28, 1754.

William, Child of Prince & Martha, 1821.

Winslow the Chield of Joshua by his wife Ruth, Oct. 28, 1759.

———— the Chield of Seth, July 15, 1750.

SOULE, Thomas H., adult, April 12, 1835.

William Thomas, son of Thomas, Dec. 11, 1836.

Ebenezer Son of Gideon, Jan 13, 1744–5.

John Ye Chield of Thoms by his wife Abigail, May 30, 1756.

SOUTHWORTH, Daniel, the Son of Thos by his Wife Abigail, Dec., 1750.

David the Son of Thos by his wife Abigail, Oct. 15, 1752.

Edward Newton, son of I. Newton, at home, sick, March 9, 1830.

Hannah, Chield of Thoms by his wife Abigail, May 14, 1749.

Mary the Daughter of Thos. by his wife Abigail, March 15, 1747.

Newton, son of Newton & Rhoda, July 29, 1849.

Rowena Augusta, dau of I. Newton, July 24, 1836.

Sarah Ye Chield of Thoms by his wife Abigail, March 4, 1759.

Sophia Wing, Rhoda Ellen, and Eli, children of Dr. Newton & Rhoda, Aug. 31, 1845.

Stephen the Son of Thoms by his wife Abigail, May 18, 1755.

Susan Eaton, dau. of Newton & Rhoda, June 26, 1853.

SPRAGUE, Paul the Chield of Noah Junr by his wife Mary at Mr. Ruggles Parish pr me I. H., March 1, 1767.

STEDSON, The Children of Nathaniel, viz. — Parnol Mitchell, Elizabeth, Nathaniel, Ansel, David, Sept. 30, 1787.

STOODLEY, Polly, Joshua, Amey, Childr of Joshua & Amey, Aug. 1, 1773.

STUDSON, Cinthia, Child of Ruth & Nathaniel her Husband, Aug. 1792.

Joseph, Son of Charles & Bathsheba, Aug. 16, 1772.

STURTEVANT, Samuel, Phebe, John Merchant, Nancy Pease, Childr of S. & L., 1808.

STUTSON, Anne the Chield of Charles by his wife Barsheba, Aug. 19, 1753.

Charles the Chield of Charles by his wife Barsheba, July 13, 1755.

Hannah the Chield of Charles by his wife Barshebah, Aug. 29, 1757.

Rebecca the Chield of Charles by his wife Barshebah, Nov. 22, 1761.

Thaddeus the Chield of Charles by his wife Barshebah, Sept. 2, 1764.

SWAIN, Benjamin Freeman, Child of ———— & Eliza, 1811.

Isaac Young, Child of ———— & Eliz., 1815.

SWIFT, Charles, Child of Jireh & ———— his wife, N. Bedford, 1802.

Eleanor Spooner, Child of Saml & ————, 1812.
All the Children of Eleanor, — Susanh, Jesse, Lucy, 1804.
———— Child of Saml & Eleanor, 1807.

TERRENT, ———— Chield to Alixandr by his Wife Mary, Aug. 13, 1749.

THACHER, Mary Ludlow, dau. of Isaiah C. and Elizabeth, June 7, 1846.

TILLY, Hannah, Child of John & Lucy, Aug., 1784.

TINKHAM, James son of James & Jane, July 29, 1849.
Nelson Blake, Child of Reuben & Salvina (?), 1821.

TOBEY, Abigail, Child of Tho & Keziah, 1895.
  Abigail, Daughter to Elisha by his wife Abigail, Sept. 17, 1749.
  Anne the Chield of Luke by his wife Anne, May 11, 1786.
  Elisha the Chield of Elisha, July 19, 1752.
  Elisha Son to Luke by his Wife Ann, Nov. 26, 1760.
  Elizabeth Child of Thomas & wife Abigail, 1789.
  Elizabeth, Child of Luke & Anna, Aug. 1, 1773.
  Isaac Son to Jonathan, Nov. 25, 1744.
  Isaac Smith, Child of Thos & Abigl, March 20, 1785.
  John the Child of Jonathan by his wife Elizabath, Aug. 7, 1742.
  John the Chield of Luke by his wife Ann, Oct. 21, 1758.
  Job Townsend Child of Smith & Rachel, April 1, 1812.
  Lemuel, Son of Thomas & Abigl, Sept., 1781.
  Luke the Chield of Luke by his wife Anne, May 9, 1756.
  Mary the Chield of Luke by his wife Anne, Feb. 14, 1768.
  Mathew, Son of Thomas & Abigail, Sept., 1787.
  Thomas, Child of Thoms & Abigl, March, 1783.
  Thoms Keziah & William the Children of Luke by his wife Abigail at his own hired House, April 10, 1754.
  William the Son of Luke by his wife Anne, Sept. 18, 1763.

TUPPER, Elizabath The Chield of Eldr Nathan by his wife Experience, Nov. 25, 1755.
  Hannah the Chield of Nathan by his wife Experience, April 2, 1749.
  Joannah Tuppr daughtr to Eldr Tupper was received into full communion with this Chh., Feb. 29, 1756.
  Medad Child of Nathan by his wife Experience, June 29, 1746.
  Martha Daughter to Deacon Nathan by his wife Experience, June 10, 1744.
  Mary the Daughter of Eldr Nathan by his wife Experience, Jan. 27, 1754.
  Mary the Chield of Nathan, June 30, 1751.

Nathan Son of Nathan by his wife Experience, April 18, 1742.

Nathan the Son of Nathan Eldr by his wife Experience, May 15, 1757.

TURNER, George Dunham, son of John V., Sept. 4, 1840.

WALLACE, John, Joseph, Elizabeth, Hannah, Abigail, Alice, Childr of Jona. (?) & Eunice, 1795.

WASHBURN, Albert, Ezra Edson, Horace Wilber, sons of Ezra and Rosamond, July 7, 1850.

Barsheba wife to Bezaleel was baptized, being upon a sick bed at her father's (Nathan) Hammond's House and Rose her sister was Baptized at the same time, making a profession of their faith. The Desires of both the above said Persons were propounded in the two Meeting-Houses the preceding Sabbath and Several of the Brethren of my Chh were present at the time of their admission & Signifyd their Consent in the Usual Way &c. nemine contradictine, March 2, 1767.

Lucy Bond, dau. of Ezra E., Aug. 25, 1839.

Sarah Allen, dau. of Ezra E., June 19, 1836.

WATER, William Bradford, Thomas Allen, Children of Eleazer, May 30, 1824.

WEEKS, Ansel Warren, Louisa, Children of Shubl & Eliza, 1807.

WEST, Asenath, Daught of Timo & Loice, March, 1781.

Jane, Nancy, Presbury, Else, Drusilla, of Timo & Loice, May, 1780.

WHITE, Samuel the Son of Samuel, of Ye other Parish, by his wife Elizabath, Nov. 1, 1747.

WHITMORE, Betty, Daughter of Richard & Deborah, July, 1777.

Sara Vaun, Welthy, Deborah, Richard, Childr, May 27, 1776.

WHITTEMORE, Benjamin, Child of Richard & Deborah, July, 1782.

Carolina. Child of Richd & Eliz: 1815.

Eunice, Hariot, Mary Hammond, Childr of Richard & Eliza, 1807.

Jane, Child of Richard & Eliz: 1790.

Jane Goodspeed, Child of Richard & Deborah, July, 1780.

WHITRIDGE, Joannah, the Daughter of Thomas by his wife Hannah, Sept. 8, 1746.

WICKS, Abiel, Townsend Child of Shubl & Elizabeth, 1807.

WILBUR, ——— the Chield of John, May, 1752.

WING, Hannah, Child of Jonathan & Hanah, Oct., 1777.

Hannah Wing, Wife to Jonathan, June 13, 1773.

Wyart, Moses, Elizabeth, Mary, Childr of Js & Hannah his Wife, July 25, 1773.

WINSLOW, Dorcas the Chield of John by his wife, July 13, 1766.

Noah the Chield of Enoch by his wife Sarah, Aug. 2, 1767.

Thankful the Child of Thoms by his wife Rebecca, June 22, 1746.
———— Daughter to Thomas, March 9, 1748.

YOUNG, Anna, Rebekah (?), and Freeman, Childr of Rekebah, Widow,
　　Sept. 3, 1780.
Eleanor, Sarah, Mary, Hannah, Solomon, John, Zaccheus Mead,
　　Children of Solomon & Hannah, March 20, 1774.　.
Hannah, an adult, wife of Solomon, Oct. 25, 1772.
Martha Olena, dau. of Henry, Nov. 13, 1833.

The following negroes are recorded as having been baptized:
Cyrus, Lot, Children of Toby & ————, May 27, 1776.
Guinea, Servant of Mr. LeBaron, Aug. 4, 1775.
Thomas, Son of Jack & Sarah, April, 14, 1776.
Violeta the Child of the Negro Woman Ann "Church," Jan. 16, 1742–3.
William, Son of Toby, & Hannah his Wife, Oct. 26, 1777.

2. MARRIAGES

The record books of the Congregational Church show the following
marriages during the years 1772 to 1864. Compiled from lists furnished
by Lemuel LeBaron Dexter, Church Clerk. For the minister who
officiated, refer to the list at the head of the section BAPTISMS, just preceding.

AKEN, Abby C. of Fairhaven and S. Bartlett Simmons of Newport,
　　R. I., Nov. 25, 1863.
ALLEN, James of Fairhaven and Mary B. Hammond, Apr. 14, 1842.
　　Joseph M. C. of London, Eng. and Sylvia Mendall, Sept. 29, 1839.
AMES, Mary T. and Caleb T. Jenny, Oct., 1832.
　　Nathaniel F. and Mary C. Townsend, Oct. 9, 1842.
ATSATT, Cynthia and George Barrows, July, 1824.
　　John T. and Mary Bolles, Nov. 17, 1835.
　　Mary H. and Isaiah Purrington, July 1, 1838.
　　Phillip and Louise Levitt, 1807.
AVERY, Deborah and Wyatt Snow, July 30, 1837.

BACON, Benjamin and Patience Crosby, 1827.
　　Deborah and Walter J. Heyer, July 26, 1832.
　　Elizabeth and Hunneman Baker, Mar. 3, 1839.
　　Selina F. and Rev. Leander Cobb of Sippican, Nov. 21, 1850.
BAKER, Hunneman and Elizabeth Bacon, Mar. 3, 1839.

BARNEY, George and Joanna Snow, 1807.
BARROWS, Ebenezer and Mary Freeman, July, 1820.
George and Cynthia Atsatt, July, 1824.
Hannah and Clemant Briggs, 1808.
Lucy and Alden Dexter, 1811.
Lucy Clarke and William Ellis, Sept. 28, 1840.
Sarah and Josiah Sears, Jr., of Dartmouth, Sept. 10, 1835.
Thomas of Brooklyn, N. Y. and Lucy Bond Washburn, Oct. 1, 1859.
BARSTOW, Benjamin and Rebekah Hammond, 1800.
Benjamin F. and Sarah F. Leach, May 12, 1834.
Caroline and Frederic W. Russell, Oct. 27, 1842.
Elizabeth P. and Charles D. Hall, Nov. 27, 1853.
George and Sally Barstow, 1801.
Georgianna and Philander D. Leonard, Nov. 1, 1854.
Henry and Mary Southworth, Jan. 2, 1842.
Jane and Daniel B. Lovering, Dec. 30, 1805.
John and Diana Bolls, Nov., 1825.
Richard and Mrs. Lurana K. Hammond, Mar. 5, 1860.
Sally and George Barstow, 1801.
Sarah and Rev. Wilbur Johnson of New Milford, Pa., Sept. 1, 1864.
Sophia and James Hezekiah Purrington, Sept. 10, 1863.
Susan C. and David H. Cannon, May 18, 1851.
Zaccheus M. and Mary J. Snow, July 31, 1853.
BARTLETT, Andrew and Eliza Hammond, 1797.
BASSET, Abigail West and Henry Taylor, Jan. 21, 1819.
BATES, Elizabeth and Ebenezer Cannon, July, 1820.
Louisa T. and Welcome Payne of Freetown, Aug. 10, 1834.
BEALLS, Charles C. and Martha C. Weaver, May 11, 1843.
BEARD, Hannah and James Purrington, Jan. 29, 1827.
BENNET, Thomas, 2nd and Sophia H. Stacy, Dec. 7, 1853.
BESSEY, Loise and William Parker, Dec. 25, 1807.
BEWEL, Edward and Clarissa Dexter, July, 1823.
BINDEN, Alfred H. of Woburn and Mary F. Sturtevant, Sept. 24, 1863.
BISHOP, Alvin and Melintha Sheraman, Feb. 1795.
BLACK, Caleb and Betsey Hammond, Feb. 9, 1794.
BOLLES, Joshua and Rachel M. Kinney, Feb. 7, 1843.
Mary and John T. Atsatt, Nov. 17, 1835.
BOLLS, Diana and John Barstow, Nov., 1825.
Mary and Elisha Tinkham, 1825.
BOWLES, Ann F. and Jesse H. Cowing, Apr. 5, 1852.
Charity and Ansel Gibbs, 1828.
Hannah and Isaac Bowles, 1798.

Isaac and Hannah Bowles, 1798.

Loise and Joseph Leavitt, June, 1794.

Zura and Phineas Hillar, March, 1812.

BRAILEY, Julia Ann and John F. Jolls, Aug. 25, 1834.

BRIGGS, Anna and John Ellis, Aug. 1794.

Clemant and Hannah Barrows, 1808.

Elisha and Mary Bolls, 1825.

George and Lois Southworth, Feb. 17, 1833.

Nathan and Mary Davis, Oct. 26, 1823.

BROWN, Julia M. and Isaac O. Pierce, Sept. 4, 1854.

BROWNEL, Hannah S. and Benjamin P. Dexter, 1826.

BROWNELL, Alexander and Polly Hatch, 1810.

BUELL, Sarah J. and John H. Meigs, June 19, 1853.

BURGES, Joanna and Israel Hammond, Nov. 15, 1831.

CANNON, Arvin and Sarah Ann LeBaron, June 12, 1834.

David H. and Susan C. Barstow, May 18, 1851.

Ebenezer and Elizabeth Bates, July, 1820.

Eunice and Stephen Snow, Oct., 1826.

Halet and Eliza W. Harlow, Apr. 13, 1845.

Hallet M. and Mary A. Hammond, Oct. 27, 1834.

Henry N. of New Bedford and Sophia Hammond, July, 1817.

Martha and John P. Carr, Sept. 21, 1843.

Melintha and Lot Jones, Sept. 19, 1833.

Silence and William Merrithew, July 13, 1834.

Thomas Jackson and Eliza Jane Purrington, Aug. 22, 1864.

Watson and Deborah S. Rogers, May 1, 1834.

CARR, John P. and Martha Cannon, Sept. 21, 1843.

CARVER, Lydia and Jesse Swift, Oct. 26, 1823.

CATHAWAY, William and Sarah Smith (Coloured), Aug. 4, 1836.

CATHEL, James and Jane Dexter, 1810.

CLAP, Sukey and Rev. Samuel Mead, 1797.

CLARK, Sarah and Andrew Southworth, Aug. 1, 1810.

Thomas, of Plymouth and Ruth Hovey, June, 1794.

CLARKE, Mary and Hallet Winslow of Dartmouth, Mar. 28, 1837.

Nathaniel and Susan M. Dean Apr. 30, 1837.

Watson C. and Drucilla H. Dexter, Jan. 31, 1837.

COBB, Carrie B. of Hartford, Me. and William G. Cowell, July 10, 1859.

Rev. Leander of Sippican and Selina F. Bacon, Nov. 21, 1850.

COLEMAN, Andrew of Nantucket and Mary Angie Jones, Nov. 24, 1859. (Thanksgiving.)

Lucy and Charles Sherman, Dec. 23, 1850.
COLLINS, E. H. and A. F. Way, July 17, 1853.
COMPTON, David Linton Little and Anna Dexter, Feb. 30, 1804.
COWELL, Hannah and James Hammond, May 12, 1836.
  William G. and Carrie B. Cobb, of Hartford, Me., July 10, 1859.
COWING, Experience and Joseph Hathaway, 1901.
  Jesse H. and Ann F. Bowles, Apr. 5, 1852.
CROSBY, Mrs. Emeline and Joshua Cushing, Nov. 25, 1849.
  Nathan and Mary Holmes, Jan. 12, 1819.
  Patience and Benjamin Bacon, 1827.
CROSS, Franklin and Catharine Leach, Apr. 18, 1850.
CUSHING, Mrs. Abby and William Robinson, May 15, 1854.
  Mrs. Alice and Josiah Sparrow, Apr. 16, 1850.
  Elizabeth and Ebenezer Holmes, Jr., June 30, 1839.
  Joshua and Mrs. Emiline Crosby, Nov. 25, 1849.
  Nathaniel and Alice Hammond, 1805.
  Phebe and Francis Nie, Dec. 1810.
CUSHMAN, Acenath and Leonard Hammond, 1813.
  Deborah and Holder Gelat, Nov. 1825.
  Ezekiel and Abigail Tobey, 1792.
  Hannah and Eben Hathaway, 1808.
  Judi and Abishai Rogers, Feb. 23, 1806.
  Mary and Moors Rogers, 1798.
  Zenas of Middleboro' and Abby Morse, Dec. 31, 1843.

DAVIS, Mary and Nathan Briggs, Oct. 26, 1823.
  Moses H. and Mary Hammond, July 19, 1832.
DEAN, Noah and Roxa Haskiel, March 19, 1813.
  Susan M. and Nathaniel Clarke, Apr. 30, 1837.
DELANO, Easter and Abraham Tinkham, 1800.
  Harper and Susanah Hammond, June, 1803.
DEWOLF, Daniel A. and Mrs. Abby G. Stetson, Dec. 31, 1846.
DEXTER, Alden and Lucy Barrows, 1811.
  Anna and Abner Hall, 1820.
  Anna and David Linton, Little Compton, Feb. 30, 1804.
  Anna and James Snow, Dec., 1795.
  Benjamin P. and Hannah S. Brownel, 1826.
  Caleb and Lydia Hillar, 1821.
  Caroline and Daniel Smith of New Bedford, Jan. 1, 1840.
  Clarissa and Edward Bewel, July, 1823.
  Drucilla H. and Watson C. Clarke, Jan. 31, 1837.
  Ebenezer and Desiah Snow, Dec., 1795.

Ephraim and Arey Snow, Oct., 1801.

Gideon and Mary Dexter, Sept., 1804.

Hannah and Eleazer Waterman, Feb. 27, 1831.

James and Sally Ellis, Jan. 21, 1819.

Jane and James Cathel, 1810.

Kezia and Ebenezer Holmes, Nov., 1805.

Lurania and Ivory Snow, 1828.

Martha M. and Noah Hammond, June 2, 1861.

Martha Mendall and Nathan Smith, Oct. 15, 1861.

Martha and Prince Snow, June, 1794.

Mary and Gideon Dexter, Sept., 1804.

Reuben and Dolly Tobey, Feb., 1796.

Sarah and Josiah Macomber, 1797.

DOTY, Sophia A. and Nathaniel Freeman, Apr. 25, 1833.

DUNHAM, Sophronia and John V. Turner of New Bedford, July 1, 1832.

DURFEY, Rachel and Cyrus Hathaway, 1801.

EATON, Solomon K. and Maria R. Rogers, Dec. 29, 1833.

EDWARDS, Jane of Falmouth and Edward Oliver of New Bedford, May 22, 1839.

ELLIS, Cordelia M. of Rochester and Charles H. Sturtevant, Feb. 11, 1863.

Cornelius and Lydia Gibbs, 1830.

John and Anna Briggs, Aug., 1794.

Mary and Harvey Fairbanks, 1816.

Nathan and Polly Shearman, 1828.

Sally and James Dexter, Jan. 21, 1819.

William and Lucy Clarke Barrows, Sept. 28, 1840.

FAIRBANKS, Harvey and Mary Ellis, 1816.

FAUNCE, Lydia Elizabeth of Plymouth and James William Tinkham, Dec. 12, 1861.

FOSTER, Shillings and Sarah Freeman, Aug., 1794.

FOWLER, Garrett and Eliza Snow, Oct., 1801.

FREEMAN, Charles Bruce and Nabby Haskiel, 1798.

Mary and Ebenezer Barrows, July, 1820.

Nathaniel and Sophia A. Doty, Apr. 25, 1833.

Olivia H. and George Purrington, Jr., Oct. 1, 1858.

Sally W. and James Shaw, Aug., 1820.

Sarah and Shillings Foster, Aug., 1794.

Sylvia A. and Abner Harlow, Nov. 6, 1842.

FULLER, Eben and Olive Standish, 1809.

GELAT, Holder and Deborah Cushman, Nov. 1825.
GIBBS, Ansel and Charity Bowles, 1828.
Lydia and Cornelius Ellis, 1830.
GIFFORD, Lydia of New Bedford and Samuel Haskins of New Bedford, Feb. 17, 1833.
Roby and Matthew Mayhew, June 28, 1846.
GOODSPEED, Theodore W. and Hannah Snow, Nov. 25, 1852.

HALL, Abner and Anna Dexter, 1820.
Charles D. and Elizabeth P. Barstow, Nov. 27, 1853.
David and Hannah Hammond, July, 1817.
Emeline and Daniel D. L. Purrington, July 3, 1842.
Emily F. and Wyat Snow, July 7, 1850.
Laura Ann and Joseph R. Taber, Jr., Sept. 28, 1843.
Martin and Arethusa Southworth, Feb. 22, 1835.
HAMOND, Mary and Mr. Potter of New Bedford, 1821.
Sophia and Henry Cannon, July, 1817.
Susanah and Harper Delano, June, 1803.
HAMMOND, Abigail and Alfred Kindrick, 1805.
Adaline and Edward Simmons, 1830.
Alice and Nathaniel Cushing, 1805.
Amitti B. and Lucinda White, Oct. 26, 1823.
Betsey and Caleb Black, Feb. 9, 1794.
Betsey and Samuel Purrington, Jan. 29, 1827.
Debby and Asa Swift, 1797.
Eliza and Andrew Bartlett, 1797.
Eliza and Ebenezer Rogers, Nov., 1795.
Eliza and Richard Whittemore, 1799.
Elizabeth and Lazarus LeBaron, July 27, 1845.
Eunice and Seth Haskell, 1812.
George F. and Abby M. Sears, June 29, 1847.
Hannah and David Hall, July, 1817.
Israel and Joanna Burges, July, 1831.
James and Hannah Cowell, May 12, 1836.
Jane E. and William Taylor, Sept. 2, 1851.
Leonard and Acenath Cushman, 1813.
Mrs. Lurana K. and Richard Barstow, Mar. 5, 1860.
Mary and Moses H. Davis, July 19, 1832.
Mary A. and Hallet M. Cannon, Oct. 27, 1834.
Mary B. and James Allen of Fairhaven, Apr. 14, 1842.

Nathaniel, Esq., and Priscilla Hammond, Oct. 30, 1808.
Noah and Abigail Palmer, Sept., 1804.
Noah and Martha M. Dexter, June 2, 1861.
Priscilla and Nathaniel Hammond, Esq., Oct. 30, 1808.
Priscilla S. and Lazarus LeBaron, July, 1816.
Rebekah and Benjamin Barstow, 1800.
Roger and Olive Hovey, 1794.
Ruth Ann of New Bedford and George R. Tabor, Nov. 28, 1850.
Waytt and Mary LeBaron, March 12, 1812.
HARLOW, Abner and Sylvia A. Freeman, Nov. 6, 1842.
Betsey and Nathaniel Harlow, June 15, 1824.
Eliza W. and Halet Cannon, Apr. 13, 1845.
Nathaniel and Betsey Harlow, June 15, 1824.
Nathaniel and Silva Lincoln, Aug., 1826.
HASKELL, Seth and Eunice Hammond, 1812.
Nabby and Charles Bruce Freeman, 1798.
HASKIEL, Roxa and Noah Dean, Mar. 19, 1813.
HASKINS, Samuel and Lydia Gifford, both of New Bedford, Feb. 17, 1833.
Samuel of New Bedford and Lydia Gifford of New Bedford, Feb. 17, 1833.
William H. and Lydia Pierce, Jan. 26, 1852.
HATCH, Nancy and Thomas Snow, Dec. 25, 1807.
Polly and Alexander Brownell, 1810.
HATHAWAY, Cyrus and Rachel Durfey, 1801.
Eben and Hannah Cushman, 1808.
· Joseph and Experience Cowing, 1801.
Royal of Newbedford and Anna Wing, Dec. 29, 1805.
HEYER, Walter J. and Deborah Bacon, July 26, 1832.
HILLAR, Lydia and Caleb Dexter, 1821.
Nathaniel and Betsey Snow, Jan. 7, 1817.
Phineas and Zura Bowles, March, 1812.
HOLMES, Charles Albert of Taunton and Mary Loring Pratt of Carver at Dr. Putnam's in Middleboro, Nov. 22, 1863.
Ebenezer and Kezia Dexter, Nov., 1805.
Ebenezer, Jr. and Elizabeth Cushing, June 30, 1839.
Lydia and Lemuel LeBaron, Sept. 22, 1836.
Mary and Nathan Crosby, Jan. 12, 1819.
Mary of Sippican and Joseph Meigs, Jr., Dec. 19, 1833.
HOWSE, Abel and Deborah Ruggles, Jan. 1, 1806.
HOWSE, Hannah and Noah Sturtevant, 1830.
HOVEY, Olive and Roger Hammond, 1794.

Ruth and Thomas Clark, of Plymouth, June, 1794.
HUBBARD, Philip G. of Brimfield and Elizabeth LeBaron, Sept. 9, 1834.

JENNEY, Caleb T. and Mary T. Ames, Oct., 1832.
JEWETT, Maximillian and Almira Tinkham, Oct. 10, 1824.
JOHNSON, Rev. Wilbur of New Milford, Pa. and Sarah Barstow, Sept. 1, 1864.
JOLLS, John F. and Julia Ann Brailey, Aug. 25, 1834.
JONES, Lot and Melintha Cannon, Sept. 19, 1833.
JONES, Mary Angie and Andrew Coleman of Nantucket, Nov. 24, 1859. (Thanksgiving.)

KINDRICK, Alfred and Abigail Hammond, 1805.
KINNEY, Rachel M. and Joshua Bolles, Feb. 7, 1843.
KNOBB, William and Elizabeth Phelps, March 14, 1813.

LACY, Lois and Henry T. Young, 1826.
LEACH, Catharine and Franklin Cross, Apr. 18, 1850.
Sarah F. and Benjamin F. Barstow, May 12, 1834.
LEAVITT, Joseph and Loise Bowles, June, 1794.
LEAVIT, Mrs. Sarah S. of Fairhaven and Capt. Levi Snow, Feb. 4, 1855.
LeBARON, Elizabeth and Philip G. Hubbard of Brimfield, Sept. 9, 1834.
Elizabeth and William LeBaron, 1810.
Enoch H. and Florilla Taber, Oct. 18, 1840.
Jane and Thomas Saunders, July 3, 1838.
John and Abigail Phillips, 1809.
John A. and Harriet Wing, July, 1817.
Lazarus and Elizabeth Hammond, July 27, 1845.
Lazarus and Priscilla S. Hammond, July, 1816.
Lemuel and Lydia Holmes, Sept. 22, 1836.
Mary and Wyatt Hammond, March 12, 1812.
Sarah Ann and Arvin Cannon, June 12, 1834.
William and Elizabeth LeBaron, 1810.
LEONARD, John H. and Sarah A. Washburn, Dec. 25, 1853.
Philander D. and Georgianna Bastow, Nov. 1, 1854.
LEVITT, Louise and Phillip Atsatt, 1807.
LEWIS, Charlotte M. and Gideon B. Spooner, June 13, 1852.
LINCOLN, Kezia and Thomas Tobey, Aug. 1794.
Silva and Nathaniel Harlow, Aug. 1826.
LOBDELL, George W. and Lucy LeB. Meigs, Dec. 26, 1848.

LORING, Mary and Weston Robinson of Fairhaven, Apr. 25, 1832.
LOVERING, Daniel B. and Jane Barstow, Dec. 30, 1805.
LUCE, Abby J. and Humphrey L. Sherman, Oct. 27, 1833.
LUMBARD, John and Susan E. Spooner of Fairhaven, Nov. 19, 1854.

McCARTY, Ellen and Thomas James Rogers, Sept. 20, 1863.
MACOMBER, Josiah and Sarah Dexter, 1797.
MANTER, Peter and Charlotte Nye Nov. 7, 1852.
MARSHALL, Rebecca and Nicholas Taber, Nov. 23, 1794.
MARTIN, Seth and Mary Peckham, June, 1832.
MATTHEWS, Richard J. and Mary Smith (coloured), May 24, 1832.
MAYHEW, Mathew and Sally A. LeBaron, July, 1816.
    Mathew and Roby Gifford, June 28, 1846.
MEAD, Rev. Samuel and Sukey Clap, 1797.
MEIGS, John H. and Sarah J. Buell, June 19, 1853.
    Joseph, Jr. and Mary Holmes of Sippican, Dec. 19, 1833.
    Lucy LeB. and George W. Lobdell, Dec. 26, 1848.
MEIGGS, Ephraim and Clarissa Rogers, Aug. 23, 1824.
MENDALL, Sylvia and Joseph M. C. Allen of London, Eng., Sept. 29,
    1839.
MERRIHEW, Edmund and Charity Simmons, Jan. 8, 1838.
    Elias and Mary Ann Nye, Nov. 11, 1838.
    Mary B. and Joseph Wilson, Mar. 16, 1837.
    William and Silence Cannon, July 13, 1834.
MORSE, Abby and Zenas Cushman of Middleboro', Dec. 31, 1843.
    Sarah D. and Calvin Rollins Weaver, both of Wareham, May 2,
    1861.
MYRICKS, Phebe and Daniel Russell of Dartmouth, 1803.

NIE, Francis and Phebe Cushing, Dec., 1810.
    William and Nancy Snow, Dec. 31, 1817.
NORTON, Eben of Farmington, Me. and Lizzie H. Shaw (dau. of
    James), Apr. 4, 1860.
NYE, Charlotte and Peter Manter, Nov. 7, 1852.
    Ebenezer of Falmouth and Koria Tobey, Jan. 1, 1806.
    Gilbert M. and Dorcas Purrington, Sept. 17, 1854.
    Mary Ann and Elias Merrithew, Nov. 11, 1838.

OLIVER, Edward of New Bedford and Jane Edwards of Falmouth,
    May 22, 1839.

PALMER, Abigail and Noah Hammond, Sept., 1804.

PARKER, William and Loise Bessey, Dec. 25, 1807.

PARLOW, Ebenezer and Drusilla Randall, 1799.

PAYNE, Phebe V. and Job P. Rounseville, Jan. 19, 1854.

Welcome of Freetown and Louisa T. Bates, Aug. 10, 1834.

PECKHAM, Mary and Seth Martin, June, 1832.

PEASE, Lydia and Samuel Sturtevant, 1799.

PEIRCE, Eliza and Ansel Weeks, Nov. 25, 1835.

Lydia and William H. Haskins, Jan. 26, 1852.

PHELPS, Elizabeth and William Knobb, March 14, 1813.

PHILLIPS, Abigail and John LeBaron, 1809.

PIERCE, Isaac O. and Julia M. Brown, Sept. 4, 1854.

William N. and Eliza J. Snow, Apr. 30, 1854.

POTTER, Mr. of New Bedford and Mary Hamond, 1821.

PRATT, Mary Loring of Carver and Charles Albert Holmes of Taunton, at Dr. Putnam's in Middleboro, Nov. 22, 1863.

PURRINGTON, Daniel D. L. and Emeline Hall, July 3, 1842.

Dorcas and Gilbert M. Nye, Sept. 17, 1854.

Eliza Jane and Thomas Jackson Cannon, Aug. 22, 1864.

George, Jr. and Olivia H. Freeman, Oct. 1, 1858.

Hattie A. and Edgar S. Silva, June 8, 1861.

Isaiah and Mary H. Atsatt, July 1, 1838.

James Hezekiah and Sophia Barstow, Sept. 10, 1863.

James and Hannah Beard, Jan. 29, 1827.

John and Minerva White, Feb. 27, 1840.

Samuel and Betsy Hammond, Jan. 29, 1827.

RANDALL, Drusilla and Ebenezer Parlow, 1799.

RANSOM, James B. of Carver and Eunice Snow, Feb. 7, 1841.

ROBINSON, Weston of Fairhaven and Mary Loring, Apr. 25, 1832.

William and Mrs. Abby Cushing, May 15, 1854.

ROGERS, Abishai and Judi Cushman, Feb. 23, 1806.

Betsey and Eli Soper, 1800.

Clarissa and Ephraim Meiggs, Aug. 23, 1824.

Deborah S. and Watson Cannon, May 1, 1834.

Ebenezer and Eliza Hammond, Nov., 1795.

Ebenezer and Rebecca Mayhew, Nov. 15, 1831.

Maria R. and Solomon K. Eaton, Dec. 29, 1833.

Moors and Mary Cushman, 1798.

Thomas James and Ellen McCarty, Sept. 20, 1863.

ROUNSEVILLE, Job P. and Phebe V. Payne, Jan. 19, 1854.

RUGGLES, Deborah and Abel House, Jan 1, 1806.

RUSSEL, Daniel of Dartmouth and Phebe Myricks, 1803.

RUSSELL, Frederic W. and Caroline Barstow, Oct. 27, 1842.

SAUNDERS, Thomas and Jane LeBaron, July 3, 1838.
SEARS, Abby M. and George F. Hammond, June 29, 1847.
  Josiah, Jr. of Dartmouth and Sarah Barrows, Sept. 10, 1835.
SHAW, James and Sally W. Freeman, Aug., 1820.
  Lizzie A., (dau. of James) and Eben Norton of Farmington, Me.,
    Apr. 4, 1860.
SHEARMAN, Melintha and Elvin Bishop, Feb., 1795.
  Polly and Nathan Ellis, 1828.
SHERMAN, Charles and Lucy Coleman, Dec. 23, 1850.
  Humphrey L. and Abby J. Luce, Oct. 27, 1833.
  Sarah M. and Charles W. Smith, Oct. 27, 1853.
SILVA, Edgar S. and Hattie A. Purrington, June 8, 1861.
SIMMONS, Charity and Edmund Merrihew, Jan. 8, 1838.
  Edward and Adaline Hammond, 1830.
  S. Bartlett of Newport, R. I. and Abby C. Aken, of Fairhaven, Nov.
    25, 1863.
SMITH, Charles W. and Sarah M. Sherman, Oct. 27, 1853.
  Daniel of New Bedford and Caroline Dexter, Jan. 1, 1840.
  Mary and Richard J. Matthews (Coloured), May 24, 1832.
  Nathan and Martha Mendall Dexter, Oct. 15, 1861.
  Sally and John Wing, 1797.
  Sarah and William Cathaway (Coloured), Aug. 4, 1836.
SNOW, Arey and Ephraim Dexter, Oct., 1801.
  Betsey and Nathaniel Hillar, Jan. 7, 1817.
  Desiah and Ebenezer Dexter, Dec., 1795.
  Eliza and Garrett Fowler, Oct., 1801.
  Eliza J. and William N. Pierce, Apr. 30, 1854.
  Eunice and James B. Ransom of Carver, Feb. 7, 1841.
  Hannah and Joshua Snow, Oct., 1792.
  Hannah and Theodore W. Goodspeed, Nov. 25, 1852.
  Ivory and Lurania Dexter, 1828.
  Ivory and Martha Snow, Nov. 17, 1833.
  James and Anna Dexter, Dec., 1795.
  Joanna and George Barney, 1807.
  Joseph and Rebekah Snow, Feb. 2, 1796.
  Joshua and Hannah Snow, Oct., 1792.
  Capt. Levi and Mrs. Sarah S. Leavit of Fairhaven, Feb. 4, 1855.
  Martha and Ivory Snow, Nov. 17, 1833.
  Mary J. and Zaccheus M. Barstow, July 31, 1853.
  Nancy and William Nie, Dec. 31, 1817.

Nathaniel and Eliza Wallace, 1803.

Prince and Martha Dexter, June, 1794.

Rachel and Wyatt Snow, Sept. 9, 1824.

Rekekah and Joseph Snow, Feb. 2, 1796.

Stephen and Eunice Cannon, Oct., 1826.

Thomas and Nancy Hatch, Dec. 25, 1807.

Wyat and Emily F. Hall, July 7, 1850.

Wyatt and Deborah Avery, July 30, 1837.

Wyatt and Rachel Snow, Sept. 9, 1824.

SPARROW, Josiah and Mrs. Alice Cushing, Apr. 16, 1850.

SOPER, Eli and Betsey Rogers, 1800.

SPOONER, Gideon B. and Charlotte M. Lewis, June 13, 1852.

Susan E. of Fairhaven and John Lumbard, Nov. 19, 1854.

SOUTHWORTH, Andrew and Sarah Clark, Aug. 1, 1810.

Arethusa and Martin Hall, Feb. 22, 1835.

Lois and George Briggs, Feb. 17, 1833.

Mary and Henry Barstow, Jan. 2, 1842.

Sarah and Josiah D. Sturtevant, 1833.

Sarah H. and Alfred M. Wright of Fairhaven, Feb. 17, 1833.

STACEY, Sophia H. and Thomas Bennet, 2nd, Dec. 7, 1853.

STANDISH, Olive and Eben Fuller, 1809.

STEPHENS, Timothy and Waty Tabor, March, 1804.

STETSON, Mrs. Abby G. and Daniel A. De Wolf, Dec. 31, 1846.

STEVENS, Charles of Boston and Thankful J. Taber, Mar. 1, 1855.

STURTEVANT, Charles H. and Cordelia M. Ellis of Rochester, Feb. 11. 1863.

Josiah D. and Sarah Southworth, 1833.

Mary F. and Alfred H. Binden of Woburn, Sept. 24, 1863.

Noah and Hannah Howse, 1830.

Samuel and Lydia Pease, 1799.

Samuel, Jr. and Mrs. Mary B. Swift of Rochester, July 31, 1859.

SWIFT, Asa and Debby Hammond, 1797.

Jesse and Lydia Carver, Oct. 26, 1823.

Mrs. Mary B. of Rochester and Samuel Sturtevant, Jr., July 31, 1859

TABER, Florilla and Enoch H. LeBaron, Oct. 18, 1840.

Joseph R., Jr. and Laura Ann Hall, Sept. 28, 1843.

Nicholas and Rebecca Marshall, Nov. 23, 1794.

Thankful J. and Charles Stevens of Boston, Mar. 1, 1855.

George R. and Ruth Ann Hammond of New Bedford, Nov. 28, 1850.

Waty and Timothy Stephens, March, 1804.

TAYLOR, Henry and Abigail West Basset, Jan. 21, 1819.

William and Jane E. Hammond, Sept. 2, 1851.

TINKHAM, Abraham and Easter Delano, 1800.

Almira and Maximillian Jewett, Oct. 10, 1824.

James William and Lydia Elizabeth Faunce of Plymouth, Dec. 12, 1861.

TOBEY, Abigail and Ezekiel Cushman, 1892.

Abigail and Francis Nye, 1816.

Dolly and Reuben Dexter, Feb., 1796.

Eliz and Shubael Wicks, 1798.

Isaac and Rachel Townsend, 1809.

Koria and Ebenezer Nye of Falmouth, Jan. 1, 1806.

Thomas and Kezia Lincoln, Aug., 1794.

TOWNSEND, Mary C. and Nathaniel F. Ames, Oct. 9, 1842.

Rachel and Isaac Tobey, 1809.

TRIPP, Emily D. and Samuel Yates, Aug. 4, 1834.

TURNER, John V. of New Bedford and Sophronia Dunham, July 1, 1832.

WALLACE, Eliza and Nathaniel Snow, 1803.

WASBHURN, Lucy Bond and Thomas Barrows of Brooklyn, N. Y., Oct. 1, 1859.

Sarah A. and John H. Leonard, Dec. 25, 1853.

WATERMAN, Eleazer and Hannah Dexter, Feb. 27, 1831.

WAY, A. F. and E. H. Collins, July 17, 1853.

WEAVER, Calvin Rollins and Sarah D. Morse, both of Wareham, May 2, 1861.

Martha C. and Charles G. Bealls, May 11, 1843.

WEEKS, Ansel and Eliza Peirce, Nov. 25, 1835.

WHITE, Lucinda and Amitti B. Hammond, Oct. 26, 1823.

Minerva and John Purrington, Feb. 27, 1840.

William S. of Boston and Eliza Ann Willis, Mar. 18, 1834.

WHITTEMORE, Richard and Eliza Hammond, 1799.

WICKS, Shubael and Eliz Tobey, 1798.

WILLIS, Eliza Ann and William S. White of Boston, Mar. 18, 1834.

WILSON, Joseph and Mary B. Merrithew, Mar. 16, 1837.

WING, Anna and Royal Hathaway of Newbedford, Dec. 29, 1805.

Harriet and John A. LeBaron, July, 1817.

John and Sally Smith, 1797.

WINSLOW, Hallet of Dartmouth and Mary Clarke, Mar. 28, 1837.
WRIGHT, Alfred M. of Fairhaven and Sarah H. Southworth, Feb. 17, 1833.

YATES, Samuel and Emily D. Tripp, Aug. 4, 1834.
YOUNG, Henry T. and Lois Lacy, 1826.

INDEX

INDEX

CPSIA information can be obtained
at www.ICGtesting.com
Printed in the USA
LVHW080949160820
663323LV00015B/324

9 781340 854850